THOMAS CARLYLE.
[From a Photograph by Elliott and Fry, London.]

REMINISCENCES

BY

THOMAS CARLYLE

EDITED BY
JAMES ANTHONY FROUDE

NEW YORK
HARPER & BROTHERS, FRANKLIN SQUARE
1881

CONTENTS.

PREFACE.

In the summer of 1871, Mr. Carlyle placed in my hands a collection of MSS. of which he desired me to take charge, and to publish, should I think fit to do so, after he was gone. They consisted of letters written by his wife to himself and to other friends during the period of her married life, with the "rudiments" of a preface of his own, giving an account of her family, her childhood, and their own experience together from their first acquaintance till her death. They were married in 1826; Mrs. Carlyle died suddenly in 1866. Between these two periods Carlyle's active literary life was comprised; and he thought it unnecessary that more than these letters contained should be made known, or attempted to be made known, about himself or his personal history. The essential part of his life was in his works, which those who chose could read. The private part of it was a matter in which the world had no concern. Enough would be found, told by one who knew him better than any one else knew him, to satisfy such curiosity as there might be. His object was rather to leave a monument to a singularly gifted woman, who, had she so pleased, might have made a name for herself, and for his sake had voluntarily sacrificed ambition and fortune.

The letters had been partially prepared for the press by short separate introductions and explanatory notes. But Carlyle warned me that before they were published they would require anxious revision. Written with the unreserve of confidential communications, they contained anecdotes, allusions, reflections, expressions of opinion and feeling, which were intended obviously for no eye save that of the person to whom they were addressed. He believed, at the time I speak of, that his own life was near its end, and, seeing the difficulty in which I might be placed, he left me at last with discretion to destroy the whole of them, should I find the task of discriminating too intricate a problem.

The expectation of an early end was perhaps suggested by the wish for it. He could no longer write. His hand was disabled by palsy. His temperament did not suit with dictation, and he was impatient of an existence which he could no longer turn to any useful purpose. He lingered on, however, year after year, and it gradually became known to him that his wishes would not protect him from biographers, and that an account of his life would certainly be tried, perhaps by more than one person. A true description of it he did not believe that any one could give, not even his closest friend: but there might be degrees of falsity; and since a biography of some kind there was to be, he decided at last to extend his original commission to me, and to make over to me all his private papers, journals, note-books, letters, and unfinished or neglected writings.

Being a person of most methodical habits, he had preserved every letter which he had ever received of not entirely trifling import. His mother, his wife, his brothers, and many of his friends had kept as carefully every letter from himself. The most remarkable of his contemporaries had been among his correspondents—English, French, Italian, German, and American. Goethe had recognized his genius, and had written to him often, advising and encouraging. His own and Mrs. Carlyle's journals were records of their most secret thoughts. All these Mr. Carlyle, scarcely remembering what they contained, but with characteristic fearlessness, gave me leave to use as I might please.

Material of such a character makes my duty in one respect an easy one. I have not to relate Mr. Carlyle's history, or describe his character. He is his own biographer, and paints his own portrait. But another difficulty arises from the extent of the resources thrown open to me. His own letters are as full of matter as the richest of his published works. His friends were not common men, and in writing to him they wrote their best. Of the many thousand letters in my possession, there is hardly one which either on its special merits, or through its connection with something which concerned him, does not deserve to be printed. Selection is indispensable; a middle way must be struck between too much and too little. I have been guided largely, however, by Carlyle's personal directions to me, and such a way will, I trust, be discovered.

Meanwhile, on examining the miscellaneous MSS., I found among them various sketches and reminiscences: one written in a note-book fifty years ago, on hearing in London of his father's death; another of Edward Irving; another of Lord Jeffrey; others (these brief and slight) of Southey and Wordsworth. In addition, there was a long narrative, or fragments of a narrative, designed as material for the introduction to Mrs. Carlyle's letters. These letters would now have to be rearranged with his own; and an introduction, under the shape which had been intended for it, would be no longer necessary. The "Reminiscences" appeared to me to be far too valuable to be broken up and employed in any composition of my own, and I told Mr. Carlyle that I thought they ought to be printed with the requisite omissions immediately after his own death. He agreed with me that it should be so, and at one time it was proposed that the type should be set up while he was still alive, and could himself revise what he had written. He found, however, that the effort would be too much for him, and the reader has here before him Mr. Carlyle's own handiwork, but without his last touches, not edited by himself, not corrected by himself, perhaps most of it not intended for publication, and written down merely as an occupation, for his own private satisfaction.

The Introductory Fragments were written immediately after his wife's death; the account of Irving belongs to the autumn and winter which followed. So singular was his condition at this time, that he was afterwards unconscious what he had done; and when, ten years later, I found the Irving MS. and asked him about it, he did not know to what I was alluding. The sketch of Jeffrey was written immediately after. Some parts of the introduction I have reserved for the biography, into which they will most conveniently fall; the rest, from the point where they form a consecutive story, I have printed with only a few occasional reservations. "Southey" and "Wordsworth," being merely detached notes of a few personal recollections, I have attached as an appendix.

Nothing more remains to be said about these papers, save to repeat, for clearness' sake, that they are published with Mr. Carlyle's consent, but without his supervision. The detailed responsibility is therefore entirely my own. I will add, for the convenience of the general public, the few chief points of his outward life. He was the son of a village mason, born at Ecclefechan, in Annandale, December 4, 1795. He was educated first at Ecclefechan school. In 1806 he was sent to the grammar-school at Annan, and in 1809 to Edinburgh University. In 1814 he was appointed mathematical usher at Annan, and in 1816 schoolmaster at Kirkcaldy. In 1818 he gave up his situation, and supported himself by taking pupils at Edinburgh. In 1822 he became private tutor in the family of Mr. Charles Buller; Charles Buller the younger, who was afterwards so brilliantly distinguished in Parliament, being his pupil. While in this capacity he wrote his "Life of Schiller," and translated "Wilhelm Meister." In 1826 he married. He lived for eighteen months at Comley Bank, on the north side of Edinburgh. He then removed to Craigenputtoch, a moorland farm in Dumfriesshire belonging to his wife's mother, where he remained for seven years, writing "Sartor Resartus" there, and nearly all his Miscellanies. In 1834 he left Scotland and settled in London, No. 5 Cheyne Row, Chelsea, and there continued without further change till his death.

REMINISCENCES

JAMES CARLYLE, OF ECCLEFECHAN, MASON

JAMES CARLYLE.*

On Tuesday, January 26, 1832, I received tidings that my dear and worthy father had departed out of this world. He was called away by a death apparently of the mildest, on Sunday morning about six. He had taken what was thought a bad cold on the Monday preceding, but rose every day and was sometimes out of doors. Occasionally he was insensible (as pain usually soon made him of late years), but when spoken to he recollected himself. He was up and at the kitchen fire (at Scotsbrig)† on the Saturday evening about six, but was evidently growing fast worse in breathing. "About ten o'clock he fell into a sort of stupor," writes my sister Jane, "still breathing higher and with greater difficulty. He spoke little to any of us, seemingly unconscious of what he did, came over to the bedside, and offered up a prayer to Heaven in such accents as it is impossible to forget. He departed almost without a struggle," adds she, "this morning at half-past six." My mother adds, in her own hand, "It is God that has done it. Be still, my dear children. Your affectionate mother. God support us all." The funeral is to be on Friday, the present date is Wednesday night. This stroke, altogether unexpected at the time, but which I have been long anticipating in general, falls heavy on me, as such needs must, yet not so as to stun me or unman me. Natural tears have come to my relief. I can look at my dear father, and that section of the past which he has made alive for me, in a certain sacred sanctified light, and give way to what thoughts rise in me without feeling that they are weak and useless.

The time till the funeral was past I instantly determined on passing with my wife only, and all others were excluded. I have written to my mother and to John,‡ have walked far and much,

---

* Written in London, in January, 1832.
† A farm near Ecclefechan occupied by James Carlyle during the last six years of his life.
‡ Mr. Carlyle's brother.

chiefly in the Regent's Park, and considered about many things, if so were that I might accomplish this problem, to see clearly what my present calamity means—what I have lost and what lesson my loss was to teach me.

As for the departed, we ought to say that he was taken home "like a shock of corn fully ripe." He "had finished the work that was given him to do" and finished it (very greatly more than the most) as became a man. He was summoned, too, before he had ceased to be interesting—to be lovable. (He was to the last the pleasantest man I had to speak with in Scotland.) For many years too he had the end ever in his eye, and was studying to make all preparation for what in his strong way he called often "that last, that awful change." Even at every new parting of late years I have noticed him wring my hand with a tenderer pressure, as if he felt that one other of our few meetings here was over. Mercifully also has he been spared me till I am abler to bear his loss; till by manifold struggles I too, as he did, feel my feet on the Everlasting rock, and, through time with its death, can in some degree see into eternity with its life. So that I have repeated, not with unwet eyes, let me hope likewise not with unsoftened heart, those old and forever true words, "Blessed are the dead that die in the Lord; they do rest from their labors, and their works follow them." Yes, their works follow them. The force that had been lent my father he honorably expended in manful well-doing. A portion of this planet bears beneficent traces of his strong hand and strong head. Nothing that he undertook to do but he did it faithfully and like a true man. I shall look on the houses he built with a certain proud interest. They stand firm and sound to the heart all over his little district. No one that comes after him will ever say, "Here was the finger of a hollow eye-servant." They are little texts for me of the gospel of man's free-will. Nor will his deeds and sayings in any case be found unworthy—not false and barren, but genuine and fit. Nay, am not I also the humble James Carlyle's work? I owe him much more than existence, I owe him a noble inspiring example (now that I can read it in that rustic character). It was he *exclusively* that determined on *educating* me; that from his small hard-earned funds sent me to school and college, and made me whatever I am or may become. Let me not mourn for my father, let me do worthily of him. So shall he still live even here in me, and his worth plant itself honorably forth into new generations.

I purpose now, while the impression is more pure and clear

within me, to mark down the main things I can recollect of my father. To myself, if I live to after-years, it may be instructive and interesting, as the past grows ever holier the farther we leave it. My mind is calm enough to do it deliberately, and to do it truly. The thought of that pale earnest face which even now lies stiffened into death in that bed at Scotsbrig, with the Infinite all of worlds looking down on it, will certainly impel me. Neither, should these lines survive myself and be seen by others, can the sight of them do harm to any one. It is good to know how a true spirit will vindicate itself with truth and freedom through what obstructions soever; how the acorn cast carelessly into the wilderness will make room for itself and grow to be an oak. This is one of the cases belonging to that class, "the lives of remarkable men," in which it has been said, "paper and ink should least of all be spared." I call a man remarkable who becomes a true workman in this vineyard of the Highest. Be his work that of palace-building and kingdom-founding, or only of delving and ditching, to me it is no matter, or *next to none*. All human work is transitory, small in itself, contemptible. Only the worker thereof, and the spirit that dwelt in him, is significant. I proceed without order, or almost any forethought, anxious only to save what I have left and mark it as it lies in me.

In several respects, I consider my father as one of the most interesting men I have known. He was a man of perhaps the very largest natural endowment of any it has been my lot to converse with. None of us will ever forget that bold glowing style of his, flowing free from his untutored soul, full of metaphors (though he knew not what a metaphor was) with all manner of potent words which he appropriated and applied with a surprising accuracy you often would not guess whence; brief, energetic, and which I should say conveyed the most perfect picture—definite, clear, not in ambitious colors, but in full white sunlight—of all the dialects I have ever listened to. Nothing did I ever hear him undertake to render visible which did not become almost ocularly so. Never shall we again hear such speech as that was. The whole district knew of it and laughed joyfully over it, not knowing how otherwise to express the feeling it gave them; emphatic I have heard him beyond all men. In anger he had no need of oaths, his words were like sharp arrows that smote into the very heart. The fault was that he exaggerated (which tendency I also inherit), yet only in description and for the sake chiefly of humorous effect. He was a man of rigid, even scrupulous, veracity. I have often heard him turn back when he thought his strong words were misleading, and correct them into mensurative accuracy.

I call him a natural man, singularly free from all manner of affectation; he was among the last of the true men which Scotland, on the old system, produced or can produce; a man healthy in body and mind, fearing God, and diligently working on God's earth with contentment, hope, and unwearied resolution. He was never visited with doubt. The old theorem of the universe was sufficient for him; and he worked well in it, and in all senses successfully and wisely—as few can do. So quick is the motion of transition becoming, the new generation almost to a man must make their belly their God, and, alas! find even that an empty one. Thus, curiously enough and blessedly, *he* stood a true man on the verge of the old, while his son stands here lovingly surveying him on the verge of the new, and sees the possibility of also being true there. God make the possibility, blessed possibility, into a reality.

A virtue he had which I should learn to imitate. He *never spoke of what was disagreeable and past.* I have often wondered and admired at this. The thing that he had nothing to do with, he did nothing with. His was a healthy mind. In like manner I have seen him always, when we young ones, half roguishly (and provokingly, without doubt), were perhaps repeating sayings of his, sit as if he did not hear us at all. Never once did I know him utter a word; only once, that I remember, give a look in such a case.

Another virtue the example of which has passed strongly into me was his settled placid indifference to the clamors or the murmurs of public opinion. For the judgment of those that had no right or power to judge him, he seemed simply to care nothing at all. He very rarely spoke of despising such things. He contented himself with altogether disregarding them. Hollow babble it was for him, a thing, as Fichte said, that did not exist—*das gar nicht existirte.* There was something truly great in this. The very perfection of it hid from you the extent of the attainment.

Or rather let us call it a new phasis of the health which in mind as in body was conspicuous in him. Like a healthy man, he wanted only to get along with his task. Whatsoever could not forward him in this (and how could public opinion and much else of the like sort do?) was of no moment to him, was not there for him.

This great maxim of philosophy he had gathered by the teaching of nature alone—that man was created to work, not to speculate or feel or dream. Accordingly, he set his whole heart thitherwards. He did work wisely and unweariedly (*ohne Hast aber Rast*), and perhaps performed more with the tools he had than any man I now know. It should have made me sadder than it did to hear the young ones sometimes complaining of his slow punctuality and thoroughness. He would leave nothing till it was done. Alas! the age of substance and solidity is gone for the time; that of show and hollow superficiality—in all senses—is in full course.

And yet he was a man of open sense; wonderfully so. I could have entertained him for days talking of any matter interesting to man. He delighted to hear of all things that were worth talking of: the mode of living men had—the mode of working; their opinions, virtues, whole spiritual and temporal environments.

It is some two years ago (in summer) since I entertained him highly—he was hoeing turnips, and perhaps I helped him—with an account of the character and manner of existence of Francis Jeffrey. Another evening he enjoyed—probably it was on this very visit—with the heartiest relish my description of the people, I think, of Turkey. The Chinese had astonished him much. In some magazine he had got a sketch of McCartney's "Embassy," the memory of which never left him. Adam Smith's "Wealth of Nations," greatly as it lay out of his course, he had also fallen in with, and admired and understood and remembered so far as he had any business with it. I once wrote him about my being in Smithfield Market seven years ago, of my seeing St. Paul's. Both things interested him heartily and dwelt with him. I had hoped to tell him much of what I saw in this second visit, and that many a long cheerful talk would have given us both some sunny hours, but *es konnte nimmer seyn.* Patience! hope!

At the same time, he had the most entire and open contempt for all idle tattle; what he called clatter. Any talk that had meaning in it he could listen to. What had no meaning in it—above all, what seemed false—he absolutely could and would not hear, but abruptly turned aside from it, or if that might not suit, with the besom of destruction swept it far away from him. Long may we remember his "I don't believe thee;" his tongue-paralyzing, cold, indifferent "Hah!" I should say of him as I did of our sister* whom we lost, that he seldom or never spoke except actually to convey an idea. Measured by quantity of words, he was a talker of fully average copiousness; by extent of meaning communicated, he was the most copious I have listened to. How in few sentences he would sketch you off an entire biography, an entire object or

---

* Margaret, who died in 1831.

transaction, keen, clear, rugged, genuine, completely rounded in!
His words came direct from the heart by the inspiration of the
moment.

"It is no idle tale," he said to some laughing rustics while stating, in his strong way, some complaint against them, and their
laughter died into silence. Dear, good father! There looked honestly through those clear earnest eyes a sincerity that compelled
belief and regard. "Moffat," said he one day to an incorrigible
reaper, "thou hast had every feature of a bad shearer — high,
rough, and little on't. Thou maun alter thy figure or slant the
bog," pointing to the man's road homewards.

He was irascible, choleric, and we all dreaded his wrath, yet passion never mastered him or maddened him. It rather inspired him
with new vehemence of insight and more piercing emphasis of
wisdom. It must have been a bold man that did not quail before
that face when glowing with indignation, grounded, for so it ever
was, on the sense of right and in resistance of wrong. More than
once has he lifted up his strong voice in tax courts and the like
before "the gentlemen" (what he knew of highest among men),
and, rending asunder official sophisms, thundered even into their
deaf ears the indignant sentence of natural justice to the conviction of all. Oh, why did we laugh at these things while we
loved them? There is a tragic greatness and sacredness in them
now.

I can call my father a brave man (*ein tapferer*). Man's face he
did not fear; God he always feared. His reverence, I think, was
considerably mixed with fear; yet not slavish fear, rather awe, as
of unutterable depths of silence through which flickered a trembling hope. How he used to speak of death, especially in late
years—or rather to be silent, and look at it! There was no feeling
in him here that he cared to hide. He trembled at the really terrible; the mock terrible he cared nought for. That last act of his
life, when in the last agony, with the thick ghastly vapors of death
rising round him to choke him, he burst through and called with
a man's voice on the great God to have mercy on him—that was
like the epitome and concluding summary of his whole life. God
gave him strength to wrestle with the King of Terrors, and, as it
were, even then to prevail. All his strength came from God, and
ever sought new nourishment there. God be thanked for it.

Let me not mourn that my father's force is all spent, that his
valor wars no longer. Has it not gained the victory? Let me
imitate him rather. Let his courageous heart beat anew in me,

that when oppression and opposition unjustly threaten, I too may rise with his spirit to front them and subdue them.

On the whole, ought I not to rejoice that God was pleased to give me such a father; that from earliest years I had the example of a real man of God's own making continually before me? Let me learn of *him*. Let me write my books as he built his houses, and walk as blamelessly through this shadow world; if God so will, to rejoin him at last. Amen.

Alas! such is the miseducation of these days, it is only among those that are called the uneducated classes—those educated by experience—that you can look for a Man. Even among these, such a sight is growing daily rarer. My father, in several respects, has not, that I can think of, left his fellow. *Ultimus Romanorum.* Perhaps among Scottish peasants what Samuel Johnson was among English authors. I have a sacred pride in my peasant father, and would not exchange him, even now, for any king known to me. Gold and the guinea stamp—the Man and the clothes of the man. Let me thank God for that greatest of blessings, and strive to live worthily of it.

Though from the heart, and practically even more than in words, an independent man, he was by no means an insubordinate one. His bearing towards his superiors I consider noteworthy—of a piece with himself. I think in early life, when working in Spring-hill for a Sir W. Maxwell—the grandfather of the present Baronet —he had got an early respect impressed upon him for the character as well as station of a gentleman. I have heard him often describe the grave wisdom and dignified deportment of that Maxwell as of a true "ruler of the people." It used to remind me of the gentlemen in Goethe. Sir William, like those he ruled over, and benignantly, or at least gracefully and earnestly, governed, has passed away. But even for the mere clothes-screens of rank my father testified no contempt. He spoke of them in public or private without acerbity; testified for them the outward deference which custom and convenience prescribed, and felt no degradation therein. Their inward claim to regard was a thing which concerned them, not him. I love to figure him addressing these men, with bared head, by the title of "your honor," with a manner respectful, yet unembarrassed; a certain manly dignity looking through his own fine face, with his noble gray head bent patiently to the, alas! unworthy. Such conduct is, perhaps, no longer possible.

Withal, he had in general a grave natural politeness. I have seen him, when the women were perhaps all in anxiety about the

disorder, etc., usher men in with true hospitality into his mean
house, without any grimace of apologies, or the smallest seeming
embarrassment.   Were the house but a cabin, it was his, and they
were welcome to him, and what it held.   This was again the man.
His life was "no idle tale;" not a lie, but a truth, which whoso
liked was welcome to come and examine.   "An earnest, toilsome
life," which had also a serious issue.

The more I reflect on it, the more I must admire how completely
nature had taught him; how completely he was devoted to his
work, to the task of his life, and content to let all pass by unheeded
that had not relation to this.   It is a singular fact, for example,
that though a man of such openness and clearness, he had never, I
believe, read three pages of Burns's poems.   Not even when all
about him became noisy and enthusiastic, I the loudest, on that
matter, did he feel it worth while to renew his investigation of
it, or once turn his face towards it.   The poetry he liked (he did
not call it poetry) was truth, and the wisdom of reality.   Burns,
indeed, could have done nothing for him.   As high a greatness
hung over his world as over that of Burns—the ever-present greatness of the Infinite itself.   Neither was he, like Burns, called to
rebel against the world, but to labor patiently at his task there,
uniting the possible with the necessary to bring out the real,
wherein also lay an ideal.   Burns could not have in any way
strengthened him in this course, and therefore was for him a phenomenon merely.   Nay, rumor had been so busy with Burns, and
destiny and his own desert had in very deed so marred his name,
that the good rather avoided him.   Yet it was not with aversion
that my father regarded Burns; at worst with indifference and
neglect.   I have heard him speak of once seeing him standing in
"Rob Scott's smithy" (at Ecclefechan, no doubt superintending
some work).   He heard one say, "There is the poet Burns."   He
went out to look, and saw a man with boots on, like a well-dressed
farmer, walking down the village on the opposite side of the burn.
This was all the relation these two men ever had ; they were very
nearly coevals.*   I knew Robert Burns, and I knew my father.
Yet were you to ask me which had the greater natural faculty, I
might perhaps actually pause before replying.   Burns had an infinitely wider education, my father a far wholesomer.   Besides, the
one was a man of musical utterance; the other wholly a man of
action, with speech subservient thereto.   Never, of all the men I

* Burns died the year after Thomas Carlyle was born.

have seen, has one come personally in my way in whom the endowment from nature and the arena from fortune were so utterly out of all proportion. I have said this often, and partly know it. As a man of speculation—had culture ever unfolded him—he must have gone wild and desperate as Burns; but he was a man of conduct, and work keeps all right. What strange shapable creatures we are!

My father's education was altogether of the worst and most limited. I believe he was never more than three months at any school. What he learned there showed what he might have learned. A solid knowledge of arithmetic, a fine antique handwriting—these, with other limited practical etceteras, were all the things he ever heard mentioned as excellent. He had no room to strive for more. Poetry, fiction in general, he had universally seen treated as not only idle, but false and criminal. This was the spiritual element he had lived in almost to old age. But greatly his most important culture he had gathered—and this, too, by his own endeavors—from the better part of the district, the religious men; to whom, as to the most excellent, his own nature gradually attached and attracted him. He was religious with the consent of his whole faculties. Without religion he would have been nothing. Indeed, his habit of intellect was thoroughly free, and even incredulous. And strongly enough did the daily example of this work afterwards on me. "Putting out the natural eye of his mind to see better with a telescope"—this was no scheme for him. But he was in Annandale, and it was above fifty years ago,* and a Gospel was still preached there to the heart of a man in the tones of a man. Religion was the pole-star for my father. Rude and uncultivated as he otherwise was, it made him and kept him " in all points a man."

Oh! when I think that all the area in boundless space he had seen was limited to a circle of some fifty miles' diameter (he never in his life was farther or elsewhere so far from home as at Craigenputtoch), and all his knowledge of the boundless time was derived from his Bible and what the oral memories of old men could give him, and his own could gather; and yet, that he was such, I could take shame to myself. I feel to my father—so great though so neglected, so generous also towards *me*—a strange tenderness, and mingled pity and reverence peculiar to the case, infinitely soft and near my heart. Was he not a sacrifice to me? Had I stood in his place, could he not have stood in mine, and more? Thou good fa-

---

* Written in 1832.

ther! well may I forever honor thy memory. Surely that act was not without its reward. And was not nature great, out of such materials to make such a man?

Though genuine and coherent, "living and life-giving," he was, nevertheless, but half developed. We had all to complain that we durst not freely love him. His heart seemed as if walled in; he had not the free means to unbosom himself. My mother has owned to me that she could never understand him; that her affection and (with all their little strifes) her admiration of him was obstructed. It seemed as if an atmosphere of fear repelled us from him. To me it was especially so. Till late years, when he began to respect me more, and, as it were, to look up to me for instruction, for protection (a relation unspeakably beautiful), I was ever more or less awed and chilled before him. My heart and tongue played freely only with my mother. He had an air of deepest gravity, even sternness. Yet he could laugh with his whole throat, and his whole heart. I have often seen him weep, too; his voice would thicken and his lips curve while reading the Bible. He had a merciful heart to real distress, though he hated idleness, and for imbecility and fatuity had no tolerance. Once — and I think once only — I saw him in a passion of tears. It was when the remains of my mother's fever hung upon her, in 1817, and seemed to threaten the extinction of her reason. We were all of us nigh desperate, and ourselves mad. He burst at last into quite a torrent of grief, cried piteously, and threw himself on the floor and lay moaning. I wondered, and had no words, no tears. It was as if a rock of granite had melted, and was thawing into water. What unknown seas of feeling lie in man, and will from time to time break through!

He was no niggard, but truly a wisely generous economist. He paid his men handsomely and with overplus. He had known poverty in the shape of actual want (in boyhood) and never had one penny which he knew not well how he had come by ("picked," as he said, "out of the hard stone"), yet he ever parted with money as a man that knew when he was getting money's worth; that could give also, and with a frank liberality when the fit occasion called. I remember with the peculiar kind of tenderness that attaches to many similar things in his life, one, or rather, I think, two times, when he sent me to buy a quarter of a pound of tobacco, to give to some old women whom he had had gathering potatoes for him. He nipped off for each a handsome leash, and handed it her by way of over and above. This was a common principle with him. I must have been twelve or thirteen when I fetched this tobacco. I love to think of it. "The little that a just man hath." The old women are now perhaps all dead. He, too, is dead, but the gift still lives.

He was a man singularly free from affectation. The feeling that he had not he could in no wise pretend to have; however ill the want of it might look, he simply would not, and did not, put on the show of it.

Singularly free from envy I may reckon him too, the rather if I consider his keen temper and the value he naturally (as a man wholly for action) set upon success in life. Others that (by better fortune; none was more industrious or more prudent) had grown richer than he did not seem to provoke the smallest grudging in him. They were going their path, he going his; one did not impede the other. He rather seemed to look at such with a kind of respect, a desire to learn from them—at lowest, with indifference.

In like manner, though he above all things (indeed, in strictness solely) admired talent, he seemed never to have measured himself anxiously against any one; was content to be taught by whomsoever could teach him. One or two men, immeasurably his inferiors in faculty, he, I do believe, looked up to and thought, with perfect composure, abler minds than himself.

Complete, at the same time, was his confidence in his own judgment when it spoke to him decisively. He was one of those few that could believe and know as well as inquire and be of opinion. When I remember how much he admired intellectual force, how much he had of it himself, and yet how unconsciously and contentedly he gave others credit for superiority, I again see the healthy spirit of the genuine man. Nothing could please him better than a well-ordered discourse of reason, the clear solution and exposition of any object, and he knew well in such cases when the nail had been hit, and contemptuously enough recognized when it had been missed. He has said of a bad preacher, "he was like a fly wading among tar." Clearness, emphatic clearness, was his highest category of man's thinking power. He delighted always to hear good argument. He would often say, "I would like to hear thee argue with him." He said this of Jeffrey and me, with an air of such simple earnestness, not two years ago (1830), and it was his true feeling. I have often pleased him much by arguing with men (as many years ago I was prone to do) in his presence. He rejoiced greatly in my success, at all events in my dexterity and manifested force. Others of us he admired for our "activity," our practical valor and skill, all of us (generally speaking) for our decent demeanor in the world. It is now one of my greatest blessings (for which I would thank Heaven from the heart) that he lived to see me, through various obstructions, attain some look of doing well. He had "educated" me against much advice, I believe, and chiefly, if not solely, from his own noble faith. James Bell, one of our wise men, had told him, "Educate a boy, and he grows up to despise his ignorant parents." My father once told me this, and added, "Thou hast not done so; God be thanked for it." I have reason to think my father was proud of me (not vain, for he never, except when provoked, openly bragged of us); that here too he lived to see the pleasure of the Lord prosper in his hands. Oh, was it not a happiness for me! The fame of all this planet were not henceforth so precious.

He was thrifty, patient, careless of outward accommodation, had a Spartan indifference to all that. When he quarrelled about such things, it was rather because some human *mismanagement* seemed to look through the evil. Food and all else were simply and solely there as the means *for doing work*. We have lived for months of old (and when he was not any longer poor), because by ourselves, on porridge and potatoes, with no other condiment than what our own cow yielded. Thus are we not now all beggars, as the most like us have become. Mother and father were assiduous, abstemious, frugal without stinginess. They shall not want their reward. Both still knew what they were doing in this world, and why they were here. "Man's chief end," my father could have answered from the depths of his soul, "is to glorify God and enjoy *him* forever." By this light he walked, choosing his path, fitting prudence to principle with wonderful skill and manliness; through "the ruins of a falling era," not once missing his footing. Go thou, whom by the hard toil of his arms and his mind he has struggled to enlighten better; go thou, and do likewise.

His death was unexpected? Not so; every morning and every evening, for perhaps sixty years, he had prayed to the Great Father in words which I shall now no more hear him impressively pronounce, "Prepare us for those solemn events, death, judgment, and eternity." He would pray also, "Forsake us not now when we are old and our heads grown gray." God did not forsake him.

Ever since I can remember, his honored head was gray; indeed, he must have been about forty when I was born. It was a noble head; very large, the upper part of it strikingly like that of the poet Goethe; the mouth again bearing marks of unrefinement, shut, indeed, and significant, yet loosely compressed (as I have seen in the firmest men if used to hard manual labor), betokening depth,

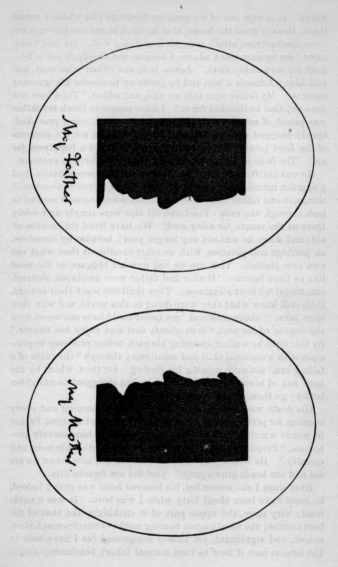

passionateness, force; all in an element not of languor, yet of toil and patient perennial endurance. A face full of meaning* and earnestness, a man of strength and a man of toil. Jane (Mrs. Carlyle) took a profile of him when she was last in Annandale. It is the only memorial we have left, and worth much to us. He was short of stature, yet shorter than usual only in the limbs; of great muscular strength, far more than even his strong-built frame gave promise of. In all things he was emphatically temperate; through life guilty, more than can be said of almost any man, of no excess.

He was born, I think, in the year 1757, at a place called Brown-knowe, a small farm not far from Burnswark Hill, in Annandale. I have heard him describe the anguish of mind he felt when leaving this place, and taking farewell of a "big stone" whereon he had been wont to sit in early boyhood tending the cattle. Perhaps there was a thorn-tree near it. His heart, he said, was like to burst; they were removing to Sibbaldry Side, another farm in the valley of Dryfe. He was come to full manhood. The family was exposed to great privations while at Brownknowe. The mother, Mary Gillespie (she had relations at Dryfesdale) was left with her children, and had not always meal to make them porridge. My father was the second son and fourth child. My grandfather, Thomas Carlyle, after whom I am named, was an honest, vehement, adventurous, but not an industrious man. He used to collect vigorously and rigorously a sum sufficient for his half-year's rent (probably some five or six pounds), lay this by, and, for the rest, leaving the mother with her little ones to manage very much as they could, would meanwhile amuse himself, perhaps hunting, most probably with the Laird of Bridekirk (a swashbuckler of those days, composer of "Bridekirk's Hunting"), partly in the character of kinsman, partly of attendant and henchman. I have heard my father describe the shifts they were reduced to at home. Once, he said, meal, which had perhaps been long scarce, and certainly for some time wanting, arrived at last late at night. The mother proceeded on the spot to make cakes of it, and had no fuel but straw that she tore from the beds (straw lies under the chaff sacks we all slept on) to do it with. The children all rose to eat. Potatoes were little in use then; a "wechtful" was stored up to be eaten perhaps about Halloween. My father often told us how he once, with a providence early manifested, got possession of four potatoes, and, think-

---

* Carlyle breaks off for a moment and writes these words: "About this hour is the funeral. Irving enters. Unsatisfactory." He then goes on.

ing that a time of want might come, hid them carefully against the evil day. He found them long after all grown together; they had not been needed. I think he once told us his first short clothes were a hull made mostly or wholly of leather. We all only laughed, for it is now long ago. Thou dear father! Through what stern obstructions was thy way to manhood to be forced, and for us and for our travelling to be made smooth!

My grandfather, whom I can remember as a slightish, wiry-looking old man, had not possessed the wisdom of his son. Yet perhaps he was more to be pitied than blamed. His mother, whose name I have forgotten, was early left a widow with two of them, in the parish, perhaps in the village, of Middlebie. Thomas, the elder, became a joiner and went to work in Lancashire, perhaps in Lancaster, where he stayed more than one season. He once returned home in winter, partly by ice — skating along the Westmoreland and Cumberland lakes. He was in Dumfriesshire in 1745; saw the Highlanders come through Ecclefechan over the Border heights as they went down; was at Dumfries among them as they returned back in flight. He had gone, by the Lady of Bridekirk's request, to look after the Laird, whom, as a Whig of some note, they had taken prisoner. His whole adventures there he had minutely described to his children (I, too, have heard him speak, but briefly and indistinctly, of them); by my uncle Frank I once got a full account of the matter, which shall perhaps be inserted elsewhere. He worked as carpenter, I know not how long, about Middlebie; then laid aside that craft (except as a side business, for he always had tools which I myself have assisted him in grinding) and went to Brownknowe to farm. In his latter days he was chiefly supported by my father, to whom I remember once hearing him say, with a half-choked tremulous palsied voice, "Thou hast been a good son to me." He died in 1804. I well remember the funeral, which I was at, and that I read (being then a good reader), "MacEwen on the Types" (which I have not seen since, but then partially understood and even liked for its glib smoothness) to the people sitting at the wake. The funeral was in time of snow. All is still very clear to me. The three brothers, my father, Frank, and Tom, spoke together in the dusk on the street of Ecclefechan, I looking up and listening. Tom proposed that he would bear the whole expense, as he had been "rather backward during his life," which offer was immediately rejected.

Old Thomas Carlyle had been proud and poor. No doubt he was discontented enough. Industry was perhaps more difficult in Aunandale then (this I do not think very likely). At all events, the man in honor (the *man*) of those days in that rude border country was a drinker and hunter; above all, a striker. My grandfather did not drink, but his stroke was ever as ready as his word, and both were sharp enough. He was a fiery man, irascible, indomitable, of the toughness and springiness of steel. An old market-brawl, called the "Ecclefechan Dog-fight," in which he was a principal, survives in tradition there to this day. My father, who in youth too had been in quarrels, and formidable enough in them, but from manhood upwards abhorred all such things, never once spoke to us of this. My grandfather had a certain religiousness; but it could not be made dominant and paramount. His life lay in two. I figure him as very miserable, and pardon (as my father did) all his irregularities and unreasons. My father liked, in general, to speak of him when it came in course. He told us sometimes of his once riding down to Annan (when a boy) behind him, on a sack of barley to be shipped, for which there was then no other mode of conveyance but horseback. On arriving at Annan bridge, the people demanded three-halfpence of toll money. This the old man would in no wise pay, for tolls were then reckoned pure imposition, got soon into argument about it, and rather than pay it turned his horse's head aside and swam the river at a dangerous place, to the extreme terror of his boy. Perhaps it was on this same occasion, while the two were on the shore about Whinnyrigg with many others on the same errand (for a boat had come in, from Liverpool probably, and the country must hasten to ship) that a lad of larger size jeered at the little boy for his ragged coat, etc. Whereupon his father, doubtless provoked too, gave him permission to fight the wrong-doer, which he did, and with victory. "Man's inhumanity to man."

I must not dwell on these things, yet will mention the other brother, my grand-uncle Francis, still remembered by his title, "the Captain of Middlebie." He was bred a shoemaker, and, like his elder brother, went to travel for work and insight. My father once described to me with pity and aversion how Francis had on some occasion taken to drinking and to gaming "far up in England" (Bristol?), had lost all his money, and gone to bed drunk. He awoke next morning in horrors, started up, stung by the serpent of remorse, and flinging himself out of bed, broke his leg against a table standing near, and lay there sprawling, and had to lie for weeks, with nothing to pay the shot. Perhaps this was the crisis of his life. Perhaps it was to pay the bill of this very tavern that he went and enlisted himself on board some small-craft man-of-war. A mutiny (as I have heard) took place, wherein Francis Carlyle with great daring stood by the captain and quelled the matter, for which service he was promoted to the command of a revenue ship, and sailed therein chiefly about the Solway seas, and did feats enough, of which perhaps elsewhere. He had retired with dignity on half-pay to his native Middlebie before my birth. I never saw him but once, and then rather memorably.

My grandfather and he, owing to some sort of cloud and misunderstanding, had not had any intercourse for long; in which division the two families had joined. But now, when old Thomas was lying on his probable, and as it proved actual, death-bed, the old rugged sea-captain relented, and resolved to see his brother yet once before he died.

He came in a cart to Ecclefechan (a great enterprise then, for the road was all water-cut, and nigh impassable with roughness). I chanced to be standing by when he arrived. He was a grim, broad, to me almost terrible man, unwieldy so that he could not walk. (My brother John is said to resemble him. He was my prototype of Smollett's Trunnion). They lifted him up the steep straight stairs in a chair to the room of the dying man. The two old brothers saluted each other, hovering over the brink of the grave. They were both above eighty. In some twenty minutes the arm-chair was seen again descending (my father bore one corner of it in front); the old man had parted with his brother for the last time. He went away with few words, but with a face that still dimly haunts me, and I never saw him more. The business at the moment was quite unknown to me, but I gathered it in a day or two, and its full meaning long afterwards grew clear to me. Its outward phases, now after some twenty-eight years, is plain as I have written. Old Francis also died not long afterwards.

One vague tradition I will mention, that our humble forefathers dwelt long as farmers at Burrens, the old Roman station in Middlebie. Once, in times of border robbery, some Cumberland cattle had been stolen and were chased. The traces of them disappeared at Burrens, and the angry Cumbrians demanded of the poor farmer what had become of them. It was vain for him to answer and aver (truly) that he knew nothing of them, had no concern with them. He was seized by the people, and despite his own desperate protestations, despite his wife's shriekings and his children's cries, he was hanged on the spot. The case even in those days was thought piteous, and a perpetual gift of the little farm was made to the poor widow as some compensation. Her children and children's children continued to possess it till their title was questioned by the Duke (of Queensberry), and they (perhaps in my great-grand-father's time, about 1720) were ousted. Date and circumstances for the tale are all wanting. This is my remotest outlook into the past, and itself but a cloudy half or whole hallucination; farther on there is not even a hallucination. I now return. These things are secular and unsatisfactory.

Bred up in such circumstances, the boys were accustomed to all manner of hardship, and must trust for upbringing to nature, to the scanty precepts of their poor mother, and to what seeds or influences of culture were hanging, as it were, in the atmosphere of their environment. Poor boys! they had to scramble, scraffle for their very clothes and food. They knit, they thatched for hire, above all, they hunted. My father had tried all these things almost in boyhood. Every dell and burn-gate and cleugh of that district he had traversed, seeking hares and the like. He used to tell of these pilgrimages. Once I remember his gun-flint was tied on with a hat-band. He was a real hunter, like a wild Indian, from necessity. The hare's flesh was food. Hare-skins (at some six-pence each) would accumulate into the purchase-money of a coat. All these things he used to speak of without either boasting or complaining, not as reproaches to us, but as historical merely. On the whole, he never complained either of the past, the present, or the future. He observed and accurately noted all: he made the most and the best of all. His hunting years were not useless to him. Misery was early training the rugged boy into a stoic, that one day he might be the assurance of a Scottish man.

One Macleod, Sandy Macleod, a wandering pensioner invalided out of some Highland regiment (who had served in America, I must think with General Wolfe), had strayed to Brownknowe with his old wife and taken a cottage of my grandfather. He, with his wild foreign legends and strange, half-idiotic, half-genial ways, was a great figure with the young ones, and I think acted not a little on their character, — least of any, however, on my father, whose early turn for the practical and real made him more heed-less of Macleod and his vagaries. The old pensioner had quaint sayings not without significance. Of a lachrymose, complaining man, for example, he said (or perhaps to him), "he might be thank-ful he was not in purgatory."

The quaint fashion of speaking, assumed for humor, and most noticeable in my uncle Frank, least or hardly at all in my father, was, no doubt, partly derived from this old wanderer, who was much about their house, working for his rent and so forth, and was partly laughed at, partly wondered at, by the young ones. Tinkers also, nestling in outhouses, making pot-metal, and with rude feuds and warfare, often came upon the scene. These, with passing Highland drovers, were perhaps their only visitors. Had there not been a natural goodness and indestructible force in my father, I see not how he could have bodied himself forth from these mean impediments. I suppose good precepts were not wanting. There was the Bible to read. Old John Orr, the schoolmaster, used from time to time to lodge with them; he was religious and enthusiastic (though in practice irregular with drink). In my grandfather, also, there seems to have been a certain geniality; for instance, he and a neighbor, Thomas Hogg, read "Anson's Voyages;" also the "Arabian Nights," for which latter my father, armed with zealous conviction, scrupled not to censure them openly. By one means and another, at an early age he had acquired principles, lights that not only flickered, but shone steadily to guide his way.

It must have been in his teens, perhaps rather early, that he and his elder brother John, with William Bell (afterwards of Wylie Hill, and a noted drover) and his brother, all met in the kiln at Relief to play cards. The corn was dried then at home. There was a fire, therefore, and perhaps it was both heat and light. The boys had played, perhaps, often enough for trifling stakes, and always parted in good humor. One night they came to some disagreement. My father spoke out what was in him about the folly, the sinfulness, of quarrelling over a perhaps sinful amusement. The earnest mind persuaded other minds. They threw the cards into the fire, and (I think the younger Bell told my brother James) no one of the four ever touched a card again through life. My father certainly never hinted at such a game since I knew him. I cannot remember that I, at that age, had any such force of belief. Which of us can?

[*Friday night.* My father is now in his grave, sleeping by the side of his loved ones, his face to the east, under the hope of meeting the Lord when He shall come to judgment, when the times shall be fulfilled. Mysterious life! Yes, there is a God in man. Silence! since thou hast no voice. To imitate him, I will pause here for the night. God comfort my brother. God guard them all.]

Of old John Orr I must say another word. My father, who often spoke of him, though not so much latterly, gave me copious de-

scription of that and other antiquarian matters in one of the pleasantest days I remember, the last time but one (or perhaps two) that
we talked together. A tradition of poor old Orr, as of a man of boundless love and natural worth, still faintly lives in Annandale. If I
mistake not, he worked also as a shoemaker. He was heartily devout, yet subject to fits of irregularity. He would vanish for
weeks into obscure tippling-houses; then reappear, ghastly and
haggard in body and mind, shattered in health, torn with gnawing
remorse. Perhaps it was in some dark interval of this kind (he
was already old) that he bethought him of his father, and how he
was still lying without a stone of memorial. John had already ordered a tombstone for him, and it was lying worked, and, I suppose, lettered and ready, at some mason's establishment (up the
water of Mein), but never yet carried to the place. Probably Orr
had not a shilling of money to hire any carter with, but he hurried off to the spot, and desperately got the stone on his back. It
was a load that had nigh killed him. He had to set it down ever
and anon and rest, and get it up again. The night fell. I think
some one found him desperately struggling with it near Main Hill,
and assisted him, and got it set in its place.

Though far above all quackery, Orr was actually employed to
exorcise a house; some house or room at Orchard, in the parish of
Hoddam. He entered the haunted place; was closeted in it for
some time, speaking and praying. The ghost was really and truly
laid, for no one heard more of it. Beautiful reverence, even of the
rude and ignorant, for the infinite nature of wisdom in the infinite
life of man.

Orr, as already said, used to come much about Brownknowe, being habitually itinerant, and (though schoolmaster of Hoddam)
without settled home. He commonly, my father said, slept with
some of the boys; in a place where, as usual, there were several
beds. He would call out from the bed to my grandfather, also in
his, "Gudeman, I have found it;" found the solution of some problem or other, perhaps arithmetical, which they had been struggling
with; or, "Gudeman, what d'ye think of this?"

I represent him to myself as a squat, pursy kind of figure, grim,
dusky; the blandest and most bounteous of cynics. Also a form of
the past. He was my father's sole teacher in schooling.

It might be in the year, I think, 1773, that one William Brown, a
mason from Peebles, came down into Annandale to do some work;
perhaps boarded in my grandfather's house; at all events, married
his eldest daughter's child, my now old and vehement, then young

and spirited, aunt Fanny. This worthy man, whose nephew is still minister of Eskdalemuir (and author of a book on the Jews), proved the greatest blessing to that household. My father would, in any case, have saved himself. Of the other brothers, it may be doubted whether William Brown was not the primary preserver. *They all learned to be masons from him,* or from one another; instead of miscellaneous laborers and hunters, became regular tradesmen, the best in all their district, the skilfullest and faithfullest, and the best-rewarded every way. Except my father, none of them attained a decisive religiousness. But they all had prudence and earnestness, love of truth, industry, and the blessings it brings. My father, before my time, though not the eldest, had become, in all senses, the head of the house. The eldest was called John. He early got asthma, and for long could not work, though he got his share of the wages still. I can faintly remember him as a pallid, sickly figure; and even one or two insignificant words, and the breathless tone he uttered them in. When seized with extreme fits of sickness, he used to gasp out, "Bring Jamie; do send for Jamie." He died, I think, in 1802. I remember the funeral, and perhaps a day before it, how an ill-behaving servant wench lifted up the coverlid from off his pale, ghastly, befilleted head to show it to some crony of hers; unheeding of me, who was alone with them, and to whom the sight gave a new pang of horror. He was the father of two sons and a daughter, beside whom our boyhood was passed, none of whom have come to anything but insignificance. He was a well-doing man, and left them well; but their mother was not wise, nor they decidedly so. The youngest brother—my uncle Tom—died next; a fiery, passionate, self-secluded, warm, loving, genuine soul, without fear and without guile : of whom it is recorded, he never, from the first tones of speech, "told any lies." A true old-Roman soul, yet so marred and stunted, who well deserves a chapter to himself, especially from me, who so lovingly admired him. He departed in my father's house, in my presence, in the year 1815, the first death I had ever understood and laid with its whole emphasis to heart. Frank followed next, at an interval of some five years; a quaint, social, cheerful man, of less earnestness but more openness, fond of genealogies, old historic poems, queer sayings, and all curious and humane things he could come at.

This made him the greatest favorite. The rest were rather feared; my father, ultimately at least, universally feared and respected. Frank left two sons, as yet young; one of whom, my namesake, gone to be a lawyer, is rather clever, how clever I have not fully seen. All these brothers were men of evidently rather peculiar endowment. They were (consciously) noted for their brotherly affection and coherence, for their hard sayings and *hard strikings*, which only my father ever grew heartily to detest. All of them became prosperous; got a name and possessions in their degree. It was a kindred warmly liked, I believe, by those *near* it; by those at a distance, viewed at worst and lowest, as something dangerous to meddle with, something not to be meddled with.

What are the rich or the poor? and how do the simple annals of the poor differ from the complex annals of the rich, were they never so rich? What is thy attainment compared with an Alexander's, a Mahomet's, a Napoleon's? And what was theirs? A temporary fraction of this planetkin, the whole round of which is but a sandgrain in the all, its whole duration but a moment in eternity. The poorer life or the rich one are but the larger or smaller (very little smaller) letters in which we write the apothegms and golden sayings of life. It may be a false saying or it may be a true one. *There* lies it all. This is of quite infinite moment; the rest is, verily and indeed, of next to none.

Perhaps my father was William Brown's first apprentice. Somewhere about his sixteenth year, early in the course of the engagement, work grew scarce in Annandale. The two "slung their tools" (mallets and irons hung in two equipoised masses over the shoulder), and crossed the hills into Nithsdale to Auldgarth, where a bridge was building. This was my father's most foreign adventure. He never again, or before, saw anything so new; or, except when he came to Craigenputtoch on visits, so distant. He loved to speak of it. That talking day we had together I made him tell it me all over again from the beginning, as a whole, for the first time. He was a "hewer," and had some few pence a day. He could describe with the lucidest distinctness how the whole work went on, and "headers" and "closers," solidly massed together, made an impregnable pile. He used to hear sermons in Closeburn church; sometimes too in Dunscore. The men had a refreshment of ale, for which he too used to table his twopence; but the grown-up men generally, for the most part, refused them. A superintendent of the work, a mason from Edinburgh, who did nothing but look on, and, rather decidedly, insist on terms of contract, "took a great notion" of him; was for having him to Edinburgh along with him. The master builder, pleased with his ingenious diligence, once laid a shilling on his "banker" (stone bench for hewing on), which he rather ungraciously refused. A flood once carried off all the centres and woodwork. He saw the master anxiously, tremulously, watch through the rain as the waters rose. When they prevailed, and all went headlong, the poor man, wringing his hands together, spread them out with open palms down the river, as if to say, "There!"

It was a noble moment, which I regret to have missed, when my father going to look at Craigenputtoch saw this work for the first time again after a space of more than fifty years. How changed was all else, this thing yet the same. Then he was a poor boy, now he was a respected old man, increased in worldly goods, honored in himself and in his household. He grew alert (Jamie said) and eagerly observant, eagerly yet with sadness. Our country was all altered; browsing knowes were become seed-fields; trees, then not so much as seeds, now waved out broad boughs. The houses, the fields, the men, were of another fashion. There was little that he could recognize. On reaching the bridge itself, he started up to his knees in the cart, sat wholly silent, and seemed on the point of weeping.

Well do I remember the first time I saw this bridge twelve years ago in the dusk of a May day. I had walked from Muirkirk, sickly, forlorn, of saddest mood (for it was then my days of darkness). A rustic answered me, "Auldgarth." There it lay, silent, red in the red dusk. It was as if half a century of past time had fatefully for moments turned back.

The master builder of this bridge was one Stewart of Minniyve, who afterwards became my uncle John Aitken's father-in-law. Him I once saw. My Craigenputtoch mason, James Hainning's father, was the smith that "sharpened the tools." A noble craft it is, that of a mason; a good building will last longer than most books, than one book of a million. The Auldgarth bridge still spans the water silently, defies its chafing. There hangs it, and will hang, grim and strong, when of all the cunning hands that piled it together, perhaps the last now is powerless in the sleep of death. O Time! O Time! wondrous and fearful art thou; yet there is in man what is above thee.

Of my father's youth and opening manhood, and with what specialities this period was marked, I have but an imperfect notion. He was now master of his own actions, possessed of means by his own earning, and had to try the world on various sides, and ascertain wherein his own "chief end" in it actually lay. The first impulse of man is to seek for enjoyment. He lives with more or less impetuosity, more or less irregularity, to conquer for himself a home and blessedness of a mere earthly kind. Not till later (in how many cases never!) does he ascertain that on earth there is no such home : that his true home lies beyond the world of sense, is a celestial home. Of these experimenting and tentative days my father did not speak with much pleasure; not at all with exultation. He considered them days of folly, perhaps sinful days. Yet I well know that his life even then was marked by temperance (in all senses), that he was abstemious, prudent, industrious as very few.

I have a dim picture of him in his little world. In summer season diligently, cheerfully laboring with trowel and hammer, amused by grave talk and grave humor with the doers of the craft. Building, walling, is an operation that beyond most other manual ones requires incessant consideration — even new invention. I have heard good judges say that he excelled in it all persons they had seen. In the depth of winter I figure him with the others gathered round his father's hearth (now no longer so poor and desolate), hunting (but now happily for amusement, not necessity), present here and there at some merry meetings and social doings, as poor Annandale, for poor yet God-created men, might then offer. Contentions occur. In these he was no man to be played with : fearless, formidable (I think to all).

In after-times he looked back with sorrow on such things—yet to me they were not, and are not, other than interesting and innocent—scarcely ever, perhaps never, to be considered as *aggressions*, but always as defences, manful assertions of man's rights against men that would infringe them—and victorious ones. I can faintly picture out one scene which I got from him many years ago; perhaps it was at some singing-school; a huge rude peasant was rudely insulting and defying the party my father belonged to, and the others quailed and bore it till he could bear it no longer, but clutches his rough adversary (who had been standing, I think, at some distance on some sort of height) by the two *flanks*, swings him with ireful force round in the air, hitting his feet against some open door, and hurled him to a distance, supine, lamed, vanquished, and utterly humbled. The whole business looks to me to have passed physically in a troubless moonlight.

In the same environment and hue does it now stand in my memory, sad and stern. He could say of such things, "I am wae to think on't:" wae from repentance. Happy he who has nothing worse to repent of.

In the vanities and gallantries of life (though such as these would come across him), he seems to have very sparingly mingled. One Robert Henderson, a dashing projector and devotee, with a dashing daughter, came often up in conversation. This was perhaps (as it were) my father's introduction to the "pride of life:" from which, as his wont was, he appears to have derived little but *instruction*, but expansion and experience. I have good reason to know he never addressed any woman except with views that were pure and manly. But happily he had been enabled very soon in this choice of the false and present against the true and future, to "choose the better part." Happily there still existed in Annandale an influence of goodness, pure emblems of a religion. There were yet men living from whom a youth of earnestness might learn by example how to become a man. Old Robert Brand, my father's maternal uncle, was probably of very great influence on him in this respect. Old Robert was a rigorous religionist, thoroughly filled with a celestial philosophy of this earthly life, which showed impressively through his stout decision and somewhat cross-grained deeds and words. Sharp sayings of his are still recollected there, not unworthy of preserving. He was a man of iron firmness, a just man, and of wise insight. I think my father, consciously and unconsciously, may have learnt more from him than from any other individual. From the time when he connected himself openly with the religious, became a Burgher (strict, not strictest species of Presbyterian Dissenter), may be dated his spiritual majority; his earthly life was now enlightened and overcanopied by a heavenly. He was henceforth a man.

Annandale had long been a lawless Border country. The people had ceased from foray riding, but not from its effects. The "gallant man" of those districts was still a wild, natural, almost animal man. A select few had only of late united themselves. They had built a little meeting-house at Ecclefechan, thatched with heath, and chosen them a priest, by name John Johnston, the priestliest man I ever, under any ecclesiastical guise, was privileged to look upon. He, in his last years, helped me well with my Latin (as he had done many), and otherwise produced me far higher benefit. This pleasant union, this little heath-thatched house, this simple evangelist, together constituted properly the church of that district. They were the blessing and the saving of many. On me too their pious heaven-sent influences still rest and live. Let them employ them well. There was in those days a "teacher of the people." He sleeps not far from my father (who built his monument) in the Ecclefechan church-yard; the teacher and the taught. "Blessed," I again say, "are the dead that die in the Lord. They do rest from their labors; their works follow them."

My father, I think, was of the second race of religious men in Annandale. Old Robert Brand, an ancient herdsman, old John Britton, and some others that I have seen, were perhaps among the first. *There is no third rising.* Time sweeps all away with it so fast at this epoch. The Scottish Church has been short-lived, and was late in reaching thither.

Perhaps it was in 1791 that my father married one Janet Carlyle, a very distant kinswoman of his own (her father yet, I believe, lives, a professor of religion, but long time suspected to be none of the most perfect, though not without his worth). She brought him one son, John, at present a well-doing householder at Cockermouth. She left him and this little life in little more than a year. A mass of long fair woman's hair which had belonged to her long lay in a secret drawer at our house (perhaps still lies); the sight of it used to give me a certain faint horror. It had been cut from her head near death, when she was in the height of fever. She was delirious, and would let none but my father cut it. He thought himself sure of infection, nevertheless consented readily, and escaped. Many ways, I have understood, he had much to suffer then, yet he never spoke of it, or only transiently, and with an historical stoicism. Let me here mention the reverent custom the old men had in Annandale of treating death even in their loosest thoughts. It is now passing away; with my father it was quite invariable. Had he occasion to speak in the future, he would say I will do so and so, never failing to add (were it only against the morrow), " if I be spared," " if I live." The dead, again, he spoke of with perfect freedom, only with serious gravity (perhaps a lowering of the voice), and always, even in the most trivial conversation, adding, " that's gane ;" " my brother John that's gane" did so and so. *Ernst ist das Leben.*

He married again, in the beginning of 1795, my mother, Margaret Aitken (a woman of to me the fairest descent—that of the pious, the just, and wise). She was a faithful helpmate to him, toiling unweariedly at his side; to us the best of all mothers; to whom, for body and soul, I owe endless gratitude. By God's great mercy she is still left as a head and centre to us all, and may yet cheer us with her pious heroism through many toils, if God so please. I am the eldest child, born in 1795, December 4, and trace deeply in myself the character of both parents, also the upbringing and example of both; the inheritance of their natural health, had not I and the time beat on it too hard.

It must have been about the period of the first marriage that my

father and his brothers, already master masons, established themselves in Ecclefechan. They all henceforth began to take on a civil
existence, to "accumulate" in all senses, to grow. They were
among the best and truest men of their craft (perhaps the very best)
in that whole district, and recompensed accordingly. Their gains
were the honest wages of industry, their savings were slow, but
constant, and in my father's, continued (from one source or other)
to the end. He was born and brought up the poorest; by his own
right hand he had become wealthy, as he accounted wealth, and in
all ways plentifully supplied. His household goods, valued in
money, may perhaps somewhat exceed £1000. In real inward
worth that value was greater than that of most kingdoms, than all
Napoleon's conquests, which did not endure. He saw his children
grow up round him to guard him and to do him honor. He had,
ultimately, a hearty respect from all; could look forward from his
verge of this earth, rich and increased in goods, into an everlasting
country, where, through the immeasurable deeps, shone a solemn,
sober hope. I must reckon my father one of the most prosperous
men I have ever in my life known.

Frugality and assiduity, a certain grave composure, an earnestness (not without its constraint, then felt as oppressive a little, yet
which now yields its fruit), were the order of our household. We
were all particularly taught that work (temporal or spiritual) was
the only thing we had to do, and incited always by precept and example to do it well. An inflexible element of authority surrounded
us all. We felt from the first (a useful thing) that our own wish
had often nothing to say in the matter.

It was not a joyful life (what life is?), yet a safe, quiet one; above
most others (or any other I have witnessed) a wholesome one. We
were taciturn rather than talkative. But if little was said, that
little had generally a meaning. I cannot be thankful enough for
my parents. My early, yet not my earliest, recollections of my father have in them a certain awe which only now or very lately has
passed into free reverence. I was parted from him in my tenth
year, and never *habitually* lived with him afterwards. Of the very
earliest I have saved some, and would not for money's worth lose
them. All that belongs to him has become very precious to me.

I can remember his carrying me across Mein Water, over a pool
some few yards below where the present Meinfoot bridge stands.
Perhaps I was in my fifth year. He was going to Luce, I think,
to ask after some joiner. It was the loveliest summer evening I
recollect. My memory dawns (or grows light) at the first aspect

of the stream; of the pool spanned by a wooden bow without railing, and a single plank broad. He lifted me against his thigh with his right hand, and walked careless along till we were over. My face was turned rather downwards. I looked into the deep, clear water and its reflected skies with terror, yet with confidence that he could save me. Directly after, I, light of heart, asked of him what those little black things were that I sometimes seemed to create by rubbing the palms of my hands together; and can at this moment (the mind having been doubtless excited by the past peril) remember that I described them in these words, "little penny rows" (rolls), "but far less." He explained it wholly to me; "my hands were not clean." He was very kind, and I loved him. All around this is dusk or night before and after. It is not my earliest recollection, not even of him. My earliest of all is a mad passion of rage at my elder brother John (on a visit to us likely from his grandfather) in which my father too figures, though dimly, as a kind of cheerful comforter and soother. I had broken my little brown stool, by madly throwing it at my brother, and felt, for perhaps the first time, the united pangs of loss and of remorse. I was perhaps hardly more than two years old, but can get no one to fix the date for me, though all is still quite legible for myself with many of its features. I remember the first "new half-pence" (brought from Dumfries by my father and mother for Alick and me), and words that my uncle John said about it, in 1799! Backwards beyond all, dim ruddy images of deeper and deeper brown shade into the dark beginnings of being.

I remember, perhaps in my fifth year, his teaching me arithmetical things, especially how to divide (my letters, taught me by my mother, I have no recollection of whatever; of reading scarcely any). He said, This is the *divider* (divisor); this, etc.; and gave me a quite clear notion how to do it. My mother said I would forget it all; to which he answered, "Not so much as they that have never learnt it." Five years or so after, he said to me once, "Tom, I do not grudge thy schooling now, when thy uncle Frank owns thee to be a better arithmetician than himself."

He took me down to Annan Academy on the Whitsunday morning, 1806; I trotting at his side in the way alluded to in Teufelsdröckh. It was a bright morning, and to me full of movement, of fluttering, boundless hopes, saddened by parting with mother, with home, and which afterwards were cruelly disappointed. He called once or twice in the grand schoolroom, as he chanced to have business at Annan; once sat down by me (as the master was out) and asked whether I was all well. The boys did not laugh, as I feared; perhaps durst not.

He was always generous to me in my school expenses; never by grudging look or word did he give me any pain. With a noble faith he launched me forth into a world which himself had never been permitted to visit. Let me study to act worthily of him there.

He wrote to me duly and affectionately while I was at college. Nothing that was good for me did he fail with his best ability to provide. His simple, true counsel and fatherly admonitions have now first attained their fit sacredness of meaning. Pity for me if they be thrown away.

His tolerance for me, his trust in me, was great. When I declined going forward into the church (though his heart was set upon it), he respected my scruples, my volition, and patiently let me have my way. In after-years, when I had peremptorily ceased from being a schoolmaster, though he inwardly disapproved of the step as imprudent, and saw me in successive summers lingering beside him in sickliness of body and mind, without outlook towards any good, he had the forbearance to say at worst nothing, never once to whisper discontent with me.

If my dear mother, with the trustfulness of a mother's heart, ministered to all my woes, outward and inward, and even against hope kept prophesying good, he, with whom I communicated far less, who could not approve my schemes, did nothing that was not kind and fatherly. His roof was my shelter, which a word from him (in those sour days of wounded vanity) would have deprived me of. He patiently let me have my way, helping when he could, when he could not help never hindering. When hope again dawned for me, how hearty was his joy, yet how silent! I have been a happy son.

On my first return from college (in the spring, 1810), I met him in the Langlands road, walking out to try whether he would not happen to see me coming. He had a red plaid about him; was recovering from a fit of sickness (his first severe one) and there welcomed me back. It was a bright April day. Where is it now?

The great world-revolutions send in their disturbing billows to the remotest creek, and the overthrow of thrones more slowly overturns also the households of the lowly. Nevertheless, in all cases the wise man adjusts himself. Even in these times the hand of the diligent maketh rich. My father had seen the American War, the French Revolution, the rise and fall of Napoleon. The last arrested him strongly. In the Russian Campaign he bought a London newspaper, which I read aloud to a little circle twice weekly. He was struck with Napoleon, and would say and look pregnant things about him. Empires won and empires lost (while his little household held together), and now it was all vanished like a tavern brawl. For the rest, he never meddled with politics. He was not there to govern, but to be governed; could still live, and therefore did not revolt. I have heard him say in late years, with an impressiveness which all his perceptions carried with them, that the lot of a poor man was growing worse and worse; that the world would not and could not last as it was; that mighty changes of which none saw the end were on the way. To him, as one about to take his departure, the whole was but of secondary moment. He was looking towards "a city that had foundations."

In the "dear years" (1799 and 1800) when the oatmeal was as high as ten shillings a stone, he had noticed the laborers (I have heard him tell) retire each separately to a brook, and there drink instead of dining, without complaint, anxious only to hide it.

At Langholm he once saw a heap of smuggled tobacco publicly burned. Dragoons were ranged round it with drawn swords; some old women stretched through their old withered arms to snatch a little of it, and the dragoons did not hinder them. A natural artist!

The largest sum he ever earned in one year was, *I think*, £100, by the building of Cressfield House. He wisely quitted the mason trade at the time when the character of it had changed, when universal poverty and vanity made show and cheapness (here as everywhere) be preferred to substance; when, as he said emphatically, honest trade "was done." He became farmer (of a wet, clayey spot called Main Hill) in 1815, that so "he might keep all his family about him," struggled with his old valor, and here, too, prevailed.

Two ears of corn are now in many places growing where he found only one. Unworthy, or little worthy, men for the time reap the benefit; but it was a benefit done to God's earth, and God's mankind will year after year get the good of it.

In his contention with an unjust, or, perhaps, only a mistaken, landlord, he behaved with prudent resolution, not like a vain braggart, but like a practically brave man. It was I that innocently (by my settlement at Hoddam Hill) had involved him in it. I must admire now his silence, while we were all so loud and vituperative. He spoke nothing in that matter except only what had practical meaning in it, and in a practical tone. His answers to un-

just proposals, meanwhile, were resolute as ever, memorable for
their emphasis. "I will not do it," said he, once; "I will rather
go to Jerusalem seeking farms, and die without finding one." "We
can live without Sharpe," said he once in my hearing (such a thing,
only once) "and the whole Sharpe creation." On getting to Scotsbrig, the rest of us all triumphed—not he. He let the matter stand
on its own feet; was there, also, not to talk, but to work. He even
addressed a conciliatory letter to General Sharpe (which I saw right
to write for him, since he judged prudence better than pride); but
it produced no result except, indeed, the ascertainment that none
could be produced, which itself was one.

When he first entered our house at Craigenputtoch, he said, in
his slow, emphatic way, with a certain rustic dignity, to my wife
(I had entered without introducing him), "I am grown an *old fellow*" (never can we forget the pathetic slow earnestness of these
two words); "I am grown an *old fellow*, and wished to see ye all
once more while I had opportunity." Jane* was greatly struck
with him, and still farther opened my eyes to the treasure I possessed in a father.

The last thing I gave him was a cake of Cavendish tobacco, sent
down by Alick about this time twelvemonth. Through life I had
given him very little, having little to give. He needed little, and
from me expected nothing. Thou who wouldst give, give quickly.
In the grave thy loved one can receive no kindness. I once bought
him a pair of silver spectacles, of the receipt of which and the letter that accompanied them (John told me), he was very glad, and
nigh weeping. "What I gave, I have." He read with these spectacles till his last days, and, no doubt, sometimes thought of me in
using them.

The last time I saw him was about the first of August last, a few
days before departing hither. He was very kind, seemed prouder
of me than ever. What he had never done the like of before, he
said, on hearing me express something which he admired, "Man,
it's surely a pity that thou shouldst sit yonder with nothing but
the eye of Omniscience to see thee, and thou with such a gift to
speak." His eyes were sparkling mildly, with a kind of deliberate
joy. Strangely, too, he offered me on one of those mornings (knowing that I was poor) "two sovereigns" which he had of his own,
and pressed them on my acceptance. They were lying in his desk;
none knew of them. He seemed really anxious and desirous that

---

* Miss Jane Welsh, whom Carlyle married.

I should take them, should take his little hoard, his *all* that he had to give. I said, jokingly, afterwards, that surely he was FEY. So it has proved.

I shall now no more behold my dear father with these bodily eyes. With him a whole threescore and ten years of the past has doubly died for me. It is as if a new leaf in the great book of time were turned over. Strange time—endless time; or of which I see neither end nor beginning. All rushes on. Man follows man. His life is as a tale that has been told; yet under Time does there not lie Eternity? Perhaps my father, all that essentially was my father, is even now near me, with me. Both he and I are with God. Perhaps, if it so please God, we shall in some higher state of being meet one another, recognize one another. As it is written, We shall be forever with God. The possibility, nay (in some way), the certainty, of perennial existence daily grows plainer to me. "The essence of whatever was, is, or shall be, even now is." God is great. God is good. His will be done, for it will be right.

As it is, I can think peaceably of the departed love. All that was earthly, harsh, sinful, in our relation has fallen away; all that was holy in it remains. I can see my dear father's life in some measure as the sunk pillar on which mine was to rise and be built; the waters of time have now swelled up round his (as they will round mine); I can see it all transfigured, though I *touch* it no longer. I might almost say his spirit seems to have entered into me (so clearly do I discern and love him); I seem to myself only the continuation and second volume of my father. These days that I have spent thinking of him and of his end are the peaceablest, the only Sabbath that I have had in London. One other of the universal destinies of man has overtaken me. Thank Heaven, I know, and have known, what it is to be a son; to love a father, as spirit can love spirit. God give me to live to my father's honor and to His. And now, beloved father, farewell for the last time in this world of shadows! In the world of realities may the Great Father again bring us together in perfect holiness and perfect love! Amen!

Sunday night, Jan. 29, 1832.

EDWARD IRVING

EDWARD IRVING.

Cheyne Row, Autumn, 1866.

EDWARD IRVING died thirty-two years ago (December, 1834) in
the first months of our adventurous settlement here. The memory of him is still clear and vivid with me in all points: that of his
first and only visit to us in this house, in this room, just before leaving for Glasgow (October, 1834), which was the last we saw of him,
is still as fresh as if it had been yesterday; and he has a solemn,
massive, sad, and even pitiable though not much blamable, or in heart
even blamable, and to me always dear and most friendly aspect, in
those vacant kingdoms of the past. He was scornfully forgotten
at the time of his death, having, indeed, sunk a good while before
out of the notice of the more intelligent classes. There has since
been, and now is, in the new theological generation, a kind of re-
vival of him, on rather weak and questionable terms, sentimental
mainly, and grounded on no really correct knowledge or insight.
Which, however, seems to bespeak some continuance of bygone remembrances for a good while yet by that class of people and the
many that hang by them. Being very solitary, and, except for converse with the spirits of my vanished ones, very idle in these hours
and days, I have bethought me of throwing down (the more rapidly the better) something of my recollections of this, to me, very
memorable man, in hopes they may by possibility be worth something by-and-by to some—not worth less than nothing to anybody
(viz. not true and candid according to my best thoughts) if I can
help it.

The Irvings, Edward's father and uncles, lived all within a few
miles of my native place, and were of my father's acquaintance.
Two of the uncles, whose little farm establishments lay close upon
Ecclefechan, were of his familiars, and became mine more or less,
especially one of them (George, of Bogside), who was further a co-
religionist of ours (a "Burgher Seceder," not a "Kirkman," as the
other was). They were all cheerfully quiet, rational, and honest

people, of good - natured and prudent turn. Something of what might be called a kindly vanity, a very harmless self-esteem, doing pleasure to the proprietor and hurt to nobody else, was traceable in all of them. They were not distinguished by intellect, any of them, except it might be intellect in the unconscious or instinctive condition (coming out as prudence of conduct, etc.), of which there were good indications; and of Uncle George, who was prudent enough, and successfully diligent in his affairs (no bad proof of "intellect" in some shape), though otherwise a most taciturn, dull, and almost stupid-looking man, I remember this other fact, that he had one of the *largest heads* in the district, and that my father, he, and a clever and original Dr. Little, their neighbor, never could be fitted at a hat-shop in the village, but had always to send their measure to Dumfries to a hat-maker there. Whether George had a round head or a long, I don't recollect. There was a fine little spice of innocent, faint, but genuine and kindly banter in him now and then. Otherwise I recollect him only as heavy, hebetated, elderly or old, and more inclined to quiescence and silence than to talk of or care about anything exterior to his own interests, temporal or spiritual.

Gavin, Edward's father (name pronounced Gavin=Guyon, as Edward once remarked to me), a tallish man of rugged countenance, which broke out oftenest into some innocent fleer of merriment, or readiness to be merry when you addressed him, was a prudent, honest-hearted, rational person, but made no pretension to superior gifts of mind, though he too, perhaps, may have had such in its undeveloped form. Thus, on ending his apprenticeship, or by some other lucky opportunity, he had formed a determination of seeing a little of England in the first place, and actually got mounted on a stout pony, accoutrements succinctly complete (road-money in a belt round his own body), and rode and wandered at his will deliberately southward, I think, for about six weeks, as far as Wiltshire at least, for I have heard him speak of Devizes, "The Devizes" he called it, as one of his halting-places. What his precise amount of profit from this was I know not at all, but it bespeaks something ingenuous and adventurous in the young man. He was by craft a tanner, had settled in Annan, soon began to be prosperous, wedded well, and continued all his life there. He was among the younger of these brothers, but was clearly the head of them, and, indeed, had been the making of the principal two, George and John, whom we knew. Gavin was baillie in Annan when the furious election sung by Burns ("There were five carlins in the south"—five burghs, namely) took place. Gavin voted the right way (Duke of Queensberry's way) and got for his two brothers each the lease of a snug Queensberry farm, which grew even the snugger as dissolute old Queensberry developed himself more and more into a cynical egoist, sensualist, and hater of his next heir (the Buccleuch, not a Douglas, but a Scott, who now holds both dukedoms), a story well known over Scotland, and of altogether lively interest in Annandale (where it meant entail - leases and large sums of money) during several years of my youth.

These people, the Queensberry farmers, seem to me to have been the happiest set of yeomen I ever came to see, not only because they sat easy as to rent, but because they *knew* fully *how* to sit so, and were pious, modest, thrifty men, who neither fell into laggard relaxation of diligence nor were stung by any madness of ambition, but faithfully continued to turn all their bits of worldly success into real profit for soul and body. They disappeared (in chancery lawsuit) fifty years ago. I have seen various kinds of farmers, scientific, etc., etc., but as desirable a set not since.

Gavin had married well, perhaps rather above his rank, a tall, black-eyed, handsome woman, sister of certian Lowthers in that neighborhood, who did most of the inconsiderable corn trade of those parts, and were considered a stiff-necked, faithful kind of people, apter to do than to speak, originally from Cumberland, I believe. For her own share, the mother of Edward Irving had much of fluent speech in her, and of management; thrifty, assiduous, wise, if somewhat fussy; for the rest, an excellent house mother, I believe, full of affection and tender anxiety for her children and husband. By degrees she had developed the modest prosperity of her household into something of decidedly "genteel" (Annan "gentility"), and having left the rest of the Irving kindred to their rustic solidities, had probably but little practical familiarity with most of them, though never any quarrel or estrangement that I heard of. Her Gavin was never careful of gentility; a roomy simplicity and freedom (as of a man in a dressing-gown) his chief aim. In my time he seemed mostly to lounge about; superintended his tanning only from afar, and at length gave it up altogether. There were four other brothers, three of them small farmers, and a fourth who followed some cattle traffic in Annan, and was well esteemed there for his honest, simple ways. No sister of theirs did I ever hear of; nor what their father had been; some honest little farmer he, too, I conclude.

Their mother, Edward Irving's aged grandmother, I well remember to have seen; once, perhaps twice, at her son George's fireside; a good old woman, half in dotage, and the only creature I ever saw spinning with a *distaff* and no other apparatus but tow or wool. All these Irvings were of blond or even red complexion—red hair a prevailing or sole color in several of their families. Gavin himself was reddish, or at least sandy blond; but all his children had beautifully coal-black hair, except one girl, the youngest of the set but two, who was carroty, like her cousins. The brunette mother with her swift black eyes had prevailed so far. Enough now for the genealogy—superabundantly enough.

One of the circumstances of Irving's boyhood ought not to be neglected by his biographer—the remarkable schoolmaster he had. "Old Adam Hope," perhaps not yet fifty in Irving's time, was all along a notability in Annan.

What had been his specific history or employment before this of schoolmastering I do not know, nor was he ever my schoolmaster except incidentally for a few weeks, once or twice, as substitute for some absentee who had the office. But I can remember on one such occasion reading in Sallust with him, and how he read it and drilled us in it; and I have often enough seen him teach, and knew him well enough. A strong-built, bony, but lean kind of man, of brown complexion, and a pair of the sharpest, not the sweetest, black eyes. Walked in a lounging, stooping figure; in the street broad-brimmed and in clean frugal rustic clothes; in his schoolroom bare-headed, hands usually crossed over back, and with his effective leather strap ("*cat*," as he called it, not *tawse*, for it was not slit at all) hanging ready over his thumb if requisite anywhere. In my time he had a couple of his front teeth quite black, which was very visible, as his mouth usually wore a settled humanly contemptuous grin. "Nothing good to be expected from you or from those you came of, ye little whelps; but we must get from you the best you have, and not complain of anything." This was what the grin seemed to say; but the black teeth (*jet-black*, for he chewed tobacco also to a slight extent, never spitting) were always mysterious to me, till at length I found they were of cork, the product of Adam's frugal penknife, and could be removed at pleasure. He was a man humanly contemptuous of the world, and valued "suffrages" at a most low figure in comparison. I should judge an extremely proud man; for the rest, an inexorable logician, a Calvinist at all points, and Burgher Scotch Seceder to the backbone. He had written a tiny *English* grammar latterly (after Irving's time and before mine) which was a very compact, lucid, and complete little piece; and was regarded by the natives, especially the young natives who had to learn from it, with a certain awe, the feat of authorship in print being then somewhat stupendous and beyond example in those parts. He did not know very much, though still a good something; geometry (of Euclid), Latin, arithmetic, English syntax. But what he did profess or imagine himself to know, he knew in every fibre, and to the very bottom. More rigorously solid teacher of the young idea, so far as he could carry it, you might have searched for through the world in vain. Self-delusion, half-knowledge, sham instead of reality, could not get existed in his presence. He had a Socratic way with him; would accept the hopeless pupil's half-knowledge, or plausible sham of knowledge, with a kind of welcome. "*Hm! hm! yes;*" and then gently enough begin a chain of inquiries more and more surprising to the poor pupil, till he had reduced him to zero—to mere *non plus ultra,* and the dismal perception that his sham of knowledge had been flat misknowledge, with a spice of dishonesty added. This was what he called "making a boy fast." For the poor boy had to sit in his place under arrest all day, or day after day, meditating those dismal new-revealed facts, and beating ineffectually his poor brains for some solution of the mystery and feasible road out. He might apply again at pleasure. "I have made it out, sir." But if again found self-deluded, it was only a new padlock to those *fastenings* of his. They were very miserable to the poor penitent, or impenitent, wretch.

I remember my father once describing to us a call he had made on Hope during the mid-day hour of interval, whom he found reading or writing something, not having cared to lock the door and to go home, with three or four bits of boys sitting prisoners, "made fast" in different parts of the room; all perfectly miserable, each with a rim of black worked out round his eye-sockets (the effect of salt tears wiped by knuckles rather dirty). Adam, though not cat-like of temper or intention, had a kind of cat-pleasure in surveying and playing with these captive mice. He was a praise and glory to well-doing boys, a beneficent terror to the ill-doing or dishonest blockhead sort; and did what was in his power to *educe* (or educate) and make available the net amount of faculty discoverable in each, and separate firmly the known from the unknown or misknown in those young heads. On Irving, who always spoke of him with mirthful affection, he had produced quietly not a little effect; prepared him well for his triumphs in geometry and Latin at college, and through life you could always notice, overhung by

such strange draperies and huge superstructures so foreign to it,
something of that primeval basis of rigorous logic and clear articulation laid for him in boyhood by old Adam Hope. Old Adam,
indeed, if you know the Annanites and him, will be curiously found
visible there to this day; an argumentative, clear-headed, sound-
hearted, if rather conceited and contentious, set of people, more
given to intellectual pursuits than some of their neighbors. I consider Adam an original meritorious kind of man, and regret to think
that his sphere was so limited. In my youngest years his brown,
quietly severe face was familiar to me in Ecclefechan Meeting-house
(my venerable Mr. Johnston's hearers on Sundays, as will be afterwards noted). Younger cousins of his, excellent honest people, I
have since met (David Hope, merchant in Glasgow; William Hope,
scholar in Edinburgh, etc.); and one tall, straight old uncle of his,
very clean always, brown as mahogany and with a head white as
snow, I remember very clearly as the picture of gravity and pious
seriousness in that poor Ecclefechan place of worship, concerning
whom I will report one anecdote and so end. Old David Hope—
that was his name—lived on a little farm close by Solway shore a
mile or two east of Annan. A wet country, with late harvests;
which (as in this year 1866) are sometimes incredibly difficult to
save. Ten days continuously pouring; then a day, perhaps two
days, of drought—part of them, it may be, of roaring wind—during
which the moments are golden for you, and perhaps you had better
work all night, as presently there will be deluges again. David's
stuff, one such morning, was all standing dry again, ready to be
saved still, if he stood to it, which was much his intention. Breakfast (wholesome hasty-porridge) was soon over, and next in course
came family worship, what they call taking the Book (or Books,
i. e. taking your Bible, Psalm and chapter always part of the service). David was putting on his spectacles when somebody rushed
in. "Such a raging wind risen as will drive the stooks (shocks)
into the sea if let alone." "Wind!" answered David, "wind canna
get ae straw that has been appointed mine. Sit down and let us
worship God" (that rides in the whirlwind)! There is a kind of
citizen which Britain used to have, very different from the millionaire Hebrews, Rothschild money-changers, Demosthenes Disraelis,
and inspired young Goschens and their "unexampled prosperity."
Weep, Britain, if the latter are among the honorable you now
have!

One other circumstance that peculiarly deserves notice in Irving's
young life, and perhaps the only other one, is also connected with

Adam Hope—Irving's young religion. Annandale was not an irreligious country, though Annan itself (owing to a drunken clergyman and the logical habits they cultivated) was more given to sceptical freethinking than other places. The greatly prevailing fashion was a decent form of devoutness, and pious theoretically anxious regard for things sacred, in all which the Irving household stood fairly on a level with its neighbors, or perhaps above most of them. They went duly to Kirk, strove still to tolerate and almost to respect their unfortunate minister (who had succeeded a father greatly esteemed in that office, and was a man of gifts himself, and of much good-nature, though so far gone astray). Nothing of profane, or of the least tendency that way, was usually seen, or would have been suffered without protest and grave rebuke in Irving's environment, near or remote. At the same time, this other fact was visible enough if you examined. A man who awoke to the belief that he actually had a soul to be saved or lost was apt to be found among the Dissenting people, and to have given up attendance on the Kirk. It was ungenteel for him to attend the meeting-house, but he found it to be altogether salutary. This was the case throughout in Irving's district and mine. As I had remarked for myself, nobody teaching me, at an early period of my investigations into men and things, I concluded it would be generally so over Scotland, but found when I went north to Edinburgh, Glasgow, Fife, etc., that it was not, or by no means so perceptibly was. For the rest, all Dissent in Scotland is merely a stricter adherence to the National Kirk in all points; and the then Dissenterage is definable to moderns simply as a *"Free Kirk, making no noise."* It had quietly (about 1760), after much haggle and remonstrance, "seceded," or walked out of its stipends, officialities, and dignities, greatly to the mute sorrow of religious Scotland, and was still, in a strict manner, on the united voluntary principle, preaching to the people what of best and sacredest it could. Not that there was not something of rigor, of severity, a lean - minded controversial spirit, among certain brethren, mostly of the laity, I think; narrow nebs (narrow of neb, i. e. of nose or bill), as the outsiders called them; of flowerage, or free harmonious beauty, there could not well be much in this system. But really, except on stated occasions (annual fast-day, for instance, when you were reminded that "a testimony had been lifted up," of which *you* were now the bearers), there was little, almost no talk, especially no preaching at all, about "patronage," or secular controversy, but all turned on the weightier and universal matters of the law, and was considerably entitled to say for itself, "Hear, all men." Very venerable are those old Seceder clergy to me now when I look back on them. Most of the chief figures among them in Irving's time and mine were hoary old men; men so like what one might call antique Evangelists in ruder vesture, and "*poor* scholars and gentlemen of Christ," I have nowhere met with in monasteries or churches, among Protestant or Papal clergy, in any country of the world. All this is altered utterly at present, I grieve to say, and gone to as good as nothing, or worse. It began to alter just about that very period, on the death of those old hoary heads, and has gone on with increasing velocity ever since. Irving and I were probably among the last products it delivered before gliding off, and then rushing off into self-consciousness, arrogancy, insincerity, jangle, and vulgarity, which, I fear, are now very much the definition of it. Irving's concern with the matter had been as follows, brief, but, I believe, ineffaceable through life.

Adam Hope was a rigid Seceder, as all his kin and connections were; and in and about Annan, equally rigid some of them, less rigid others, were a considerable number of such, who, indeed, some few years hence, combined themselves into an Annan Burgher congregation, and set up a meeting-house and minister of their own. For the present they had none, nor had thought of such a thing. Venerable Mr. Johnston of Ecclefechan, six miles off, was their only minister, and to him duly on Sunday Adam and a select group were in the habit of pilgriming for sermon. Less zealous brethren would perhaps pretermit in bad weather, but I suppose it had to be very bad when Adam and most of his group failed to appear. The distance—six miles twice—was nothing singular in this case; one family, whose streaming plaids, hung up to drip, I remember to have noticed one wet Sunday, pious Scotch weavers settled near Carlisle, I was told, were in the habit of walking fifteen miles twice for their sermon, since it was not to be had nearer. A curious phasis of things, quite vanished now, with whatever of divinity and good was in it, and whatever of merely human and not so good. From reflection of his own, aided, or perhaps awakened, by study of Adam Hope and his example (for I think there could not be direct speech or persuasion from Adam in such a matter), the boy Edward joined himself to Adam's pilgriming group, and regularly trotted by their side to Ecclefechan for sermon-listening, and occasionally joining in their pious discourse thither and back. He might be then in his tenth year; distinguished hitherto, both his elder brother John and he, by their wild love of sport as well as readiness in school lessons. John had quite refused this Ecclefechan adventure. And, no doubt, done what he could to prevent it; for father and mother looked on it likewise with dubious or disapproving eyes—"Why run into these ultra courses, sirrah?"—and Edward had no furtherance in it except from within. How long he persisted I do not know, possibly a year or two, or occasionally, almost till he went to college. I have heard him speak of the thing long afterwards in a genially mirthful way; well recognizing what a fantastic, pitifully pedantic, and serio-ridiculous set these road companions of his mostly were. I myself remember two of them who were by no means heroic to me. "Willie Drummond," a little man with mournful goggle-eyes, a tailor, I almost think, and "Joe Blacklock" (Blai-lock), a rickety stocking-weaver, with protruding chin and one leg too short for the other short one, who seemed to me an abundantly solemn and much too infallible and captious little fellow. Edward threw me off with gusto outline likenesses of these among the others, and we laughed heartily without malice. Edward's religion in after-years, though it ran always in the blood and life of him, was never shrieky or narrow; but, even in his last times, with their miserable troubles and confusions, spoke always with a sonorous deep tone, like the voice of a man frank and sincere addressing men. To the last, or almost to the last, I could occasionally raise a genial old Annandale laugh out of him which is now pathetic to me to remember.

I will say no more of Irving's boyhood. He must have sat often enough in Ecclefechan meeting-house along with me, but I never noticed or knew, and had not indeed heard of him till I went to Annan school (1806; a new "Academy," forsooth, with Adam Hope for "English master"), and Irving, perhaps two years before, had left for college. I must bid adieu also to that poor temple of my childhood, to me more sacred at this moment than perhaps the biggest cathedral then extant could have been; rude, rustic, bare—no temple in the world was more so—but there were sacred lambencies, tongues of authentic flame from heaven, which kindled what was best in one, what has not yet gone out. Strangely vivid to me some twelve or twenty of those old faces whom I used to see every Sunday, whose names, employments, precise dwelling-places, I never knew, but whose portraits are yet clear to me as a mirror—their heavy-laden, patient, ever-attentive faces. Fallen solitary most of them. Children all away, wife away forever, or, it might be, wife still there (one such case I well remember), constant like a shadow, and grown very like her old man—the thrifty, cleanly poverty of these good people, their well-saved old coarse clothes (tailed waistcoats down to mid-thigh, a fashion quite dead twenty years before); all this I occasionally see as with eyes sixty or sixty-five years off, and hear the very voice of my mother upon it when sometimes I would be questioning about the persons of the drama and endeavoring to describe and identify them to her for that purpose. O ever-miraculous time! O death! O life!

Probably it was in 1808, April or May, after college time, that I first saw Irving. I had got over my worst miseries in that doleful and hateful "Academy" life of mine, which lasted three years in all; had begun, in spite of precept, to strike about me, to defend myself by hand and voice; had made some comradeship with one or two of my own age, and was reasonably becoming alive in the place and its interests. I remember to have felt some human curiosity and satisfaction when the noted Edward Irving, English Mr. Hope escorting—introduced himself in our Latin class-room one bright forenoon. Hope was essentially the introducer; this was our rector's class-room. Irving's visit to the school had been specially to Adam Hope, his own old teacher, who now brought him down nothing loath. Perhaps our mathematics gentleman, one Morley (an excellent Cumberland man, whom I loved much and who taught me well), had also stepped in in honor of such a stranger. The road from Adam's room to ours lay through Mr. Morley's. Ours was a big airy room lighted from both sides, desks and benches occupying scarcely the smaller half of the floor; better half belonged to the rector, and to the classes he called up from time to time. It was altogether vacant at that moment, and the interview perhaps of ten to fifteen minutes transacted itself in a standing posture there. We were all of us attentive with eye and ear, or as attentive as we durst be, while by theory "preparing our lessons." Irving was scrupulously dressed; black coat, ditto tight pantaloons in the fashion of the day; clerically black his prevailing hue; and looked very neat, self-possessed, and enviable. A flourishing slip of a youth, with coal-black hair, swarthy clear complexion, very straight on his feet, and, except for the glaring squint alone, decidedly handsome. We didn't hear everything; indeed, we heard nothing that was of the least moment or worth remembering. Gathered, in general, that the talk was all about Edinburgh, of this professor and of that, and their merits and method ("wonderful world up yonder, and this fellow has been in it and can talk of it in that easy cool way"). The last professor touched upon, I think, must have been mathematical Leslie (at that time totally non-extant to me), for the one particular I clearly recollect was something from Irving about new doctrines by somebody (doubtless Leslie) " concerning the circle," which last word he pronounced " circul" with a certain preciosity which was noticeable slightly in other parts of his behavior.   Shortly after this of " circul," he courteously (had been very courteous all the time, and unassuming in the main) made his bow, and the interview melted instantly away.   For years I don't remember to have seen Irving's face again.

Seven years come and gone.   It was now the winter of 1815.   I had myself been in Edinburgh College, and above a year ago had duly quitted it.   Had got (by competition at Dumfries, summer 1814) to be " mathematical master " in Annan Academy, with some potential outlook on divinity as ultimatum (a rural divinity student visiting Edinburgh for a few days each year, and " delivering" certain " discourses ").   Six years of that would bring you to the church gate, as four years of continuous " divinity hall " would ; unlucky only that in my case I had never had the least enthusiasm for the business (and there were even grave prohibitive doubts more and more rising ahead): both branches of my situation flatly contradictory to all ideals or wishes of mine, especially the Annan one, as the closely actual and the daily and hourly pressing on me, while the other lay theoretic, still well ahead and perhaps avoidable.   One attraction—one only—there was in my Annan business.   I was supporting myself, even saving some few pounds of my poor £60 or £70 annually, against a rainy day, and not a burden to my ever-generous father any more.   But in all other points of view I was abundantly lonesome, uncomfortable, and out of place there.   Didn't go and visit the people there. (Ought to have pushed myself in a little silently, and sought invitations.   Such their form of special politeness, which I was far too shy and proud to be able for.)   Had the character of morose dissociableness ; in short, thoroughly detested my function and position, though understood to be honestly doing the duties of it, and held for solacement and company to the few books I could command, and an accidental friend I had in the neighborhood (Mr. Cherch and his wife, of Hitchill ; Rev. Henry Duncan, of Ruthwell, and ditto.   These were the two bright and brightest houses for me.   My thanks to them, now and always).   As to my schoolmaster function, it was never said I *misdid* it much ; a clear and correct expositor and enforcer.   But from the first, especially with such adjuncts, I disliked it, and by swift degrees grew to hate it more and more. Some four years in all I had of it; two in Annan, two in Kirkcaldy under much improved social accompaniments. And at the end my solitary desperate conclusion was fixed: that I, for my own part, would prefer to perish in the ditch, if necessary, rather than continue living by such a trade, and peremptorily gave it up accordingly. This long preface will serve to explain the small passage of collision that occurred between Irving and me on our first meeting in this world.

I had heard much of Irving all along; how distinguished in studies, how splendidly successful as teacher, how two professors had sent him out to Haddington, and how his new Academy and new methods were illuminating and astonishing everything there. (Alas! there was one little pupil he had there, with her prettiest little *penna pennœ* from under the table, and let *me* be a boy, too, papa! who was to be of endless moment, and who alone was of any moment to me in all that!) I don't remember any malicious envy whatever towards this great Irving of the distance. For his greatness in study and learning I certainly might have had a tendency, hadn't I struggled against it, and tried to make it emulation: "Do the like, do thou the like under difficulties!" As to his schoolmaster success, I cared little about that, and easily flung that out when it came across me. But naturally all this betrumpeting of Irving to me (in which I could sometimes trace some touch of malice to myself) had not awakened in me any love towards this victorious man. "Ich gönnte ihn," as the Germans phrase it; but, in all strictness, nothing more.

About Christmas-time (1815) I had gone with great pleasure to see Edinburgh again, and read in Divinity Hall a Latin discourse —"exegesis" they call it there—on the question "*Num detur religio naturalis?*" It was the second, and proved to be the last, of my performances on that treatise. My first, an English sermon on the words "Before I was afflicted I went astray, but now," etc., etc., a very weak, flowery, and sentimental piece, had been achieved in 1814, a few months after my leaving for Annan. Piece second, too, I suppose, was weak enough, but I still remember the kind of innocent satisfaction I had in turning it into Latin in my solitude, and my slight and momentary (by no means deep or sincere) sense of pleasure in the bits of compliments and flimsy approbation from comrades and professors on both these occasions. Before Christmas-day I had got rid of my exegesis, and had still a week of holiday ahead for old acquaintances and Edinburgh things, which was the real charm of my official errand thither.

One night I had gone over to Rose Street, to a certain Mr. (afterwards Dr.) Waugh's there, who was a kind of maternal cousin or half-cousin of my own. Had been my school comrade; several years older; item: my predecessor in the Annan "mathematical mastership;" immediate successor he of Morley, and a great favorite in Annan society in comparison with some; and who, though not without gifts, proved gradually to be intrinsically a fool, and, by his insolvencies and confused futilities as doctor there in his native place, has left a kind of remembrance, ludicrous, partly contemptuous, though not without kindliness, too, and even something of respect. His father, with whom I had been boarded while a scholar at Annan, was one of the most respectable and yet laughable of mankind; a ludicrous caricature of originality, honesty, and faithful discernment and practice—all in the awkward form. Took much care of his money, however, which this, his only son, had now inherited, and did not keep very long. Of Waugh senior, and even of Waugh junior, there might be considerable gossiping and quizzical detailing. They failed not to rise now and then, especially Waugh senior did not, between Irving and me, always with hearty ha-ha's, and the finest recognition on Irving's part when we came to be companions afterwards. But whither am I running with so interminable a preface to one of the smallest incidents conceivable?

I was sitting in Waugh junior's that evening, not too vigorously conversing, when Waugh's door went open, and there stepped in Irving, and one Nichol, a mathematical teacher in Edinburgh, an intimate of his, a shrewd, merry, and very social kind of person, whom I did not then know, except by name. Irving was over, doubtless from Kirkcaldy, on his holidays, and had probably been dining with Nichol. The party was to myself not unwelcome, though somewhat alarming. Nichol, I perceived, might be by some three or four years the eldest of us; a sharp man, with mouth rather quizzically close. I was by some three or four years the youngest; and here was Trismegistus Irving, a victorious bashaw, while poor I was so much the reverse. The conversation in a minute or two became quite special, and my unwilling self the centre of it; Irving directing upon me a whole series of questions about Annan matters, social or domestic mostly; of which I knew little, and had less than no wish to speak, though I strove politely to answer succinctly what I could. In the good Irving all this was very natural, nor was there in him, I am well sure, the slightest notion to hurt me or be tyrannous to me. Far the reverse his mood at all

3

times towards all men. But there was, I conjecture, something of
conscious unquestionable superiority, of careless natural *de haut en
bas* which fretted on me, and might be rendering my answers
more and more and more succinct. Nay, my small knowledge
was failing; and I had more than once on certain points—as "Has
Mrs. —— got a baby? is it son or daughter?" and the like—answered candidly, "I *don't* know."

I think three or two such answers to such questions had followed
in succession, when Irving, feeling uneasy, and in a dim manner
that the game was going wrong, answered in gruffish yet not ill-
natured tone, "You seem to know nothing!" To which I with
prompt emphasis, somewhat provoked, replied, "Sir, by what right
do you try my knowledge in this way? Are you grand inquisitor,
or have you authority to question people and cross-question at discretion? I have had no interest to inform myself about the births
in Annan, and care not if the process of birth and generation there
should cease and determine altogether!" "A bad example that,"
cried Nichol, breaking into laughter; "that would never do for me
(a fellow that needs pupils);" and laughed heartily, joined by
Waugh, and perhaps Irving, so that the thing passed off more
smoothly than might have been expected; though Irving, of course,
felt a little hurt, and, I think, did not altogether hide it from me
while the interview still lasted, which was only a short while.
This was my first meeting with the man whom I had afterwards,
and very soon, such cause to love. We never spoke of this small unpleasant passage of fence, I believe, and there never was another
like it between us in the world. Irving did not want some due
heat of temper, and there was a kind of joyous swagger traceable
in his manner in this prosperous young time; but the basis of him
at all times was fine manly sociality, and the richest, truest good-
nature. Very different from the new friend he was about picking up.
No swagger in this latter, but a want of it which was almost still
worse. Not sanguine and diffusive he, but biliary and intense. "Far
too sarcastic for a young man," said several in the years now coming.

Within six or eight months of this, probably about the end of
July, 1816, happened a new meeting with Irving. Adam Hope's
wife had died of a sudden. I went up the second or third evening
to testify my silent condolence with the poor old man. Can still
remember his gloomy look, speechless, and the thankful pressure
of his hand. A number of people were there; among the rest, to
my surprise, Irving—home on his Kirkcaldy holidays—who seemed
to be kindly taking a sort of lead in the little managements. He

conducted worship, I remember, "taking the Book," which was the only fit thing he could settle to; and he did it in a free, flowing, modest, and altogether appropriate manner, "*precenting*," or leading off the Psalm too himself, his voice melodiously strong, and his tune, "St. Paul's," truly sung, which was a new merit in him to me. Quite beyond my own capacities at that time. If I had been in doubts about his reception of me, after that of Rose Street, Edinburgh, he quickly and forever ended them by a friendliness which, in wider scenes, might have been called chivalrous. At first sight he heartily shook my hand, welcomed me as if I had been a valued old acquaintance, almost a brother, and before my leaving, after worship was done, came up to me again, and with the frankest tone said, "You are coming to Kirkcaldy to look about you in a month or two. You know I am there. My house and all that I can do for you is yours: two Annandale people must not be strangers in Fife!" The "doubting Thomas" durst not quite believe all this, so chivalrous was it, but felt pleased and relieved by the fine and sincere tone of it, and thought to himself, "Well, it would be pretty!"

But to understand the full chivalry of Irving, know first what my errand to Kirkcaldy now was.

Several months before this, rumors had come of some break-up in Irving's triumphant Kirkcaldy kingdom. "A terribly severe master, isn't he? Brings his pupils on amazingly. Yes, truly, but at such an expense of cruelty to them. Very proud, too; no standing of him;" him, the least cruel of men, but obliged and expected to go at high-pressure speed, and no resource left but that of spurring on the laggard. In short, a portion, perhaps between a third and fourth part, of Irving's Kirkcaldy patrons, feeling these griefs, and finding small comfort or result in complaining to Irving, had gradually determined to be off from him, and had hit upon a resource which they thought would serve. "Buy off the old parish head schoolmaster," they said; "let Hume have his £25 of salary and go, the lazy, effete old creature. We will apply again to Professors Christison and Leslie, the same who sent us Irving, to send us another 'classical and mathematical' who can start fair." And accordingly, by a letter from Christison, who had never noticed me while in his class, nor could distinguish me from another Mr. Irving Carlyle, an older, considerably bigger boy, with red hair, wild buck-teeth, and scorched complexion, and the *worst Latinist* of all my acquaintance (so dark was the good professor's class-room, physically and otherwise), I learned, much to my surprise and gratification, " that Professor Leslie had been with him; that, etc., etc., as above; and, in brief, that I was the nominee if I would accept." Several letters passed on the subject, and it had been settled, shortly before this meeting with Irving, that I was in my near vacation-time — end of August — to visit Kirkcaldy, take a personal view of everything, and then say yes if I could, as seemed likely.

Thus stood matters when Irving received me in the way described. Noble, I must say, when you put it all together! Room for plenty of the vulgarest peddling feelings there was, and there must still have been between us, had either of us, especially had Irving, been of peddler nature. And I can say there could no two Kaisers, nor Charlemagne and Barbarossa, had they neighbored one another in the empire of Europe, have been more completely rid of all that *sordes* than were we two schoolmasters in the burgh of Kirkcaldy. I made my visit, August coming, which was full of interest to me. Saw St. Andrews, etc.; saw a fine, frank, wholesome-looking people of the Burgher grandees; liked Irving more and more, and settled to return in a couple of months " for good," which I may well say it was, thanks to Irving principally.

George Irving, Edward's youngest brother (who died in London as M.D., beginning practice about 1833), had met me as he returned from his lessons, when I *first* came along the street of Kirkcaldy on that sunny afternoon (August, 1816), and with blithe looks and words had pointed out where his brother lived—a biggish, simple house on the sands. The *when* of my first call there I do not now remember, but have still brightly in mind how exuberantly good Irving was; how he took me into his library, a rough, littery, but considerable collection—far beyond what I had—and said, cheerily flinging out his arms, "Upon all these you have will and waygate," an expressive Annandale phrase of the completest welcome, which I failed not of using by-and-by. I also recollect lodging with him for a night or two nights about that time. Bright moonshine; waves all dancing and glancing out of window, and beautifully humming and lullabying on that fine long sandy beach, where he and I so often walked and communed afterwards. From the first we honestly liked one another and grew intimate; nor was there ever, while we both lived, any cloud or grudge between us, or an interruption of our feelings for a day or hour. Blessed conquest of a friend in this world! That was mainly all the wealth I had for five or six years coming, and it made my life in Kirkcaldy (i. e., till near 1819, I think) a happy season in comparison, and a genially

EARLY PORTRAIT OF THOMAS CARLYLE.

useful. Youth itself—healthy, well-intending youth—is so full of opulences. I always rather liked Kirkcaldy to this day. *Annan* the reverse rather still when its *gueuseries* come into my head, and my solitary quasi-enchanted position among them—unpermitted to kick them into the sea.

Irving's library was of great use to me; Gibbon, Hume, etc. I think I must have read it almost through. Inconceivable to me now with what ardor, with what greedy velocity, literally above ten times the speed I can now make with any book. Gibbon, in particular, I recollect to have read at the rate of a volume a day (twelve volumes in all); and I have still a fair recollection of it, though seldom looking into it since. It was, of all the books, perhaps the most impressive on me in my then stage of investigation and state of mind. I by no means completely admired Gibbon, perhaps not more than I now do; but his winged sarcasms, so quiet and yet so conclusively transpiercing and killing dead, were often admirable potent and illuminative to me. Nor did I fail to recognize his great power of investigating, ascertaining, grouping, and narrating; though the latter had always, then as now, something of a Drury Lane character, the colors strong but coarse, and set off by lights from the side scenes. We had books from Edinburgh College Library, too. (I remember Bailly's "Histoire de l'Astronomie," ancient and also modern, which considerably disappointed me.) On Irving's shelves were the small Didot French classics in quantity. With my appetite sharp, I must have read of French and English (for I don't recollect much classicality, only something of mathematics in intermittent spasms) a great deal during those years.

Irving himself, I found, was not, nor had been, much of a reader; but he had, with solid ingenuity and judgment, by some briefer process of his own, fished out correctly from many books the substance of what they handled, and of what conclusions they came to. This he possessed, and could produce in an "honest" manner, always when occasion came. He delighted to hear me give accounts of my reading, which were often enough a theme between us, and to me as well a profitable and pleasant one. He had gathered by natural sagacity and insight, from conversation and inquiry, a great deal of practical knowledge and information on things extant round him, which was quite defective in me the recluse. We never wanted for instructive and pleasant talk while together. He had a most hearty, if not very refined, sense of the ludicrous; a broad genial laugh in him always ready. His wide just sympathies, his native sagacity, honest-heartedness, and good-humor, made him the most delightful of companions. Such colloquies and such rovings about in bright scenes, in talk or in silence, I have never had since.

The beach of Kirkcaldy in summer twilights, a mile of the smoothest sand, with one long wave coming on gently, steadily, and breaking in gradual explosion into harmless melodious white, at your hand all the way; the break of it rushing along like a mane of foam, beautifully sounding and advancing, ran from south to north, from the West Burn to Kirkcaldy harbor, through the whole mile's distance. This was a favorite scene, beautiful to me still, in the far away. We roved in the woods too, sometimes till all was dark. I remember very pleasant strolls to Dysart, and once or twice to the caves and queer old salt-works of Wemyss. Once, on a memorable Saturday, we made a pilgrimage to hear Dr. Chalmers at Dunfermline the morrow. It was on the inducting young *Mr.* Chalmers as minister there; Chalmers minimus, as he soon got named. The great Chalmers was still in the first flush of his long and always high popularity. "Let us go and hear him once more," said Irving. The summer afternoon was beautiful; beautiful exceedingly our solitary walk by Burntisland and the sands and rocks to Inverkeithing, where we lodged, still in a touchingly beautiful manner (host the schoolmaster, one Douglas from Haddington, a clever old acquaintance of Irving's, in after-years a Radical editor of mark; whose wife, for thrifty order, admiration of her husband, etc., etc., was a model and exemplar). Four miles next morning to Dunfermline and its crowded day, Chalmers maximus not disappointing; and the fourteen miles to Kirkcaldy ending in late darkness, in rain, and thirsty fatigue, which were cheerfully borne.

Another time, military tents were noticed on the Lomond Hills (on the eastern of the two). "Trigonometrical survey," said we; "Ramsden's theodolite, and what not;" let us go. And on Saturday we went. Beautiful the airy prospect from that eastern Lomond far and wide. Five or six tents stood on the top; one a black-stained cooking one, with a heap of coals close by, the rest all closed and occupants gone, except one other, partly open at the eaves, through which you could look in and see a big circular mahogany box (which we took to be the theodolite), and a saucy-looking, cold official gentleman, diligently walking for exercise, no observation being possible, though the day was so bright. No admittance, however. Plenty of fine country-people had come up, to whom the official had been coldly monosyllabic, as to us also he was. Polite, with a shade of contempt, and unwilling to let himself into speech. Irving had great skill in these cases. He remarked—and led us into remarking—courteously, this and that about the famous Ramsden and his instrument, about the famous Trigonometrical Survey, and so forth, till the official, in a few minutes, had to melt; invited us exceptionally in for an actual inspection of his theodolite, which we reverently enjoyed, and saw through it the signal column, a great, broad plank, he told us, on the top of Ben Lomond, sixty miles off, wavering and shivering like a bit of loose tape, so that no observation could be had.

We descended the hill *re factâ*. Were to lodge in Leslie with the minister there, where, possibly enough, Irving had engaged to preach for him next day. I remember a sight of Falkland ruined palace, black, sternly impressive on me, as we came down ; like a black old bit of coffin or "protrusive shin-bone," sticking through from the soil of the dead past. The kirk, too, of next day, I remember, and a certain tragical Countess of Rothes. She had been at school in London; fatherless. In morning walk in the Regent's Park she had noticed a young gardener, had transiently glanced into him, he into her; and had ended by marrying him, to the horror of society, and ultimately of herself, I suppose; for he seemed to be a poor little commonplace creature, as he stood there beside her. She was now an elderly, a stately woman, of resolute look, though slightly sad, and didn't seem to solicit pity. Her I clearly remember, but not who preached, or what; and, indeed, both ends of this journey are abolished to me as if they had never been.

Our voyage to Inchkeith one afternoon was again a wholly pleasant adventure, though one of the rashest. There were three of us; Irving's assistant the third, a hardy, clever kind of man named Donaldson, of Aberdeen origin—Professor Christison's nephew—whom I always rather liked, but who before long, as he could never burst the shell of expert schoolmastering and gerund-grinding, got parted from me nearly altogether. Our vessel was a row-boat belonging to some neighbors; in fact, a trim yawl with two oars in it and a bit of helm, reputed to be somewhat crazy and cranky hadn't the weather been so fine. Nor was Inchkeith our original aim. Our aim had been as follows. A certain Mr. Glen, Burgher minister at Annan, with whom I had lately boarded there, and been domestically very happy in comparison, had since, after very painful and most undeserved treatment from his congregation, seen himself obliged to quit the barren wasp's nest of a thing altogether, and with his wife and young family embark on a missionary career, which had been his earliest thought, as conscience now reminded him, among other considerations. He was a most pure and excellent man, of correct superior intellect, and of much modest piety and amiability. Things were at last all ready, and he and his were come to Edinburgh to embark for Astrachan; where, or whereabouts, he continued diligent and zealous for many years; and was widely esteemed, not by the missionary classes alone. Irving, as well as I, had an affectionate regard for Glen, and, on Saturday eve of Glen's last Sunday in Edinburgh, had come across with me to bid his brave wife and him farewell; Edinburgh from Saturday afternoon till the last boat on Sunday evening. This was every now and then a cheery little adventure of ours, always possible again after due pause. We found the Glens in an inn in the Grass Market, only the mistress, who was a handsome, brave, and cheery-hearted woman, altogether keeping up her spirits. I heard Glen preach for the last time in " Peddie's Meeting-house," a large, fine place behind Bristo Street—night just sinking as he ended, and the tone of his voice betokening how full the heart was. At the door of Peddie's house I stopped to take leave. Mrs. Glen alone was there for me (Glen not to be seen farther). She wore her old bright saucily - affectionate smile, fearless, superior to trouble; but, in a moment, as I took her hand and said, "Farewell, then, good be ever with you," she shot all pale as paper, and we parted mournfully without a word more. This sudden paleness of the spirited woman stuck in my heart like an arrow. All that night and for some three days more I had such a bitterness of sorrow as I hardly recollect otherwise. "Parting sadder than by death," thought I, in my foolish inexperience; "these good people are to live, and we are never to behold each other more." Strangely, too, after about four days it went quite off, and I felt it no more. This was, perhaps, still the third day; at all events, it was the day of Glen's sailing for St. Petersburg, while Irving and I went watching from Kirkcaldy sands the Leith ships outward bound, afternoon sunny, tide ebbing, and settled with ourselves which of the big ships was Glen's. "That one surely," we said at last; "and it bends so much this way one might, by smart rowing, cut into it, and have still a word with the poor Glens." Of nautical conclusions none could be falser, more ignorant, but we instantly set about executing it; hailed Donaldson, who was somewhere within reach, shoved "Robie Greg's" poor green-painted, rickety yawl into the waves (Robie, a good creature who would rejoice to have obliged us), and pushed out with our best speed to intercept that outward-bound big ship. Irving, I think, though the strongest of us, rather preferred the helm part then and afterwards, and did not much take the oar when he could honorably help it. His steering, I doubt not, was perfect, but in the course of half an hour it became ludicrously apparent that we were the tortoise chasing the hare, and that we should or could in no wise ever intercept that big ship. Short counsel thereupon, and determination, probably on my hint, to make for Inchkeith at least, and treat ourselves to a visit there.

We prosperously reached Inchkeith, ran ourselves into a wild, stony little bay (west end of the island towards the lighthouse), and stept ashore. Bay in miniature was prettily savage, every stone in it, big or little, lying just as the deluges had left them in ages long gone. Whole island was prettily savage. Grass on it mostly wild and scraggy, but equal to the keep of seven cows. Some patches (little bedquilts as it were) of weak dishevelled barley trying to grow under difficulties; these, except perhaps a square yard or two of potatoes equally ill off, were the only attempt at crop. Inhabitants none except these seven cows, and the lighthouse-keeper and his family. Conies probably abounded, but these were *feræ naturæ*, and didn't show face. In a slight hollow about the centre of the island (which island I think is traversed by a kind of hollow of which our little bay was the western end) were still traceable some ghastly remnants of "Russian graves," graves from a Russian squadron which had wintered thereabouts in 1799 and had there buried its dead. Squadron we had often heard talked of, what foul creatures these Russian sailors were, how (for one thing) returning from their sprees in Edinburgh at late hours, they used to climb the lamp-posts in Leith Walk and drink out the train oil irresistible by vigilance of the police, so that Leith Walk fell ever and anon into a more or less eclipsed condition during their stay! Some rude wooden crosses, rank wild grass, and poor sad grave hillocks almost abolished, were all of memorial they had left. The lighthouse was curious to us; the only one I ever saw before or since. The "revolving light" not produced by a single lamp on its axis, but by ten or a dozen of them all set in a wide glass cylinder, each with its hollow mirror behind it, cylinder alone slowly turning, was quite a discovery to us. Lighthouse-keeper too in another sphere of inquiry was to me quite new; by far the most life-weary looking mortal I ever saw. Surely no lover of the picturesque, for in nature there was nowhere a more glorious view. He had seven cows too, was well fed, I saw, well clad, had wife and children fairly eligible looking. A shrewd healthy Aberdeen native; his lighthouse, especially his cylinder and lamps, all kept

3*

shining like a new shilling—a kindly man withal—yet in every feature of face and voice telling you, " Behold the victim of un-speakable ennui." We got from him down below refection of the best, biscuits and new milk I think almost better in both kinds than I have tasted since. A man not greedy of money either. We left him almost sorrowfully, and never heard of him more.

The scene in our little bay, as we were about proceeding to launch our boat, seemed to me the beautifullest I had ever beheld. Sun about setting just in face of us, behind Ben Lomond far away. Edinburgh with its towers; the great silver mirror of the Frith girt by such a framework of mountains; cities, rocks and fields and wavy landscapes on all hands of us; and reaching right un-derfoot, as I remember, came a broad pillar as of gold from the just sinking sun; burning axle as it were going down to the centre of the world ! But we had to bear a hand and get our boat launched, daylight evidently going to end by-and-by. Kirkcaldy was some five miles off, and probably the tide not in our favor. Gradually the stars came out, and Kirkcaldy crept under its coverlid, show-ing not itself but its lights. We could still see one another in the fine clear gray, and pulled along what we could. We had no ac-cident; not the least ill-luck. Donaldson, and perhaps Irving too, I now think, wore some air of anxiety. I myself by my folly felt nothing, though I now almost shudder on looking back. We leapt out on Kirkcaldy beach about eleven P.M., and then heard sufficient-ly what a misery and tremor for us various friends had been in.

This was the small adventure to Inchkeith. Glen and family re-turned to Scotland some fifteen years ago; he had great approval from his public, but died in a year or two, and I had never seen him again. His widow, backed by various Edinburgh testimoni-als, applied to Lord Aberdeen (Prime Minister) for a small pension on the "Literary list." Husband had translated the Bible (or New Testament) into Persic, among other public merits non-literary : and through her son solicited and urged me to help, which I did zealously, and by continual dunning of the Duke of Argyll (whom I did not then personally know, and who was very good and patient with me), an annual £50 was at last got; upon which Mrs. Glen, adding to it some other small resources, could frugally but comfort-ably live. This must have been in 1853. I remember the young Glen's continual importunity in the midst of my *Friedrich* incipi-encies was not always pleasant, and my chief comfort in it was the pleasure which success would give my mother. Alas, my good mother did hear of it, but pleasure even in this was beyond her in the dark valley she was now travelling! When she died (Christmas, 1853), one of my reflections was: "Too late for *her* that little bit of kindness; my last poor effort, and it came too late." Young Glen with his too profuse thanks, etc., was again rather importunate. Poor young soul, he is since dead. His mother appeared in person one morning at my door in Edinburgh (last spring [1866], in those Rector hurries and hurlyburlies now so sad to me); T. Erskine just leading me off somewhither. An aged decent widow, looking kindly on me and modestly thankful; so changed I could not have recognized a feature of her. How *tragic* to one is the sight of "old friends;" a thing I always really shrink from. Such my lot has been!

Irving's visits and mine to Edinburgh were mostly together, and had always their attraction for us in the meeting with old acquaintances and objects of interest, but except from the books procured could not be accounted of importance. Our friends were mere ex-students, cleverish people mostly, but of no culture or information; no aspiration beyond (on the best possible terms) bread and cheese. Their talk in good part was little else than gossip and more or less ingenious giggle. We lived habitually by their means in a kind of Edinburgh element, not in the still baser Kirkcaldy one, and that was all. Irving now and then perhaps called on some city clergyman, but seemed to have little esteem of them by his reports to me afterwards. I myself by this time was indifferent on that head. On one of those visits my last feeble tatter of connection with Divinity Hall affairs or clerical outlooks was allowed to snap itself and fall definitely to the ground. Old Dr. Ritchie "not at home" when I called to enter myself. "Good!" answered I; "let the omen be fulfilled." Irving on the contrary was being licensed—probably through Annan Presbytery; but I forget the when and where, and indeed conjecture it may have been before my coming to Kirkcaldy. What alone I well remember is his often and ever notable preaching in those Kirkcaldy years of mine. This gave him an interest in conspicuous clergymen—even if stupid—which I had not. Stupid those Edinburgh clergy were not at all by any means; but narrow, ignorant, and barren to us two, they without exception were.

In Kirkcaldy circles (for poor Kirkcaldy had its circles and even its West end, much more genial to me than Annan used to be) Irving and I seldom or never met; he little frequented them, I hardly at all. The one house where I often met him, besides his own, was the Manse, Rev. Mr. Martin's, which was a haunt of his, and where, for his sake partly, I was always welcome. There was a feeble intellectuality current here; the minister was a precise, innocent, didactic kind of man, and I now and then was willing enough to step in, though various boys and girls went cackling about, and Martin himself was pretty much the only item I really liked. The girls were some of them grown up, not quite ill-looking, and all thought to be or thinking themselves "clever and learned;" yet even these, strange to say, in the great rarity of the article and my ardent devotion to it, were without charm to me. They were not the best kind of children; none of them I used to think quite worthy of such a father. Martin himself had a kind of cheery grace and sociality of way (though much afflicted by dyspepsia), a clear-minded, brotherly, well-intentioned man, and bating a certain glimmer of vanity which always looked through, altogether honest, wholesome as Scotch oatmeal. His wife, who had been a beauty, perhaps a wit, and was now grown a notable manager of house and children, seemed to me always of much inferior type, visibly proud as well as vain, of a snappish rather uncomfortable manner, betokening, even in her kindness, steady egoism and various splenetic qualities. A big burly brother of hers, a clergyman whom I have seen, a logical enough, sarcastic, swashing kind of man in his sphere, struck me as kneaded out of precisely the same clay. All Martin's children, I used to fancy, had this bad cross in the birth; it is certain that none of them came to much good. The eldest Miss Martin, perhaps near twenty by this time, was of bouncing, frank, gay manners and talk, studious to be amiable, but never quite satisfactory on the side of *genuineness*. Something of affected you feared always in these fine spirits and smiling discourses, to which however you answered with smiles. She was very ill-looking withal; a skin always under blotches and discolorment; muddy gray eyes, which for their part never laughed with the other features; pock-marked, ill-shapen triangular kind of face, with hollow cheeks and long chin; decidedly unbeautiful as a young woman. In spite of all which (having perhaps the arena much to herself) she had managed to charm poor Irving for the time being, and it was understood they were engaged, which unfortunately proved to be the fact. Her maternal ill-qualities came out in her afterwards as a bride (an engaged young lady), and still more strongly as a wife. Poor woman, it was never with her will; you could perceive she had always her father's strong and true wish to be good, had not her difficulties been quite too strong. But it was and is very visible to me, she (unconsciously for much the greater part) did a good deal aggravate all that was bad in Irving's "London position," and impeded his wise profiting by what was really good in it. Let this be *enough said* on that subject for the present.

Irving's preachings as a licentiate (or probationer waiting for fixed appointment) were always interesting to whoever had acquaintance with him, especially to me who was his intimate. Mixed with but little of self-comparison or other dangerous ingredient, indeed with loyal recognition on the part of most of us, and without any grudging or hidden envy, we enjoyed the broad potency of his delineations, exhortations, and free flowing eloquences, which had all a manly and original turn; and then afterwards there was sure to be on the part of the public a great deal of criticising pro and contra, which also had its entertainment for us. From the first Irving read his discourses, but not in a servile manner; of attitude, gesture, elocution there was no neglect. His voice was very fine; melodious depth, strength, clearness, its chief characteristics. I have heard more pathetic voices, going more direct to the heart both in the way of indignation and of pity, but recollect none that better filled the ear. He affected the Miltonic or old English Puritan style, and strove visibly to imitate it more and more till almost the end of his career, when indeed it had become his own, and was the language he used in utmost heat of business for expressing his meaning. At this time and for years afterwards there was something of preconceived intention visible in it, in fact of real affectation, as there could not well help being. To his example also I suppose I owe something of my own poor affectations in that matter, which are now more or less visible to me, much repented of or not. We were all taught at that time by Coleridge, etc., that the old English dramatists, divines, philosophers, judicious Hooker, Milton, Sir Thomas Browne, were the genuine exemplars, which I also tried to believe, but never rightly could *as a whole*. The young must learn to speak by imitation of the older who already do it, or have done it. The ultimate rule is: learn so far as possible to be intelligible and transparent—no notice taken of your style, but solely of what you express by it. This is your clear rule, and if you have anything which is not quite trivial to express to your contemporaries, you will find such rule a great deal more difficult to follow than many people think.

On the whole, poor Irving's style was sufficiently surprising to his hidebound public, and this was but a slight circumstance to the novelty of the matter he set forth upon them. Actual practice.

"If this thing is true, why not do it? You had better do it. There will be nothing but misery and ruin in not doing it." That was the gist and continual purport of all his discoursing, to the astonishment and deep offence of hidebound mankind. There was doubtless something of rashness in the young Irving's way of preaching; not perhaps quite enough of pure, complete, and serious conviction (which ought to have lain silent a good while before it took to speaking). In general I own to have felt that there was present a certain inflation or spiritual bombast in much of this, a trifle of unconscious playactorism (highly unconscious but not quite absent) which had been unavoidable to the brave young prophet and reformer. But brave he was, and bearing full upon the truth if not yet quite attaining it. And as to the offence he gave, our withers were unwrung. I for one was perhaps rather entertained by it, and grinned in secret to think of the hides it was piercing! Both in Fife and over in Edinburgh, I have known the offence very rampant. Once in Kirkcaldy Kirk, which was well filled and all dead silent under Irving's grand voice, the door of a pew a good way in front of me (ground floor—right-hand as you fronted the preacher), banged suddenly open, and there bolted out of it a middle-aged or elderly little man (an insignificant baker by position), who with long swift strides, and face and big eyes all in wrath, came tramping and sounding along the flags close past my right hand, and vanished out of doors with a slam; Irving quite victoriously disregarding. I remember the violently angry face well enough, but not the least what the offence could have been. A kind of "Who are you, sir, that dare to tutor *us* in that manner, and harrow up our orthodox quiet skin with your novelties?" Probably that was all. In Irving's preaching there was present or prefigured generous opulence of ability in all kinds (except perhaps the very highest kind not even prefigured), but much of it was still crude; and this was the reception it had for a good few years to come; indeed, to the very end he never carried all the world along with him, as some have done with far fewer qualities.

In vacation time, twice over, I made a walking tour with him. First time I think was to the Trosachs, and home by Loch Lomond, Greenock, Glasgow, etc., many parts of which are still visible to me. The party generally was to be of four; one Piers, who was Irving's housemate or even landlord, schoolmaster of Abbotshall, i. e., of "The Links," at the southern extra-burghal part of Kirkcaldy, a cheerful scatterbrained creature who went ultimately as preacher or professor of something to the Cape of Good Hope, and one Brown (James Brown), who had succeeded Irving in Haddington, and was now tutor somewhere. The full rally was not to be till Stirling; even Piers was gone ahead; and Irving and I, after an official dinner with the burghal dignitaries of Kirkcaldy, who strove to be pleasant, set out together one gray August evening by Forth sands towards Torryburn. Piers was to have beds ready for us there, and we cheerily walked along our mostly dark and intricate twenty-two miles. But Piers had nothing serviceably ready; we could not even discover Piers at that dead hour (2 A.M.), and had a good deal of groping and adventuring before a poor inn opened to us with two coarse clean beds in it, in which we instantly fell asleep. Piers did in person rouse us next morning about six, but we concordantly met him with mere ha-ha's! and inarticulate hootings of satirical rebuke, to such extent that Piers, convicted of nothing but heroic punctuality, flung himself out into the rain again in momentary indignant puff, and strode away for Stirling, where we next saw him after four or five hours. I remember the squalor of our bedroom in the dim rainy light, and how little we cared for it in our opulence of youth. The sight of giant Irving in a shortish shirt on the sanded floor, drinking patiently a large tankard of "penny whaup" (the smallest beer in creation) before beginning to dress, is still present to me as comic. Of sublime or tragic, the night before a mysterious great red glow is much more memorable, which had long hung before us in the murky sky, growing gradually brighter and bigger, till at last we found it must be Carron Ironworks, on the other side of Forth, one of the most impressive sights. Our march to Stirling was under pouring rain for most part, but I recollect enjoying the romance of it; Kincardine, Culross (Cu'ros), Clackmannan, here they are then; what a wonder to be here! The Links of Forth, the Ochills, Grampians, Forth itself, Stirling, lion-shaped, ahead, like a lion couchant with the castle for his crown; all this was beautiful in spite of rain. Welcome too was the inside of Stirling, with its fine warm inn and the excellent refection and thorough drying and refitting we got there, Piers and Brown looking pleasantly on. Strolling and sight-seeing (day now very fine—Stirling all washed) till we marched for Doune in the evening (Brig of Teith, "blue and arrowy Teith," Irving and I took that byway in the dusk); breakfast in Callander next morning, and get to Loch Katrine in an hour or two more. I have not been in that region again till August last year, four days of magnificently perfect hospitality with Stirling of Keir. Almost surprising how mournful it was to "look on this picture and on that" at interval of fifty years.

Irving was in a sort the captain of our expedition: had been there before, could recommend everything; was made, unjustly by us, responsible for everything. The Trosachs I found really grand and impressive, Loch Katrine exquisitely so (my first taste of the beautiful in scenery). Not so, any of us, the dirty smoky farm hut at the entrance, with no provision in it but bad oatcakes and unacceptable whiskey, or the "Mrs. Stewart" who somewhat royally presided over it, and dispensed these dainties, expecting to be flattered like an independency as well as paid like an innkeeper. Poor Irving could not help it; but in fine, the rains, the hardships, the ill diet was beginning to act on us all, and I could perceive that we were in danger of splitting into two parties. Brown, leader of the Opposition—myself considerably flattered by him, though not seduced by him into factious courses, only led to see how strong poor Piers was for the Government interest. This went to no length, never bigger than a summer cloud or the incipiency of one. But Brown in secret would never quite let it die out (a jealous kind of man, I gradually found; had been much commended to us by Irving, as of superior intellect and honesty; which qualities I likewise found in him, though with the above abatement), and there were divisions of vote in the walking parliament, two against two; and had there not been at this point, by a kind of outward and legitimate reason, which proved very sanatory in the case, an actual division of routes, the folly might have lasted longer and become audible and visible—which it never did. Sailing up Loch Katrine in top or unpicturesque part, Irving and Piers settled with us that only we two should go across Loch Lomond, round by Tarbert, Roseneath, Greenock, they meanwhile making direct for Paisley country, where they had business. And so on stepping out and paying our boatmen they said adieu, and at once struck leftwards, we going straight ahead; rendezvous to be at Glasgow again on such and such a day. (What feeble trash is all this. . . . Ah me! no better than Irving's penny whaup with the gas *gone out* of it. Stop to-day, October 4, 1866.)

The heath was bare, trackless, sun going almost down. Brown and I (our friends soon disappearing) had an interesting march, good part of it dark, and flavored just to the right pitch with something of anxiety and something of danger. The sinking sun threw his reflexes on a tame-looking house with many windows some way to our right, the *"Kharrison* of Infersnaidt," an ancient anti-Rob Roy establishment, as two rough Highland wayfarers had lately informed us. Other house or persons we did not see, but made for the shoulder of Benlomond and the boatman's hut, partly, I think, by the stars. Boatman and huthold were in bed, but he, with a ragged little sister or wife, cheerfully roused themselves; cheerfully and for most part in silence, rowed us across (under the spangled vault of midnight; which, with the lake waters silent as if in deep dream, several miles broad here, had their due impression on us) correctly to Tarbert, a most hospitable, clean, and welcome little country inn (now a huge "hotel" I hear, worse luck to it, with its nasty "Hotel Company limited"). On awakening next morning, I heard from below the sound of a churn; prophecy of new genuine butter, and even of ditto rustic buttermilk.

Brown and I did very well on our separate branch of pilgrimage; pleasant walk and talk down to the west margin of the loch (incomparable among lakes or lochs yet known to me); past Smollett's pillar; emerge on the view of Greenock, on Helensburgh, and across to Roseneath Manse, where with a Rev. Mr. Story, not yet quite inducted, whose "Life" has since been published, who was an acquaintance of Brown's, we were warmly welcomed and well entertained for a couple of days. Story I never saw again, but he, acquainted in Haddington neighborhood, saw some time after incidentally a certain bright figure, to whom I am obliged to him at this moment for speaking favorably of me. "Talent plenty; fine vein of satire in him!" something like this. I suppose they had been talking of Irving, whom both of them knew and liked well. Her, probably at that time I had still never seen, but she told me long afterwards.

At Greenock I first saw *steamers* on the water; queer little dumpy things with a red sail to each, and legible name, "Defiance," and such like, bobbing about there, and making continual passages to Glasgow as their business. Not till about two years later (1819 if I mistake not) did Forth see a steamer; Forth's first was far bigger than the Greenock ones, and called itself "The Tug," being intended for towing ships in those narrow waters, as I have often seen it doing; *it* still, and no rival or congener, till (in 1825) Leith, spurred on by one Bain, a kind of scientific half-pay Master R. N., got up a large finely appointed steamer, or pair of steamers, for London; which, so successful were they, all ports then set to imitating. London alone still held back for a good few years; London was notably shy of the steamship, great as are its doings now in that line. An old friend of mine, the late Mr. Strachey,* has told me that in his school days he at one time—early in the Nineties I should guess, say 1793—used to see, in crossing Westminster Bridge, a little model steamship paddling to and fro between him and Blackfriars Bridge, with steam funnel, paddle wheels, and the other outfit, exhibiting and recommending itself to London and whatever scientific or other spirit of marine adventure London might have. London entirely dead to the phenomenon—which had to duck under and dive across the Atlantic before London saw it again, when a new generation had risen. The real inventor of steamships, I have learned credibly elsewhere, the maker and proprietor of that fruitless model on the Thames, was Mr. Miller, Laird of Dalswinton in Dumfriesshire (Poet Burns's landlord), who spent his life and his estate in that adventure, and is not now to be heard of in those parts; having had to sell Dalswinton and die quasi-bankrupt (and I should think broken-hearted) after that completing of his painful invention and finding London and mankind dead to it. Miller's assistant and work-hand for many years was John Bell, a joiner in the neighboring village of Thornhill. Miller being ruined, Bell was out of work and connection: emigrated to New York, and there speaking much of his old master, and glorious unheeded invention well known to Bell in all its outlines or details, at length found one Fulton to listen to him; and by "Fulton and Bell" (about 1809) an actual packet steamer was got launched, and, lucratively plying on the Hudson River, became the miracle of Yankee-land, and gradually of all lands. These I believe are essentially the facts. Old Robert M'Queen of Thornhill, Strachey of the India House, and many other bits of good testimony and indication, once far apart, curiously coalescing and corresponding for me. And as, possibly enough, the story is not now known in whole to anybody but myself, it may go in here as a digression—à propos of those brisk little Greenock steamers which I first saw, and still so vividly remember; little "Defiance," etc., saucily bounding about with their red sails in the sun, on this my tour with Irving.

Those old three days at Roseneath are all very vivid to me, and marked in white. The quiet blue mountain masses, giant Cobler overhanging, bright seas, bright skies, Roseneath new mansion (still unfinished and standing as it did), the grand old oaks, and a

---

* Late Charles Buller's uncle. Somersetshire gentleman, ex-Indian, died in 1831, an examiner in the India House; colleague of John S. Mill and his father there.

certain handfast, middle-aged, practical and most polite "Mr. Campbell" (the Argyll factor there) and his two sisters, excellent lean old ladies, with their wild Highland accent, wiredrawn but genuine good manners and good principles, and not least their astonishment, and shrill interjections at once of love and fear, over the talk they contrived to get out of me one evening and perhaps another when we went across to tea; all this is still pretty to me to remember. They are all dead, the good souls—Campbell himself, the Duke told me, died only lately, very old—but they were to my rustic eyes of a superior, richly furnished stratum of society; and the thought that I too might perhaps be "one and somewhat" (*Ein und Etwas*) among my fellow creatures by-and-by, was secretly very welcome at their hands. We rejoined Irving and Piers at Glasgow; I remember our glad embarkation towards Paisley by canal trackboat; visit preappointed for us by Irving, in a good old lady's house, whose son was Irving's boarder; the dusty, sunny Glasgow evening; and my friend's joy to see Brown and me. Irving was very good and jocund-hearted : most blithe his good old lady, whom I had seen at Kirkcaldy before. We had a pleasant day or two in those neighborhoods; the picturesque, the comic, and the genially common all prettily combining; particulars now much forgotten. Piers went to eastward, Dunse, his native country; "born i' Dunse," equal in sound to born a dunce, as Irving's laugh would sometimes remind him; "opposition party" (except it were in the secret of Brown's jealous heart) there was now none; Irving in truth was the natural king among us, and his qualities of captaincy in such a matter were indisputable.

Brown, he, and I went by the Falls of Clyde; I do not recollect the rest of our route, except that at New Lanark, a green silent valley, with cotton works turned by Clyde waters, we called to see Robert Owen, the then incipient arch-gomeril, "model school," and thought it (and him, whom after all we did not see, and knew only by his pamphlets and it) a thing of wind not worth considering farther; and that after sight of the Falls, which probably was next day, Irving came out as captain in a fine new phase. The Falls were very grand and stormful—nothing to say against the Falls; but at the last of them, or possibly at Bothwell Banks farther on, a woman who officiated as guide and cicerone, most superfluous, unwilling too, but firmly persistent in her purpose, happened to be in her worst humor; did nothing but snap and snarl, and being answered by bits of quiz, towered at length into foam. She intimated she would bring somebody who would ask us how we could so treat an unprotected female, and vanished to seek the champion or champions. As our business was done, and the woman paid too, I own (with shame if needed) my thought would have been to march with decent activity on our way, not looking back unless summoned to do it, and prudently evading discrepant circles of that sort. Not so Irving, who drew himself up to his full height and breadth, cudgel in hand, and stood there, flanked by Brown and me, waiting the issue.

Issue was, a thickish kind of man, seemingly the woman's husband, a little older than any of us, stept out with her, calmly enough surveying, and at a respectful distance; asked if we would buy apples? Upon which with negatory grin we did march. I recollect too that we visited lead hills and descended into the mines; that Irving prior to Annan must have struck away from us at some point. Brown and I, on arriving at Mainhill, found my dear good mother in the saddest state; dregs of a bad fever hanging on her; my profound sorrow at which seemed to be a surprise to Brown, according to his letters afterwards. With Brown, for a year or two ensuing, I continued to have some not unpleasant correspondence; a conscientious, accurate, clear-sighted, but rather narrow and unfruitful man, at present tutor to some Lockhart of Lee, and wintering in Edinburgh. Went afterwards to India as Presbyterian clergyman somewhere, and shrank gradually, we heard, into complete aridity, phrenology, etc., etc., and before long died there. He had, after Irving, been my dear little Jeannie's teacher and tutor; she never had but these two, and the name of her, like a bright object far above me like a star, occasionally came up between them on that journey; I dare say at other times. She retained a child's regard for James Brown, and in this house he was always a memorable object.

My second tour with Irving had nothing of circuit in it: a mere walk homeward through the Peebles-Moffat moor country, and is not worth going into in any detail. The region was without roads, often without foot-tracks, had no vestige of an inn, so that there was a kind of knight-errantry in threading your way through it; not to mention the romance that naturally lay in its Ettrick and Yarrow, and old melodious songs and traditions. We walked up Meggat Water to beyond the sources, emerged into Yarrow, not far above St. Mary's Loch; a charming secluded shepherd country, with excellent shepherd population—nowhere setting up to be picturesque, but everywhere honest, comely, well done to, peaceable and useful. Nor anywhere without its solidly characteristic features, hills, mountains, clear rushing streams, cosy nooks and homesteads, all of fine rustic type; and presented to you *in naturâ,* not as in a Drury Lane with stage-lights and for a purpose; the vast and yet not savage solitude as an impressive item, long miles from farm to farm, or even from one shepherd's cottage to another. No company to you but the rustle of the grass underfoot, the tinkling of the brook, or the voices of innocent primæval things. I repeatedly walked through that country up to Edinburgh and down by myself in subsequent years, and nowhere remember such affectionate, sad, and thoughtful, and in fact, interesting and salutary journeys. I have had days clear as Italy (as in this Irving case), days moist and dripping, overhung with the infinite of silent gray—and perhaps the latter were the preferable in certain moods. You had the world and its waste imbroglios of joy and woe, of light and darkness, to yourself alone. You could strip barefoot if it suited better, carry shoes and socks over shoulder, hung on your stick; clean shirt and comb were in your pocket; *omnia mea mecum porto.* You lodged with shepherds who had clean solid cottages; wholesome eggs, milk, oatbread, porridge, clean blankets to their beds, and a great deal of human sense and unadulterated natural politeness. Canty, shrewd and witty fellows, when you set them talking; knew from their hill tops every bit of country between Forth and Solway, and all the shepherd inhabitants within fifty miles, being a kind of confraternity of shepherds from father to son. No sort of peasant laborers I have ever come across seemed to me so happily situated, morally and physically well-developed, and deserving to be happy, as those shepherds of the Cheviots. *O fortunatos nimium!* But perhaps it is all altered not a little now, as I sure enough am who speak of it!

Irving's course and mine was from bonny Yarrow onwards by Loch Skene and the "Grey Mare's Tail" (finest of all cataracts, lonesome, simple, grand, that are now in my memory) down into Moffat dale where we lodged in a shepherd's cottage. Caplegill, old Walter Welsh's farm, must have been near, though I knew not of it then. From the shepherd people came good talk; Irving skilful to elicit topography; Poet Hogg (who was then a celebrity), "Shirra Scott" (Sir Walter, Sheriff of Selkirkshire, whose borders we had just emerged from); then gradually stores of local anecdote, personal history, etc. These good people never once asked us whence, whither, or what are you? but waited till perhaps it voluntarily came, as generally chanced. Moffat dale with its green holms and hill ranges, "Correyran Saddle-yoke" (actual

quasi-saddle, you can sit astride anywhere, and a stone dropped
from either hand will roll and bound a mile), with its pleasant
groves and farmsteads, voiceful limpid waters rushing fast *for Annan*, all was very beautiful to us; but what I most remember is
Irving's arrival at Mainhill with me to tea, and how between my
father and him there was such a mutual recognition. My father
had seen Loch Skene, the Grey Mare's Tail, etc., in his youth, and
now gave in few words such a picture of it, forty years after sight,
as charmed and astonished Irving; who on his side was equally
unlike a common man, definitely true, intelligent, frankly courteous, faithful in whatever he spoke about. My father and he saw
one another (on similar occasions) twice or thrice again, always
with increasing esteem; and I rather think it was from Irving on
this particular occasion that I was first led to compare my father
with other men, and see how immensely superior he, altogether unconsciously, was. No intellect equal to his, in certain important
respects, have I ever met with in the world. Of my mother, Irving
never made any reading for himself, or could well have made, but
only through me, and that too he believed in and loved well; generally all recognizing Irving.

The Kirkcaldy population were a pleasant, honest kind of fellow-
mortals; something of quietly fruitful, of good *old Scotch* in their
works and ways; more *vernacular*, peaceable, fixed, and almost genial in their mode of life than I had been used to in the Border
home-land. Fife generally we liked, those ancient little burghs
and sea villages, with their poor little havens, salt pans, and weath-
erbeaten bits of Cyclopean breakwaters and rude innocent machineries, are still kindly to me to think of. Kirkcaldy itself had
many looms, had Baltic trade, had whale-fishery, etc., and was a
solidly diligent, yet by no means a panting, puffing, or in any way
gambling "Lang Town." The flaxmill-machinery, I remember,
was turned mainly by *wind;* and curious blue painted wheels, with
oblique vans (how working I never saw) rose from many roofs for
that end. We all, I in particular, always rather liked the people,
though from the distance chiefly, chagrined and discouraged by the
sad *trade* one had! Some hospitable human firesides I found, and
these were at intervals a fine little element, but in general we were
but onlookers (the one real society our books and our few selves).
Not even with the bright "young ladies" (which was a sad feature)
were we on speaking terms. By far the cleverest and brightest,
however, an ex-pupil of Irving's, and genealogically and otherwise
(being poorish, proud, and well-bred) a kind of alien in the place, I

did at last make some acquaintance with (at Irving's first, I think, though she rarely came thither); some acquaintance, and it might easily have been more, had she and her aunt and our economics and other circumstances liked. She was of the fair-complexioned, softly elegant, softly grave, witty and comely type, and had a good deal of gracefulness, intelligence, and other talent. Irving too, it was sometimes thought, found her very interesting, could the Miss Martin bonds have allowed, which they never would. To me who had only known her for a few months, and who within twelve or fifteen months saw the last of her, she continued for perhaps some three years a figure hanging more or less in my fancy on the usual romantic, or latterly quite elegiac and silent terms, and to this day there is in me a goodwill to her, a candid and gentle pity for her, if needed at all. She was of the Aberdeenshire Gordons, a far-off Huntly I doubt not; "Margaret Gordon," born I think in New Brunswick, where her father, probably in some official post, had died young and poor. Her accent was prettily English and her voice very fine. An aunt (widow in Fife, childless, with limited resources, but of frugal cultivated turn, a lean, proud elderly dame, once a "Miss Gordon" herself, sang Scotch songs beautifully, and talked shrewd *Aberdeenish* in accent and otherwise) had adopted her and brought her hither over seas; and here as Irving's ex-pupil, she now, cheery though with dim outlooks, was. Irving saw her again in Glasgow one summer, touring, etc., he himself accompanying joyfully, not joining (so I understood it) the retinue of suitors or potential suitors, rather perhaps indicating gently "No, I must not," for the last time. A year or so after we heard the fair Margaret had married some rich insignificant Aberdeen Mr. Something, who afterwards got into Parliament, thence out to "Nova Scotia" (or so) as "Governor," and I heard of her no more, except that lately she was still living about Aberdeen, childless, as the Dowager Lady, her Mr. Something having got knighted before dying. Poor Margaret! Speak to her since the "good-bye then" at Kirkcaldy in 1819 I never did or could. I saw her, recognizably to me, here in her London time, twice (1840 or so), once with her maid in Piccadilly, promenading, little altered; a second time, that same year or next, on horseback both of us, and meeting in the gate of Hyde Park, when her eyes (but that was all) said to me almost touchingly, "Yes, yes, that is you." Enough of that old matter, which but half concerns Irving and is now quite extinct.

In the space of two years we had all got tired of schoolmastering and its mean contradictions and poor results: Irving and I quite resolute to give it up for good; the headlong Piers disinclined for it on the then terms longer, and in the end of 1818 we all three went away; Irving and I to Edinburgh, Piers to his own east country, whom I never saw again with eyes, poor, good rattling soul. Irving's outlooks in Edinburgh were not of the best, considerably checkered with dubiety, opposition, and even flat disfavor in some quarters; but at least they were far superior to mine, and indeed, I was beginning my four or five most miserable, dark, sick, and heavy-laden years; Irving, after some staggerings aback, his seven or eight healthiest and brightest. He had as one item several good hundreds of money to wait upon. My *peculium* I don't recollect, but it could not have exceeded £100. I was without friends, experience, or connection in the sphere of human business, was of shy humor, proud enough and to spare, and had begun my long curriculum of dyspepsia which has never ended since!

Irving lived in Bristo Street, more expensive rooms than mine, used to give breakfasts to intellectualities he fell in with, I often a guest with them. They were but stupid intellectualities, and the talk I got into there did not please me even then; though it was well enough received. A visible gloom occasionally hung over Irving, his old strong sunshine only getting out from time to time. He gave lessons in mathematics, once for a while to Captain Basil Hall, who had a kind of thin celebrity then, and did not seem to love too well that small lion or his ways with him. Small lion came to propose for me at one stage; wished me to go out with him "to Dunglas," and there do "lunars" in his name, he looking on and learning of me what would come of its own will. "Lunars" meanwhile were to go to the Admiralty, testifying there what a careful studious Captain he was, and help to get him promotion, so the little wretch smilingly told me.

I remember the figure of him in my dim lodging as a gay, crackling, sniggering spectre, one dusk, and endeavoring to seduce my affability in lieu of liberal wages into this adventure. Wages, I think, were to be smallish ("so poor are we"), but then the great Playfair is coming on visit. "You will see Professor Playfair." I had not the least notion of such an enterprise on these shining terms, and Captain Basil with his great Playfair in posse vanished for me into the shades of dusk for good. I don't think Irving ever had any other pupil but this Basil for perhaps a three months. I had not even Basil, though private teaching, to me the poorer, was much the more desirable if it would please to come; which it generally would not in the least. I was timorously aiming towards "literature," too; thought in audacious moments I might perhaps earn some trifle that way by honest labor to help my finance; but in that, too, I was painfully sceptical (talent and opportunity alike doubtful, alike incredible, to me poor downtrodden soul), and in fact there came little enough of produce or finance to me from that source, and for the first years absolutely none in spite of my diligent and desperate efforts, which are sad to me to think of even now. *Acti labores;* yes, but of such a futile, dismal, lonely, dim and chaotic kind, in a scene all ghastly-chaos to one, sad, dim and ugly as the shores of Styx and Phlegethon, as a nightmare-dream become real! No more of that; it did not conquer me, nor quite kill me, thank God. Irving thought of nothing as ultimate but a clerical career, obstacles once overcome; in the meanwhile we heard of robust temporary projects. "Tour to Switzerland," glaciers, Geneva, "Lake of Thun," very grand to think of, was one of them; none of which took effect.

I forget how long it was till the then famed Dr. Chalmers, fallen in want of an assistant, cast his eye on Irving. I think it was in the summer following our advent to Edinburgh. I heard duly about it, how Rev. Andrew Thomson, famous *malleus* of theology in that time, had mentioned Irving's name, had engaged to get Chalmers a hearing of him in his (Andrew's) church; how Chalmers heard *incognito,* and there ensued negotiation. Once I recollect transiently seeing the famed Andrew on occasion of it (something Irving had forgotten with him, and wished me to call for), and what a lean-minded, iracund, ignorant kind of man Andrew seemed to me; also much more vividly, in autumn following, one fine airy October day in Annandale, Irving on foot on his way to Glasgow for a month of actual trial. Had come by Mainhill, and picked me up to walk with him seven or eight miles farther into Dryfe Water (i. e. valley watered by clear swift Dryfe, quasi Drive, so impetuous and swift is it), where was a certain witty comrade of ours, one Frank Dickson, preacher at once and farmer (only son and heir of his father who had died in that latter capacity). We found Frank I conclude, though the whole is now dim to me, till we arrived all three (Frank and I to set Irving on his road and bid him good speed) on the top of a hill commanding all upper Annandale, and the grand mass of Moffat hills, where we paused thoughtful a few moments. The blue sky was beautifully spotted with white clouds, which, and their shadows on the wide landscape, the wind was beautifully chasing. *Like life,* I said with a kind of emotion, on which Irving silently pressed my arm with the hand near it or per-

4

haps on it, and a moment after, with no word but his "farewell" and ours, strode swiftly away. A mail coach would find him at Moffat that same evening (after his walk of about thirty miles), and carry him to Glasgow to sleep. And the curtains sink again on Frank and me at this time.

Frank was a notable kind of man, and one of the memorabilities to Irving as well as me; a most quizzing, merry, entertaining, guile-less, and unmalicious man; with very considerable logic, reading, contemptuous observation and intelligence, much real tenderness too, when not obstructed, and a mournful true affection especially for the friends he had lost by death! No mean impediment *there* any more (that was it), for Frank was very sensitive, easily moved to something of envy, and as if surprised when contempt was not possible; easy banter was what he habitually dwelt in; for the rest an honorable, bright, amiable man; alas, and his end was very tragic! I have hardly seen a man with more opulence of conver-sation, wit, fantastic bantering, ingenuity, and genial human sense of the ridiculous in men and things: Charles Buller, perhaps, but he was of far more refined, delicately managed, and less copious tone; finer by nature, I should say, as well as by culture, and had nothing of the fine *Annandale Rabelais* turn which had grown up, partly of will and at length by industry as well, in poor Frank Dickson in the valley of Dryfe amid his little stock of books and rustic phenomena. A slightly built man, nimble-looking, and yet lazy-looking, our Annandale Rabelais; thin, neatly expressive aqui-line face, gray genially laughing eyes, something sternly serious and resolute in the squarish fine brow, nose specially aquiline, thin, and rather small. I well remember the play of point and nostrils there, while his wild home - grown *Gargantuisms* went on. He rocked rather, and negligently wriggled in walking or standing, something slightly twisted in the spine, I think; but he made so much small involuntary tossing and gesticulating while he spoke or listened, you never noticed the twist. What a childlike and yet half imp-like volume of laughter lay in Frank; how he would fling back his fine head, left cheek up, not himself laughing much or loud even, but showing you such continents of inward gleesome mirth and victo-rious mockery of the dear stupid ones who had crossed his sphere of observation. A wild roll of sombre eloquence lay in him too, and I have seen in his sermons sometimes that brow and aquiline face grow dark, sad, and thunderous like the eagle of Jove. I al-ways liked poor Frank, and he me heartily. After having tried to banter me down and recognized the mistake, which he loyally did for himself and never repeated, we had much pleasant talk together first and last.

His end was very tragic, like that of a sensitive, gifted man, too much based on laughter. Having no good prospect of Kirk promotion in Scotland (I think his Edinburgh resource had been mainly that of teaching under Mathematical Nichol for certain hours daily), he perhaps about a year after Irving went to Glasgow had accepted some offer to be Presbyterian chaplain and preacher to the Scotch in Bermuda, and lifted anchor thither with many regrets and good wishes from us all. I did not correspond with him there, my own mood and posture being so dreary and empty. But before Irving left Glasgow, news came to me (from Irving I believe) that Frank, struck quite miserable and lame of heart and nerves by dyspepsia and dispiritment, was home again, or on his way home to Dryfesdale, there to lie useless, Irving recommending me to do for him what kindness I could, and not remember that he used to disbelieve and be ignorantly cruel in my own dyspeptic tribulations. This I did not fail of, nor was it burdensome, but otherwise, while near him in Annandale.

Frank was far more wretched than I had been; sunk in spiritual dubieties too, which I by that time was getting rid of. He had brought three young Bermuda gentlemen home with him as pupils (had been much a favorite in society there). With these in his rough farm-house, Belkat hill,* he settled himself to live. Farm was *his*, but in the hands of a rough-spun sister and her ploughing husband, who perhaps was not over glad to see Frank return, with new potientiality of ownership if he liked, which truly I suppose he never did. They had done some joinering, plank-flooring in the farm-house, which was weather-tight, newish though straight and dim, and there on rough rustic terms, perhaps with a little disappointment to the young gentlemen, Frank and his Bermudians lived, Frank himself for several years. He had a nimble, quick pony, rode latterly (for the Bermudians did not stay above a year or two) much about among his cousinry of friends, always halting and baiting with me when it could be managed. I had at once gone to visit him, found Bell Top Hill on the new terms as interesting as ever. A comfort to me to administer some comfort, interesting even to compare dyspeptic notes. Besides, Frank by degrees would kindle into the old coruscations, and talk as well as ever. I remember some of those visits to him, still more the lonely,

---

* Bell Top Hill, near Hook, head part of the pleasant vale of Dryfe.

silent rides thither, as humanly impressive, wholesome, not unpleasant; especially after my return from Buller tutorship, and my first London visit (in 1824), when I was at Hoddam Hill, idly high and dry like Frank (or only translating German romance, etc.), and had a horse of my own. Frank took considerably to my mother; talked a great deal of his bitter Byronic scepticism to her, and seemed to feel like oil poured into his wounds her beautifully pious contradictions of him and it. "Really likes to be contradicted, poor Frank!" she would tell me afterwards. He might be called a genuine bit of rustic dignity—modestly, frugally, in its simplest expression, gliding about among us there. This lasted till perhaps the beginning of 1826. I do not remember him at Scotsbrig ever. I suppose the lease of his farm may have run out that year, not renewed, and that he was now farther away. After my marriage, perhaps two years after it, from Craigenputtoch I wrote to him, but never got the least answer, never saw him or *distinctly* heard of him more. Indistinctly I did, with a shock, hear of him once, and then a second, a final time, thus. My brother Jamie,* riding to Moffat in 1828 or so, saw near some poor cottage (not a farm at all, a bare place for a couple of cows, perhaps it was a turnpike-keeper's cottage), not far from Moffat, a forlornly miserable-looking figure, walking languidly to and fro, parted from him by the hedge, whom in spite of this sunk condition he recognized clearly for Frank Dickson, who, however, took no notice of him. "Perhaps refuses to know me," thought Jamie; "they have lost their farm—sister and husband seem to have taken shelter here, and there is the poor gentleman and scholar Frank sauntering miserably with an old plaid over his head, slipshod in a pair of old clogs." That was Jamie's guess, which he reported to me; and a few months after grim whisper came, low but certain—no inquest of coroner there—that Frank was dead, and had gone in the Roman fashion. What other could he do now—the silent, valiant, though vanquished man? He was hardly yet thirty-five, a man richer in gifts than nine-tenths of the vocal and notable are. I remember him with sorrow and affection, native - countryman Frank, and his little life. What a strange little island fifty years off; sunny, homelike, pretty in the memory, yet with tragic thunders waiting it!

Irving's Glasgow news from the first were good. Approved of, accepted by the great Doctor and his congregation, preaching

---

* Youngest brother, ten years my junior.

heartily, laboring with the "visiting deacons" (Chalmers's grand
parochial anti-pauperism apparatus much an object with the Doctor at this time), seeing and experiencing new things on all hands
of him in his new wide element. He came occasionally to Edinburgh on visit. I remember him as of prosperous aspect; a little
more carefully, more clerically dressed than formerly (ample black
frock, a little longer skirted than the secular sort, hat of gravish
breadth of brim, all very simple and correct). He would talk
about the Glasgow Radical weavers, and their notable receptions
of him and utterances to him while visiting their lanes; was not
copious upon his great Chalmers, though friendly in what he did
say. All this of his first year must have been in 1820 or late in
1819; year 1819 comes back into my mind as the year of the Radical "rising" in Glasgow; and the kind of altogether imaginary
"fight" they attempted on Bonny Muir against the Yeomanry
which had assembled from far and wide. A time of great rages
and absurd terrors and expectations, a very fierce Radical and
anti-Radical time. Edinburgh endlessly agitated by it all round
me, not to mention Glasgow in the distance—gentry people full of
zeal and foolish terror and fury, and looking disgustingly busy and
important. Courier hussars would come in from the Glasgow region covered with mud, breathless, for head-quarters, as you took
your walk in Princes Street; and you would hear old powdered
gentlemen in silver spectacles talking with low-toned but exultant
voice about "cordon of troops, sir," as you went along. The mass
of the people, not the populace alone, had a quite different feeling,
as if the danger from those West-country Radicals was small or
imaginary, and their grievances dreadfully real; which was with
emphasis my own private notion of it. One bleared Sunday morning, perhaps seven or eight A.M., I had gone out for my walk. At
the riding-house in Nicholson Street was a kind of straggly group,
or small crowd, with red-coats interspersed. Coming up I perceived it was the "Lothian Yeomanry," Mid or East I know not,
just getting under way for Glasgow to be part of "the cordon."
I halted a moment. They took their way, very ill ranked, not numerous or very dangerous-looking men of war; but there rose from
the little crowd by way of farewell cheer to them the strangest
shout I have heard human throats utter, not very loud, or loud
even for the small numbers; but it said as plain as words, and with
infinitely more emphasis of sincerity, " May the devil go with *you*,
ye peculiarly contemptible and dead to the distresses of your fellow-creatures." Another morning, months after, spring and sun

now come, and the "cordon," etc., all over, I met an advocate slightly of my acquaintance hurrying along musket in hand towards the
Links, there to be drilled as item of the "gentlemen" volunteers
now afoot. "You should have the like of this," said he, cheerily
patting his musket. "H'm, yes; but I haven't yet quite settled on
which side"—which probably he hoped was quiz, though it really
expressed my feeling. Irving too, and all of us juniors, had the
same feeling in different intensities, and spoken of only to one another; a sense that revolt against such a load of unveracities, im-
postures, and quietly inane formalities would one day become indispensable; sense which had a kind of rash, false, and quasi-inso-
lent joy in it; mutiny, revolt, being a light matter to the young.

Irving appeared to take great interest in his Glasgow visitings
about among these poor weavers and free communings with them
as man with man. He was altogether human we heard and could
well believe; he broke at once into sociality and frankness, would
pick a potato from their pot, and in eating it get at once into free
and kindly terms. "Peace be with you here" was his entering sal-
utation one time in some weaving-shop which had politely paused
and silenced itself on sight of him; "peace be with you." "Ay,
sir, if there's plenty wi't!" said an angry little weaver who happened to be on the floor, and who began indignant response and
remonstrance to the minister and his fine words. "Quite angry
and fiery," as Irving described him to us; a fine thoughtful brow,
with the veins on it swollen and black, and the eyes under it sparkling and glistening, whom however he succeeded in pacifying, and
parting with on soft terms. This was one of his anecdotes to us.
I remember that fiery little weaver and his broad brow and swollen
veins, a vanished figure of those days, as if I had myself seen him.

By-and-by, after repeated invitations, which to me were permis-
sions rather, the time came for my paying a return visit. I well
remember the first visit and pieces of the others; probably there
were three or even four in all, each of them a real holiday to me.
By steamer to Bo'ness and then by canal. Skipper of canal-boat
and two Glasgow scamps of the period, these are figures of the first
voyage; very vivid these, the rest utterly out. I think I always
went by Bo'ness and steam *so far*, coach the remainder of the road
in all subsequent journeys. Irving lived in Kent Street, eastern
end of Glasgow, ground floor, tolerably spacious room. I think he
sometimes gave up his bedroom (me the bad sleeper) and went out
himself to some friend's house. David Hope (cousin of old Adam's,
but much younger, an excellent guileless man and merchant) was

warmly intimate and attached; the like William Graham of Burns-wark, Annandale, a still more interesting character; with both of whom I made or renewed acquaintance which turned out to be agreeable and lasting. These two were perhaps Irving's most domestic and practically trusted friends, but he had already many in the better Glasgow circles; and in generous liking and appreciation tended to excess, never to defect, with one and all of them. "Philosophers" called at Kent Street whom one did not find so extremely philosophical, though all were amiable and of polite and partly religious turn; and in fact these reviews of Glasgow in its streets, in its jolly Christmas dining-rooms and drawing-rooms, were cordial and instructive to me; the solid style of comfort, freedom, and plenty was new to me in that degree. The Tontine (my first evening in Glasgow) was quite a treat to my rustic eyes; several hundreds of such fine, clean, opulent, and enviable or amiable-looking good Scotch gentlemen sauntering about in truthful gossip or solidly reading their newspapers. I remember the shining bald crowns and serene white heads of several, and the feeling, *O fortunatos nimium*, which they generally gave me. Irving was not with me on this occasion; had probably left me there for some half-hour, and would come to pick me up again when ready. We made morning calls together too, not very many, and found once, I recollect, an exuberant bevy of young ladies which I (silently) took as sample of great and singular privilege in my friend's way of life. Oftenest it was crotchety, speculative, semi-theological elderly gentlemen whom we met, with curiosity and as yet without weariness on my part, though of course their laughing, chatting daughters would have been better. The Glasgow women of the young lady stamp seemed to me well-looking, clever enough, good-humored : but I noticed (for my own behoof and without prompting of any kind) that they were not so *well dressed* as their Edinburgh sisters; something flary, glary, colors too flagrant and ill-assorted, want of the harmonious transitions, neatnesses, and soft Attic art which I now recognized or remembered for the first time.

Of Dr. Chalmers I heard a great deal; naturally the continual topic, or one of them; admiration universal, and as it seemed to me slightly wearisome, and a good deal indiscriminate and over-done, which probably (though we were dead silent on that head) was on occasions Irving's feeling too. But the great man was himself truly lovable, truly loved; and nothing personally could be more modest, intent on his good industries, not on himself or his fame. Twice that I recollect I specially saw him; once at his own

house, to breakfast; company Irving, one Crosby, a young licentiate, with glaring eyes and no speculation in them, who went afterwards to Birmingham, and thirdly myself. It was a cold vile
smoky morning; house and breakfast-room looked their worst in
the dismal light. Doctor himself was hospitably kind, but spoke
little and engaged none of us in talk. Oftenest, I could see, he
was absent, wandering in distant fields of abstruse character, to
judge by the sorrowful glaze which came over his honest eyes and
face. I was not ill-pleased to get away, *ignotus*, from one of whom
I had gained no new knowledge. The second time was in a fine
drawing-room (a Mr. Parker's) in a rather solemn evening party,
where the doctor, perhaps bored by the secularities and trivialities
elsewhere, put his chair beside mine in some clear space of floor,
and talked earnestly for a good while on some scheme he had for
proving Christianity by its visible fitness for human nature. " All
written in us already," he said, "*in sympathetic ink*. Bible awakens
it; and you can read." I listened respectfully, not with any real
conviction, only with a clear sense of the geniality and goodness of
the man. I never saw him again till within a few months of his
death, when he called here, and sate with us an hour, very agreeable to *her* and to me after the long abeyance. She had been with
him once on a short tour in the Highlands; me too he had got an
esteem of—liked the " Cromwell" especially, and Cromwell's self
ditto, which I hardly reckoned creditable of him. He did not
speak of that, nor of the Free Kirk war, though I gave him a
chance of that which he soon softly let drop. The now memorablest point to me was of Painter Wilkie, who had been his familiar
in youth, and whom he seemed to me to understand well. " Painter's language," he said, " was stinted and difficult." Wilkie had
told him how in painting his *Rent Day* he thought long, and to no
purpose, by what means he should signify that the sorrowful woman with the children there, had left no husband at home, but was
a widow under tragical self-management; till one morning, pushing along the Strand, he met a small artisan family going evidently on excursion, and in one of their hands or pockets somewhere
was visible the *house-key*. "That will do," thought Wilkie, and
prettily introduced the house-key as *coral* in the poor baby's
mouth, just drawn from poor mammy's pocket, to keep her unconscious little orphan peaceable. He warmly agreed with me in
thinking Wilkie a man of real genius, real vivacity and simplicity.
Chalmers was himself very beautiful to us during that hour, grave
—not too grave—earnest, cordial face and figure very little altered,

only the head had grown white, and in the eyes and features you could read something of a serene sadness, as if evening and star-crowned night were coming on, and the hot noises of the day growing unexpectedly insignificant to one. We had little thought this would be the last of Chalmers; but in a few weeks after he suddenly died. . . . He was a man of much natural dignity, ingenuity, honesty, and kind affection, as well as sound intellect and imagination. A very eminent vivacity lay in him, which could rise to complete impetuosity (growing conviction, passionate eloquence, fiery play of heart and head), all in a kind of *rustic* type, one might say, though wonderfully true and tender. He had a burst of genuine fun, too, I have heard, of the same honest but most plebeian broadly natural character; his laugh was a hearty low guffaw; and his tones in preaching would rise to the piercingly pathetic — no preacher ever went so into one's heart. He was a man essentially of little culture, of narrow sphere, all his life; such an intellect professing to be educated, and yet so ill *read*, so ignorant in all that lay beyond the horizon in place or in time, I have almost nowhere met with. A man capable of much soaking indolence, lazy brooding and do-nothingism, as the first stage of his life well indicated; a man thought to be timid almost to the verge of cowardice, yet capable of impetuous activity and blazing audacity, as his latter years showed.

I suppose there will never again be such a preacher in any Christian church.

[A slip from a newspaper is appended here, with a note to it in Carlyle's hand.

"It is a favorite speculation of mine that if spared to sixty we then enter on the seventh decade of human life, and that this if possible should be turned into the Sabbath of our earthly pilgrimage and spent sabbatically, as if on the shores of an eternal world, or in the outer courts as it were of the temple that is above, the tabernacle in Heaven. What enamors me all the more of this idea is the retrospect of my mother's widowhood. I long, if God should spare me, for such an old age as she enjoyed, spent as if at the gate of heaven, and with such a fund of inward peace and hope as made her nine years' widowhood a perfect feast and foretaste of the blessedness that awaits the righteous."—*Dr. Chalmers.*

Carlyle writes:

"Had heard it before from Thomas Erskine (of Linlathen), with pathetic comment as to what Chalmers's own sabbath-decade had been."]

4*

Irving's discourses were far more opulent in ingenious thought
than Chalmers's, which indeed were usually the triumphant on-rush
of *one* idea with its satellites and supporters.   But Irving's wanted
in definite *head* and *backbone*, so that on arriving you might see
clearly where and how.   That was mostly a defect one felt in trav-
ersing those grand forest-avenues of his with their multifarious outlooks to right and left.   He had many thoughts pregnantly expressed, but they did not tend all one way.   The reason was there were
in him infinitely more thoughts than in Chalmers, and he took far
less pains in setting them forth.   The uniform custom was, he shut
himself up all Saturday, became invisible all that day; and had his
sermon ready before going to bed.   Sermon an hour long or more;
it could not be done in one day, except as a kind of *extempore* thing.
It flowed along, not as a swift flowing river, but as a broad, deep,
and bending or meandering one.   Sometimes it left on you the impression almost of a fine noteworthy *lake*.   Noteworthy always;
nobody could mistake it for the discourse of other than an uncommon man.   Originality and truth of purpose were undeniable in it,
but there was withal, both in the matter and the manner, a something which might be suspected of affectation, a noticeable preference and search for striking quaint and ancient locutions; a style
modelled on the Miltonic old Puritan; something too in the delivering which seemed elaborate and of forethought, or might be suspected of being so.   He (still) always read, but not in the least
slavishly; and made abundant rather strong gesticulations in the
right places; voice one of the finest and powerfullest, but not a
power quite on the heart as Chalmers's was, which you felt to be
coming direct *from* the heart.   Irving's preaching was accordingly
a thing not above criticism to the Glasgowites, and it got a good
deal on friendly terms, as well as admiration plenty, in that tem-
pered form; not often admiration pure and simple, as was now
always Chalmers's lot there.   Irving no doubt secretly felt the dif-
ference, and could have wished it otherwise; but the generous
heart of him was incapable of envying any human excellence, and
instinctively would either bow to it and to the rewards of it withal,
or rise to loyal emulation of it and them.   He seemed to be much
liked by many good people; a fine friendly and wholesome element
I thought it for him; and the criticisms going, in connection with
the genuine admiration going, might be taken as handsomely *near*
the mark.

To me, for his sake, his Glasgow friends were very good, and I
liked their ways (as I might easily do) much better than some I had

been used to. A romance of novelty lay in them too. It was the *first* time I had looked into opulent burgher life in any such completeness and composed solidity as here. We went to Paisley several times, to certain "Carliles" (so they spelt their name; Annan people of a century back), rich enough old men of religious moral turn, who received me as "a cousin;" their daughters good if not pretty, and one of the sons (Warrand Carlile, who afterwards became a clergyman) not quite uninteresting to me for some years coming. He married the youngest sister of Edward Irving, and I think is still preaching somewhere in the West Indies. Wife long since died, but one of their sons, "Gavin Carlile" (or now Carlyle), a Free Kirk minister here in London, editing his uncle's select works just now (1866). David Hope, of Glasgow, always a little stuck to me afterwards, an innocent, cheerful Nathaniel, ever ready to oblige. The like much more emphatically did William Graham of Burnswark, whom I first met in the above city under Irving's auspices, and who might in his way be called a friend both to Irving and me so long as his life lasted, which was thirty odd years longer. Other conquests of mine in Glasgow I don't recollect. Graham of Burnswark perhaps deserves a paragraph.

Graham was turned of fifty when I first saw him, a lumpish, heavy, but stirring figure; had got something lamish about one of the knees or ankles, which gave a certain rocking motion to his gait; firm jocund affectionate face, rather reddish with good cheer, eyes big, blue and laughing, nose defaced with snuff, fine bald broad-browed head, ditto almost always with an ugly brown scratch wig. He was free of hand and of heart, laughed with sincerity at not very much of fun, liked widely yet with some selection, and was widely liked. The history of him was curious. His father, first some small farmer in "Corrie Water" perhaps, was latterly for many years (I forget whether as farmer or as shepherd, but guess the former) stationary at Burnswark, a notable tabular hill, of no great height, but detached a good way on every side, far seen almost to the shores of Liverpool, indeed commanding all round the whole of that large *saucer*, fifty to thirty miles in radius, the brother point of which is now called Gretna ("Gretan How," Big Hollow, at the head of Solway Frith); a Burnswark beautiful to look on and much noted from of old. Has a glorious Roman camp on the south flank of it, "the best preserved in Britain except one" (says General Roy); velvet sward covering the whole, but trenches, prætorium (three conic mounds), etc., not altered otherwise; one of the finest limpid *wells* within it; and a view to Liverpool as was said,

and into Tynedale, to the Cumberland and even Yorkshire mountains on the one side, and on the other into the Moffat ditto and
the Selkirkshire and Eskdale.

The name "Burnswark" is probably Birrenswark (or fortifica-
tion work).   Three Roman stations, with Carlisle (Caer Lewel, as
old as King Solomon) for mother: Netherbie, Middlebie, and Ower-
bie (or Upperby) in Eskdale.   The specific Roman town of Middlebie is about half a mile below the Kirk (i. e. eastward of it) and is
called by the country people "the Birrens" (i. e. the Scrags or Haggles, I should think), a place lying all in dimples and wrinkles, with
ruined houses if you dig at all, grassy but inarable part of which is
still kept sacred *in lea* by "the Duke" (of Queensberry, now of
Buccleuch and Queensberry), while the rest has been all dug to
powder in the last sixty or seventy years by the adjoining little
lairds.   Many altars, stone figures, tools, axes, etc., were got out of
the dug part, and it used to be one of the tasks of my boyhood to
try what I could do at reading the *inscriptions* found there; which
was not much, nor almost ever *wholly* enough, though the country
folk were thankful for my little Latin faithfully applied, like the
light of a damp windlestraw to them in what was total darkness.
The fable went that from Birrens to Birrenswark, two and a half
miles, there ran a "subterranean passage," complete *tunnel*, equal
to *carts*, perhaps, but nobody pretended even to have seen a trace
of it, or indeed did believe it.

In my boyhood, passing Birrens for the first time, I noticed a
small conduit (cloaca, I suppose) abruptly ending or issuing in the
then recent precipice which had been left by those diggers, and
recollect nothing more, except my own poor awe and wonder at the
strange scene, strange face to face vestige of the vanished æons.
The Caledonian Railway now screams and shudders over this dug
part of Birrens; William Graham, whom I am (too idly) writing of,
was born at the north-east end of Burnswark, and passed in labor, but in health, frugality, and joy, the first twenty-five years of
his life.

Graham's father and mother seem to have been of the best kind
of Scottish peasant; he had brothers two or perhaps three, of whom
William was the youngest, who were all respected in their state,
and who all successively emigrated to America on the following
slight first-cause.   John Graham, namely the eldest of the brothers,
had been balloted for the militia (Dumfriesshire Militia), and on
private consideration with himself preferred expatriation to soldier-
ing, and quietly took ship to push his fortune in the New World

instead. John's adventures, which probably were rugged enough, are not on record for me; only that in no great length of time he found something of success, a solid merchant's clerkship or the like, with outlooks towards merchant's business of his own one day; and invited thither one by one all his brothers to share with him or push like him there. Philadelphia was the place, at least the ultimate place, and the firm of "Graham Brothers" gradually rose to be a considerable and well-reputed house in that city. William, probably some fifteen years junior of John, was the last brother that went; after him their only sister, parents having now died at Burnswark, was sent for also, and kept house for William or for another of the bachelor brothers—one at least of them had wedded and has left Pennsylvanian Grahams. William continued bachelor for life; and this only sister returned ultimately to Annandale, and was William's house-manager there. I remember her well, one of the amiablest of old maids; kind, true, modestly polite to the very heart; and in such a curious style of polite culture; Pennsylvanian Yankee grafted on Annandale Scotch. Used to "expect" instead of "suppose," would "guess" now and then, and commonly said pastor (which she pronounced "paustor") to signify clergyman or minister.

The Graham Brothers house growing more and more prosperous and opulent in Philadelphia, resolved at last to have a branch in Glasgow (year 1814 or so) and despatched William thither, whose coming I dimly remember was heard of in Annandale by his triumphant purchase for himself in fee simple of the farm and hill of Burnswark, which happened to come into the market then. His tradings and observations in Glasgow were extensive, not unskilful that I heard of, and were well looked on, as he himself still more warmly was, but at length (perhaps a year or more before my first sight of him) some grand cargo from or to Philadelphia, some whole fleet of cargoes, all mostly of the same commodity, had by sudden change of price during the voyage ruinously misgone, and the fine house of Graham Brothers came to the ground. William was still in the throes of settlement, just about quitting his fine well-appointed mansion in Vincent Street, in a cheerfully stoical humor, and only clinging with invincible tenacity to native Burnswark, which of course was no longer his except on bond with securities, with interest, etc., all of excessive extent, his friends said, but could not persuade him, so dear to his heart was that native bit of earth, with the fond improvements, planting and the like, which he had begun upon it.

Poor Graham kept iron hold of Burnswark, ultimately as plain tenant; good sheep farm at a fair rent; all attempts otherwise, and they were many and strenuous, having issued in non-success, and the hope of ever recovering himself, or it, being plainly futile. Graham never merchanted more; was once in America on exploratory visit, where his brothers were in some degree set up again, but had no £8,000 to spare for his Burnswark. He still hung a little to Glasgow, tried various things, rather of a "projector" sort, all of which miscarried, till happily he at length ceased visiting Glasgow, and grew altogether rustic, a successful sheep-farmer at any rate, fat, cheery, happy, and so for his last twenty years rode visiting about among the little lairds of an intelligent turn, who liked him well, but not with entire acquiescence in all the copious quasi-intelligent talk he had. Irving had a real love for him, with silent deductions in the unimportant respects; he an entire loyalty and heart-devotedness to Irving. Me also he took up in a very warm manner, and for the first few years was really pleasant and of use to me, especially in my then Annandale summers. Through him I made acquaintance with a really intellectual modest circle, or rather pair of people, a Mr. and Mrs. Johnston, at their place called Grange, on the edge of the hill country, seven or eight miles from my father's. Mrs. Johnston was a Glasgow lady, of fine culture, manners, and intellect; one of the smallest voices, and most delicate, gently smiling figure; had been in London, etc. Her husband was by birth laird of this pretty Grange, and had modestly withdrawn to it, finding merchanthood in Glasgow ruinous to weak health. The elegance, the perfect courtesy, the simple purity and beauty I found in both these good people, was an authentic attraction and profit to me in those years, and I still remember them, and the bright little environment of them, with a kind of pathetic affection. I as good as lost them on my leaving Annandale. Mr. Johnston soon after died; and with Mrs. Johnston there could only be at rare intervals a flying call, sometimes only the attempt at such, which amounted to little.

Graham also I practically more and more lost from that epoch (1826), ever memorable to me otherwise. He hung about me studiously, and with unabating good-will, on my Annandale visits to my mother, to whom he was ever attentive and respectful for my sake and her own. Dear good mother! best of mothers! He pointed out the light of her "end window," *gable* window, one dark night to me, as I convoyed him from Scotsbrig. " Will there ever be in the world for you a prettier light than that?" He was once or more with us at Craigenputtoch, ditto at London, and wrote long letters, not unpleasant to read and *burn*. But his sphere was shrinking more and more into dark safety and monstrous rusticity, mine the reverse in respect of safety and otherwise—nay, at length his faculties were getting hebetated, wrapt in lazy eupeptic fat. The last time I ever, strictly speaking, saw him (for he was grown more completely stupid and oblivious every subsequent time) was at the ending of my mother's funeral (December, 1853), day bitterly cold, heart bitterly sad, at the gate of Ecclefechan kirkyard. He was sitting in his gig just about to go, I ready to mount for Scotsbrig, and in a day more for London; he gazed on me with his big innocent face, big heavy eyes, as if half-conscious, half-frozen in the cold, and we shook hands nearly in silence.

In the Irving Glasgow time, and for a while afterwards, there went on at Edinburgh too a kind of cheery visiting and messaging from these good Graham-Hope people. I do not recollect the visits as peculiarly successful, none of them except *one*, which was on occasion of George IV.'s famed "visit to Edinburgh," when Graham and Hope (I think both of them together) occupied my rooms with grateful satisfaction. I myself *not there*. I had grown disgusted with the fulsome "loyalty" of all classes in Edinburgh towards this approaching George Fourth visit; whom, though called and reckoned a "king," I in my private radicalism of mind could consider only as a—what shall I call him? and loyalty was not the feeling I had towards any part of the phenomenon. At length reading one day in a public placard from the magistrates (of which there had been several) that on His Majesty's advent it was expected that everybody would be carefully well-dressed, "black coat and white duck trousers," if at all convenient, I grumbled to myself, "scandalous flunkeys! I, if I were changing my dress at all, should incline rather to be in white coat and black trousers;" but resolved rather to quit the city altogether, and be absent and silent in such efflorescence of the flunkeyisms, which I was—for a week or more in Annandale, at Kirkchrist with the Churches in Galloway; ride to Lochinbrack Well by Kenmore Lake, etc., how vivid still! and found all comfortably rolled away at my return to Edinburgh.

It was in one of those visits by Irving himself,[*] without any company, that he took me out to Haddington (as recorded elsewhere), to what has since been so momentous through all my subsequent life. We walked and talked a good sixteen miles in the sunny sum-

---

[*] June, 1821.

mer afternoon. He took me round by Athelstanford ("Elshinford") parish, where John Home wrote his "Douglas," in case of any enthusiasm for Home or it, which I secretly had not. We leapt the solitary kirkyard wall, and found close by us the tombstone of "old Skirring," a more remarkable person, author of the strangely vigorous doggrel ballad on "Preston Pans Battle" (and the ditto answer to a military *challenge* which ensued thereupon), "one of the most athletic and best natured of men," said his epitaph. This is nearly all I recollect of the journey; the end of it, and what I saw there, will be memorable to me while life or thought endures. Ah me! ah me!—I think there had been before this on Irving's own part some movements of negotiation over to Kirkcaldy for *release* there, and of hinted hope towards Haddington, which was so infinitely miserable! and something (as I used to gather long afterwards) might have come of it had not Kirkcaldy been so peremptory and stood by its bond (as spoken or as written), "bond or utter ruin, sir!" upon which Irving had honorably submitted and resigned himself. He seemed to be quite composed upon the matter by this time.* I remember in an inn at Haddington that first night a little passage. We had just seen in the minister's house (whom Irving was to preach for) a certain shining Miss Augusta, tall, shapely, airy, giggly, but a consummate fool, whom I have heard called "Miss Disgusta" by the satirical. We were now in our double-bedded room, George Inn, Haddington, stripping, or perhaps each already in his bed, when Irving jocosely said to me, "What would you take to marry Miss Augusta now?" "Not for an entire and perfect chrysolite the size of this terraqueous globe," answered I at once, with hearty laughter from Irving. "And what would you take to marry Miss Jeannie, think you?" "Hah, I should not be so hard to deal with there I should imagine!" upon which another bit of laugh from Irving, and we composedly went to sleep. I was supremely dyspeptic and out of health during those three or four days, and they were the beginning of a new life to me.

The notablest passage in my Glasgow visits was probably the year before this Edinburgh-Haddington one on Irving's part. I was about quitting Edinburgh for Annandale, and had come round by Glasgow on the road home. I was utterly out of health as usual, but had otherwise had my enjoyments. We had come to Paisley as finale, and were lodging pleasantly with the Carliles. Warrand Carlile, hearing I had to go by Muirkirk in Ayrshire, and Irving to

---

* Carlyle was mistaken here. Irving's hopes at this time were at their brightest.

return to Glasgow, suggested a convoy of me by Irving and himself, furthered by a fine riding horse of Warrand's, on the ride-and-tie principle. Irving had cheerfully consented. "You and your horse as far as you can; I will go on to Drumclog Moss with Carlyle; then turn home for Glasgow in good time, he on to Muirkirk, which will be about a like distance for him." "Done, done!" To me of course nothing could be welcomer than this improvised convoy, upon which we entered accordingly; early A.M., a dry brisk April day, and one still full of strange dim interest to me. I never rode and tied (especially with three) before or since, but recollect we had no difficulty with it.

Warrand had settled that we should breakfast with a Rev. Mr. French some fifteen miles off, after which he and horse would return. I recollect the Mr. French, a fat, apoplectic-looking old gentleman, in a room of very low ceiling, but plentifully furnished with breakfast materials; who was very kind to us, and seemed glad and ready to be invaded in this sudden manner by articulate speaking young men. Good old soul! I never saw him or heard mention of him again.

Drumclog Moss (after several hours fallen vacant and wholly dim) is the next object that survives, and Irving and I sitting by ourselves under the silent bright skies among the "peat-hags" of Drumclog with a world all silent round us. These peat-hags are still pictured in me; brown bog, all pitted and broken into heathy remnants and bare abrupt wide holes, four or five feet deep, mostly dry at present; a flat wilderness of broken bog, of quagmire not to be trusted (probably wetter in old days there, and wet still in rainy seasons). Clearly a good place for Cameronian preaching, and dangerously difficult for Claverse and horse soldiery if the suffering remnant had a few old muskets among them! Scott's novels had given the Claverse skirmish here, which all Scotland knew of already, a double interest in those days. I know not that we talked much of this; but we did of many things, perhaps more confidentially than ever before. A colloquy the sum of which is still mournfully beautiful to me, though the details are gone. I remember us sitting on the brow of a peat-hag, the sun shining, our own voices the one sound. Far, far away to the westward, over our brown horizon, towered up white and visible at the many miles of distance a high irregular pyramid. "Ailsa Craig," we at once guessed, and thought of the seas and oceans over yonder. But we did not long dwell on that. We seem to have seen no human creature after French (though of course our very road would

have to be inquired after); to have had no bother and no need of
human assistance or society, not even of refection, French's breakfast perfectly sufficing us. The talk had grown ever friendlier,
more interesting. At length the declining sun said plainly, you
must part. We sauntered slowly into the Glasgow-Muirkirk highway. Masons were building at a wayside cottage near by, or were
packing up on ceasing for the day. We leant our backs to a dry
stone fence ("stone dike," dry stone wall, very common in that
country), and looking into the western radiance, continued in talk
yet a while, loth both of us to go. It was just here, as the sun
was sinking, Irving actually drew from me by degrees, in the softest manner, the confession that I did not think as he of the Christian religion, and that it was vain for me to expect I ever could or
should. This, if this was so, he had pre-engaged to take well of
me, like an elder brother, if I would be frank with him. And
right loyally he did so, and to the end of his life we needed no con-
cealments on that head, which was really a step gained.

The sun was about setting when we turned away each on his
own path. Irving would have had a good space further to go than
I (as now occurs to me), perhaps fifteen or seventeen miles, and
would not be in Kent Street till towards midnight. But he feared
no amount of walking, enjoyed it rather, as did I in those young
years. I felt sad, but affectionate and good, in my clean, utterly
quiet little inn at Muirkirk, which, and my feelings in it, I still well
remember. An innocent little Glasgow youth (young bagman on
his first journey, I supposed) had talked awhile with me in the
otherwise solitary little sitting-room. At parting he shook hands,
and with something of sorrow in his tone said, "Good-night, I
shall not see *you* again." A unique experience of mine in inns.

I was off next morning by four o'clock, Muirkirk, except possibly its pillar of furnace smoke, all sleeping round me, concerning
which, I remembered in the silence something I had heard from my
father in regard to this famed iron village (famed long before, but
still rural, natural, not all in a roaring state, which, as I imagine, it
is now). This is my father's picture of an incident he had got to
know and never could forget. On the platform of one of the furnaces a solitary man (stoker, if they call him so) was industriously minding his business, now throwing in new fuel and ore, now
poking the white-hot molten mass that was already in. A poor old
maniac woman silently joined him and looked, whom also he was
used to and did not mind. But after a little, his back being towards
the furnace mouth, he heard a strange thump or cracking puff;

and turning suddenly, the poor old maniac woman was not there, and on advancing to the furnace-edge he saw the figure of her red-hot, semi-transparent, floating as ashes on the fearful element for some moments! This had printed itself on my father's brain; twice perhaps I had heard it from him, which was rare, nor will it ever leave my brain either.

That day was full of mournful interest to me in the waste moors, there in bonny Nithsdale (my first sight of it) in the bright but palish, almost pathetic sunshine and utter loneliness. At eight P.M. I got well to Dumfries, the longest walk I ever made, fifty-four miles in one day.

Irving's visits to Annandale, one or two every summer, while I spent summers (for cheapness' sake and health's sake) in solitude at my father's there, were the sabbath times of the season to me; by far the beautifullest days, or rather the only beautiful I had! Unwearied kindness, all that tenderest anxious affection could do, was always mine from my incomparable mother, from my dear brothers, little clever active sisters, and from every one, brave father in his tacit grim way not at all excepted. There was good talk also, with mother at evening tea, often on theology (where I did at length contrive, by judicious endeavor, to speak piously and *agreeably* to one so pious, *without* unveracity on my part). Nay it was a kind of interesting exercise to wind softly out of those anxious affectionate cavils of her dear heart on such occasions, and get real sympathy, real assent under borrowed forms. Oh, her patience with me! oh, her never-tiring love! Blessed be "poverty" which was never indigence in any form, and which has made all that tenfold more dear and sacred to me! With my two eldest brothers also, Alick and John, who were full of ingenuous curiosity, and had (especially John) abundant intellect, there was nice talking as we roamed about the fields in *gloaming* time after their work was done; and I recollect noticing (though probably it happened various times) that little Jean ("Craw" as we called her, she alone of us not being blond but blackhaired), one of the cleverest children I ever saw (then possibly about six or seven), had joined us for her private behoof, and was assiduously trotting at my knee, cheek, eyes, and ear assiduously turned up to me! Good little soul! I thought it and think it very pretty of her. She alone of them had nothing to do with milking; I suppose her charge would probably be ducks or poultry, all safe to bed now, and was turning her bit of leisure to this account instead of another. She was hardly longer than my leg by the whole head and neck. There was a younger

sister (Jenny) who is now in Canada, of far inferior speculative intellect to Jean, but who has proved to have (we used to think)
superior *housekeeping* faculties to hers. The same may be said of
Mary, the next elder to Jean. Both these, especially Jenny, got
husbands, and have dexterously and loyally made the most of them
and their families and households. Henning, of Hamilton, Canada
West; Austin, of the Gill, Annan, are now the names of these two.
Jean is Mrs. Aitken, of Dumfries, still a clever, speculative, ardent,
affectionate and discerning woman, but much *zersplittert* by the cares
of life; *zersplittert;* steadily denied acumination or definite consist-
ency and direction to a point; a "tragedy" often repeated in this
poor world, the more the pity for the world too!

   All this was something, but in all this I gave more than I got,
and it left a sense of isolation, of sadness; as the rest of my impris-
oned life all with emphasis did. I kept daily studious, reading
diligently what few books I could get, learning what was possible,
German, etc. Sometimes Dr. Brewster turned me to account (on
most frugal terms always) in wretched little translations, compi-
lations, which were very welcome too, though never other than
dreary. Life was all dreary, "eerie" (Scotticè), tinted with the
hues of imprisonment and impossibility; hope practically not there,
only obstinacy, and a grim steadfastness to strive without hope as
with. To all which Irving's advent was the pleasant (temporary)
contradiction and *reversal*, like sunrising to night, or impenetrable
fog, and its spectralities! The time of his coming, the how and
when of his movements and possibilities, were always known to me
beforehand. On the set day I started forth better dressed than
usual, strode along for Annan which lay pleasantly in sight all the
way (seven miles or more from Mainhill). In the woods of Mount
Annan I would probably meet Irving strolling towards me; and
then what a talk for the three miles down that bonny river's bank,
no sound but our own voices amid the lullaby of waters and the
twittering of birds! We were sure to have several such walks,
whether the first day or not, and I remember none so well as some
(chiefly *one* which is not otherwise of moment) in that fine locality.

   I generally stayed at least one night, on several occasions two or
even more, and I remember no visits with as pure and calm a pleasure. Annan was then at its culminating point, a fine, bright, self-
confident little town (gone now to dimness, to decay, and almost
grass on its streets by railway transit). Bits of travelling notabilities were sometimes to be found alighted there. Edinburgh
people, Liverpool people, with whom it was interesting for the re-

cluse party to "measure minds" for a little, and be on your best behavior, both as to matter and to manner. Musical Thomson (memorable, more so than venerable, as the publisher of Burns's songs), him I saw one evening sitting in the reading-room, a clean-brushed, commonplace old gentleman in scratch wig, whom we spoke a few words to and took a good look of. Two young Liver-pool brothers, Nelson their name, scholars just out of Oxford, were on visit one time in the Irving circle, specially at Provost Dixon's, Irving's brother-in-law's. These were very interesting to me night after night; handsome, intelligent, polite young men, and the first of their species I had seen. Dixon's on other occasions was usual-ly my lodging, and Irving's along with me, but would not be on this (had I the least remembrance on that head), except that I seem to have been always beautifully well lodged, and that Mrs. Dixon, Irving's eldest sister, and very like him *minus* the bad eye, and *plus* a fine *dimple* on the bright cheek, was always beneficent and fine to me. Those Nelsons I never saw again, but have heard once in late years that they never *did* anything, but continued ornamentally lounging with Liverpool as head-quarters; which seemed to be something like the prophecy one might have gathered from those young aspects in the Annandale visit, had one been intent to scan them. A faded Irish dandy once picked up by us is also present; one fine clear morning Irving and I found this figure lounging about languidly on the streets. Irving made up to him, invited him home to breakfast, and home he politely and languidly went with us; "bound for some cattle fair," he told us, Norwich perhaps, and waiting for some coach; a parboiled, insipid "agricultural dandy" or old fogie, of Hibernian type; wore a superfine light green frock, snow-white corduroys; age about fifty, face colorless, crow-footed, feebly conceited; proved to have nothing in him, but especially nothing *bad*, and we had been human to him. Break-fast this morning, I remember, was at Mrs. Ferguson's (Irving's third sister; there were four in all, and there had been three broth-ers, but were now only two, the youngest and the eldest of the set). Mrs. F.'s breakfast—tea—was praised by the Hibernian pilgrim, and well deserved it.

Irving was generally happy in those little Annandale "sunny islets" of his year; happier perhaps than ever elsewhere. All was quietly flourishing in this his natal element; father's house neat and contented; ditto, ditto, or perhaps blooming out a little far-ther, those of his daughters, all nestled close to it in place withal; a very prettily thriving group of things and objects in their limited, in their safe seclusion; and Irving was silently but visibly in the hearts of all the flower and crowning jewel of it. He was quiet, cheerful, genial. Soul unruffled and clear as a mirror, honestly loving and loved all round. His time too was so *short*, every moment valuable. Alas, and in so few years after, ruin's ploughshare had run through it all, and it was prophesying to you, "Behold, in a little while the last trace of me will not be here, and I shall have vanished tragically, and fled into oblivion and darkness like a bright dream." As is long since mournfully the fact, when one passes, pilgrim-like, those old houses still standing there, which I have once or twice done.

Our dialogues did not turn very much or long on personal topics, but wandered wide over the world and its ways—new men of the travelling conspicuous sort whom he had seen in Glasgow, new books sometimes, my scope being short in that respect; all manner of interesting objects and discoursings; but to me the personal, when they did come in course, as they were sure to do now and then in fit proportion, were naturally the gratefullest of all. Irving's voice was to me one of blessedness and new hope. He would not hear of my gloomy prognostications; all nonsense that I never should get out of these obstructions and impossibilities; the real impossibility was that such a talent, etc., should not cut itself clear one day. He was very generous to everybody's "talent," especially to mine; which to myself was balefully dubious, nothing but bare scaffold poles, weather-beaten corner-pieces of perhaps a "potential talent," even visible to me. His predictions about what I was to be flew into the completely incredible; and however welcome, I could only rank them as devout imaginations and quiz them away. "You will see now," he would say, "one day we two will shake hands across the brook, you as first in literature, I as first in divinity, and people will say, 'Both these fellows are from Annandale. Where is Annandale?'" This I have heard him say more than once, always in a laughing way, and with self-mockery enough to save it from being barrenly vain. He was very sanguine, I much the reverse; and had his consciousness of power, and his generous ambitions and forecastings. Never ungenerous, never ignoble; only an enemy could have called him vain, but perhaps an enemy could or at least would, and occasionally did. His pleasure in being *loved* by others was very great, and this if you looked well was manifest in him when the case offered; never more or worse than this in any case, and this too he had well in check at all times. If this was vanity, then he might by some be called a little vain, if not not. To trample on the smallest mortal or be tyrannous even towards the basest of caitiffs was never at any moment Irving's turn. No man that I have known had a sunnier type of character, or so little of hatred towards any man or thing. On the whole, *less* of rage in him than I ever saw combined with such a fund of courage and conviction. Noble Irving! he was the faithful elder brother of my life in those years; generous, wise, beneficent, all his dealings and discoursings with me were. Well may I recollect as blessed things in my existence those Annan and other visits, and feel that beyond all other men he was helpful to me when I most needed help.

Irving's position at Glasgow, I could dimly perceive, was not without its embarrassments, its discouragements; and evidently enough it was nothing like the ultimatum he was aiming at, in the road to which I suppose he saw the obstructions rather multiplying than decreasing or diminishing. Theological Scotland above all things is dubious and jealous of originality, and Irving's tendency to take a road of his own was becoming daily more indisputable. He must have been severely *tried in the sieve* had he continued in Scotland. Whether that might not have brought him out clearer, more pure and victorious in the end, must remain forever a question. Much suffering and contradiction it would have cost him, mean enough for most part, and *possibly* with loss of patience, with mutiny, etc., for ultimate result, but one may now regret that the experiment was never to be made.

Of course the invitation to London was infinitely welcome to him, summing up, as it were, all of good that had been in Glasgow (for it was the rumors and reports from Glasgow people that had awakened Hatton Garden to his worth), and promising to shoot him aloft over all that had been obstructive there into wider new elements. The negotiations and correspondings had all passed at a distance from me, but I recollect well our final practical parting on that occasion. A dim night, November or December, between nine and ten, in the coffee-room of the Black Bull Hotel. He was to start by early coach to-morrow. Glad I was bound to be, and in a sense was, but very sad I could not help being. He himself looked hopeful, but was agitated with anxieties too, doubtless with regrets as well; more clouded with agitation than I had ever seen the fine habitual solar light of him before. I was the last friend he had to take farewell of. He showed me old Sir Harry Moncrieff's testimonial; a Reverend Presbyterian Scotch Baronet of venerable quality (the last of his kind), whom I knew well by sight, and by his universal character for integrity, honest orthodoxy, shrewdness, and veracity. Sir Harry testified with brevity, in stiff, firm, ancient hand, several important things on Irving's behalf; and ended by saying, "All this is my true opinion, and meant to be understood as it is written." At which we had our bit of approving laugh, and thanks to Sir Harry. Irving did not laugh that night; laughter was not the mood of either of us. I gave him as road-companion a bundle of the best cigars (gift of Graham to me) I almost ever had. He had no practice of smoking, but a little by a time, and agreed that on the coach roof, where he was to ride night and day, a cigar now and then might be tried with advantage. Months afterwards I learnt he had begun by losing every cigar of them; left the whole bundle lying on the seat in the stall of the coffee-room; this cigar gift being probably our last transaction there. We said farewell; and I had in some sense, according to my worst anticipations, lost my friend's society (not my friend himself ever) from that time.

For a long while I saw nothing of Irving after this. Heard in the way of public rumors or more specific report, chiefly from Graham and Hope of Glasgow, how grandly acceptable he had been at Hatton Garden, and what negotiating, deliberating, and contriving had ensued in respect of the impediments there ("preacher ignorant of Gaelic; our fundamental law requires him to preach half the Sunday in that language," etc.), and how at length all these were got over or tumbled aside, and the matter settled into adjustment. "Irving, our preacher, *talis qualis*," to the huge contentment of his congregation and all onlookers, of which latter were already in London a select class; the chief religious people getting to be aware that an altogether uncommon man had arrived here to speak to them.

On all these points, and generally on all his experiences in London, glad enough should I have been to hear from him abundantly, but he wrote nothing on such points, nor in fact had I expected anything; and the truth was, which did a little disappoint me at the time, our regular correspondence had here suddenly come to *finis!* I was not angry, how could I be? I made no solicitation or remonstrance, nor was any poor pride kindled (I think), except strictly, and this in silence, so far as was proper for self-defence; but I was always sorry more or less, and regretted it as a great loss I had by ill-luck undergone. Taken from me by ill-luck! but then had it not been given me by good ditto? Peace, and be silent! In the first month Irving, I doubt not, had intended much correspondence with me, were the hurly-burly done; but no sooner was it so in some measure, than his flaming popularity had begun, spreading, mounting without limit, and instead of business hurly-burly there was whirlwind of conflagration.

Noble, good soul! In his last weeks of life, looking back from that grim shore upon the safe sunny isles and smiling possibilities now forever far behind, he said to Henry Drummond, "I should have kept Thomas Carlyle closer to me; his counsel, blame, or praise, was always faithful, and few have such eyes." These words, the first part of them *ipsissima verba*, I know to have been verily his. Must not the most blazing indignation (had the least vestige of such been ever in me for one moment) have died almost into tears at the sound of them? Perfect absolution there had long been without inquiring after penitence. My ever-generous, loving, and noble Irving! . . .

If in a gloomy moment I had fancied that my friend was lost to me because no letters came from him, I had shining proof to the contrary very soon. It was in these first months of Hatton Garden and its imbroglio of affairs, that he did a most signal benefit to me; got me appointed tutor and intellectual guide and guardian to the young Charles Buller, and his boy-brother, now Sir Arthur, and an elderly ex-Indian of mark. The case had its comic points too, seriously important as it was to me for one. Its pleasant real history is briefly this: Irving's preaching had attracted Mrs. Strachey, wife of a well-known Indian official of Somersetshire kindred, then an "examiner" in the India House, and a man of real worth, far diverse as his worth and ways were from those of his beautiful, enthusiastic, and still youngish wife. A bright creature she, given wholly (though there lay silent in her a great deal of fine childlike mirth and of innocent grace and gift) to things sacred and serious, emphatically what the Germans call a *schöne Seele*. She had brought Irving into her circle, found him good and glorious there, almost more than in the pulpit itself; had been speaking of him to her elder sister, Mrs. Buller (a Calcutta fine lady, and princess of the kind worshipped there, a once very beautiful, still very witty, graceful, airy, and ingenuously intelligent woman of the gossamer kind), and had naturally winded up with "Come and dine with us; come and see this uncommon man." Mrs. Buller came, saw (I dare say with much suppressed quizzing and wonder) the uncommon man; took to him. She also in her way recognized, as did her husband too, the robust, practical common-sense that was in him; and after a few meetings began speak-

ing of a domestic intricacy there was with a clever but too mer-
curial and unmanageable eldest son of hers, whom they knew not
what to do with.

Irving took sight and survey of this dangerous eldest lad, Charles
Buller, junior, namely—age then about fifteen, honorably done with
Harrow some weeks or months ago, still too young for college on
his own footing, and very difficult to dispose of. Irving perceived
that though perfectly accomplished in what Harrow could give
him, this hungry and highly ingenious youth had fed hitherto on
Latin and Greek husks, totally unsatisfying to his huge appetite;
that being a young fellow of the keenest sense for everything, from
the sublime to the ridiculous, and full of airy ingenuity and fun, he
was in the habit in quiet evenings at home of starting *theses* with
his mother in favor of Pierce Egan and "Boxiana," as if the annals
of English boxing were more nutritive to an existing man than
those of the Peloponnesian war, etc. Against all which, etc., as his
mother vehemently argued, Charles would stand on the defensive,
with such swiftness and ingenuity of fence, that frequently the
matter kindled between them; and both being of hot though most
placable temper, one or both grew loud; and the old gentleman,
Charles Buller, senior, who was very deaf, striking blindly in at this
point would embroil the whole matter into a very bad condition!
Irving's recipe after some consideration was, "Send this gifted, un-
guided youth to Edinburgh College. I know a young man there
who could lead him into richer spiritual pastures and take effective charge of him." Buller thereupon was sent, and his brother
Arthur with him; boarded with a good old Dr. Fleming (in George
Square), then a clergyman of mark: and I (on a salary of £200 a
year) duly took charge. This was a most important thing to me
in the economies and practical departments of my life, and I owe
it wholly to Irving. On this point I always should remember he
did "write" copiously enough to Dr. Fleming and other parties,
and stood up in a gallant and grandiloquent way for every claim
and right of his "young literary friend," who had nothing to do
but wait silent while everything was being adjusted completely to
his wish or beyond it.

From the first I found my Charles a most manageable, intelligent,
cheery, and altogether welcome and intelligent phenomenon; quite
a bit of sunshine in my dreary Edinburgh element. I was in waiting for his brother and him when they landed at Fleming's. We
set instantly out on a walk, round by the foot of Salisbury Crags,
up from Holyrood, by the Castle and Law Courts, home again to

George Square; and really I recollect few more pleasant walks in my life! So all-intelligent, seizing everything you said to him with such a recognition; so loyal-hearted, chivalrous, guileless, so delighted (evidently) with me, as I was with him. Arthur, two years younger, kept mainly silent, being slightly deaf too; but I could perceive that he also was a fine little fellow, honest, intelligent, and kind, and that apparently I had been much in luck in this didactic adventure, which proved abundantly the fact. The two youths took to me with unhesitating liking, and I to them; and we never had anything of quarrel or even of weariness and dreariness between us; such "teaching" as I never did in any sphere before or since! Charles, by his qualities, his ingenuous curiosities, his brilliancy of faculty and character, was actually an entertainment to me rather than a labor. If we walked together, which I remember sometimes happening, he was the best company I could find in Edinburgh. I had entered him of Dunbar's, in third Greek class at college. In Greek and Latin, in the former in every respect, he was far my superior; and I had to prepare my lessons by way of keeping him to his work at Dunbar's. Keeping him to work was my one difficulty, if there was one, and my essential function. I tried to guide him into reading, into solid inquiry and reflection. He got some mathematics from me, and might have had more. He got in brief what expansion into such wider fields of intellect and more manful modes of thinking and working as my poor possibilities could yield him; and was always generously grateful to me afterwards. Friends of mine in a fine frank way, beyond what I could be thought to merit, he, Arthur, and all the family continued till death parted us.

This of the Bullers was the product for me of Irving's first months in London, begun and got under way in the spring and summer of 1822, which followed our winter parting in the Black Bull Inn. I was already getting my head a little up; translating "Legendre's Geometry" for Brewster; my outlook somewhat cheerfuller. I still remember a happy forenoon (Sunday, I fear) in which I did a *Fifth Book* (or complete "doctrine of proportion") for that work, complete really and lucid, and yet one of the briefest ever known. It was begun and done that forenoon, and I have (except correcting the press next week) never seen it since; but still feel as if it were right enough and felicitous in its kind! I got only £50 for my entire trouble in that "Legendre," and had already ceased to be in the least proud of *mathematical* prowess; but it was an honest job of work honestly done, though perhaps for bread and water wages, such an improvement upon wages producing (in Jean Paul's phrase) only water without the bread! Towards autumn the Buller family followed to Edinburgh, Mr. and Mrs. B. with a third very small son, Reginald, who was a curious, gesticulating, pen-drawing, etc., little creature, *not* to be under my charge, but who generally *dined* with me at luncheon time, and who afterwards turned out a lazy, hebe-tated fellow, and is now parson of Troston, a fat living in Suffolk. These English or Anglo-Indian gentlefolks were all a new species to me, sufficiently exotic in aspect; but we recognized each other's quality more and more, and did very well together. They had a house in India Street, saw a great deal of company (of the ex-Indian accidental English gentleman, and native or touring *lion* genus for which Mrs. B. had a lively appetite). I still lodged in my old half-rural rooms, 3 Moray Place, Pilrig Street; attended my two pupils during the day hours (lunching with "Regie" by way of dinner), and rather seldom, yet to my own taste amply often enough, was of the "state dinners;" but walked home to my books and to my brother John, who was now lodging with me and attending college. Except for dyspepsia I could have been extremely content, but that did dismally forbid me now and afterwards! Irving and other friends always treated the "ill-health" item as a light matter which would soon vanish from the account; but I had a pre-sentiment that it would stay there, and be the Old Man of the Sea to me through life, as it has too tragically done, and will do to the end. Woe on it, and not for my own poor sake alone; and yet perhaps a benefit has been in it, priceless though hideously painful!

Of Irving in these two years I recollect almost nothing personal, though all round I heard a great deal of him; and he must have been in my company at least once prior to the advent of the elder Bullers, and been giving me counsel and light on the matter; for I recollect his telling me of Mrs. Buller (having no doubt portrayed Mr. Buller to me in acceptable and clearly intelligible lineaments) that she—she too, was a worthy, honorable, and quick-sighted lady, but not without fine-ladyisms, crotchets, caprices—"somewhat like Mrs. Welsh,* you can fancy, but good too, like her." Ah me! this I perfectly remember, this and nothing more, of those Irving inter-courses; and it is a memento to me of a most important province in my poor world at that time! I was in constant correspondence (weekly or oftener sending books, etc., etc.) with Haddington, and heard often of Irving, and of things far more interesting to me from

---

* Mrs. Welsh, of Haddington, mother of Jane Welsh, afterwards Mrs. Carlyle.

that quarter. Gone silent, closed forever—so sad, so strange it all is now! Irving, I think, had paid a visit there, and had certainly sent letters; by the above token I too must have seen him at least once. All this was in his first London year, or half-year, some months before his "popularity" had yet taken *fire*, and made him for a time the property of all the world rather than of his friends.

The news of this latter event, which came in vague, vast, fitful, and decidedly *fuliginous* forms, was not quite welcome to any of us, perhaps in secret not welcome at all. People have their envies, their pitiful self-comparisons, and feel obliged sometimes to profess from the teeth outwards more "joy" than they really have; not an agreeable duty or quasi-duty laid on one. For myself I can say that there was first something of real joy; ("success to the worthy of success;") second, something, probably not yet much, of honest question for his sake, "Can he guide it in that huge element, as *e. g.* Chalmers has done in this smaller one?" and third, a noticeable quantity of *Quid tui interest?* What business hast thou with it, poor, suffering, handcuffed wretch? To me these great doings in Hatton Garden came only on wings of rumor, the exact nature of them uncertain. To me for many months back Irving had fallen totally silent, and this seemed a seal to its being a permanent silence. I had been growing steadily worse in health too, and was in habitual wretchedness, ready to say, "Well, whoever is happy and gaining victory, thou art and art like to be very miserable, and to gain none at all." These were, so far as I can now read, honestly my feelings on the matter. My love to Irving, now that I look at it across those temporary vapors, had not abated, never did abate : but he seemed for the present flown (or mounted if that was it) far away from me, and I could only say to myself, "Well, well then, so it must be."

One heard too, often enough, that in Irving there was visible a certain joyancy and frankness of triumph; that he took things on the high key and nothing doubting; and foolish stories circulated about his lofty sayings, sublimities of manner, and the like : something of which I could believe (and yet kindly interpret too); all which might have been, though it scarcely was, some consolation for our present silence towards one another. For what could I have said in the circumstances that would have been on both sides agreeable and profitable?

It was not till late in autumn 1823, nearly two years after our parting in the Black Bull Inn, that I fairly, and to a still memorable measure, saw Irving again. He was on his marriage jaunt, Miss

Martin of Kirkcaldy now become his life-partner; off on a tour to
the Highlands; and the generous soul had determined to pass near
Kinnaird (right bank of Tay, a mile below the junction of Tummel
and Tay), where I then was with the Bullers, and pick me up to accompany as far as I would. I forget where or how our meeting
was (at Dunkeld probably). I seem to have lodged with them two
nights in successive inns, and certainly parted from them at Taymouth, Sunday afternoon, where my horse by some means must have
been waiting for me. I remember baiting him* at Aberfeldy, and
to have sate in a kindly and polite yet very huggermugger cottage,
among good peasant kirk-people, refreshing themselves, returning
home from sermon; sate for perhaps some two hours, till poor Dolph
got rested and refected like his fellow-creatures there. I even remember something like a fraction of scrag of mutton and potatoes
eaten by myself—in strange contrast, had I thought of that, to
Irving's nearly simultaneous dinner which would be with my lord
at Taymouth Castle. After Aberfeldy cottage the curtain falls.

Irving, on this his wedding-jaunt, seemed superlatively happy,
as was natural to the occasion, or more than natural, as if at the
top of Fortune's wheel, and in a sense (a generous sense, it must be
owned, and not a *tyrannous* in any measure) striking the stars with
his sublime head. Mrs. I. was demure and quiet, though doubtless
not less happy at heart, really comely in her behavior. In the
least beautiful she never could be; but Irving had loyally taken
her as the consummate flower of all his victory in the world—poor
good tragic woman—better probably than the fortune she had after all.

My friend was kind to me as possible, and bore with my gloomy
humors (for I was ill and miserable to a degree), nay perhaps as
foil to the radiancy of his own sunshine he almost enjoyed them.
I remember jovial bursts of laughter from him at my surly sarcastic and dyspeptic utterances. "Doesn't this subdue you, Carlyle?"
said he, somewhat solemnly; we were all three standing at the
Falls of Aberfeldy (amid the "Birks" of ditto, and memories of
song) silent in the October dusk, perhaps with moon rising—our
ten miles to Taymouth still ahead—"Doesn't this subdue you?"
"Subdue me? I should hope not. I have quite other things to
front with defiance in this world than a gush of bog-water tumbling over crags as here!" which produced a joyous and really kind

---

* Excellent cob or pony Dolph, i. e. Bardolph, bought for me at Lilliesleaf fair
by my dear brother Alick, and which I had ridden into the Highlands for health.

laugh from him as sole answer. He had much to tell me of London, of its fine literary possibilities for a man, of its literary stars, whom he had seen or knew of, Coleridge in particular, who was in the former category, a marvellous sage and man ; Hazlitt, who was in the latter, a fine talent too, but tending towards scamphood ; was at the *Fonthill Abbey sale* the other week, "hired to attend as a *white bonnet* there," said he, with a laugh. *White bonnet* intensely vernacular, is the Annandale name for a false bidder merely appointed to raise prices, works so for his five shillings at some poor little Annandale roup,* of standing crop or hypothecate cottage furniture, and the contrast and yet kinship between these little things and the Fonthill great one was ludicrous enough. He would not hear of ill-health being any hindrance to me; he had himself no experience in that sad province. All seemed possible to him—all was joyful and running upon wheels. He had suffered much angry criticism in his late triumphs (on his "Orations" quite lately), but seemed to accept it all with jocund mockery, as something harmless and beneath him.

Wilson in "Blackwood" had been very scornful and done his bitterly enough disobliging best. Nevertheless Irving now advising with me about some detail of our motions, or of my own, and finding I still demurred to it, said with true radiancy of look, "Come now, you know I am the *judicious Hooker*," which was considered one of Wilson's cruellest hits in that Blackwood article. To myself I remember his answering, in return evidently for some criticism of my own on the orations which was not so laudatory as required, but of which I recollect nothing farther, "Well, Carlyle, I am glad to hear you say all that; it gives me the opinion of another mind on the thing ;" which, at least, beyond any doubt it did. He was in high sunny humor, good Irving. There was no trace of anger left in him; he was jovial, riant, jocose rather than serious, throughout, which was a new phasis to me. And furthermore, in the serious vein itself there was oftenest something of *falsetto* noticeable (as in that of the waterfall "subduing" one), generally speaking a new height of self-consciousness not yet sure of the manner and carriage that was suitablest for it. He affected to feel his popularity too great and burdensome ; spoke much about a Mrs. Basil Montague ; elderly, sage, lofty, whom we got to know afterwards, and to call by his name for her, " the noble lady ;" who had saved him greatly from the dashing floods of that tumultuous and

---

* Ruf, or vocal sale.

unstable element, hidden him away from it once and again; done
kind ministrations, spread sofas for him, and taught him "to rest."
The last thing I recollect of him was on our coming out from Taymouth Kirk (kirk, congregation, minister, utterly erased from me),
how in coming down the broadish little street he pulled off his big
broad hat, and walked, looking mostly to the sky, with his fleece of
copious coal-black hair flowing in the wind, and in some spittings
of rain that were beginning; how thereupon in a minute or two a
livery servant ran up, "Please, sir, aren't you the Rev. Edward Irving?" "Yes." "Then my Lord Breadalbane begs you to stop for
him one moment." Whereupon exit *flunkey*. Irving turning to us
with what look of sorrow he could, and "Again found out!" upon
which the old lord came up,* and civilly invited him to dinner.
Him and party, I suppose; but to me there was no temptation, or
on those terms less than none. So I had Bardolph saddled and
rode for Aberfeldy as above said; home, sunk in manifold murky
reflections now lost to me; and of which only the fewest and friendliest were comfortably fit for uttering to the Bullers next day. I
saw no more of Irving for this time. But he had been at Haddington, too, was perhaps again corresponding a little there, and I heard
occasionally of him in the beautiful bright and kindly quizzing style
that was natural there.

I was myself writing "Schiller" in those months; a task Irving
had encouraged me in and prepared the way for, in the "London
Magazine." Three successive parts there were, I know not how far
advanced, at this period; knew only that I was nightly working at
the thing in a serious, sad and *totally solitary* way. My two rooms
were in the old "Mansion" of Kinnaird, some three or four hundred
yards from the new, and on a lower level, overshadowed with wood.
Thither I always retired directly after tea, and for most part had
the edifice all to myself; good candles, good wood fire, place dry
enough, tolerably clean, and such silence and total absence of company, good or bad, as I never experienced before or since. I remember still the grand *sough* of those woods; or, perhaps, in the stillest
times, the distant ripple of Tay. Nothing else to converse with but
this and my own thoughts, which never for a moment pretended to
be joyful, and were sometimes pathetically sad. I was in the miserablest dyspeptic health, uncertain whether I ought not to *quit*
on that account, and at times almost resolving to do it; driven far
away from all my loved ones. My poor "Schiller," nothing consid-

---

* Father of the last, or later, Free Kirk one, whom I have sometimes seen.

erable of a work even to my own judgment, had to be steadily persisted in as the only protection and resource in this inarticulate huge
" wilderness," actual and symbolical. My editor, I think, was complimentary; but I knew better. The "Times" newspaper once
brought me, without commentary at all, an "eloquent" passage re-
printed (about the tragedy of noble literary life), which I remember
to have read with more pleasure in this utter isolation, and as the
"first" public nod of approval I had ever had, than any criticism
or laudation that has ever come to me since. For about two hours
it had lighted in the desolation of my inner man a strange little
glow of illumination; but here too, on reflection, I "knew better,"
and the winter afternoon was not over when I saw clearly how very
small this conquest was, and things were in their *statu quo* again.

"Schiller" done, I began "Wilhelm Meister," a task I liked perhaps rather better, too scanty as my knowledge of the element, and
even of the language, still was. Two years before I had at length,
after some repulsions, got into the heart of "Wilhelm Meister," and
eagerly read it through; my sally out, after finishing, along the vacant streets of Edinburgh, a windless, scotch-misty Saturday night,
is still vivid to me. "Grand, surely, harmoniously built together,
far seeing, wise and true. When, for many years, or almost in my
whole life before, have I read such a book?" Which I was now,
really in part as a kind of duty, conscientiously translating for my
countrymen, if they would read it—as a select few of them have
ever since kept doing.

I finished it the next spring, not at Kinnaird but at Mainhill. A
month or two there with my best of nurses and of hostesses—my
mother; blessed voiceless or low-voiced time, still sweet to me;
with London now silently ahead, and the Bullers there, or to be
there. Of Kinnaird life they had now had enough, and of my miserable health far more than enough some time before! But that is
not my subject here. I had ridden to Edinburgh, there to consult
a doctor, having at last reduced my complexities to a single question: "Is this disease curable by medicine, or is it chronic, incurable
except by regimen, if even so?" This question I earnestly put; got
response, "It is all tobacco, sir; give up tobacco." Gave it instantly and strictly up. Found, after long months, that I might as well
have ridden sixty miles in the opposite direction, and poured my
sorrows into the long hairy ear of the first jackass I came upon, as
into this select medical man's, whose name I will not mention.

After these still months at Mainhill my printing at Edinburgh
was all finished, and I went thither with my preface in my pocket;

5*

finished that and the rest of the "Meister" business (£180 of payment the choicest part of it!) rapidly off; made a visit to Haddington; what a retrospect to me, now encircled by the silences and
the eternities; most beautiful, most sad! I remember the "gimp
bonnet" she wore, and her anxious silent thoughts, and my own;
mutually legible, both of them, in part; my own little darling now
at rest, and far away!—which was the last thing in Scotland. Of
the Leith smack, every figure and event in which is curiously present, though so unimportant, I will say nothing; only that we entered London River on a beautiful June morning; scene very impressive to me, and still very vivid in me; and that, soon after mid-day,
I landed safe in Irving's, as appointed.

Irving lived in Myddelton Terrace, *hodie* Myddelton Square, Islington, No. 4. It was a new place; houses bright and smart, but
inwardly bad, as usual. Only one side of the now square was built
—the western side—which has its back towards Battle Bridge region. Irving's house was fourth from the northern end of that,
which, of course, had its *left hand* on the New Road. The place was
airy, not uncheerful. Our chief prospect from the front was a good
space of green ground, and in it, on the hither edge of it, the big
open *reservoir* of Myddelton's "New River," now above two centuries old for that matter, but recently made new again, and all cased
in tight masonry; on the spacious expanse of smooth flags surround-
ing which it was pleasant on fine mornings to take an early promenade, with the free sky overhead, and the New Road, with its lively
traffic and vehiculation, seven or eight good yards below our level.
I remember several pretty strolls here, ourselves two, while breakfast was getting ready close by; and the esplanade, a high little
island, lifted free out of the noises and jostlings, was all our own.

Irving had received me with the old true friendliness; wife and
household eager to imitate him therein. I seem to have stayed a
good two or three weeks with them at that time. Buller arrangements not yet ready; nay, sometimes threatening to become uncertain altogether! and off and on during the next ten months I saw
a great deal of my old friend and his new affairs and posture. That
first afternoon, with its curious phenomena, is still very lively in
me. Basil Montague's eldest son,* Mr. Montague, junior, accidental
guest at our neat little early dinner, my first specimen of the London dandy—broken dandy; very mild of manner, who went all to

---

* Noble lady's step-son. She was Basil's third wife, and had four kinds of children at home—a most sad miscellany, as I afterwards found.

shivers, and died miserable soon after. This was novelty first. Then, during or before his stay with us, dash of a brave carriage driving up, and entry of a strangely-complexioned young lady, with soft brown eyes and floods of bronze-red hair, really a pretty-looking, smiling, and amiable, though most foreign bit of magnificence and kindly splendor, whom they welcomed by the name of "dear Kitty." Kitty Kirkpatrick, Charles Buller's cousin or half-cousin, Mrs. Strachey's full cousin, with whom she lived; her birth, as I afterwards found, an Indian *romance*, mother a sublime *Begum*, father a ditto English official, mutually adoring, wedding, living withdrawn in their own private paradise, romance famous in the East. A very singular "dear Kitty," who seemed bashful withal, and soon went away, twitching off in the lobby, as I could notice not without wonder, the loose label which was sticking to my trunk or bag, still there as she tripped past, and carrying it off in her pretty hand. With what imaginable object then, in heaven's name? To show it to Mrs. Strachey I afterwards guessed, to whom privately poor I had been prophesied of in the most grandiloquent terms. This might be called novelty second, if not first, and far greatest. Then after dinner in the drawing-room, which was prettily furnished, the *romance* of said furnishing, which had all been done as if by beneficent fairies in some temporary absence of the owners. "We had decided on not furnishing it," Irving told me, "not till we had more money ready; and on our return this was how we found it. The people here are of a nobleness you have never before seen." "And don't you yet guess at all who can have done it?" "H'm, perhaps we guess vaguely, but it is their secret, and we should not break it against their will." It turned out to have been Mrs. Strachey and dear Kitty, both of whom were rich and open-handed, that had done this fine stroke of art magic, one of the many munificences achieved by them in this new province. Perhaps the "noble lady" had at first been suspected, but how innocently she! Not flush in that way at all, though notably so in others! The talk about these and other noble souls and new phenomena, strange to me and half incredible in such interpretation, left me wondering and confusedly guessing over the much that I had heard and seen this day.

Irving's London element and mode of existence had its questionable aspects from the first; and one could easily perceive, here as elsewhere, that the ideal of fancy and the actual of fact were two very different things. It was as the former that my friend, according to old habit, strove to represent it to himself, and to *make it be;*

and it was as the latter that it obstinately continued being! There were beautiful items in his present scene of life; but a great majority which, under specious figure, were intrinsically poor, vulgar, and importunate, and introduced largely into one's existence the character of *huggermugger*, not of greatness or success in any real sense.

He was inwardly, I could observe, nothing like so happy as in old days; inwardly confused, anxious, dissatisfied; though as it were denying it to himself, and striving, if not to talk big, which he hardly ever did, to *think* big upon all this. We had many strolls together, no doubt much dialogue, but it has nearly all gone from me; probably not so worthy of remembrance as our old communings were. Crowds of visitors came about him, and ten times or a hundred times as many would have come if allowed; well-dressed, decorous people, but for most part tiresome, ignorant, weak, or even silly and absurd. He persuaded himself that at least he "loved their love;" and of this latter, in the kind they had to offer him, there did seem to be no lack. He and I were walking one bright summer evening, somewhere in the outskirts of Islington, in what was or had once been *fields*, and was again coarsely green in general, but with symptoms of past devastation by bricklayers, who have now doubtless covered it all with their dirty human "dog-hutches of the period;" when, in some smoothish hollower spot, there suddenly disclosed itself a considerable company of altogether fine-looking young girls, who had set themselves to dance; all in airy bonnets, silks, and flounces, merrily alert, nimble as young fawns, tripping it to their own rhythm on the light fantastic toe, with the bright beams of the setting sun gilding them, and the hum and smoke of huge London shoved aside as foil or background. Nothing could be prettier. At sight of us they suddenly stopped, all looking round; and one of the prettiest, a dainty little thing, stept radiantly out to Irving. "Oh! oh! Mr. Irving!" and, blushing and smiling, offered her pretty lips to be kissed, which Irving gallantly stooped down to accept as well worth while. Whereupon, after some benediction or pastoral words, we went on our way. Probably I rallied him on such opulence of luck provided for a man, to which he could answer properly as a spiritual shepherd, not a secular.

There were several Scotch merchant people among those that came about him, substantial city men of shrewd insight and good honest sense, several of whom seemed truly attached and reverent. One, William Hamilton, a very shrewd and pious Nithsdale man, who wedded a sister of Mrs. Irving's by-and-by, and whom I knew till his death, was probably the chief of these, as an old good Mr. Dinwiddie, very zealous, very simple, and far from shrewd, might perhaps be reckoned at or near the other end of the series. Sir Peter Laurie, afterwards of aldermanic and even mayoral celebrity, came also pretty often, but seemed privately to look quite from the aldermanic point of view on Irving and the new "Caledonian Chapel" they were struggling to get built—old Mr. Dinwiddie especially struggling; and indeed once to me at Paris, a while after this, he likened Irving and Dinwiddie to Harlequin and Blast, whom he had seen in some farce then current; Harlequin conjuring up the most glorious possibilities, like this of their "Caledonian Chapel," and Blast loyally following him with swift destruction on attempting to help. Sir Peter rather took to me, but not I much to him. A long-sighted satirical ex-saddler I found him to be, and nothing better; nay, something of an ex-Scotchman too, which I could still less forgive. I went with the Irvings once to his house (Crescent, head of Portland Place) to a Christmas dinner this same year. Very sumptuous, very cockneyish, strange and unadmirable to me; and don't remember to have met him again. On our coming to live in London he had rather grown in civic fame and importance, and possibly, for I am not quite sure, on the feeble chance of being of some help, I sent him some indication or other;* but if so, he took no notice; gave no sign. Some years afterwards I met him in my rides in the Park, evidently recognizant, and willing or wistful to speak, but it never came to effect, there being now no charm in it. Then again, years afterwards, when "Latter-day Pamphlets" were coming out, he wrote me on that of *Model Prisons* a knowing, approving, kindly and civil letter, to which I willingly responded by a kindly and civil. Not very long after that I think he died, riding diligently almost to the end. Poor Sir Peter! he was nothing of a bad man, very far other indeed; but had lived in a loud roaring, big, pretentious, and intrinsically barren sphere, unconscious wholly that he might have risen to the top in a considerably nobler and fruitfuller one. What a tragic, treacherous stepdame is vulgar Fortune to her children! Sir Peter's wealth has gone now in good part to somebody concerned in discovering, not for the first time, the source of the Nile (blessings on it!)—a Captain Grant, I think, companion to Speke, having married Sir Peter's Scotch niece and lady heiress, a good clever girl, once of "Hadding-

---

* A project belike—and my card with it—one of several air-castles I was anxiously building at that time before taking to *French Revolution*.

ton," and extremely poor, who made her way to my loved one on the ground of common country in late years, and used to be rather liked here in the few visits she made.

Grant and she, who are now gone to India, called after marriage, but found nobody; nor now ever will.

By far the most distinguished two, and to me the alone important, of Irving's London circle, were Mrs. Strachey (Mrs. Buller's younger sister), and the "noble lady" Mrs. Basil Montague, with both of whom and their households I became acquainted by his means. One of my first visits was along with him to Goodenough House, Shooter's Hill, where the Stracheys oftenest were in summer. I remember once entering the little winding avenue, and seeing, in a kind of open conservatory or verandah on our approaching the house, the effulgent vision of "dear Kitty" buried among the roses and almost buried under them; who on sight of us glided hastily in. The before and after and all other incidents of that first visit are quite lost to me, but I made a good many visits there and in town, and grew familiar with my ground.

Of Mrs. Strachey I have spoken already. To this day, long years after her death, I regard her as a singular pearl of a woman, pure as dew, yet full of love, incapable of unveracity to herself or others. Examiner Strachey had long been an official (judge, etc.) in Bengal, where brothers of his were, and sons still are. Eldest son is now master, by inheritance, of the family estate in Somersetshire. One of the brothers had translated a curious old Hindoo treatise on algebra, which had made his name familiar to me. Edward (that I think was the examiner's name) might be a few years turned of fifty at this time; his wife twenty years younger, with a number of pretty children, the eldest hardly fourteen, and only one of them a girl. They lived in Fitzroy Square, a fine-enough house, and had a very pleasant country establishment at Shooter's Hill; where, in summer time, they were all commonly to be found. I have seldom seen a pleasanter place; a panorama of green, flowery, clear, and decorated country all round; an umbrageous little park, with roses, gardens; a modestly - excellent house; from the drawing - room window a continual view of ships, multiform and multitudinous, sailing up or down the river (about a mile off); smoky London as background; the clear sky overhead; and within doors honesty, good-sense, and smiling seriousness the rule, and not the exception. Edward Strachey was a genially-abrupt man, a Utilitarian and Democrat by creed; yet beyond all things he loved Chaucer, and kept reading him; a man rather tacit than discursive, but willing to speak, and doing it well, in a fine, tinkling, mellow-toned voice, in an ingenious, aphoristic way; had, withal, a pretty vein of quiz, which he seldom indulged in; a man sharply impatient of pretence, of sham and untruth in all forms; especially contemptuous of quality pretensions and affectations, which he scattered grinningly to the winds. Dressed in the simplest form, he walked daily to the India House and back, though there were fine carriages in store for the woman part; scorned cheerfully "the general humbug of the world," and honestly strove to do his own bit of duty, spiced by Chaucer and what else of inward harmony or condiment he had. Of religion in articulate shape he had none, but much respected his wife's, whom and whose truthfulness in that as in all things he tenderly esteemed and loved; a man of many qualities comfortable to be near. At his house, both in town and here, I have seen pleasant, graceful people, whose style of manners, if nothing else, struck me as new and superior.

Mrs. Strachey took to me from the first, nor ever swerved. It strikes me now more than it then did, she silently could have liked to see "dear Kitty" and myself come together, and so continue near her, both of us, through life. The good, kind soul! And Kitty, too, was charming in her beautiful Begum sort; had wealth abundant, and might, perhaps, have been charmed? None knows. She had one of the prettiest smiles, a visible sense of humor, the slight, merry curl of her upper lip (right side of it only), the carriage of her head and eyes on such occasions, the quiet little things she said in that kind, and her low-toned hearty laugh were noticeable. This was perhaps her most spiritual quality. Of developed intellect she had not much, though not wanting in discernment; amiable, affectionate, graceful; might be called attractive; not slim enough for the title "pretty," not tall enough for "beautiful;" had something low-voiced, languidly harmonious, placid, sensuous; loved perfumes, etc.; a half-*Begum;* in short, an interesting specimen of the semi-oriental Englishwoman. Still lives!— near Exeter; the wife of some ex-captain of Sepoys, with many children, whom she watches over with a passionate instinct; and has not quite forgotten me, as I had evidence once in late years, thanks to her kind little heart.

The Montague establishment (25 Bedford Square) was still more notable, and as unlike this as possible; might be defined, not quite satirically, as a most singular, social, and spiritual ménagerie; which, indeed, was well known and much noted and criticised in certain literary and other circles. Basil Montague, a chancery barrister in excellent practice, hugely a *sage*, too, busy all his days upon "Bacon's Works," and continually preaching a superfinish morality about benevolence, munificence, health, peace, unfailing happiness. Much a bore to you by degrees, and considerably a humbug if you probed too strictly. Age at this time might be about sixty; good middle stature, face rather fine under its grizzled hair, brow very prominent; wore oftenest a kind of smile, not false or consciously so, but insignificant, and as if feebly defensive against the intrusions of a rude world. On going to Hinchinbrook long after, I found he was strikingly like the dissolute, questionable Earl of Sandwich (Foote's "Jeremy Diddler"); who, indeed, had been father of him in a highly tragic way. His mother, pretty Miss Reay, carefully educated for that function; Rev. ex-dragoon Hackman taking this so dreadfully to heart that, being if not an ex-lover, a lover (bless the mark!), he shot her as she came out of Drury Lane Theatre one night, and got well-hanged for it. The story is musty rather, and there is a loose, foolish old book upon it called "Love and Madness," which is not worth reading. Poor Basil! no wonder he had his peculiarities, coming by such a genesis, and a life of his own which had been brimful of difficulties and confusions! It cannot be said he managed it ill, but far the contrary, all things considered. Nobody can deny that he wished all the world rather well, could wishing have done it. Express malice against anybody or anything he seldom or never showed. I myself experienced much kind flattery (if that were a benefit), much soothing treatment in his house, and learned several things there which were of use afterwards, and not alloyed by the least harm done me. But it was his wife, the "noble lady," who in all senses presided there, to whom I stand debtor, and should be thankful for all this.

Basil had been thrice married. Children of all his marriages, and one child of the now Mrs. Montague's own by a previous marriage, were present in the house; a most difficult miscellany. The one son of B.'s first marriage we have already dined with, and indicated that he soon ended by a bad road. Still worse the three sons of the second marriage, dandy young fellows by this time, who went all and sundry to the bad, the youngest and luckiest soon to a *madhouse*, where he probably still is. Nor were the two boys of Mrs. Montague Tertia a good kind; thoroughly vain or even proud, and with a spice of angry falsity discernible amid their showy talents. They grew up only to go astray and be unlucky. Both long since are dead, or gone out of sight. Only the eldest child,

Emily, the single daughter Basil had, succeeded in the world; made a good match (in Turin country somewhere), and is still doing well. Emily was Basil's only daughter, but she was not his wife's only one. Mrs. Montague had by her former marriage, which had been brief, one daughter, six or eight years older than Emily Montague. Anne Skepper the name of this one, and York or Yorkshire her birthplace; a brisk, witty, prettyish, sufficiently clear-eyed and sharp-tongued young lady; bride, or affianced, at this time, of the poet "Barry Cornwall," i. e. Brian W. Procter, whose wife, both of them still prosperously living (1860), she now is. Anne rather liked me; I her; an evidently true, sensible, and practical young lady in a house considerably in want of such an article. She was the fourth genealogical species among those children, visibly the eldest, all but Basil's first son now gone; and did, and might well pass for, the flower of the collection.

Ruling such a miscellany of a household, with Basil Montague at the head, and an almost still stranger miscellaneous society that fluctuated through it, Mrs. Montague had a problem like few others. But she, if any one, was equal to it. A more constant and consummate artist in that kind you could nowhere meet with; truly a remarkable and partly a high and tragical woman; now about fifty, with the remains of a certain queenly beauty which she still took strict care of. A tall, rather thin figure; a face pale, intelligent, and penetrating; nose fine, rather large, and decisively Roman; pair of bright, not soft, but sharp and small black eyes, with a cold smile as of inquiry in them; fine brow; fine chin (both rather prominent); thin lips—lips always gently shut, as if till the inquiry were completed, and the time came for something of royal speech upon it. She had a slight Yorkshire accent, but spoke— Dr. Hugh Blair could not have picked a hole in it—and you might have printed every word, so queen-like, gentle, soothing, measured, prettily royal towards subjects whom she wished to love her. The voice was modulated, low, not inharmonious; yet there was something of metallic in it, akin to that smile in the eyes. One durst not quite love this high personage as she wished to be loved! Her very dress was notable; always the same, and in a fashion of its own; kind of widow's cap fastened below the chin, darkish puce-colored silk all the rest, and (I used to hear from one who knew!) was admirable, and must have required daily the fastening of sixty or eighty pins.

There were many criticisms of Mrs. Montague—often angry ones; but the truth is she did love and aspire to human excellence, and her road to it was no better than a steep hill of jingling boulders and sliding sand. There remained therefore nothing, if you still aspired, but to succeed ill and put the best face on it. Which she amply did. I have heard her speak of the Spartan boy who let the fox hidden under his robe eat him, rather than rob him of his honor from the theft.

In early life she had made some visit to Nithsdale (to the "Craiks of Arligsland"), and had seen Burns, of whom her worship continued fervent, her few recollections always a jewel she was ready to produce. She must have been strikingly beautiful at that time, and Burns's recognition and adoration would not be wanting; the most royally courteous of mankind she always defined him, as the first mark of his genius. I think I have heard that, at a ball at Dumfries, she had frugally constructed some dress by sewing real flowers upon it; and shone by that bit of art, and by her fine bearing, as the cynosure of all eyes. Her father, I gradually understood, not from herself, had been a man of inconsiderable wealth or position, a wine-merchant in York, his name Benson. Her first husband, Mr. Skepper, some young lawyer there, of German extraction; and that the *romance* of her wedding Montague, which she sometimes touched on, had been prosaically nothing but this. Seeing herself, on Skepper's death, left destitute with a young girl, she consented to take charge of Montague's motherless confused family under the name of "governess," bringing her own little Anne as appendage. Had succeeded well, and better and better, for some time, perhaps some years, in that ticklish capacity; whereupon at length offer of marriage, which she accepted. Her sovereignty in the house had to be soft, judicious, politic, but it was constant and valid, felt to be beneficial withal. "She is like one in command of a mutinous ship which is ready to take fire," Irving once said to me. By this time he had begun to discover that this "noble lady" was in essentiality an artist, and hadn't perhaps so much loved him as tried to buy love from him by soft ministrations, by the skilfullest flattery liberally laid on. He continued always to look kindly towards her, but had now, or did by-and-by, let drop the old epithet. Whether she had done him good or ill would be hard to say; ill perhaps! In this liberal London, pitch your sphere one step lower than yourself, and you can get what amount of flattery you will consent to. Everybody has it, like paper money, for the printing, and will buy a small amount of ware by any quantity of it. The generous Irving did not find out this so soon as some surlier fellows of us!

On one of the first fine mornings, Mrs. Montague, along with Irving, took me out to see Coleridge at Highgate. My impressions of the man and of the place are conveyed faithfully enough in the "Life of Sterling;" that first interview in particular, of which I had expected very little, was idle and unsatisfactory, and yielded me nothing. Coleridge, a puffy, anxious, obstructed-looking, fattish old man, hobbled about with us, talking with a kind of solemn emphasis on matters which were of no interest (and even *reading* pieces in proof of his opinions thereon). I had him to myself once or twice, in various parts of the garden walks, and tried hard to get something about *Kant* and Co. from him, about "reason" versus "understanding" and the like, but in vain. Nothing came from him that was of use to me that day, or in fact any day. The sight and sound of a sage who was so venerated by those about me, and whom I too would willingly have venerated, but could not—this was all. Several times afterwards, Montague, on Coleridge's "Thursday evenings," carried Irving and me out, and returned blessing Heaven (I not) for what he had received. Irving and I walked out more than once on mornings too, and found the Dodona oracle humanly ready to act, but never to me, or Irving either I suspect, explanatory of the question put. Good Irving strove always to think that he was getting priceless wisdom out of this great man, but must have had his misgivings. Except by the Montague-Irving channel, I at no time communicated with Coleridge. I had never on my own strength had much esteem for him, and found slowly in spite of myself that I was getting to have less and less. Early in 1825 was my last sight of him ; a print of Porson brought some trifling utterance : " Sensuality such a *dissolution* of the features of a man's face ;" and I remember nothing more. On my second visit to London (autumn 1830) Irving and I had appointed a day for a pilgrimage to Highgate, but the day was one rain deluge and we couldn't even try. Soon after our settling here (late in 1834) Coleridge was reported to be dying, and died; I had seen the last of him almost a decade ago.

A great "worship of genius" habitually went on at Montague's, from self and wife especially ; Coleridge the head of the Lares there, though he never appeared in person, but only wrote a word or two of note on occasions. A confused dim miscellany of "geniuses" (mostly nondescript and harmlessly useless) hovered fitfully about the establishment ; I think those of any reality had tired and gone away. There was much talk and laud of Charles Lamb and his Pepe, etc., but he never appeared. At his own house I saw him once; once I gradually felt to have been enough for me. Poor Lamb! such a "divine genius" you could find in the London world only! Hazlitt, whom I had a kind of curiosity about, was not now of the "admitted" (such the hint); at any rate kept strictly away. There was a "Crabbe Robinson," who had been in Weimar, etc., who was first of the "Own Correspondents" now so numerous. This is now his real distinction. There was a Mr. Fearn, "profound in metaphysics" ("dull utterly and dry"). There was a *Dr*. Sir Anthony Carlile, of name in medicine, native of Durham and a hard-headed fellow, but Utilitarian to the bone, who had defined poetry to Irving once as "the *prodooction* of a rude *aage*." We were clansmen, he and I, but had nothing of mutual attraction, nor of repulsion either, for the man didn't want for shrewd sense in his way. I heard continual talk and admiration of "the grand old English writers" (Fuller, Sir Thomas Browne, and various others—Milton more rarely); this was the orthodox strain. But there was little considerable of actual knowledge, and of critical appreciation almost nothing at the back of it anywhere; and in the end it did one next to no good, yet perhaps not quite none, deducting in accurate balance all the ill that might be in it.

Nobody pleased me so much in this miscellany as Procter (Barry Cornwall), who for the fair Anne Skepper's sake was very constantly there. Anne and he were to have been, and were still to be married, but some disaster or entanglement in Procter's attorney business had occurred (some partner defalcating or the like), and Procter, in evident distress and dispiritment, was waiting the slow conclusion of this; which and the wedding thereupon happily took place in the winter following. A decidedly rather pretty little fellow, Procter, bodily and spiritually; manners prepossessing, slightly London-elegant, not unpleasant; clear judgment in him, though of narrow field; a sound honorable morality, and airy friendly ways; of slight neat figure, vigorous for his size; fine genially rugged little face, fine head; something curiously dreamy in the eyes of him, lids drooping at the *outer* ends into a cordially meditative and drooping expression; would break out suddenly now and then into opera attitude and a *Là ci darem la mano* for a moment; had something of real fun, though in London style. Me he had invited to "his garret," as he called it, and was always good and kind and so continues, though I hardly see him once in a quarter of a century.

The next to Procter in my esteem, and the considerably more important to me just then, was a young Mr. Badams, in great and

"BARRY CORNWALL" (B. W. PROCTER).

romantic estimation there, and present every now and then, though his place and business lay in Birmingham; a most cheery, gifted, really amiable man, with whom not long afterwards I more or less *romantically* went to Birmingham, and though not cured of "dyspepsia" there (alas! not the least) had two or three singular and interesting months, as will be seen.

Irving's preaching at Hatton Garden, which I regularly attended while in his house, and occasionally afterwards, did not strike me as superior to his Scotch performances of past time, or, in private fact, inspire me with any complete or pleasant feeling. Assent to them I could not, except under very wide reservations, nor, granting all his postulates, did either matter or manner carry me captive, or at any time perfect my admiration. The force and weight of what he urged was undeniable; the potent faculty at work, like that of a Samson heavily striding along with the gates of Gaza on his shoulders; but there was a want of spontaneity and simplicity, a something of strained and aggravated, of elaborately intentional, which kept gaining on the mind. One felt the bad element to be and to have been unwholesome to the honorable soul. The doors were crowded long before opening, and you got in by ticket; but the first sublime rush of what once seemed more than popularity, and had been nothing more—Lady Jersey "sitting on the pulpit steps," Canning, Brougham, Mackintosh, etc., rushing day after day—was now quite over, and there remained only a popularity of " the people;" not of the *plebs* at all, but never higher than of the well-dressed *populus* henceforth, which was a sad change to the sanguine man. One noticed that he was not happy, but anxious, struggling, questioning the future; happiness, alas, he was no more to have, even in the old measure, in this world! At sight of Canning, Brougham, Lady Jersey and Co., crowding round him and listening week after week as if to the message of salvation, the noblest and joyfullest thought (I know this on perfect authority) had taken possession of his noble, too sanguine, and too trustful mind: "that the Christian religion was to be a truth again, not a paltry form, and to rule the world, he unworthy, even he, the chosen instrument." Mrs. Strachey, who had seen him in her own house in these moods, spoke to me once of this, and only once, reporting some of his expressions with an affectionate sorrow. Cruelly blasted all these hopes were, but Irving never to the end of his life could consent to give them up. That was the key to all his subsequent procedures, extravagances, aberrations, so far as I could understand them. Whatever of blame (and there was on the surface a fond credulity, or perhaps, farther down, and as root to such credulity, some excess of *self-love*, which I define always as love that others should love him, *not* as any worse kind), with that degree of blame Irving must stand charged, with that and with no more, so far as I could testify or understand.

Good Mrs. Oliphant, and probably her public, have much mistaken me on this point. That Irving to the very last had abundant "popularity," and confluence of auditors sufficient for the largest pulpit "vanity," I knew and know, but also that his own immeasurable and quasi-celestial hope remained cruelly blasted, refusing the least *bud* farther, and that without this all else availed him nothing. Fallacious semblances of bud it did shoot out again and again, under his continual fostering and forcing, but real bud never more, and the case in itself is easy to understand.

He had much quiet seriousness, beautiful piety and charity, in this bud time of agitation and disquietude, and I was often honestly sorry for him. Here was still the old true man, and his new element seemed so false and abominable. Honestly, though not so purely, sorry as now—now when element and man are alike gone, and all that was or partook of paltry in one's own view of them is also mournfully gone! He had endless patience with the mean people crowding about him and jostling his life to pieces ; hoped always they were not so mean; never complained of the uncomfortable huggermugger his life was now grown to be; took everything, wife, servants, guests, by the most favorable handle. He had infinite delight in a little baby boy there now was ; went dandling it about in his giant arms, tick-ticking to it, laughing and playing to it; would turn seriously round to me with a face sorrowful rather than otherwise, and say, "Ah, Carlyle, this little creature has been sent to me to soften my hard heart, which did need it."

Towards all distressed people not absolutely criminals, his kindness, frank helpfulness, long suffering, and assiduity were in truth wonderful to me; especially in one case, that of a Reverend Mr. Macbeth, which I thought ill of from the first, and which did turn out hopeless. Macbeth was a Scotch preacher, or licentiate, who had failed of a kirk, as he had deserved to do, though his talents were good, and was now hanging very miscellaneously on London, with no outlooks that were not bog meteors, and a steadily increasing tendency to strong drink. He knew town well, and its babble and bits of temporary cynosures, and frequented haunts good and perhaps bad; took me one evening to the poet Campbell's, whom I had already seen, but not successfully.

Macbeth had a sharp, sarcastic, clever kind of tongue; not much real knowledge, but was amusing to talk with on a chance walk through the streets; older than myself by a dozen years or more. Like him I did not; there was nothing of wisdom, generosity, or worth in him, but in secret, evidently discernible, a great deal of bankrupt vanity which had taken quite the malignant shape. Undeniable envy, spite, and bitterness looked through every part of him. A tallish, slouching, lean figure, face sorrowful, malignant, black, not unlike the picture of a devil. To me he had privately much the reverse of liking. I have seen him in Irving's and elsewhere (perhaps with a little drink on his stomach, poor soul!) break out into oblique little spurts of positive spite, which I understood to mean merely, "Young Jackanapes, getting yourself noticed and honored while a mature man of genius is" etc., etc., and took no notice of, to the silent comfort of self and neighbors.

This broken Macbeth had been hanging a good while about Irving, who had taken much earnest pains to rescue and arrest him on the edge of the precipices, but latterly had begun to see that it was hopeless, and had rather left him to his own bad courses. One evening, it was in dirty winter weather and I was present, there came to Irving or to Mrs. Irving, dated from some dark tavern in the Holborn precincts, a piteous little note from Macbeth. "Ruined again (tempted, oh how cunningly, to my old sin); been drinking these three weeks, and now have a chalk-score and no money, and can't get out. Oh, help a perishing sinner!" The majority was of opinion, "Pshaw! it is totally useless!" but Irving after some minutes of serious consideration decided, "No, not totally!" and directly got into a hackney coach, wife and he, proper moneys in pocket, paid the poor devil's tavern score (some £2 10s. or so, if I remember), and brought him groaning home out of his purgatory again: for he was in much bodily suffering too. I remember to have been taken up to see him one evening in his bedroom (comfortable airy place) a week or two after. He was in clean dressing-gown and night-cap, walking about the floor; affected to turn away his face and be quite "ashamed" when Irving introduced me, which as I could discern it to be painful hypocrisy merely, forbade my visit to be other than quite brief. Comment I made none here or down-stairs; was actually a little sorry, but without hope, and rather think this was my last sight of Macbeth. Another time, which could not now be distant, when he lay again under chalk-score and bodily sickness in his drinking shop, there would be no deliverance but to the hospital; and there I suppose the poor creature tragically ended. He was not without talent, had written a "Book on the Sabbath," better or worse, and I almost think was understood, with all his impenitences and malignities, to have real love for his poor old Scotch mother. After that night in his clean airy bedroom I have no recollection or tradition of him— a vanished quantity, hardly once in my thoughts for above forty years past. There were other disastrous or unpleasant figures whom I met at Irving's; a Danish fanatic of Calvinistic species (repeatedly, and had to beat him off), a good many fanatics of different kinds—one insolent "Bishop of Toronto," triumphant Canadian but Aberdeen by dialect (once only, from whom Irving defended me), etc., etc.; but of these I say nothing. Irving, though they made his house-element and life-element continually muddy for him, was endlessly patient with them all.

This my first visit to London lasted with interruptions from early June, 1824, till March, 1825, during which I repeatedly lodged for a little while at Irving's, his house ever open to me like a brother's, but cannot now recollect the times or their circumstances. The above recollections extend vaguely over the whole period, during the last four or five months of which I had my own rooms in Southampton Street near by, and was still in almost constant familiarity. My own situation was very wretched; primarily from a state of health which nobody could be expected to understand or sympathize with, and about which I had as much as possible to be silent. The accursed hag "Dyspepsia" had got me bitted and bridled, and was ever striving to make my waking living day a thing of ghastly nightmares. I resisted what I could; never did yield or surrender to her; but she kept my heart right heavy, my battle very sore and hopeless. One could not call it hope, but only desperate obstinacy refusing to flinch that animated me. "Obstinacy as *of ten mules*" I have sometimes called it since; but in candid truth there was something worthily *human* in it too; and I have had through life, among my manifold unspeakable blessings, no other real bower anchor to ride by in the rough seas. Human "obstinacy," grounded on real faith and insight, is good and the *best*.

All was change, too, at this time with me, all uncertainty. Mrs. Buller, the bright, the ardent, the airy, was a changeful lady! The original programme had been, we were all to shift to Cornwall, live in some beautiful Buller cottage there was about East Looe or West (on her eldest brother-in-law's property). With this as a fixed thing I had arrived in London, asking myself " what kind of a thing will it be ?" It proved to have become already a thing of all the winds; gone like a dream of the night (by some accident or other). For four or five weeks coming there was new scheme, followed always by newer and newest, all of which proved successively inexecutable, greatly to my annoyance and regret, as may be imagined. The only thing that did ever take effect was the shifting of Charles and me out to solitary lodgings at Kew Green, an isolating of us two (*pro tempore*) over our lessons there, one of the dreariest and uncomfortablest things to both of us. It lasted for about a fortnight, till Charles, I suppose privately pleading, put an end to it as intolerable and useless both (for one could not " study " but only pretend to do it in such an element). Other wild projects rose rapidly, rapidly vanished futile. The end was, in a week or two after, I deliberately counselled that Charles should go direct for Cambridge next term, in the mean time making ready under some fit college "grinder;" I myself not without regret taking leave of the enterprise. Which proposal, after some affectionate resistance on the part of Charles, was at length (rather suddenly, I recollect) acceded to by the elder people, and one bright summer morning (still vivid to me) I stept out of a house in Foley Place, with polite farewell sounding through me, and the thought, as I walked along Regent Street, that here I was without employment henceforth. Money was no longer quite wanting, enough of money for some time to come, but the question what to do next was not a little embarrassing, and indeed was intrinsically abstruse enough.

I must have been lodging again with Irving when this finale came. I recollect Charles Buller and I, a day or some days after quitting Kew, had rendezvoused by appointment in Regent Square (St. Pancras), where Irving and a great company were laying the foundation of " Caledonian Chapel " (which still stands there), and Irving of course had to deliver an address. Of the address, which was going on when we arrived, I could hear nothing, such the confusing crowd and the unfavorable locality (a muddy chaos of rubbish and excavations, Irving and the actors shut off from us by a circle of rude bricklayers' planks); but I well remember Irving's glowing face, streaming hair, and deeply moved tones as he spoke ; and withal that Charles Buller brought me some new futility of a proposal, and how sad he looked, good youth, when I had directly to reply with " No, alas! I cannot, Charles." This was but a few days before the Buller finale.

Twenty years after, riding discursively towards Tottenham one summer evening, with the breath of the wind from northward, and London hanging to my right hand like a grim and vast sierra, I saw among the peaks, as easily ascertainable, the high minarets of that chapel, and thought with myself, " Ah, you fatal *tombstone* of my lost friend! and did a soul so strong and high avail only to build *you?*" and felt sad enough and rather angry in looking at the thing.

It was not many days after this of the Regent Square address, which was quickly followed by termination with the Bullers, that I found myself one bright Sunday morning on the top of a swift coach for Birmingham, with intent towards the Mr. Badams above mentioned, and a considerable visit there, for health's sake mainly. Badams and the Montagues had eagerly proposed and counselled this step. Badams himself was so eager about it, and seemed so frank, cheery, ingenious, and friendly a man that I had listened to his pleadings with far more regard than usual in such a case, and without assenting had been seriously considering the proposal for some weeks before (during the Kew Green seclusion and perhaps earlier). He was in London twice or thrice while things hung in deliberation, and was each time more eager and persuasive on me. In fine I had assented, and was rolling along through sunny Eng-land—the first considerable space I had yet seen of it—with really pleasant recognition of its fertile beauties and air of long-continued cleanliness, contentment, and well being. Stony Stratford, Fenny Stratford, and the good people coming out of church, Coventry, etc., etc., all this is still a picture. Our coach was of the swiftest in the world ; appointments perfect to a hair ; one and a half minutes the time allowed for changing horses ; our coachman, in dress, etc., resembled a "sporting gentleman," and scornfully called any groundling whom he disliked, "You Radical!" for one symptom. I don't remember a finer ride, as if on the arrow of Abaris, with lips shut and nothing to do but look. My reception at Ashsted (west end of Birmingham, not far from the great Watts' house of that name), and instalment in the Badams' domesticities, must have well corresponded to my expectations, as I have now no memory of it. My visit in whole, which lasted for above three months, may be pronounced interesting, idle, pleasant, and success-ful, though singular.

Apart from the nimbus of Montague romance in the first accounts I had got of Badams, he was a gifted, amiable, and remarkable man, who proved altogether friendly and beneficent, so far as he went, with

me, and whose final history, had I time for it, would be tragical in
its kind. He was eldest boy of a well-doing but not opulent mas-
ter-workman (plumber, I think) in Warwick town; got marked for
the ready talents he showed, especially for some picture he had on
his own resources and unaided inventions copied in the Warwick
Castle gallery with " wonderful success;" and in fine was taken
hold of by the famous Dr. Parr and others of that vicinity, and
lived some time as one of Parr's scholars in Parr's house; learning
I know not what, not taking very kindly to the *Œolic digamma* department I should apprehend! He retained a kindly and respectful remembrance about this Trismegistus of the then pedants, but
always in brief quizzical form. Having declared for medicine, he
was sent to Edinburgh College, studied there for one session or
more; but "being desirous to marry some beautiful lady-love"
(said the Montagues), or otherwise determined on a shorter road to
fortune, he now cut loose from his patrons, and modestly planted
himself in Birmingham, with purpose of turning to account some
chemical ideas he had gathered in the classes here; rivalling of
French green vitriol by purely English methods ("no *husks of
grapes* for you and your vitriol, ye English; your vitriol only half
the selling price of ours!") that I believe was it, and Badams had
fairly succeeded in it and in other branches of the color business,
and had a manufactory of twenty or fewer hands, full of thrifty and
curious ingenuity; at the outer corner of which, fronting on two
streets, was his modest but comfortable dwelling-house, where I
now lived with him as guest. Simplicity and a pure and direct
aim at the essential (aim good and generally successful), that was
our rule in this establishment, which was and continued always innocently comfortable and home-like to me. The lowest floor, opening rearward of the manufactory, was exclusively given up to an
excellent Mrs. Barnet (with husband and family of two), who in
perfection and in silence kept house to us; her husband, whom
Badams only tolerated for her sake, working out of doors among
the twenty. We lived in the two upper floors, entering from one
street door, and wearing a modestly civilized air. Everything has
still a living look to me in that place; not even the bad Barnet,
who never showed his badness, but has claims on me; still more
the venerable lean and brown old grandfather Barnet, who used to
"go for our letters," and hardly ever spoke except by his fine and
mournful old eyes. These Barnets, with the workmen generally,
and their quiet steady ways, were pleasant to observe, but especially our excellent, sad, pure, and silent Mrs. Barnet, correct as an

eight-day clock, and making hardly as much noise! Always
dressed in modest black, tall, clean, well-looking, light of foot and
hand. She was very much loved by Badams as a friend of his
mother's and a woman of real worth, bearing well a heavy enough
load of sorrows (chronic disease of the heart to crown them he
would add). I remember the sight of her, one afternoon, in some
lighted closet there was, cutting out the bit of bread for the children's luncheon, two dear pretty little girls who stood looking up
with hope, her silence and theirs, and the fine human relation between them, as one of my pleasant glimpses into English humble
life. The younger of these pretty children died within few years;
the elder, "Bessy Barnet," a creature of distinguished faculties who
has had intricate vicissitudes and fortunate escapes, stayed with us
here as our first servant (servant and friend both in one) for about
a year, then went home, and after long and complete disappearance
from our thoughts and affairs, re-emerged, most modestly triumphant, not very long ago, as wife of the accomplished Dr. Blakiston
of Leamington ; in which capacity she showed a generous exaggerated "gratitude" to her old mistress and me, and set herself and
her husband unweariedly to help in that our sad Leamington season of woe and toil, which has now ended in eternal peace to one
of us. Nor can Dr. B.'s and his "Bessy's" kindness in it ever be
forgotten while the other of us still lingers here! Ah me! ah me!

My Birmingham visit, except as it continually kept me riding
about in the open air, did nothing for me in the anti-dyspeptic
way, but in the social and spiritually consolatory way it was really
of benefit. Badams was a horse fancier, skilful on horseback, kept
a choice two or three of horses here, and in theory professed the
obligation to "ride for health," but very seldom by himself did it
—it was always along with me, and not one-tenth part so often as
I during this sojourn. With me red "Taffy," the briskest of Welsh
ponies, went galloping daily far and wide, unless I were still better
mounted (for exercise of the other high-going sort), and many were
the pleasant rides I had in the Warwickshire lanes and heaths,
and real good they did me, if Badams's medicinal and dietetic formalities (to which I strictly conformed) did me little or none. His
unaffected kindness, and cheerful human sociality and friendliness,
manifest at all times, could not but be of use to me too. Seldom
have I seen a franker, trustier, cheerier form of human kindliness
than Badams's. How I remember the laughing eyes and sunny
figure of him breaking into my room on mornings, himself half-
dressed (waistband in hand was a common aspect, and hair all fly-

ing). "What! not up yet, monster?" The smile of his eyes, the sound of his voice, were so bright and practically true on these occasions. A tight, middle-sized, handsome kind of man, eyes blue, sparkling soft, nose and other features inclining to the pointed, complexion, which was the weak part, tending rather to bluish, face always shaven bare and no whiskers left; a man full of hope, full of natural intellect, ingenuity, invention, essentially a gentleman; and really looked well and jauntily aristocratic when dressed for riding or the like, which was always a careful preliminary. Slight rusticity of accent rather did him good; so prompt, mildly emphatic and expressive were the words that came from him. His faults were a too sanguine temper, and a defective inner *sternness of veracity:* true he was, but not sternly enough, and would listen to imagination and delusive hopes when Fact said No—for which two faults, partly recognizable to me even then, I little expected he would by-and-by pay so dear.

We had a pleasant time together, many pleasant summer rides, and outdoor talks and in; to Guy's Cliff, Warwick Castle, Sutton Coldfield, or Kenilworth, etc., on holidays; or miscellaneously over the furzy heaths and leafy ruralities on common evenings. I remember well a ride we made to Kenilworth one Saturday afternoon by the "wood of Arden" and its monstrous old oaks, on to the famous ruin itself (*fresh* in the Scott novels then), and a big jolly farmer of Badams's, who lodged us—nice polite wife and he in a finely human way—till Monday morning, with much talk about old Parr, in whose parish (Hatton) we then were. Old Parr would have been desirabler to me than the great old ruin (now mainly a skeleton, part of it a coarse farm-house, which was the most interesting part). But Badams did not propose a call on his old pedant friend, and I could not be said to regret the omission; a saving of so much trouble withal. There was a sort of pride felt in their Dr. Parr all over this region; yet everybody seemed to consider him a ridiculous old fellow, whose strength of intellect was mainly gone to self-will and fantasticality. They all mimicked his *lisp,* and talked of wig and tobacco-pipe. (No pipe, no Parr! his avowed principle when asked to dinner among fine people). The old man came to Edinburgh on a visit to Dr. Gregory, perhaps the very next year; and there, too, for a year following there lingered traditions of good-natured grins and gossip, which one heard of; but the man himself I never saw, nor, though rather liking him, sensibly cared to see.

Another very memorable gallop (we always went at galloping or cantering pace, and Badams was proud of his cattle and their really great prowess), was one morning out to Hagley; to the top of the Clent Hill for a view, after breakfast at Hagley Tap, and then return. Distance from Birmingham about seventeen miles. "The Leasowes" (Poet Shenstone's place) is about midway (visible enough to left in the level sun-rays as you gallop out); after which comes a singular *Terra di Lavóro*—or wholly metallic country—Hales Owen the heart of it. Thick along the wayside, little forges built of single brick, hardly bigger than sentry-boxes; and in each of them, with bellows, stake, and hammer a woman busy making nails; fine, tall young women several of them, old others, but all in clean aprons, clean white calico jackets (must have been Monday morning), their look industrious and patient. Seems as if all the nails in the world were getting made here on very unexpected terms! Hales Owen itself had much sunk under the improved highway, but was cheerfully jingling as we cantered through. Hagley Tap and its quiet green was all our own; not to be matched out of England. Lord Lyttelton's mansion I have ever since in my eye as a noble-looking place, when his lordship comes athwart me; a rational, ruggedly-considerate kind of man whom I could have liked to see there (as he was good enough to wish), had there been a *Fortunatus* travelling carpet at my disposal. Smoke pillars many, in a definite straight or spiral shape; the Dudley "Black Country," under favorable omens, visible from the Clent Hill; after which, and the aristocratic roof works, attics, and grand chimney-tops of Hagley mansion, the curtain quite drops.

Of persons also I met some notable or quasi-notable. "Joe" Parkes, then a small Birmingham attorney, afterwards the famous Reform Club ditto, was a visitor at Badams's on rare evenings; a rather pleasant-talking, shrewd enough little fellow, with bad teeth, and a knowing, flighty satirical way; whom Badams thought little of, but tolerated for his (Joe's) mother's sake, as he did Parkes senior, who was her second husband. The famous Joe I never saw again, though hearing often of his preferments, performances, and him, till he died, not long since, writing a new "Discovery of Junius," it was rumored; fit enough task for such a man. Bessy Parkes (of the Rights of Women) is a daughter of his. There were Phipsons, too, "Unitarian people," very good to me. A young fellow of them, still young though become a pin manufacturer, had been at *Erlangen* University, and could float along in a light, airy, anecdotic fashion by a time. He re-emerged on me four or five years ago, living at Putney; head grown white from red, but heart still light; introducing a chemical son of his, whom I thought not unlikely to push himself in the world by that course. Kennedy of Cambridge, afterwards great as "master of Shrewsbury school," was polite to me, but unproductive. Others—but why should I speak of them at all? Accidentally, one Sunday evening, I heard the famous Dr. Hall (of Leicester) preach; a flabby, puffy, but massy, earnest, forcible-looking man, *homme alors célèbre!* Sermon extempore; text, "God who cannot lie." He proved beyond shadow of doubt, in a really forcible but most superfluous way, that God never lied (had no need to do it, etc.). "As good prove that God never fought a duel," sniffed Badams, on my reporting at home.

Jemmy Belcher was a smirking little dumpy Unitarian bookseller, in the Bull-ring, regarded as a kind of curiosity and favorite among these people, and had seen me. One showery day I took shelter in his shop; picked up a new magazine, found in it a cleverish and completely hostile criticism of my "Wilhelm Meister," of my Goethe, and self, etc., read it faithfully to the end, and have never set eye on it since. On stepping out of my bad spirits did not feel much elevated by the dose just swallowed, but I thought with myself, "This man is perhaps right on some points; if so, let him be admonitory!" And he was so (on a Scotticism, or perhaps two); and I did reasonably soon (in not above a couple of hours), dismiss him to the devil, or to Jericho, as an ill-given, unserviceable kind of entity in my course through this world. It was De Quincey, as I often enough heard afterwards from foolish-talking persons. "What matter who, ye foolish-talking persons?" would have been my *silent* answer, as it generally pretty much was. I recollect, too, how in Edinburgh a year or two after, poor De Quincey, whom I wished to know, was reported to tremble at the thought of such a thing; and did fly pale as ashes, poor little soul, the first time we actually met. He was a pretty little creature, full of wire-drawn ingenuities, bankrupt enthusiasms, bankrupt pride, with the finest silver-toned low voice, and most elaborate gently-winding courtesies and ingenuities in conversation. "What wouldn't one give to have him in a box, and take him out to talk!" That was Her criticism of him, and it was right good. A bright, ready, and melodious talker, but in the end an inconclusive and long-winded. One of the smallest man figures I ever saw; shaped like a pair of tongs, and hardly above five feet in all. When he sate, you would have taken him, by candlelight, for the beautifullest little child; blue-eyed, sparkling face, had there not been a something, too, which said "*Eccovi*—this child has been in hell." After leaving Edinburgh I never saw him, hardly ever heard of him. His fate, owing to opium, etc., was hard and sore, poor fine-strung weak creature, launched *so* into the literary career of ambition and mother of dead dogs. That peculiar kind of "meeting" with him was among the phenomena of my then Birmingham ("Bromwich-ham," "Bruma-gem," as you were forced to call it).

Irving himself, once, or perhaps twice, came to us, in respect of a Scotch Chapel newly set on foot there, and rather in tottering condition. Preacher in it one Crosbie, whom I had seen once at Glasgow in Dr. Chalmers's, a silent guest along with me, whose chief characteristic was helpless dispiritment under *dyspepsia*, which had come upon him, hapless innocent lazy soul. The people were very kind to him, but he was helpless, and I think soon after went away. What became of the Chapel since I didn't hear. The Rev. Mr. Martin of Kirkcaldy, with his reverend father, and perhaps a sister, passed through Birmingham, bound for London to christen some new child of Irving's; and being received in a kind of gala by those Scotch Chapel people, caused me a noisy not pleasant day. Another day, positively painful though otherwise instructive, I had in the Dudley "Black Country" (which I had once seen from the distance), roving about among the coal and metal mines there, in company or neighborhood of Mr. Airy, now "Astronomer Royal," whom I have never seen since. Our party was but of four. Some opulent retired Dissenting Minister had decided on a holiday ova-tion to Airy, who had just issued from Cambridge as chief of Wran-glers and mathematical wonder, and had come to Birmingham on visit to some footlicker whose people lived there. "I will show Airy our mine country," said the reverend old friend of enlighten-ment, "and Mr. G., Airy's footlicker, shall accompany!" That was his happy thought; and Badams hearing it from him, had suggested me (not quite unknown to him) as a fourth figure. I was ill in health, but thought it right to go. We inspected black furnaces, descended into coal mines; poked about industriously into nature's and art's sooty arcana all day (with a short recess for luncheon), and returned at night in the Reverend's postchaise, thoroughly wearied and disgusted, one of us at least. Nature's sooty arcana was welcome and even pleasant to me; art's also, more or less. Thus in the belly of the deepest mine, climbing over a huge jingle of new-loosened coal, there met me on the very summit a pair of small cheerful human *eyes* (face there was none discernible at first, so totally black was *it*, and so dim were our candles), then a ditto ditto of lips, internally red; which I perceived, with a comic inter-est, were begging beer from me! Nor was Airy himself in the least

THOMAS DE QUINCEY.

an offence, or indeed sensibly a concern. A hardy little figure, of edacious energetic physiognomy, eyes hard, strong, not fine; seemed three or four years younger than I, and to be in secret serenely, not insolently, enjoying his glory, which I made him right welcome to do on those terms. In fact he and I hardly spoke together twice or thrice, and had as good as no relation to each other. The old Reverend had taken possession of Airy, and was all day at his elbow. And to me, fatal allotment, had fallen the "footlicker," one of the foolishest, most conceited, ever-babbling blockheads I can remember to have met.

What a day of *boring* (not of the mine strata only!) I felt as if driven half crazy, and mark it to this hour with *coal!*

But enough, and far more than enough, of my Birmingham reminiscences! Irving himself had been with us. Badams was every few weeks up in London for a day or two. Mrs. Strachey, too, sometimes wrote to me. London was still, in a sense, my headquarters. Early in September (it must have been), I took kind leave of Badams and his daily kind influences; hoping, both of us, it might be only temporary leave; and revisited London, at least passed through it, to Dover and the sea-coast, where Mrs. Strachey had contrived a fine sea party, to consist of herself, with appendages of the Irvings and of me, for a few bright weeks! I remember a tiny bit of my journey, solitary on the coach-roof, between Canterbury and Bridge. Nothing else whatever of person or of place from Birmingham to that, nor anything immediately onwards from that! The Irvings had a dim but snuggish house, rented in some street near the shore, and I was to lodge with them. Mrs. Strachey was in a brighter place near by; detached new *row*, called *Liverpool Terrace* at that time (now buried among streets, and hardly discernible by me last autumn when I pilgrimed thither again after forty-two years).

Mrs. Strachey had Kitty with her, and was soon expecting her husband. Both households were in full action, or gradually getting into it, when I arrived.

We walked, all of us together sometimes, at other times in threes or twos. We dined often at Mrs. Strachey's; read commonly in the evenings at Irving's, Irving *reader*, in Phineas Fletcher's "Purple Island" for one thing; over which Irving strove to be solemn, and Kitty and I rather *not*, throwing in now and then a little spice of laughter and quiz. I never saw the book again, nor in spite of some real worth it had, and of much half-real laudation, cared greatly to see it. Mrs. Strachey, I suspect, didn't find the sea party

so idyllic as her forecast of it.   In a fortnight or so Strachey came,
and then there was a new and far livelier element of anti-humbug,
anti-*ennui*, which could not improve matters.   She determined on
sending Strachey, Kitty, and me off on a visit to Paris for ten days,
and having the Irvings all to herself.   We went accordingly ; saw
Paris, saw a bit of France—nothing like so common a feat as now ;
and the memory of that is still almost complete, if it were a legitimate part of my subject.

The journey out, weather fine and novelty awaiting young curiosity at every step, was very pleasant.   Montreuil, Noailles, Abbé-
ville, Beauvais, interesting names, start into facts.   Sterne's "Sentimental Journey" (especially) is alive in one from the first stage
onwards.   At Nampont, on the dirty little street, you almost expect to see the dead ass lying!   Our second night was at Beauvais ;
glimpses of the old cathedral next morning went for nothing, was
in fact nothing to me ; but the glimpse I had had the night before,
as we drove in this way, of the *Coffee-house* near by, and in it no
company but one tall, sashed, epauletted, well-dressed officer striding dismally to and fro, was, and still is, impressive on me, as an
almost unrivalled image of human *ennui*.   I sate usually outside,
fair Kitty sometimes, and Strachey oftener, sitting by me on the
hindward seat.   Carriage I think was Kitty's own, and except her
maid we had no servants.   Postilion could not tell me where
"Crécy" was, when we were in the neighborhood.   Country in
itself, till near Paris, ugly, but all gilded with the light of young
lively wonder.   Little scrubby boys playing at ball on their scrubby patch of parish green ; how strange!   "*Charité, madame, pour
une pauvre misérable, qui, elle, en a bien besoin!*" sang the poor lame
beggar girls at the carriage door.   None of us spoke French well.
Strachey grew even worse as we proceeded, and at length was
quite an amusement to hear.   At Paris he gave it up altogether,
and would speak nothing but English ; which, aided by his vivid
looks and gestures, he found in shops and the like to answer much
better.   "*Quelque chose à boire, monsieur,*" said an exceptional respectful postilion at the coach window, before quitting.   "*Nong,
vous avez drivé devilish slow,*" answered Strachey, readily, and in a
positive, half-quizzing tone.   This was on the way home, followed
by a storm of laughter on our part, and an angry blush on the
postilion's.

From about Montmorency (with the shadow of Rousseau), especially from St. Denis to Paris, the drive was quite beautiful, and
full of interesting expectation.   Magnificent broad highway, great

old trees and then potherb gardens on each hand, all silent too in the brilliant October afternoon; hardly one vehicle or person met, till, on mounting the shoulder of Montmarte, an iron gate, and douanier with his brief question before opening, and Paris, wholly and at once, lay at our feet. A huge bowl or deepish *saucer* of seven miles in diameter; not a breath of smoke or dimness anywhere; every roof, and dome, and spire, and chimney-top clearly visible, and the skylight sparkling like diamonds. I have never, since or before, seen so fine a view of a town. I think the fair Miss Kitty was sitting by me; but the curious *speckled straw hats* and costumes and physiognomies of the Faubourg St. (fashionable, I forget it at this moment), are the memorablest circumstances to me. We alighted in the Rue de la Paix (clean and good hotel, not now a hotel), admired our rooms, all covered with mirrors; our grates, or grate backs, each with a *cupidon* cast on it; and roved about the Boulevards in a happy humor till sunset or later. Decidedly later, in the still dusk, I remember sitting down in the Place Vendôme, on the steps of the Column, there to smoke a cigar. Hardly had I arranged myself when a bustle of military was heard round me; clean, trim, handsome soldiers, blue and white, ranked themselves in some quality, drummers and drums especially faultless, and after a *shoulder arms* or so, marched off in parties, drums fiercely and finely clangouring their rantan-plan. Setting the watch or watches of this human city, as I understood it. "Ha! my tight little fellows in blue, you also have got drums then, none better; and all the world is of kin whether it all agree or not!" was my childlike reflection as I silently looked on.

Paris proved vastly entertaining to me. "Walking about the streets would of itself (as Gray the poet says) have amused me for weeks." I met two young Irishmen who had seen me once at Irving's, who were excellent *ciceroni*. They were on their way to the liberation of Greece, a totally wildgoose errand as then seemed to me, and as perhaps they themselves secretly guessed, but which entitled them to call on everybody for an "autograph to our album," their main employment just now. They were clever enough young fellows, and soon came home again out of Greece. Considerably the taller and cleverer, black-haired and with a strong Irish accent, was called Tennent, whom I never saw again. The milky, smaller blondine figure, cousin to him, was Emerson, whom I met twenty-five years afterwards at Allan Cunningham's, as *Sir* Emerson *Tennent*, late Governor of Ceylon, and complimented, simpleton that I was! on the now finely *brown* color of his *hair!* We have not met

since.   There was also of their acquaintances a pleasant Mr. Malcolm, ex-lieutenant of the 42nd, native of the Orkney Islands, only
son of a clergyman there, who as a young ardent lad had joined
Wellington's army at the *Siege of St. Sebastian*, and got badly wounded (lame for life) at the battle of Thoulouse that same season.
Peace coming, he was invalided on half-pay, and now lived with
his widowed mother in some clean upper floor in Edinburgh on
frugal kind and pretty terms, hanging loosely by literature, for
which he had some talent.   We used to see him in Edinburgh
with pleasure and favor, on setting up our own poor household
there.   He was an amiable, intelligent little fellow, of lively talk
and speculation, always cheerful and with a traceable vein of humor and of pathos withal (there being much of sadness and affection hidden in him), all kept, as his natural voice was, in a fine low
melodious tone.   He wrote in annuals and the like vehicles really
pretty verses, and was by degrees establishing something like a
real reputation, which might have risen higher and higher in that
kind, but his wound still hung about him and he soon died, a year
or two after our quitting Edinburgh ; which was the last we saw
of him.

Poor little Malcolm! he quietly loved his mother very much, his
vanished father too, and had pieties and purities very alien to the
wild reckless ways of practice and of theory which the army had
led him into.   Most of his army habitudes (with one private exception, I think, nearly *all*) he had successfully washed off from
him.   To the reprobate "theories" he had never been but heartily
abhorrent.   "No God, I tell you, and I will prove it to you on the
spot," said some elder blackguard Lieutenant among a group of
them in their tent one evening (a Hanoverian, if I recollect)—"on
the spot—none."   "How then ?" exclaimed Ensign Malcolm, much
shocked.   The Hanoverian lifted his canteen, turned the bottom of
it up.   "Empty ; you see we have no more rum."   Then holding
it aloft into the air, said in a tone of request, "Fill us that ;" paused
an instant, turned it bottom up empty still, and with a victorious
glance at his companions, set it down again as a thing that spoke
for itself.   This was one of Malcolm's war experiences, of which he
could pleasantly report a great many.   These and the physical agonies and horrors witnessed and felt had given him a complete disgust for war.   He could not walk far, always had a marked halt in
walking, but was otherwise my pleasantest companion in Paris.

Poor *Louis Dix-huit* had been "lying in state" as we passed
through St. Denis ; Paris was all plastered with placards, "*Le Roi*

est mort; vive le Roi!" announcing from Châteaubriand a pamphlet of that title. I made no effort to see Châteaubriand, did not see his pamphlet either; in the streets, galleries, *cafés*, I had enough and to spare. Washington Irving was said to be in Paris, a kind of lion at that time, whose books I somewhat esteemed. One day the Emerson Tennent people bragged that they had engaged him to breakfast with us at a certain *café* next morning. We all attended duly, Strachey among the rest, but no Washington came. "Couldn't rightly come," said Malcolm to me in a judicious *aside*, as we cheerfully breakfasted without him. I never saw Washington at all, but still have a mild esteem of the good man. To the Louvre Gallery, alone or accompanied, I went often; got rather faintish good of the pictures there, but at least no *harm*, being mute and deaf on the subject. Sir Peter Laurie came to me one day; took me to dinner, and plenty of hard-headed London talk.

Another day, nobody with me and very few in the gallery at all, there suddenly came storming past, with dishevelled hair and large besoms in their hands, which they shoved out on any bit of paper or the like, a row of wild Savoyards, distractedly proclaiming "Le Roi!" "le Roi!" and almost oversetting people in their fierce speed to clear the way. Le Roi, *Charles Dix* in person, soon appeared accordingly, with three or four attendants, very ugly people, especially one of them (who had blear eyes and small bottle nose, never identifiable to my inquiries since). Charles himself was a swart, slightish, insipid-looking man, but with much the air of a gentleman, insipidly endeavoring to smile and be popular as he walked past; sparse public indifferent to him, and silent nearly all. I had a real sympathy with the poor gentleman, but could not bring up the least Vive le Roi in the circumstances. We understood he was going to look at a certain picture or painting now on the easel, in a room at the very end (entrance end) of the gallery which one had often enough seen, generally with profane mockery if with any feeling. Picture of, or belonging to, the birth or baptism of what they called the child of miracle (the assassinated Duc de Berri's posthumous child, *hodie* Henri V. *in partibus*). Picture as yet distressingly ugly, mostly in a smear of dead colors, brown and even green, and with a kind of horror in the subject of it as well. How tragical are men once more; how merciless withal to one another! I had not the least real pity for *Charles Dix's* pious pilgriming to such an object; the poor mother of it and her immense hopes and pains, I did not even think of then. This was all I ever saw of the legitimate Bourbon line, with which and its tragedies I was to have more concern within the next ten years.

My reminiscences of Paris and its old aspects and localities were of visible use to me in writing of the *Revolution* by-and-by; the rest could only be reckoned under the head of amusement, but had its vague profits withal, and still has. Old Legendre, the mathematician (whose Geometry I had translated in Edinburgh), was the only man of real note with whom I exchanged a few words; a tall, bony, gray old man, who received me with dignity and kindness; introduced me to his niece, a brisk little brown gentlewoman who kept house for him; asked about my stay here, and finding I was just about to go, answered "*Diantre!*" with an obliging air of regret. His rugged sagacious, sad and stoical old face is still dimly present with me. At a meeting of the *Institut* I saw and well remember the figure of Trismegistus Laplace; the skirt of his long blue-silk dressing-gown (such his costume, unique in the place, his age and his fame being also unique) even touched me as he passed on the session's rising. He was tall, thin, clean, serene, his face, perfectly smooth, as a healthy man of fifty's, bespoke intelligence keen and ardent, rather than deep or great. In the eyes was a dreamy smile, with something of pathos in it, and perhaps something of contempt. The session itself was profoundly stupid; some lout of a provincial reading about *Vers à soie*, and big Vauquelin the chemist (noticed by me) fallen sound asleep. Strachey and I went one evening to call upon M. de Chézy, Professor of *Persic*, with whom he, or his brother and he, had communicated while in India. We found him high aloft, but in a clean snug apartment, burly, hearty, glad enough to see us, only that Strachey would speak no French, and introduced himself with some shrill-sounding sentence, the first word of which was clearly *salaam*. Chézy tried lamely for a pass or two what Persian he could muster, but hastened to get out of it, and to talk even to me, who owned to a little French, since Strachey would own to none. We had rather an amusing twenty minutes; Chézy a glowing and very emphatic man; "*ce hideux reptile de Langlès*" was a phrase he had once used to Strachey's brother, of his chief French rival in the Persic field! I heard Cuvier lecture one day; a strong German kind of face, ditto intelligence as manifested in the lecture, which reminded me of one of old Dr. Gregory's in Edinburgh. I was at a sermon in Ste. Geneviève's; main audience 500 or so of serving-maids; preacher a dizened fool in *hour-glass hat*, who ran to and fro in his balcony or pulpit, and seemed much contented with himself; heard another foolish preacher, Protestant, at the Oratoire (*console-toi, O France!* on the death of *Louis Dix-huit*). Looked silently into the *Morgue* one morning (infinitely better *sermon* that stern old gray-haired corpse lying there!); looked into the Hôtel Dieu and its poor sick-beds once; was much in the Pont-Neuf region (*on tond les chiens et coupe les chats, et va en ville,* etc., etc.); much in the Palais Royal and adjacencies; and the night before leaving found I ought to visit one theatre, and by happy accident came upon Talma playing there. A heavy, shortish numb-footed man, face like a warming-pan for size, and with a strange most ponderous yet delicate expression in the big dull-glowing black eyes and it. Incomparably the best actor I ever saw. Play was "Œdipe" (Voltaire's very first); place the Théâtre Français. Talma died within about a year after.

Of the journey home I can remember nothing but the French part, if any part of it were worth remembering. At Dover I must still have found the Irvings, and poor outskirts and insignificant fractions of solitary dialogues on the Kent shore (far inferior to our old Fife ones) have not yet entirely vanished; e. g. strolling together on the beach one evening, we had repeatedly passed at some distance certain building operations, upon which by-and-by the bricklayers seemed to be getting into much vivacity, crowding round the last gable top; in fact just about finishing their house then. Irving grasped my arm, said in a low tone of serious emotion, "See, they are going to bring out their topstone with shouting!" I inquired of a poor man what it was; "You see, sir, they gets allowance," answered he; that was all — a silent deglutition of some beer. Irving sank from his Scriptural altitudes; I no doubt profanely laughing rather. There are other lingering films of this sort, but I can give them no date of before or after, and find nothing quite distinct till that of our posting up to London. I should say of the Stracheys posting, who took me as guest, the Irvings being now clearly gone. Canterbury and the (site of the) shrine of St. Thomas I did see, but it must have been before. We had a pleasant drive throughout, weather still sunny though cool, and about nine or ten P.M. of the second day I was set down at a little tavern on Shooter's Hill, where some London mail or diligence soon picked me up, and speedily landed me within reach of hospitable Pentonville, which gave me a welcome like itself. There I must have stayed a few days, and not above a few.

I was now again in London (probably about the middle of November); hither after much sad musing and moping I had decided on returning for another while. My "Schiller" (of which I felt then the intrinsic wretchedness or utter leanness and commonplace) was to be stitched together from the "London Magazine," and put forth with some trimmings and additions as a book; £100 for it on publication in that shape (zero till then), that was the bargain made, and I had come to fulfil that, almost more uncertain than ever about all beyond. I soon got lodgings in Southampton Street, Islington, in Irving's vicinity, and did henceforth with my best diligence endeavor to fulfil that, at a far slower rate than I had expected. I frequently called on Irving (he never or not often on me, which I did not take amiss), and frequently saw him otherwise, but have already written down miscellaneously most of the remembrances that belong to this specific date of months. On the whole, I think now he felt a good deal unhappy, probably getting deeper and deeper sunk in manifold cares of his own, and that our communications had not the old copiousness and flowing freedom; nay, that even since I left for Birmingham there was perhaps a diminution. London "pulpit popularity," the smoke of that foul witches' cauldron: there was never anything else to blame. I stuck rigorously to my work, to my Badams regimen, though it did but little for me, but I was sick of body and of mind, in endless dubiety, very desolate and miserable, and the case itself, since nobody could help, admonished me to silence. One day on the road down to Battle Bridge I remember recognizing Irving's broad hat, atop amid the tide of passengers, and his little child sitting on his arm, wife probably near by. "Why should I hurry up? They are parted from me, the old days are no more," was my sad reflection in my sad humor.

Another morning, what was wholesomer and better, happening to notice, as I stood looking out on the bit of green under my bedroom window, a trim and rather pretty hen actively paddling about and picking up what food might be discoverable. "See," I said to myself; "look, thou fool! Here is a two-legged creature with scarcely half a thimbleful of poor brains; thou call'st thyself a man with nobody knows how much brain, and reason dwelling in it; and behold how the one *life* is regulated and how the other! In God's name concentrate, collect whatever of reason thou hast, and direct it on the one thing needful." Irving, when we did get into intimate dialogue, was affectionate to me as ever, and had always to the end a great deal of sense and insight into things about him, but he could not much help me; how could anybody but myself? By degrees I was doing so, taking counsel of that *symbolic* HEN!

and settling a good few things. First, and most of all, that I would, renouncing ambitions, "fine openings," and the advice of all bystanders and friends, *who didn't know;* go *home* to Annandale, were this work done; provide myself a place where I could ride, follow regimen, and be free of *noises* (which were unendurable) till if possible I could recover a little health. Much followed out of that, all manner of adjustments gathering round it. As head of these latter I had offered to let my dearest be free of me, and of any virtual engagement she might think there was; but she would not hear of it, not of that, the noble soul! but stood resolved to share my dark lot along with me, be it what it might. Alas! her love was never completely known to me, and how celestial it was, till I had lost her. "Oh, for five minutes more of her!" I have often said, since April last, to tell her with what perfect love and admiration, as of the beautifullest of known human souls, I did intrinsically always regard her! But all minutes of the time are inexorably past; be wise, all ye living, and remember that time *passes* and does not return.

Apart from regular work upon "Schiller," I had a good deal of talking with people and social moving about which was not disagreeable. With Allan Cunningham I had made ready acquaintance; a cheerful social man; "solid Dumfries mason with a surface polish given him," was one good judge's definition years afterwards! He got at once *into Nithsdale* when you talked with him, which, though he was clever and satirical, I didn't very much enjoy. Allan had sense and shrewdness on all points, especially the practical; but *out* of Nithsdale, except for his perennial good-humor and quiet cautions (which might have been exemplary to me) was not instructive. I was at the christening of one of Allan's children over in Irving's, where there was a cheery evening, and the Cunninghams to sleep there; one other of the guests, a pleasant enough Yorkshire youth, going with me to a spare room I could command. My commonest walk was fieldward, or down into the city (by many different old lanes and routes), more rarely by Portland Place (Fitzroy Square and Mrs. Strachey's probably first), to Piccadilly and the West End. One muddy evening there came to me, what enlightened all the mirk and mud, by the Herren Grafen von Bentincks' servant, a short letter from Goethe in Weimar! It was in answer to the copy of "Wilhelm Meister" which (doubtless with some reverent bit of note) I had despatched to him six months ago, without answer till now. He was kind though distant brief, apologized, by his great age (*hohen Jahren*), for the delay, till at length the Herren Grafen von Bentincks' passage homewards had operated on him as a hint to do the needful, and likewise to procure for both parties, Herren Grafen and self, an agreeable acquaintance, of which latter naturally neither I nor the Herren Grafen ever heard more. Some twenty years afterwards a certain Lord George Bentinck, whom newspapers called the "stable minded" from his previous *turf* propensities, suddenly quitting all these and taking to statistics and Tory politics, became famous or noisy for a good few months, chiefly by intricate *statistics* and dull vehemence, so far as I could see, a stupid enough phenomenon for me, till he suddenly died, poor gentleman! I then remembered that this was probably one of the Herren Grafen von Bentinck whose acquaintance I had missed as above.

One day Irving took me with him on a curious little errand he had. It was a bright summer morning; must therefore have preceded the Birmingham and Dover period. His errand was this. A certain loquacious extensive Glasgow publisher* was in London for several weeks on business, and often came to Irving, wasting (as I used to think) a good deal of his time in zealous discourse about many vague things; in particular about the villany of common publishers, how, for example, on their "*half profits* system," they would show the poor authors a printer's account pretending to be paid in full, printer's signature visibly appended, printer having really touched a sum *less* by 25 per cent., and *sic de cæteris*. All an arranged juggle to cheat the poor author, and sadly convince him that his moiety was nearly or altogether zero divided by two! Irving could not believe it; denied stoutly on behalf of his own printer, one Bensley, a noted man in his craft, and getting nothing but negatory smiles and kindly but inexorable contradiction, said he would go next morning and see. We walked along somewhere Holbornwards, found Bensley and wife in a bright, quiet, comfortable room, just finishing breakfast; a fattish, solid, rational, and really amiable-looking pair of people, especially the wife, who had a plump, cheerfully experienced matronly air. By both of whom we, i.e. Irving (for I had nothing to do but be silent), were warmly and honorably welcomed, and constrained at least to sit, since we would do nothing better. Irving with grave courtesy laid the case before Bensley, perhaps showed him his old signature and account, and asked if that was or was not really the sum he had received.

---

* Dr. Chalmers's especially; had been a school-master; Collin perhaps his name.

Bensley, with body and face writhed uneasily; evidently loath to lie, but evidently obliged by the laws of trade to do it. "Yes, on the whole, that was the sum!" upon which we directly went our ways; both of us convinced, I believe, though only one of us said so. Irving had a high opinion of men, and was always mortified when he found it in any instance no longer tenable.

Irving was sorrowfully occupied at this period, as I now perceive, in scanning and surveying the *wrong* side of that immense popularity, the outer or right side of which had been so splendid and had given rise to such sacred and glorious hopes. The crowd of people flocking round him continued in abated but still superabundant quantity and vivacity; but it was not of the old high quality any more. The thought that the Christian religion was again to dominate all minds, and the world to become an Eden by his thrice-blessed means, was fatally declaring itself to have been a dream; and he would not consent to believe it such: never he! That was the secret of his inward quasi-desperate resolutions; out into the wild struggles and clutchings towards the unattainable, the unregainable, which were more and more conspicuous in the sequel. He was now, I gradually found, listening to certain interpreters of prophecy, thinking to cast his own great faculty into that hopeless quagmire along with them. These and the like resolutions, and the dark humor which was the mother of them, had been on the growing hand during all this first London visit of mine, and were fast coming to outward development by the time I left for Scotland again.

About the beginning of March, 1825, I had at length, after fierce struggling and various disappointments from the delay of others, got my poor business winded up; "Schiller" published, paid for, left to the natural neglect of mankind (which was perfect so far as I ever heard or much cared), and in humble but condensed resolute and quiet humor was making my bits of packages, bidding my poor adieus, just in act to go. Everybody thought me headstrong and foolish; Irving less so than others, though he too could have no understanding of my dyspeptic miseries, my intolerable sufferings from noises, etc., etc. He was always kind, and spoke hope if personal topics turned up. Perhaps it was the very day before my departure, at least it is the last I recollect of him, we were walking in the streets multifariously discoursing: a dim gray day, but dry and airy. At the corner of Cockspur Street we paused for a moment, meeting Sir John Sinclair ("Statistical Account of Scotland," etc.), whom I had never seen before and never saw again. A lean old man, tall but stooping, in tartan cloak, face very wrinkly, nose blue, physiognomy vague and with distinction as one might have expected it to be. He spoke to Irving with benignant respect, whether to me at all I don't recollect. A little farther on in Parliament Street, somewhere near the Admiralty (that now is, and perhaps then was), we ascended certain stairs, narrow newish wooden staircase the last of them, and came into a bare, clean, comfortless, official little room (fire gone out), where an elderly official little gentleman was seated within rails, busy in the red-tape line. This was the Honorable Something or other, great in Scripture prophecy; in which he had started some sublime new idea, well worth prosecuting as Irving had assured me. Their mutual greetings were cordial and respectful; and a lively dialogue ensued on prophetic matters, especially on the sublime new idea; I, strictly unparticipant, sitting silently apart till it was done. The Honorable Something had a look of perfect politeness, perfect silliness; his face, heavily wrinkled, went smiling and shuttling about at a wonderful rate; and in the smile there seemed to me to be lodged a frozen sorrow as if bordering on craze. On coming out I asked Irving, perhaps too markedly, "Do you really think that gentleman can throw any light to you on anything whatever?" To which he answered good-naturedly, but in a grave tone, "Yes, I do." Of which the fruits were seen before long. This is the last thing I can recollect of Irving in my London visit; except perhaps some gray shadow of him giving me "Farewell" with express "blessing."

I paused some days at Birmingham; got rich gifts sent after me by Mrs. Strachey; beautiful desk, gold pencil, etc., which were soon *Another's*, ah me! and are still here. I saw Manchester too, for the first time (strange *bagman* ways in the Palace Inn there); walked to Oldham; savage-looking scene of Sunday morning; old school-fellow of mine, very stupid but very kind, being Curate there. Shot off too over the Yorkshire moors to Marsden, where another boy and college friend of mine was (George Johnson, since surgeon in Gloucester); and spent three dingy but impressive days in poking into those mute wildernesses and their rough habitudes and populations. At four o'clock, in my Palace Inn (Boots having forgotten me), awoke by good luck of myself, and saved my place on the coach roof. Remember the Blackburns, Boltons, and their smoke clouds, to right and left grimly black, and the gray March winds; Lancashire was not all smoky then, but only smoky in parts. Remember the Bush Inn at Carlisle, and quiet luxurious shelter it yielded for the night, much different from now. ("Betty, a pan o' cooals!" shouted the waiter, an Eskdale man by dialect, and in five minutes the trim Betty had done her feat, and your clean sleek bed was comfortably warm.) At Ecclefechan, next day, within two miles or so of my father's, while the coach was changing horses, I noticed through the window my little sister Jean earnestly looking up for me; she, with Jenny, the youngest of us all, was at school in the village, and had come out daily of late to inspect the coach in hope of me, always in vain till this day; her bonny little blush and radiancy of look when I let down the window and suddenly disclosed myself are still present to me. In four days' time I now (December 2, 1866), hope to see this brave Jean again (now "Mrs. Aitken," from Dumfries, and a hardy, hearty wife and mother). Jenny, poor little thing, has had her crosses and difficulties, but has managed them well; and now lives, contented enough and industrious as ever, with husband and three or two daughters, in Hamilton, Canada West, not far from which are my brother Alick too, and others dear to me. "Double, double, toil and trouble"—such, with result or without it, are our wanderings in this world."

My poor little establishment at Hoddam Hill* (close by the "Tower of Repentance," as if symbolically!) I do not mean to speak of here; a neat compact little farm, rent £100, which my father had leased for me, on which was a prettyish-looking cottage for dwelling-house (had been the factor's place, who was retiring), and from the windows such a "view" (fifty miles in radius, from beyond Tyndale to beyond St. Bees, Solway Frith, and all the fells to Ingleborough inclusive), as Britain or the world could hardly have matched! Here the ploughing, etc., etc., was already in progress (which I often rode across to see), and here at term day (May 26th, 1825) I established myself, set up my books and bits of implements and Lares, and took to doing "German Romance" as my daily work, "ten pages daily" my stint, which, barring some rare accidents, I faithfully accomplished. Brother Alick was my practical *farmer;* ever-kind and beloved mother, with one of the little girls, was generally there; brother John, too, oftenest, who had just taken his degree. These, with a little man and ditto maid, were our establishment. It lasted only one year, owing, I believe, to indistinctness of bargain first of all, and then to arbitrary high-handed temper of our landlord (used to a rather prostrate style of obedi-

---

* A house with small farm attached, three miles from Mainhill, and visible from the fields at the back of it.

ence, and not finding it here, but a polite appeal to fair-play instead). One whole summer and autumn were defaced by a great deal of paltry bother on that head, superadded to the others; and at last, lease of Mainhill, too, being nearly out, it was decided to quit said landlord's territories altogether, and so end his controversies with us.

Next 26th of May we went all of us to Scotsbrig (a much better farm, which was now bidden for and got), and where, as turned out, I continued only a few months, wedded, and to Edinburgh in October following. Ah me! what a *retrospect* now!

With all its manifold petty troubles, this year at Hoddam Hill has a rustic beauty and dignity to me, and lies now like a not ignoble russet-coated idyll in my memory; one of the quietest, on the whole, and perhaps the most triumphantly important of my life. I lived very silent, diligent, had long solitary rides (on my wild Irish horse "Larry," good for the dietetic part), my meditatings, musings, and reflections were continual; my thoughts went wandering (or travelling) through eternity, through time, and through space, so far as poor I had scanned or known, and were now to my endless solacement coming back with tidings to me! This year I found that I had conquered all my scepticisms, agonizing doubtings, fearful wrestlings with the foul and vile and soul-murdering Mud-gods of my epoch; had escaped as from a worse than Tartarus, with all its Phlegethons and Stygian quagmires, and was emerging free in spirit into the eternal blue of ether, where, blessed be heaven! I have for the spiritual part ever since lived, looking down upon the welterings of my poor fellow-creatures, in such multitudes and millions still stuck in that fatal element, and have had no concern whatever in their Puseyisms, ritualisms, metaphysical controversies and cobwebberies, and no feeling of my own except honest silent pity for the serious or religious part of them, and occasional indignation, for the poor world's sake, at the frivolous secular and impious part, with their universal suffrages, their Nigger emancipations, sluggard and scoundrel Protection societies, and "unexampled prosperities" for the time being! What my pious joy and gratitude then was, let the pious soul figure. In a fine and veritable sense, I, poor, obscure, without outlook, almost without worldly hope, had become independent of the world. What was death itself, from the world, to what I had come through? I understood well what the old Christian people meant by "*conversion*," by God's infinite mercy to them. I had, in effect, gained an immense victory, and for a number of years had, in spite of nerves and chagrins, a constant inward happiness that was quite royal and supreme, in which all temporal evil was transient and insignificant, and which essentially remains with me still, though far oftener *eclipsed* and lying deeper *down* than then. Once more, thank Heaven for its highest gift. I then felt, and still feel, endlessly indebted to Goethe in the business. He, in his fashion, I perceived, had travelled the steep rocky road before me, the first of the moderns. Bodily health itself seemed improving. Bodily health was all I had really lost in this grand spiritual battle now gained; and that, too, I may have hoped would gradually return altogether, which it never did, and was far enough from doing! Meanwhile my thoughts were very peaceable, full of pity and humanity as they had never been before. Nowhere can I recollect of myself such pious musings, communings silent and spontaneous with Fact and Nature, as in these poor Annandale localities. The sound of the kirk-bell once or twice on Sunday mornings, from Hoddam kirk, about a mile off on the plain below me, was strangely touching, like the departing voice of eighteen hundred years. Frank Dickson at rare intervals called in passing. Nay, once for about ten days my dearest and beautifullest herself came across out of Nithsdale to "pay my mother a visit," when she gained all hearts, and we mounted our swift little horses and careered about! No wonder I call that year idyllic, in spite of its russet coat. My darling and I were at the Grange (Mrs. Johnston's), at Annan (Mrs. Dickson's), and we rode together to Dumfries, where her aunts and grandmother were, whom she was to pause with on this her road home to Templand.* How beautiful, how sad and strange all that now looks! Her beautiful little heart was evidently much cast down, right sorry to part, though we hoped it was but for some short while. I remember the heights of Mousewold, with Dumfries and the granite mountains lying in panorama seven or eight miles off to our left, and what she artlessly yet finely said to me there. Oh, my darling, not Andromache dressed in all the art of a Racine looks more high and queenly to me, or is more of a *tragic poem* than thou and thy noble pilgrimage beside me in this poor thorny, muddy world!

I had next to no direct correspondence with Irving; a little note or so on business, nothing more. Nor was Mrs. Montague much more instructive on that head, who wrote me high-sounding amiable things which I could not but respond to more or less,

---

* House in Nithsdale where Miss Urleh's grandfather lived.

though dimly aware of their quality. Nor did the sincere and ardent Mrs. Strachey, who wrote seldomer, almost ever touch upon Irving; but by some occasional unmelodious *clang* in all the newspapers (twice over I think in this year), we could sufficiently and with little satisfaction construe his way of life. Twice over he had leaped the barrier, and given rise to criticism of the customary idle sort, loudish universally, and nowhere accurately just. Case first was of preaching to the London Missionary Society ("Missionary" I will call it, though it might be "Bible" or another). On their grand anniversary these people had appointed to him the honor of addressing them, and were numerously assembled expecting some flourishes of eloquence and flatteries to their illustrious divinely-blessed Society, ingeniously done and especially with fit *brevity*, dinner itself waiting, I suppose, close in the rear. Irving emerged into his speaking place at the due moment, but instead of treating men and office-bearers to a short comfortable dose of honey and butter, opened into strict sharp inquiries, Rhadamanthine expositions of duty and ideal, issuing perhaps in actual criticism and admonition, gall and vinegar instead of honey; at any rate keeping the poor people locked up there for "above two hours" instead of one hour or less, with dinner *hot* at the end of it. This was much criticised; "plainly wrong, and produced by love of singularity and too much pride in oneself," voted everybody. For, in fact, a man suddenly holding up the naked inexorable Ideal in face of the clothed, and in England generally plump, comfortable, and pot-bellied Reality, is doing an unexpected and a questionable thing!

The next escapade was still worse. At some public meeting, of probably the same "Missionary Society," Irving again held up his ideal, I think not without murmurs from former sufferers by it, and ended by solemnly putting down, not his name to the subscription list, but an actual gold watch, which he said had just arrived to him from his beloved brother lately dead in India.* That of the gold watch tabled had in reality a touch of rash ostentation, and was bitterly crowed over by the able editors for a time. On the whole, one could gather too clearly that Irving's course was beset with pitfalls, barking dogs, and dangers and difficulties unwarned

---

* This brother was John, the eldest of the three, an Indian army surgeon, whom I remember once meeting on a "common stair" in Edinburgh, on return, I suppose, from some call on a comrade higher up; a taller man than even Edward, and with a blooming, placid, not very intelligent face, and no squint, whom I easily recognized by family likeness, but never saw again or before.

of, and that for one who took so little counsel with prudence he perhaps carried his head too high. I had a certain harsh kind of sorrow about poor Irving, and my loss of him (and his loss of *me* on such poor terms as these seemed to be!), but I carelessly trusted in his strength against whatever mistakes and impediments, and felt that for the present it was better to be absolved from corresponding with him.

That same year, late in autumn, he was at Annan, only for a night and day, returning from some farther journey, perhaps to Glasgow or Edinburgh; and had to go on again for London next day. I rode down from Hoddam Hill before nightfall; found him sitting in the snug little parlor beside his father and mother, beautifully domestic. I think it was the last time I ever saw those good old people. We sate only a few minutes, my thoughts sadly contrasting the beautiful affectionate safety here, and the wild tempestuous hostilities and perils yonder. He left his blessing to each, by name, in a low soft voice. There was something almost tragical to me as he turned round (hitting his hat on the little door lintel), and the next moment was on the dark street, followed only by me. We stept over to Robert Dickson's, his brother-in-law's, and sat there, still talking, for perhaps an hour. Probably his plan of journey was to catch the Glasgow-London mail at Gretna, and to walk thither, the night being dry, and time at discretion.

Walk I remember he did, and talk in the interim (three or at most four of us now), not in the least downhearted. Told us, probably in answer to some question of mine, that the projected "London University" (now of Gower Street) seemed to be progressing towards fulfilment, and how at some meeting Poet Campbell, arguing loudly for a purely *secular* system, had, on sight of Irving entering, at once stopt short, and in the politest way he could, sate down, without another word on the subject. "It will be unreligious, secretly anti-religious all the same," said Irving to us. Whether he reported of the projected Athenæum Club (dear to Basil Montague, among others), I don't recollect; probably not, as he or I had little interest in that. When the time had come for setting out, and we were all on foot, he called for his three little nieces, having their mother by him; had them each successively set standing on a chair, laid his hand on the head first of one, with a "Mary Dickson, the Lord bless you!" then of the next by name, and of the next, "The Lord bless you!" in a sad and solemn tone (with something of elaborate noticeable in it, too), which was painful and dreary to me. A dreary visit altogether, though an unabatedly affectionate

7

on both sides. In what a contrast, thought I, to the old sunshiny visits, when Glasgow was head-quarters, and everybody was obscure, frank to his feelings, and safe! Mrs. Dickson, I think, had tears in her eyes. Her, too, he doubtless blessed, but without hand on head. Dickson and the rest of us escorted him a little way; would then take leave in the common form; but even that latter circumstance I do not perfectly recall, only the fact of our escorting, and before the visit and after it all is now fallen dark.

Irving did not re-emerge for many months, and found me then in very greatly changed circumstances. His next visit was to *us* at Comley Bank,* Edinburgh, not to *me* any longer! It was probably in spring, 1827, a visit of only half-an-hour, more resembling a "call" from neighbor on neighbor. I think it was connected with Scripture prophecy work, in which he was now deep. At any rate, he was now preaching and communing on something or other to numbers of people in Edinburgh, and we had heard of him for perhaps a week before as shiningly busy in that way, when in some interval he made this little run over to Comley Bank and us. He was very friendly, but had a look of trouble, of haste, and confused controversy and anxiety, sadly unlike his old good self. In dialect, too, and manner, things had not bettered themselves, but the contrary. He talked with an undeniable self-consciousness, and something which you could not but admit to be religious mannerism. Never quite recovered out of that, in spite of our, especially of her, efforts while he stayed. At parting he proposed "to pray" with us, and did, in standing posture, ignoring or conscientiously defying our pretty evident reluctance. "Farewell!" he said soon after; "I must go then and suffer persecution as my fathers have done." Much painful contradiction he evidently had from the world about him, but also much zealous favor; and was going that same evening to a public dinner given in honor of him, as we and everybody knew.

This was, I think, the *nadir* of my poor Irving, veiled and hooded in these miserable manifold crapes and formulas, so that his brave old self never once looked fairly through, which had not been nor was again quite the case in any other visit or interview. It made one drearily sad. "Dreary," that was the word; and we had to consider ourselves as not a little divorced from him, and bidden "shift for yourselves."

We saw him once again in Scotland, at Craigenputtoch,† and had

---

* Where Carlyle and his wife lived for the first eighteen months after their marriage.

† A lonely house on the moor, at the head of Nithsdale, ten miles from Dumfries.

him for a night, or I almost think for two, on greatly improved terms. He was again on some kind of church business, but it seemed to be of cheerfuller and wider scope than that of Scriptural prophecy last time. Glasgow was now his goal, with frequent preaching as he went along, the regular clergy actively countenancing. I remember dining with him at our parish minister's, good Mr. Bryden's, with certain Reverends of the neighborhood (the Dow of "Irongray" one of them, who afterwards went crazy on the "Gift of Tongues" affair). I think it must have been from Bryden's that I brought him up to Craigenputtoch, where he was quite alone with us, and franker and happier than I had seen him for a long time. It was beautiful summer weather, pleasant to saunter in with old friends in the safe green solitudes, no sound audible but that of our own voices, and of the birds and woods. He talked to me of Henry Drummond as of a fine, a great, evangelical yet courtly and indeed universal gentleman, whom prophetic studies had brought to him, whom I was to *know* on my next coming to London, more joy to me! We had been discoursing of religion with mildly worded but entire frankness on my part as usual, and something I said had struck Irving as unexpectedly orthodox, who thereupon ejaculated, "Well, I am right glad to hear that, and will not forget it when it may do you good with one whom I know of;" with Henry Drummond namely, which had led him into that topic, perhaps not quite for the first time. There had been big "prophetic conferences," etc., held at Drummond's house (Albury, Surrey), who continued ever after an ardent Irvingite, and rose by degrees in the "Tongues" business to be hierophant, and chief over Irving himself. He was far the richest of the sect, and alone belonged to the aristocratic circles, abundant in speculation as well as in money; a sharp, elastic, haughty kind of man; had considerable ardor, disorderly force of intellect and character, and especially an insatiable love of shining and figuring. In a different element I had afterwards plentiful knowledge of Henry Drummond, and if I got no good of him got also no mischief, which might have been extremely possible.

We strolled pleasantly, in loose group, Irving the centre of it, over the fields. I remember an excellent little portraiture of *Methodism* from him on a green knoll where we had loosely sat down. "Not a good religion, sir," said he, confidentially shaking his head in answer to my question; "far too little of spiritual conscience, far too much of temporal appetite; goes hunting and watching after its own emotions, that is, mainly its own *nervous system;* an essentially sensuous religion, depending on the body, not on the soul!" "Fit only for a gross and vulgar-minded people," I perhaps added; "a religion so called, and the essence of it principally *cowardice* and *hunger*, terror of pain and appetite for pleasure both carried to the infinite;" to which he would sorrowfully assent in a considerable degree. My brother John, lately come home from Germany, said to me next day, "That was a pretty little *Schilderung* (portraiture) he threw off for us, that of the Methodists, wasn't it ?"

At Dunscore, in the evening, there was sermon and abundant rustic concourse, not in the kirk but round it in the kirkyard for convenience of room. I attended with most of our people (*one* of us not—busy she at home "field marshalling," the noble little soul!). I remember nothing of sermon or subject, except that it went flowingly along like true discourse, direct from the inner reservoirs, and that everybody seemed to listen with respectful satisfaction. We rode pleasantly home in the dusk, and soon afterwards would retire, Irving having to "catch the Glasgow coach" early next day. Next day, correct to time, he and I were on horseback soon after breakfast, and rode leisurely along towards Auldgirth Bridge, some ten miles from us, where the coach was to pass. Irving's talk, or what of it I remember, turned chiefly, and in a cheerful tone, upon touring to the Continent, a beautiful six weeks of rest which he was to have in that form (and I to be taken with him as *dragoman*, were it nothing more!), which I did not at the time believe in, and which was far enough from ever coming. On nearing the goal he became a little anxious about his coach, but we were there in perfect time, "still fifteen minutes to spare," and stept into the inn to wait over a real, or (on my part) theoretic glass of ale. Irving was still but midway in his glass when the coach, sooner than expected, was announced. "Does not *change* here, changes at Thornhill!" so that there was not a moment to be lost. Irving sprang hastily to the coach roof (no other seat left), and was at once bowled away, waving me his kind farewell, and vanishing among the woods. This was probably the last time I ever had Irving as my guest; nay, as guest for nights or even a night it was probably the first time. In Scotland I never saw him again. Our next meeting was in London, autumn of the year 1831.

By that time there had been changes both with him and me. With him a sad enough change, namely, *deposition* from the Scottish Established Kirk, which he felt to be a sore blow, though to me it seemed but the whiff of a *telum imbelle* for such a man. What the particulars of his heresy were I never knew, or have totally forgotten. Some doctrine he held about the human nature of the Divine Man; that Christ's human nature was liable to sin like our own, and continually tempted thereto, which by His divine nobleness He kept continually perfect and pure from sin. This doctrine, which as an impartial bystander, I, from Irving's point of view and from my own, entirely assented to, Irving had by voice and pen been publishing, and I remember hearing vaguely of its being much canvassed up and down, always with impatience and a boundless contempt, when I did hear of it. "The gig of respectability again!" I would say or think to myself. "They consider it more honorable to their Supreme of the world to have had his work done for him than to have done it himself. Flunkeys irredeemable, carrying their *plush* into highest heaven!" This I do remember, but whether this was the damning heresy, this or some other, I do not now know. Indeed, my own grief on the matter, and it had become a chronic dull and perennial grief, was that such a soul had anything to do with "heresies" and mean puddles of that helpless sort, and was not rather working in his proper sphere, infinite spaces above all that! Deposed he certainly was, the fact is still recorded in my memory, and by a kind of accident I have the approximate *date* of it too, Allan Cunningham having had a public dinner given him in Dumfries, at which I with great effort attended, and Allan's first talk to me on meeting having been about Irving's late troubles, and about my own soon coming to London with a MS. book in my pocket, with "Sartor Resartus" namely! The whole of which circumstances have naturally imprinted themselves on me, while so much else has faded out.

The first genesis of "Sartor" I remember well enough, and the very spot (at Templand) where the notion of astonishment at *clothes* first struck me. The book had taken me in all some nine months, which are not present now, except confusedly and in mass, but that of being wearied with the fluctuations of *review* work, and of having decided on London again, with "Sartor" as a book to be offered there, is still vivid to me; vivid above all that dinner to Allan, whither I had gone not against my deliberate will, yet with a very great repugnance, knowing and hating the multiplex bother of it, and that I should have some kind of speech to make. "Speech" done, however (*taliter qualiter*, some short rough words upon Burns, which did well enough), the thing became not unpleasant, and I still well remember it all. Especially how at length, probably near midnight, I rose to go, decisively resisting all invitations to "sleep at Dumfries;" must and would drive home (knowing well who was waiting for me there!) and drove accordingly, with only one circumstance now worth mention.

Dumfries streets, all silent, empty, were lying clear as day in the purest moonlight, a very beautiful and shiny midnight, when I stept down with some one or two for escort of honor, got into my poor old gig—brother Alick's gift or procurement to me—and with brief farewell rattled briskly away. I had sixteen good miles ahead, fourteen of them parish road, narrower than highway, but otherwise not to be complained of, and the night and the sleeping world seemed all my own for the little enterprise. A small black mare, nimble, loyal, wise,* this was all my team. Soon after leaving the highway, or perhaps it was almost before, for I was well wrapt up, warm enough, contented to be out of my affair, wearied too with so much noise and sipping of wine, I too, like the world, had fallen sound asleep, must have sate in deep, perfect sleep (probably with the reins hung over the whip and its case), for about ten miles! There were ascents, descents, steep enough, dangerous fenceless parts, narrow bridges with little parapet (especially one called "rowting," i. e. bellowing or roaring, "Brig," spanning a grand, loud cataract in quite an intricate way, for there was abrupt turn just at the end of it with rapid descent, and wrong road to be avoided); "Rowting Brig," "Milltown Brig" (also with intricacy of wrong roads), not very long after which latter, in the bottom of Glenesland, roads a little rumbly there owing to recent inundation, I awoke, safe as if Jehu had been driving me, and within four miles of home; considerably astonished, but nothing like so grateful as I now am, on looking back on the affair, and my little mare's performance in it. Ah me! in this creation rough and honest, though not made for our sake only, how many things, lifeless and living, living *persons* some of them, and *their* life beautiful as azure and heaven, beneficently help us forward while we journey together, and have not yet bidden sorrowful farewell! My little darling sate waiting for me in the depths of the desert, and, better or worse, the Dumfries dinner was over. This must have been in July, 1831.

Thirteen months before there had fallen on me, and on us all, a very great, most tender, painful, and solemn grief, the death of my eldest sister Margaret, who, after some struggles, had quitted us in the flower of her youth, age about twenty-five. She was the charm

---

* Whom I well remember. "As useful a beast," said my dear mother once, in fine expressive Scotch, as we drove together, "as ever one little skin covered."

of her old father's life, deeply respected as well as loved by her mother and all of us, by none more than me; and was, in fact, in the simple, modest, comely, and rustic form as intelligent, quietly valiant, quietly wise and heroic a young woman as I have almost ever seen. Very dear and estimable to my Jeannie, too, who had zealously striven to help her, and now mourned for her along with me. "The shortest night of 1830," that was her last in this world. The year before for many months she had suffered nameless miseries with a stoicism all her own. Doctors, unable to help, saw her with astonishment rally and apparently recover, "by her own force of character," said one of them. Never shall I forget that bright summer evening (late summer 1829), when contemplatively lounging with my pipe outside the window, I heard unexpectedly the sound of horses' feet, and up our little "avenue," pacing under the trees overhung by the yellow sunlight, appeared my brother John and she unexpectedly from Scotsbrig, bright to look upon, cheery of face, and the welcomest interruption to our solitude. "Dear Mag, dear Mag, once more!" Nay, John had brought me from Dumfries post-office a long letter from Goethe, one of the finest I ever had from him; son's death perhaps mentioned in it; all so white, so pure, externally and internally, so high and heroic. This, too, seemed bright to me as the summer sunset in which I stood reading it. Seldom was a cheerfuller evening at Craigenputtoch. Margaret stayed perhaps a fortnight, quietly cheerful all the time, but was judged (by a very quick eye in such things) to be still far from well. She sickened again in March or April next, on some cold or accident, grew worse than ever, herself now falling nearly hopeless. "Cannot stand a second bout like last year," she once whispered to one of her sisters. We had brought her to Dumfries in the hope of better medical treatment, which was utterly vain. Mother and sister Mary waited on her with trembling anxiety; I often there. Few days before the end my Jeannie (in the dusk of such a day of gloomy hurlyburly to us all!) carried her on her knees in a *sedan* to some suburban new garden lodging we had got (but did not then tell me what the dying one had said to her). In fine, towards midnight, June 21–22, I alone still up, an express from Dumfries rapped on my window. "Grown worse; you and your brother wanted yonder!" Alick and I were soon on horseback, rode diligently through the slumbering woods—ever memorable to me that night, and its phenomena of moon and sky!—found all finished hours ago, only a weeping mother and sister left, with whom neither of us could help weeping. Poor Alick's face, when

I met him at the door with such news (he had stayed behind me getting rid of the horses); the mute struggle, mute and vain, as of the rugged rock not to dissolve itself, is still visible to me. Why do I evoke these bitter sorrows and miseries which have mercifully long lain as if asleep? I will not farther. That day, June 22, 1830, full of sacred sorrow and of paltry botheration of business— for we had, after some hours and a little consultation, sent Mary and my mother home—is to be counted among the painfullest of my life; and in the evening, having at last reached the silence of the woods, I remember fairly lifting up my voice and weeping aloud a long time.

All this has little to do with Irving, little even with the journey I was now making towards him, except that in the tumultuous agitations of the latter it came all in poignant clearness and completeness into my mind again, and continued with me in the background or the foreground during most of the time I was in London.

From Whitehaven onwards to Liverpool, amid the noise and jostle of a crowd of high-dressed vulgar-looking people who joined us there, and with their "hot brandies," dice-boxes, etc., down below, and the blaring of brass bands, and idle babblers and worshippers of the nocturnal picturesque, made deck and cabin almost equally a delirium,—this, all this of fourteen months ago, in my poor head and heart, was the one thing awake, and the saturnalia round it a kind of mad nightmare *dream*. At London too, perhaps a week or so after my arrival, somebody had given me a ticket to see Macready, and stepping out of the evening sun I found myself in Drury Lane Theatre, which was all darkened, carefully lamp-lit, play just beginning or going to begin. Out of my gratis box—front box on the lower tier—I sat gazing into that painted scene and its mimings, but heard nothing, saw nothing;—her green grave and Ecclefechan silent little kirkyard far away, and how the evening sun at this same moment would be shining *there*, generally that was the main thing I saw or thought of, and tragical enough that was, without any Macready! Of Macready that time I remember nothing, and suppose I must have come soon away.

Irving was now living in Judd Street, New Road, a bigger, much better old house than the former new one, and much handier for the new "Caledonian Chapel," which stood spacious and grand in Regent Square, and was quite dissevered from Hatton Garden and its concerns. I stept over to him on the evening of my arrival; found him sitting quiet and alone, brotherly as ever in his reception of me. Our talk was good and edifying.

[Mr. Carlyle's MS. is here interrupted.   Early in December, 1866, he went to Mentone, where he remained for several months. *December* 27 he resumes in the new environment.]*

He was by this time deep in prophecy and other aberrations, surrounded by weak people, mostly echoes of himself and his inaudible notions; but he was willing to hear me too on secularities, candid like a second self in judging of what one said in the way of opinion, and wise and even shrewd in regard to anything of business if you consulted him on that side.   He objected clearly to my Reform Bill notions, found *Democracy* a thing forbidden, leading down to outer darkness; I, a thing inevitable, and obliged to lead whithersoever it could.   We had several colloquies on that subject, on which, though my own poor convictions are widened, not altered, I should now have more sympathy with his than was then the case. We also talked on religion and Christianity "evidences," our notions of course more divergent than ever.   "It is sacred, my friend, we can call it sacred; such a *Civitas Dei* as was never built before, wholly the grandest series of work ever hitherto done by the human soul; the highest God, doubt it not, assenting and inspiring all along."   This I remember once saying plainly, which was not an encouragement to prosecute the topic.   We were in fact hopelessly divided, to what tragical extent both of us might well feel! But something still remained, and this we (he, at least, for I think in friendship he was the nobler of the two) were only the more anxious to retain and make good.   I recollect breakfasting with him, a strange set of ignorant conceited fanatics forming the body of the party, and greatly spoiling it for me.   Irving's own kindness was evidently in essence unabated; how sorrowful, at once provoking and pathetic, that I or he could henceforth get so little good of it!

We were to have gone and seen Coleridge together, had fixed a day for that object; but the day proved a long deluge, no stirring

---

* Ceased in London perhaps three weeks ago, mere hubbub and uncertainty intervening; begins again at Mentone on the *Riviera Occidentale,* whither I have been pushed and pulled in the most unheard of way, Professor Tyndall, Lady Ashburton, friends, foes, all conspiring, a journey like "chaos come again," and an arrival and a continuance hitherto still *liker* ditto.   Wakeful nights each, especially the one just gone; in which strange circumstances—bright sun shining, blue sea faintly murmuring, orange groves glowing out of window, Mentone hidden, and Ventimiglia Cape in view, all earth a kind of Paradise, inhabitants a kind of quasi-Satan—I endeavor to proceed the best I can.

out possible, and we did not appoint another. I never saw Coleridge more. He died the year after our final removal to London, a man much pitied and recognized by me; never excessively esteemed in any respect, and latterly, on the intellectual or spiritual side, less and less. The father of Puseyism and of much vain phantasmal moonshine which still vexes this poor earth, as I have already described him. Irving and I did not, on the whole, see much of one another during this "Sartor Resartus" visit, our circumstances, our courses and employments were so altogether diverse. Early in the visit he walked me to Belgrave Square to dine with Henry Drummond; beautiful promenade through the crowd and stir of Piccadilly, which was then somewhat of a novelty to me. Irving, I heard afterwards, was judged, from the broad hat, brown skin, and flowing black hair, to be in all probability the one-string fiddler Paganini—a tall, lean, taciturn, abstruse-looking figure—who was then, after his sort, astonishing the idle of mankind. Henry Drummond—house all in summer *deshabille*, carpets up, etc.—received us with abundance of respect, and of aristocratic pococurantism withal (the latter perhaps rather in a conscious condition); gave us plenty of talk, and received well what was given; chiefly on the rotten social state of England, on the "Swing" outrages (half the year raising wheat and the other half burning it), which were then alarming everybody—all rather in epigrammatic exaggerative style, and with "wisdom" sometimes sacrificed to "wit." Gave us, in short, a pleasant enough dinner and evening, but left me, as Mazzini used to describe it, "cold." A man of elastic, pungent decisive nature, full of fine qualities and capabilities, but well nigh cracked by an enormous conceit of himself, which, both as pride and vanity (in strange partnership mutually agreeable), seemed to pervade every fibre of him, and render his life a restless inconsistency. That was the feeling he left in me; nor did it alter afterwards when I saw a great deal more of him, without sensible increase or diminution of the little love he at first inspired in me. Poor Henry! he shot fiery arrows about too, but they told nowhere. I was never tempted to become more intimate with him, though he now and then seemed willing enough: *ex nihilo nihil fit.* He, without unkindness of intention, did my poor Irving a great deal of ill; me never any, such my better luck. His last act was, about eight or nine years ago, to ask us both* out to Albury on a mistaken day, when he himself was not there! Happily my darling had at

---

* Carlyle and his wife.

SAMUEL T. COLERIDGE.

the eleventh hour decided not to go, so that the ugly confusion fell all on me, and in a few months more Henry was himself dead, and no mistake possible again. Albury, the ancient Earl of Arundel's, the recent scene of prophet conferences, etc., I had seen for the first and most likely for the last time. My *double-goer*, T. Carlyle, "Advocate," who had for years been "Angel" there, was lately dead; and the numerous mistakes, wilful and involuntary, which he, from my fifteenth year onwards, had occasioned me, selling his pamphlets as mine, getting my letters as his, and *vice versâ;* nay, once or more with some ambassador at Berlin *dining* in my stead; foolish vain fellow, who called me Antichrist withal in his serious moments! were likewise at an end. All does end.

My business lay with the bookseller or publishing world; my chief intercourse was with the lighter literary figures: in part, too, with the political, many of whom I transiently saw at Jeffrey's (who was then Lord Advocate), and all of whom I might hear of through him. Not in either kind was my appetite very keen, nor did it increase by what it fed on. Rather a "feast of shells," as perhaps I then defined it; people of biggish names, but of substance mainly spilt and wanting. All men were full of the *Reform Bill;* nothing else talked of, written of, the air loaded with *it* alone, which occasioned great obstruction in the publishing of my "Sartor," I was told. On that latter point I could say much, but will forbear. Few men ever more surprised me than did the great Albemarle Street Murray, who had published for Byron and all the great ones for many years, and to whom Jeffrey sent me recommended. Stupider man than the great Murray, in look, in speech, in conduct, in regard to this poor "Sartor" question, I imagined I had seldom or never seen! Afterwards it became apparent to me that partly he was sinking into the heaviness of old age, and partly, still more important, that in regard to this particular "Sartor" question his position was an impossible one; position of a poor old man endeavoring to answer yes *and* no! I had striven and pushed for some weeks with him and others on those impossible principles, till at length discovering how the matter stood, I with brevity demanded back my poor MS. from Murray, received it with some apologetic palaver (enclosing an opinion from his taster, which was subsequently printed in our edition), and much hope, etc., etc.; locked it away into fixity of silence for the present (my Murray into ditto forever), and decided to send for the dear one I had left behind me, and let her too see London, which I knew she would like, before we went farther. Ah me! this sunny Riviera which we sometimes vaguely thought of, she does not see along with me, and my thoughts of her here are too sad for words. I will write no more to-day. Oh, my darling, my lost darling, may the great God be good to thee! Silence, though! and "hope" if I can!

My Jeannie came about the end of September. Brother John, by industry of hers and mine (hers chiefly), acting on an opportunity of Lord Advocate Jeffrey's, had got an appointment for Italy (travelling physician, by which he has since made abundance of money, and of work may be said to have translated Dante's "Inferno," were there nothing more!). We shifted from our uncomfortable lodging* into a clean, quiet, and modestly comfortable one in Ampton Street (same St. Pancras region), and there, ourselves two—brother John being *off* to Italy—set up for the winter under tolerable omens. My darling was, as ever, the guardian spirit of the establishment, and made all things bright and smooth. The daughter of the house, a fine young Cockney specimen, fell quite in love with her, served like a fairy. Was next year, long after we were gone, for coming to us at Craigenputtoch to be "maid of all work"—an impossible suggestion; and did, in effect, keep up an adoring kind of intercourse till the fatal day of April last, never changing at all in her poor tribute of love. A fine outpouring of her grief and admiring gratitude, written after that event,† was *not* thrown into the fire half-read, or unread, but is still lying in a drawer at Chelsea, or perhaps adjoined to some of the things I was writing there, as a genuine human utterance, not without some sad value to me. My poor little woman had often indifferent health, which seemed rather to worsen than improve while we continued; but her spirit was indefatigable, ever cheery, full of grace, ingenuity, dexterity; and she much enjoyed London, and the considerable miscellany of people that came about us—Charles Buller, John Mill, several professed "admirers" of mine (among whom was, and for aught I know still is, the mocking Hayward!); Jeffrey almost daily, as an admirer of hers; not to mention Mrs. Montague and Co., certain Holcrofts (Badams married to one of them, a certain Captain Kenny married to the mother of them, at whose house I once saw Godwin, if that was any-

---

* At Irving's youngest brother George's; an incipient surgeon, amiable and clear superficially, who soon after died.

† Letter to me, signed "Eliza Snowden;" *Miles* was her maiden name. "Snowden," once a clerk with her uncle, is now himself, for long years back, a prosperous upholsterer; and the sylph-like Eliza, grown fat enough of shape, is the mother of six or seven prosperous children to him.

thing), Allan Cunningham from time to time, and fluctuating foreigners, etc., etc. We had company rather in superabundance than otherwise, and a pair of the clearest eyes in the whole world were there to take note of them all, a judgment to compare and contrast them (as I afterwards found she had been doing, the dear soul!) with what was already all her own. Ah me! Ah me!

Soon after New Year's Day a great sorrow came, unexpected news of my father's death. He had been in bed, as ill, only a few hours, when the last hour proved to be there, unexpectedly to all, except perhaps to himself; for ever since my sister Margaret's death he had been fast failing, though none of us took notice enough, such had been his perfection of health almost all through the seventy-three years he lived. I sat plunged in the depths of natural grief, the pale kingdoms of eternity laid bare to me, and all that was sad and grand and dark as death filling my thoughts exclusively day after day. How beautiful She was to me, how kind and tender! Till after the funeral my father's noble old face —one of the finest and strongest I have ever seen—was continually before my eyes. In these and the following days and nights I hastily wrote down some memorials of him,* which I have never since seen, but which still exist somewhere; though, indeed, they were not worth preserving, still less are after I have done with them. "Posterity!" that is what I never thought of appealing to. What possible use can there be in appealing *there*, or in *appealing* anywhere, except by absolute silence to the High Court of Eternity, which can do no error, poor sickly transciencies that we are, coveting we know not what! In the February ensuing I wrote "Johnson" (the "Bozzy" part was published in "Fraser" for March). A week or two before, we had made acquaintance, by Hunt's own goodness, with Leigh Hunt, and were much struck with him. Early in April we got back to Annandale and Craigenputtoch. Sadly present to my soul, most sadly, yet most beautifully, all that, even now!

In the course of the winter sad things had occurred in Irving's history. His enthusiastic studies and preachings were passing into the practically "miraculous," and to me the most doleful of all phenomena. The "Gift of Tongues" had fairly broken out among the crazed and weakliest of his wholly rather dim and weakly flock. I was never at all in his church during this visit, being at once grieved and angered at the course he had fallen into; but once

---

* The first "Reminiscence" in this volume.

or twice poor Eliza Miles came running home from some evening sermon there was, all in a tremor of tears over these same
"Tongues," and a riot from the *dissenting* majority opposing them.
"All a tumult yonder, oh me!" This did not happen above twice
or so; Irving (never himself a "Tongue" performer) having taken
some order with the thing, and I think discouraged and nearly suppressed it as *unfit* during church service. It was greatly talked of
by some persons, with an inquiry, "Do you believe in it?" "Believe
it? As much as I do in the high priest of Otaheite!" answered
Lockhart once to Fraser, the inquiring bookseller, in my hearing.
Sorrow and disgust were naturally my own feeling. "How are
the mighty fallen! my own high Irving come to this, by paltry
popularities and Cockney admirations puddling such a head!" We
ourselves saw less and less of Irving; but one night in one of our
walks we did make a call, and actually heard what they called the
Tongues. It was in a neighboring room, larger part of the drawing-room belike. Mrs. Irving had retired thither with the devo-
tees. Irving for our sake had stayed, and was pacing about the
floor, dandling his youngest child, and talking to us of this and
that, probably about the Tongues withal, when there burst forth
a shrieky hysterical "Lah lall lall!" (little or nothing else but *l*'s
and *a*'s continued for several minutes) to which Irving, with singular calmness, said only, "There, hear you, there are the Tongues!"
And we too, except by our looks, which probably were eloquent,
answered him nothing, but soon came away, full of distress, provocation, and a kind of shame. "Why was there not a bucket
of cold water to fling on that *lah-lalling* hysterical madwoman?"
thought we, or said to one another. "Oh, heaven, that it should
come to this!" I do not remember any call that we made there afterwards. Of course there was a farewell call; but that too I recollect only obliquely by my Jeannie's distress and disgust at Mrs.
Irving's hypocritical final *kiss;* a "kiss" of the untruest, which
really ought to have been spared. Seldom was seen a more tragical
scene to us than this of Irving's London life was now becoming!

One other time we did see Irving, at our lodging, where he had
called to take leave of us a day or two before our quitting London.
I know not whether the interview had been preconcerted between
my darling and me for the sake of our common friend, but it was
abundantly serious and affecting to us all, and none of the three, I
believe, ever forgot it again. Preconcerting or not, I had privately
determined that I must tell Irving plainly what I thought of his
present course and posture. And I now did so, breaking in by the

first opportunity, and leading the dialogue wholly into that channel, till with all the delicacy, but also with all the fidelity possible to me, I put him fully in possession of what my real opinion was. *She*, my noble Jeannie, said hardly anything, but her looks, and here and there a word, testified how deep her interest was, how complete her assent. I stated plainly to him that he must permit me a few words for relief of my conscience before leaving him for we know not what length of time, on a course which I could not but regard as full of danger to him. That the 13*th of the Corinthians* to which he always appealed, was surely too narrow a basis for so high a tower as he was building upon it, a high lean tower, or quasi-*mast*, piece added to piece, till it soared far above all human science and experience, and flatly contradicted all that, founded solely on a little text of *writing* in an ancient book! No sound judgment on such warranty could venture on such an enterprise. Authentic "writings" of the Most High, were they found in old books only? They were in the stars and on the rocks, and in the brain and heart of every mortal; not dubious these to any person, as this 13*th of Corinthians* very greatly was. That it did not beseem him, Edward Irving, to be hanging on the rearward of mankind, struggling still to chain them to old notions not now well tenable, but to be foremost in the van, leading on by the light of the eternal stars across this hideous delirious wilderness where we all were, towards promised lands that lay ahead. Bethink you, my friend, I said, is not that your plainly commanded duty, more plain than any 13th of Corinthians can be? I bid you pause and consider; that verily is my solemn advice to you! I added that, as he knew well, it was in the name of old friendship I was saying all this. That I did not expect he would at once, or soon, renounce his fixed views, connections, and methods for any words of mine; but perhaps at some future time of crisis and questioning dubiety in his own mind he might remember the words of a well-affected soul, and they might then be a help to him.

During all this, which perhaps lasted about twenty minutes, Irving sat opposite to me, within a few feet; my wife to his right hand and to my left, silent and sad-looking, in the middle of the floor, Irving, with head downcast, face indicating great pain, but without the slightest word or sound from him till I had altogether ended. He then began with the mildest low tone, and face full of kindness and composed distress—"dear friend," and endeavored to make his apology and defence, which did not last long or do anything to convince me, but was in a style of modesty and friendly magnanimity which no mortal could surpass, and which remains to me at this moment dear and memorable and worthy of all honor. Which done, he went silently his way, no doubt with kindest farewell to us, and I remember nothing more. Possibly we had already made farewell call in Judd Street the day before, and found *him* not there.

This was, in a manner, the last visit I ever made to Irving, the last time either of *us* ever freely saw him, or spoke with him at any length. We had to go our way, he his; and his soon proved to be precipitous, full of chasms and plunges, which rapidly led him to the close. Our journey homewards—I have spoken of it elsewhere, and of the dear reminiscences it leaves, ever sad, but also ever blessed to me now. We were far away from Irving in our solitary moors, stayed there still above two years (one of our winters in Edinburgh), and heard of Irving and his catastrophes only from a distance. He had come to Annan and been expelled from the Scottish Kirk. That scene I remember reading in some newspaper with lively conception and emotion. A poor aggregate of Reverend Sticks in black gown, sitting in Presbytery, to pass formal condemnation on a man and a cause which might have been tried in Patmos under presidency of St. John without the right truth of it being got at! I knew the "Moderator" (one Roddick, since gone mad), for one of the stupidest and barrenest of living mortals; also the little phantasm of a creature—Sloane his name—who went niddy-noddying with his head, and was infinitely conceited and phantasmal, by whom Irving was rebuked with the "Remember where you are, sir!" and got answer, "I have not forgotten where I am; it is the church where I was baptized, where I was consecrated to preach Christ, where the bones of my dear ones lie buried." Condemnation under any circumstances had to follow; "*le droit de me damner te reste toujours !*" as poor Danton said in a far other case.

The feeling of the population was, too, strong and general for Irving. Reverends Sloane and Roddick were not without their apprehensions of some tumult perhaps, had not the people been so reverent of the place they were in. Irving sent us no word of himself, made no appeal to any, friend or foe, unless his preaching to the people up and down for some days, partly perhaps in the way of defence, though mostly on general Gospel subjects, could be taken as such. He was followed by great crowds who eagerly heard him. My brother Jamie, who had been at several of those open-air preachings in different parts of the Annan neighborhood, and who much admired and pitied the great Irving, gave me the last notice I ever had of that tragic matter, "Irving's vocal *appellatio ad populum,*" when Presbytery had condemned him. This time the gathering was at Ecclefechan, probably the final one of all, and the last time he ever preached to Annandale men. The assemblage was large and earnest, gathered in the Middlebie road, a little way off the main street and highway. The preacher stood on some table or chair, which was fixed against the trunk of a huge, high, strong, and many-branched elm tree, well known to me and to everyone that passes that way. The weather was of proper February quality, grimly fierce, with windy snow showers flying. Irving had a woollen comforter about his neck, skirts of comforter, hair, and cloak tossing in the storms ; eloquent voice well audible under the groaning of the boughs and piping of the wind. Jamie was on business in the village and had paused awhile, much moved by what he saw and heard. It was our last of Irving in his native Annandale. Mrs. Oliphant, I think, relates that on getting back to London he was put under a kind of arrest by certain Angels or authorities of his New "Irvingite" Church (just established in Newman Street, Oxford Street), for disobeying regulations—perhaps in regard to those volunteer preachings in Annandale—and sat with great patience in some penitential place among them, dumb for about a week, till he had expiated that sin. Irving was now become wholly tragical to us, and the least painful we could expect in regard to him was what mainly happened, that we heard no news from that side at all. His health we vaguely understood was becoming uncertain, news naturally worse than none, had we much believed it ; which, knowing his old herculean strength, I suppose we did not.

In 1834 came our own removal to London, concerning which are heavy fields of memory, laborious, beautiful, sad and sacred (oh, my darling lost one!) were this the place for them, which it is not. Our winter in Edinburgh, our haggles and distresses (badness of servants mainly), our bits of diligences, strenuous and sometimes happy, brought in fine the clear resolution that we ought to go. I had been in correspondence with London—with John Mill, Leigh Hunt, Mrs. Austin, etc.—ever since our presence there. "Let us burn our ships," said my noble one, and " get on march!" I went as precursor early in May, ignorantly thinking this was, as in Scotland, the general and sole term for getting houses in London, and that after May 26 there would be none but leavings! We were not very practically advised, I should think, though there were counsellors many. However, I roved hastily about seeking houses for the next three weeks, while my darling was still busier at home, getting all things packed and put under way.

What endless toils for her, undertaken with what courage, skill, and cheery heroism! By the time of her arrival I had been far and wide round London, seeking houses. Had found out that the western suburb was in important respects the fittest, and had seen nothing I thought so eligible there as a certain *one* of three cheap houses; which *one* she on survey agreed to be the best, and which is in fact No. 5 Great Cheyne Row, where the rest of our life was to be passed together. Why do I write all this? It is too sad to me to think of it, broken down and solitary as I am, and the lamp of my life, which "covered everything with gold" as it were, gone out, gone out!

It was on one of those expeditions, a week or more after my arrival, expedition to take survey of the proposed No. 5, in company with Mrs. Austin, whom I had taken up in Bayswater, where she lived, and with whom, attended also by Mrs. Jamieson, not known to me before, but found by accident on a call there, we were proceeding towards Chelsea in the middle of a bright May day, when I noticed well down in Kensington Gardens a dark male figure sitting between two white female ones under a tree; male figure, which abruptly rose and stalked towards me, whom, seeing it was Irving, I disengaged myself and stept out to meet. It was indeed Irving, but how changed in the two years and two months since I had last seen him! In look he was almost friendlier than ever; but he had suddenly become an old man. His head, which I had left raven-black, was grown gray, on the temples almost snow-white. The face was hollow, wrinkly, collapsed; the figure, still perfectly erect, seemed to have lost all its elasticity and strength. We walked some space slowly together, my heart smitten with various emotions; my speech, however, striving to be cheery and hopeful. He was very kind and loving. It seemed to be a kind of tender grief and regret that my Jeannie and I were taking so important a step, and he not called at all to assist, rendered unable to assist. Certainly in all England there was no heart, and in all Scotland only two or three, that wished us half as well. He admitted his weak health, but treated it as temporary; it seemed of small account to him. Friends and doctors had advised him to shift to Bayswater for better air, had got him a lodging there, a stout horse to ride. Summer they expected would soon set him up again. His tone was not despondent, but it was low, pensive, full of silent sorrow. Once, perhaps twice, I got a small bit of Annandale laughter from him, strangely genuine, though so lamed and overclouded. This was to me the most affecting thing of all, and still is when I recall it. He gave me his address in Bayswater, his house as near as might be, and I engaged to try and find him there; I, him, which seemed the likelier method in our widely diverse elements, both of them so full of bustle, interruption, and uncertainty. And so adieu, my friend, adieu! Neither of us had spoken with the women of the other, and each of us was gone his several road again, mine not specially remembered farther.

It seems to me I never found Irving in his Bayswater lodging. I distinctly recollect seeing him one dusty evening about eight at the door there, mount his horse, a stout fine bay animal, of the kind called cob, and set out towards Newman Street, whither he rode perhaps twice or thrice a day for church services there were; but this and his friendly regret at being obliged to go is all I can recall of interview farther. Neither at the Bayswater lodging nor at his own house in Newman Street when he returned thither, could I for many weeks to come ever find him "at home." In Chelsea, we poor pair of immigrants had, of course, much of our own to do, and right courageously we marched together, my own brave darling (what a store of humble, but high and sacred memories to me!) victoriously carrying the flag. But at length it struck me there was something questionable in these perpetual "not-at-home's" of Irving, and that perhaps his poor, jealous, anxious, and much-bewildered wife had her hand in the phenomenon—as proved to be the fact accordingly. I applied to William Hamilton (excellent City Scotsman, married, not over well I doubt, to a sister of Mrs. Irving), with a brief statement of the case, and had immediate remedy; an appointment to dinner at Newman Street on a given day, which I failed not to observe. None but Irving and his wife, besides myself, were there. The dinner (from a good joint of roast beef, in a dim but quite comfortable kind of room) was among the pleasantest of dinners to me, Madam herself wearing nothing but smiles, and soon leaving us together to a fair hour or two of free talk. I think the main topic must have been my own outlooks and affairs, my project of writing on the *French Revolution*, which Irving warmly approved of (either then or some other time). Of his church matters we never spoke. I went away gratified, and for my own share glad, had not the outlooks on his side been so dubious and ominous. He was evidently growing weaker, not stronger, wearing himself down, as to me seemed too clear, by spiritual agitations, which would kill him unless checked and ended. Could he but be got to Switzerland, to Italy, I thought, to some pleasant country of which the language was unknown to him, where he would be *forced to silence*, the one

salutary medicine for him in body and in soul! I often thought of
this, but he had now no brother, no father, on whom I could practically urge it, as I would with my whole strength have done, feeling
that his life now lay on it. I had to hear of his growing weaker
and weaker, while there was nothing whatever that I could do.

With himself I do not recollect that there was anything more of
interview since that dinner in Newman Street, or that I saw him
again in the world, except once only, to be soon noticed. Latish
in the autumn some of the Kirkcaldy Martins had come. I remember speaking to his father-in-law at Hamilton's in Cheapside one
evening, and very earnestly on the topic that interested us both.
But in Martin, too, there was nothing of help, "Grows weaker and
weaker," said he, "and no doctor can find the least disease in him;
so weak now he cannot lift his little baby to his neck!" In my
desperate anxiety at this time I remember writing a letter on my
Switzerland or Italy scheme to Henry Drummond, whom I yet knew
nothing more of, but considered to be probably a man of sense and
practical insight; letter stating briefly my sad and clear belief that,
unless carried into some element of *perfect silence,* poor Irving would
soon die; letter which lay some days on the mantelpiece at Chelsea,
under some misgivings about sending it, and was then thrown into
the fire. We heard before long that it was decided he should journey slowly into Wales, paying visits—perhaps into Scotland, which
seemed the next best to what I would have proposed, and was of
some hope to us. And late one afternoon, soon after, we had a short
farewell visit from him; his first visit to Cheyne Row and his last;
the last we two ever saw of him in this world. It was towards
sunset, had there been any sun that damp, dim October day. He
came ambling gently on his bay horse, sate some fifteen or twenty
minutes, and went away while it was still daylight. It was in the
ground-floor room, where I still write (thanks to her last service
to me, shifting me thither again, the darling ever-helpful one!)
Whether she was sitting with me on his entrance I don't recollect,
but I well do his fine chivalrous demeanor to *her,* and how he
complimented her, as he well might, on the pretty little room she
had made for her husband and self, and running his eye over her
dainty bits of arrangements, ornamentations, all so frugal, simple,
full of grace, propriety, and ingenuity as they ever were, said, smiling, "You are like an Eve, and make a little Paradise wherever you
are!" His manner was sincere, affectionate, yet with a great suppressed sadness in it, and as if with a feeling that he must not
linger. It was perhaps on this occasion that he expressed to me
his satisfaction at my having taken to "writing history" ("French

Revolution" now begun, I suppose); study of history, he seemed to intimate, was the study of things real, practical, and actual, and would bring me closer upon all reality whatever. With a fine simplicity of lovingness he bade us farewell. I followed him to the door, held his bridle (doubtless) while he mounted, no groom being ever with him on such occasions, stood on the steps as he quietly walked or ambled up Cheyne Row, quietly turned the corner (at Wright's door, or the Rector's back *garden* door) into Cook's grounds, and had vanished from my eyes for evermore! In this world neither of us ever saw him again. He was off northward in a day or two, died at Glasgow in December following, age only forty-three, and except weakness, no disease traceable.

Mrs. Oliphant's narrative is nowhere so true and touching to me as in that last portion, where it is drawn almost wholly from his own letters to his wife. All there is true to the life, and recognizable to me as perfect *portraiture;* what I cannot quite say of any other portion of the book. All Mrs. Oliphant's delineation shows excellent diligence, loyalty, desire to be faithful, and indeed, is full of beautiful sympathy and ingenuity; but nowhere else are the features of Irving or of his environment and life recognizably hit, and the pretty picture, to one who knew his looks throughout, is more or less romantic *pictorial*, and "not like" till we arrive here, at the grand close of all, which to me was of almost Apocalyptic impressiveness when I first read it some years ago. What a falling of the curtain! upon what a drama! Rustic Annandale begins it, with its homely honesties, rough vernacularities, safe, innocently kind, ruggedly mother-like, cheery, wholesome, like its airy hills and clear-rushing streams; prurient corrupted London is the middle part, with its volcanic stupidities and bottomless confusions; and in the end is terrible, mysterious, godlike, and awful; what Patmos could be more so? It is as if the vials of Heaven's wrath were pouring down upon a man, yet not wrath alone, for his heart was filled with trust in Heaven's goodness withal. It must be said Irving nobly expiates whatever errors he has fallen into. Like an antique evangelist he walks his stony course, the fixed thought of his heart at all times, "Though he slay me, yet will I trust in Him;" and these final deluges of sorrow are but washing the faithful soul of him clear.

He sent from Glasgow a curious letter to his "Gift of Tongues" congregation; full of questionings, dubieties upon the *Tongues,* and such points, full of wanderings in deep waters, with one light fixed on high: "Humble ourselves before God, and he will show us;" letter indicating a sincerity as of very death, which these New

Church people (Henry Drummond and Co.) first printed for useful private circulation, and then afterwards zealously suppressed and destroyed, till almost everybody but myself had forgotten the existence of it. Luckily, about two years ago I still raked out a copy of it from "Rev. Gavin Carlile,"* by whom I am glad to know it has been printed and made prominent, as a document honorable and due to such a memory. Less mendacious soul of a man than my noble Irving's there could not well be.

It was but a little while before this that he had said to Drummond, what was mentioned above, "I ought to have seen more of T. Carlyle, and heard him more clearly than I have done." And there is one other thing which dates several years before, which I always esteem highly honorable to Irving's memory, and which I will note here as my last item, since it was forgotten at its right date. Right date is that of "German Romance," early 1826. The report is from my brother John, to whom Irving spoke on the subject, which with me he had always rather avoided. Irving did not much know Goethe; had generally a dislike to him as to a kind of heathen ungodly person and idle singer, who had considerably seduced *me* from the right path, as one sin. He read "Wilhelm Meister's Travels" nevertheless, and he said to John one day, "Very curious! in this German poet there are some pages about Christ and the Christian religion, which as I study and re-study them have more sense about that matter than I have found in all the theologians I have ever read!" Was not this a noble thing for such a man to feel and say? I have a hundred times recommended that passage in "Wilhelm Meister" to inquiring and devout souls, but I think never elsewhere met with one who so thoroughly recognized it. One of my last letters, flung into the fire just before leaving London, was from an Oxford self-styled "religious inquirer," who asks me if in those pages of "Meister" there is not a wonderfully distinct foreshadow of Comte and *Positivism!* Phœbus Apollo, god of the sun, foreshadowing the miserablest phantasmal *algebraic ghost* I have yet met with among the ranks of the living!

I have now ended, and am sorry to end, what I had to say of Irving. It is like bidding him farewell for a second and the last time. He waits in the eternities. Another, his brightest scholar, has left me and gone thither. God be about us all. Amen. Amen.

Finished at Mentone, January 2, 1867, looking towards the eastward hills, bathed in sunshine, under a brisk west wind; two P.M.

T. C.

---

* Nephew of Irving. Now editing "Irving's Select Works," or some such title.

LORD JEFFREY

LORD JEFFREY.

OF FRANCIS JEFFREY, HON. LORD JEFFREY, THE LAWYER AND REVIEWER.

Mentone: January 3, 1867.

FEW sights have been more impressive to me than the sudden one I had of the "Outer House" in Parliament Square, Edinburgh, on the evening of November 9, 1809, some hours after my arrival in that city for the first time. We had walked some twenty miles that day, the third day of our journey from Ecclefechan; my companion one "Tom Smail," who had already been to college last year, and was thought to be a safe guide and guardian to me. He was some years older than myself, had been at school along with me, though never in my class. A very innocent, conceited, insignificant, but strict-minded orthodox creature, for whom, knowing him to be of no scholarship or strength of judgment, I had privately very small respect, though civilly following him about in things he knew better than I. As in the streets of Edinburgh, for example, on my first evening there. On our journey thither he had been wearisome, far from entertaining, mostly silent, having, indeed, nothing to say. He stalked on generally some steps ahead, languidly whistling through his teeth some similitude of a wretched Irish tune, which I knew too well as that of a still more wretched doggrel song called the "Belfast Shoemaker," most melancholy to poor me, given up to my bits of reflections in the silence of the moors and hills.

How strangely vivid, how remote and wonderful, tinged with the hues of far-off love and sadness, is that journey to me now, after fifty-seven years of time! My mother and father walking with me in the dark frosty November morning through the village to set us on our way; my dear and loving mother and her tremulous affection, my etc., etc. But we must get to Edinburgh and Moffat, over Airock Stane (Burnswark visible there for the last time, and my poor little sister Margaret "bursting into tears" when

8

she heard of this in my first letter home). I hid my sorrow and my weariness, but had abundance of it, checkering the mysterious hopes and forecastings of what Edinburgh and the student element would be. Tom and I had entered Edinburgh, after twenty miles of walking, between two and three P.M., got a clean-looking, most cheap lodging (Simon Square the poor locality), had got ourselves brushed, some morsel of dinner doubtless, and Palinurus Tom sallied out into the streets with me to show the novice mind a little of Edinburgh before sundown. The novice mind was not excessively astonished all at once, but kept his eyes well open, and said nothing. What streets we went through I don't the least recollect, but have some faint image of St. Giles's High Kirk, and of the Luckenbooths there, with their strange little ins and outs, and eager old women in miniature shops of combs, shoe-laces, and trifles; still fainter image, if any whatever, of the sublime horse statue in Parliament Square hard by. Directly after which Smail audaciously (so I thought) pushed open a door free to all the world, and dragged me in with him to a scene which I have never forgotten.

An immense hall, dimly lighted from the top of the walls, and perhaps with candles burning in it here and there, all in strange *chiar-oscuro*, and filled with what I thought (exaggeratively) a thousand or two of human creatures, all astir in a boundless buzz of talk, and simmering about in every direction, some solitary, some in groups. By degrees I noticed that some were in wig and black gown, some not, but in common clothes, all well dressed; that here and there, on the sides of the hall, were little thrones with inclosures, and steps leading up, red-velvet figures sitting in said thrones, and the black-gowned eagerly speaking to them; advocates pleading to judges, as I easily understood. How they could be heard in such a grinding din was somewhat a mystery. Higher up on the walls, stuck there like swallows in their nests, sate other humbler figures. These, I found, were the sources of certain wildly plangent lamentable kinds of sounds or echoes which from time to time pierced the universal noise of feet and voices, and rose unintelligibly above it as if in the bitterness of incurable woe. Criers of the Court, I gradually came to understand. And this was Themis in her "Outer House," such a scene of chaotic din and hurly-burly as I had never figured before. It seems to me there were four times or ten times as many people in that "Outer House" as there now usually are, and doubtless there is something of fact in this, such have been the curtailments and abatements of law practice in the head courts since then, and transference of it to the county jurisdiction. Last time I was in that Outer House (some six or seven years ago, in broad daylight), it seemed like a place fallen asleep, fallen almost dead.

Notable figures, now all vanished utterly, were doubtless wandering about as part of that continual hurly-burly when I first set foot in it, fifty-seven years ago : great Law Lords this and that, great advocates *alors célèbres*, as Thiers has it ; Cranstoun, Cockburn, Jeffrey, Walter Scott, John Clerk. To me at that time they were not even names, but I have since occasionally thought of that night and place when probably they were living substances, some of them in a kind of relation to me afterward. Time with his *tenses*, what a miraculous entity is he always ! The only figure I distinctly recollect and got printed on my brain that night was John Clerk, there veritably hitching about, whose grim strong countenance, with its black far-projecting brows and look of great sagacity, fixed him in my memory. Possibly enough poor Smail named others to me, Jeffrey perhaps, if we saw him, though he was not yet quite at the tōp of his celebrity. Top was some three or four years afterwards, and went on without much drooping for almost twenty years more. But the truth is, except Clerk I carried no figure away with me ; nor do I in the least recollect how we made our exit into the streets again, or what we did next. Outer House, vivid now to a strange degree, is bordered by darkness on both hands. I recall it for Jeffrey's sake, though we see it is but potentially his, and I mean not to speak much of his law procedures in what follows.

Poor Smail, too, I may dismiss as thoroughly insignificant, conceitedly harmless. He continued in some comradeship with me (or with James Johnston and me) for perhaps two seasons more, but gained no regard from me, nor had any effect on me, good or bad. Became, with success, an insignificant flowery Burgher minister (somewhere in Galloway), and has died only within few years. Poor Jamie Johnston, also my senior by several years, was far dearer, a man of real merit, with whom about my 17th–21st years I had much genial companionship. But of him also I must not speak, the good, the honest, not the strong *enough*, much-suffering soul. He died as school-master of Haddington in a time memorable to me. *Ay de mi!*

It was about 1811 when I began to be familiar with the figure of Jeffrey, as I saw him in the courts. It was in 1812–13 that he became universally famous, especially in Dumfries-shire, by his saving from the gallows one "Nell Kennedy," a country lass who had

shocked all Scotland, and especially that region of it, by a whole-
sale murder, done on her next neighbor and all his household in
mass, in the most cold-blooded and atrocious manner conceivable
to the oldest artist in such horrors. Nell went down to Ecclefechan one afternoon, purchased a quantity of arsenic, walked back
with it towards Burnswark Leas, her father's farm, stopped at Burnswark Farm, which was old Tom Stoddart's, a couple of furlongs
short of her own home, and there sate gossiping till she pretended it was too late, and that she would now sleep with the maid.
Slept accordingly, old Tom giving no welcome, only stingy permission; rose with the family next morning, volunteered to make porridge for breakfast, made it, could herself take none of it, went
home instead, "having a headache," and in an hour or so after poor
old Tom, his wife, maid, and every living creature in the house (except a dog who had vomited, and *not* except the cat who couldn't)
was dead or lay dying. Horror was universal in those solitary
quiet regions. On the third day my father, finding no lawyer take
the least notice, sent a messenger express to Dumfries, whereupon
the due precognitions, due et ceteras, due arrest of Helen Kennedy,
with strict questioning and strict locking up as the essential element. I was in Edinburgh that summer of 1812, but heard enough
of the matter there. In the Border regions, where it was the universal topic, perhaps not one human creature doubted but Nell was
the criminal, and would get her doom. Assize time came, Jeffrey
there; and Jeffrey by such a play of advocacy as was never seen
before bewildered the poor jury into temporary deliquium or loss
of wits (so that the poor foreman, Scottice chancellor, on whose
casting vote it turned, said at last, with the sweat bursting from
his brow, Mercy, then, mercy!), and brought Nell clear off; home
that night, riding gently out of Dumfries in men's clothes to escape
the rage of the mob. The jury chancellor, they say, on awakening
next morning, smote his now dry brow with a gesture of despair
and exclaimed, "Was I mad?" I have heard from persons who
were at the trial that Jeffrey's art in examining of witnesses was
extreme, that he made them seem to say almost what he would,
and blocked them up from saying what they evidently wished to
say. His other great resource was urging the "want of motive"
on Nell's part; no means of fancying how a blousy rustic lass
should go into such a thing; thing *must* have happened otherwise!
And indeed the stagnant stupid soul of Nell, awake only to its own
appetites, and torpid as dead bacon to all else in this universe, had
needed uncommonly little motive. A blackguard young farmer of

FRANCIS JEFFREY.

the neighborhood, it was understood, had answered her in a trying circumstance : " No, oh no, I cannot marry you. Tom Stoddart has a bill against me of £50; I have no money. How can I marry ?" " Stoddart £50," thought Nell to herself; and without difficulty decided on removing that small obstacle !

Jeffrey's advocate fame from this achievement was, at last, almost greater than he wished, as indeed it might well be. Nell was next year indicted again for murdering a child she had borne (supposed to be the blackguard young farmer's). She escaped this time too, by want of evidence and by good advocacy (not Jeffrey's, but the very best that could be hired by three old miser uncles, bringing out for her their long-hoarded stock with a generosity nigh miraculous). Nell, free again, proceeded next to rob the treasure-chest of these three miraculous uncles one night, and leave them with their house on fire and singular reflections on so delectable a niece ; after which, for several years, she continued wandering in the Border by-ways, smuggling, stealing, etc.; only intermittently heard of, but steadily mounting in evil fame, till she had become the *facile princeps* of Border devils, and was considered a completely uncanny and quasi-infernal object. Was found twice over in Cumberland ships, endeavoring to get to America, sailors universally refusing to lift anchor till she were turned out; did at length, most probably, smuggle herself through Liverpool or some other place to America; at last vanished out of Annandale, and was no more talked of there. I have seen her father mowing at Scotsbrig as a common day-laborer in subsequent years, a snuffling, unpleasant, deceitful-looking body: very ill thought of while still a farmer, and before his Nell took to murdering. Nell's three miraculous uncles were maternal, and were of a very honest kin.

The merit of saving such an item of the world's population could not seem to Jeffrey very great, and it was said his brethren quizzed him upon it, and made him rather uncomfortable. Long after at Craigenputtoch my Jeannie and I brought him on the topic: which he evidently did not like too well, but was willing to talk of for our sake, and perhaps his own. He still affected to think it uncertain whether Nell was really guilty; such an intrepidity, calmness, and steadfast immovability had she exhibited, persisting in mere unshaken "No" under the severest trials by him; but there was no persuading us that he had the least real doubt, and not some real regret rather. Advocate morality was clearly on his side. It is a strange trade, I have often thought, that of advocacy. Your intellect, your highest heavenly gift, hung up in the shop window like a loaded pistol for sale; will either blow out a pestilent scoundrel's brains, or the scoundrel's salutary sheriff's officer's (in a sense), as you please to choose for your guinea! Jeffrey rose into higher and higher professional repute from this time; and to the last was very celebrated as what his satirists might have called a "felon's friend." All this, however, was swallowed among quite nobler kinds of renown, both as advocate and as "man of letters" and as member of society; everybody recognizing his honorable ingenuity, sagacity, and opulent brilliancy of mind; and nobody ascribing his felon help to anything but a pitying disposition and readiness to exercise what faculty one has.

I seem to remember that I dimly rather felt there was something trivial, doubtful, and not quite of the highest type in our Edinburgh admiration for our great lights and law sages, and poor Jeffrey among the rest; but I honestly admired him in a loose way as my neighbors were doing, was always glad to notice him when I strolled into the courts, and eagerly enough stept up to hear if I found him pleading; a delicate, attractive, dainty little figure as he merely walked about, much more if he were speaking; uncommonly bright black eyes, instinct with vivacity, intelligence, and kindly fire; roundish brow, delicate oval face full of rapid expression, figure light, nimble, pretty though so small, perhaps hardly five feet in height. He had his gown, almost never any wig, wore his black hair rather closely cropt; I have seen the back part of it jerk suddenly out in some of the rapid expressions of his face, and knew even if behind him that his brow was then puckered, and his eyes looking archly, half-contemptuously out, in conformity to some conclusive little cut his tongue was giving. His voice, clear, harmonious, and sonorous, had something of metallic in it, something almost plangent; never rose into alt, into any dissonance or shrillness, nor carried much the character of humor, though a fine feeling of the ludicrous always dwelt in him—as you would notice best when he got into Scotch dialect, and gave you, with admirable truth of mimicry, old Edinburgh incidents and experiences of his —very great upon old "Judge Baxie," "Peter Peebles," and the like. For the rest, his laugh was small and by no means Homeric; he never laughed loud (could not do it, I should think), and indeed oftener sniggered slightly than laughed in any way.

For above a dozen or fourteen years I had been outwardly familiar with the figure of Jeffrey before we came to any closer acquaintance, or, indeed, had the least prospect of any. His sphere lay far away above mine; to him, in his shining elevation, my existence down among the shadows was unknown. In May, 1814, I heard him once pleading in the General Assembly, on some poor cause there; a notable, but not the notablest thing to me, while I sate looking diligently, though mostly as dramatic spectator, into the procedure of that venerable Church Court for the first time, which proved also the last. Queer old figures there; Hill of St. Andrews, Johnston of Carmichael, Dr. Inglis with the voice jingling in perpetual unforeseen alternation between deep bass and shrill treble (ridiculous to hear, though shrewd cunning sense lay in it), Dr. Chalmers once, etc., etc., all vanished now! Jeffrey's pleading, the first I had heard of him, seemed to me abundantly clever, full of liveliness, free flowing ingenuity; my admiration went frankly with that of others, but I think was hardly of very deep character.

This would be the year I went to Annan as teacher of mathematics; not a gracious destiny, nor by any means a joyful, indeed a hateful, sorrowful, and imprisoning one, could I at all have helped it, which I could not. My second year there at Rev. Mr. Glen's (reading Newton's "Principia" till three A.M., and voraciously many other books) was greatly more endurable, nay, in parts was genial and spirited, though the paltry trade and ditto environment for the most part were always odious to me. In late autumn, 1816, I went to Kirkcaldy in like capacity, though in circumstances (what with Edward Irving's company, what with, etc., etc.) which were far superior. There in 1818 I had come to the grim conclusion that school-mastering must end, whatever pleased to follow; that "it were better to perish," as I exaggeratively said to myself, "than continue school-mastering." I made for Edinburgh, as did Irving too, intending, I, darkly towards potential "literature," if I durst have said or thought so. But hope hardly dwelt in me on that or on any side; only fierce resolution in abundance to do my best and utmost in all honest ways, and to suffer as silently and stoically as might be, if it proved (as too likely!) that I could do *nothing*. This kind of humor, what I sometimes called of "desperate hope," has largely attended me all my life. In short, as has been enough indicated elsewhere, I was advancing towards huge installments of bodily and spiritual wretchedness in this my Edinburgh purgatory, and had to clean and purify myself in penal fire of various kinds for several years coming; the first and much the worst two or three of which were to be enacted in this once-loved city. Horrible to think of in part even yet! The bodily part of them was a kind of base agony (arising mainly in the want of any extant or discoverable *fence* between my coarser fellow-creatures and my more sensitive self), and might and could easily (had the age been pious or thoughtful) have been spared a poor creature like me. Those hideous disturbances to sleep, etc., a very little real care and goodness might prevent all that; and I look back upon it still with a kind of angry protest, and would have my successors saved from it. But perhaps one needs suffering more than at first seems, and the spiritual agonies would not have been enough! These latter seem wholly blessed in retrospect, and were infinitely worth suffering, with whatever addition *was* needful. God be thanked always.

It was still some eight or ten years before any personal contact occurred between Jeffrey and me; nor did I ever tell him what a bitter passage, known to only one party, there had been between us. It was probably in 1819 or 1820 (the coldest winter I ever knew) that I had taken a most private resolution, and executed it in spite of physical and other misery, to try Jeffrey with an actual contribution to the "Edinburgh Review." The idea seemed great, and might be tried, though nearly desperate. I had got hold somewhere (for even books were all but inaccessible to me) of a foolish enough, but new French book, a mechanical *theory of gravitation* elaborately worked out by a late foolish M. Pictet (I think that was the name) in Geneva. This I carefully read, judged of, and elaborately dictated a candid account and condemnation of, or modestly firm contradiction of (my amanuensis, a certain feeble but inquiring quasi-disciple of mine called George Dalgleish of Annan, from whom I kept my ulterior purpose quite secret). Well do I remember those dreary evenings in Bristo Street; oh, what ghastly passages and dismal successive spasms of attempt at "literary enterprise!"—"Herclii Selenographia," with poor Horrox's "Venus in Sole visa," intended for some *life* of the said Horrox—this for one other instance. I read all Saussure's four quartos of Travels in Switzerland too (and still remember much of it), I know not with what object. I was banished solitary as if to the bottom of a cave, and blindly had to try many impossible roads out! My "Review of Pictet" all fairly written out in George Dalgleish's good clerk hand, I penned some brief polite note to the great editor, and walked off with the small parcel one night to his address in George Street. I very well remember leaving it with his valet there, and disappearing in the night with various thoughts and doubts. My hopes had never risen high, or, in fact, risen at all; but for a fortnight or so they did not quite die out, and then it was in absolute *Zero;* no answer, no return of MS., absolutely no notice taken, which was a form of catastrophe more complete than even I had anticipated. There rose in my head a pungent little note which might be written to the great man, with neatly cutting considerations offered him from the small unknown ditto; but I wisely judged it was still more dignified to let the matter lie as it was, and take what I had got for my own benefit only. Nor did I ever mention it to almost anybody, least of all to Jeffrey in subsequent changed times, when at any rate it was fallen extinct. It was my second, not quite my first, attempt in that fashion. Above two years before, from Kirkcaldy, I had forwarded to some magazine editor in Edinburgh what, perhaps, was a likelier little article (of descriptive tourist kind after a real tour by Yarrow country into Annandale), which also vanished without sign; not much to my regret that first one, nor indeed very much the second either (a dull affair altogether, I could not but admit), and no third adventure of the kind lay ahead for me. It must be owned my first entrances into glorious "literature" were abundantly stinted and pitiful; but a man does enter if, even with a small gift, he persists; and perhaps it is no disadvantage if the door be several times slammed in his face as a preliminary.

In spring, 1827, I suppose it must have been, a letter came to me at Comley Bank* from Procter (Barry Cornwall, my quondam London acquaintance), offering, with some "congratulations," etc., to introduce me formally to Jeffrey, whom he certified to be a "very fine fellow," with much kindness in him, among his other known qualities. Comley Bank, except for one darling soul, whose heavenly nobleness, then as ever afterwards, shone on me, and should have made the darkest place bright (ah me! ah me! I only know now how noble she was!), was a gloomy, intricate abode to me, and in retrospect has little or nothing of pleasant but her. This of Jeffrey, however, had a practical character of some promise; and I remember striding off with Procter's introduction one evening towards George Street and Jeffrey (perhaps by appointment of hour and place by himself) in rather good spirits. "I shall see the famous man, then," thought I, "and if he can do nothing for me, why not?" I got ready admission into Jeffrey's study, or rather "office," for it had mostly that air—a roomy, not overneat, apartment on the ground-floor, with a big baize-covered table, loaded with book rows and paper bundles. On one, or perhaps two, of

* Carlyle's first home after his marriage; a suburb of Edinburgh.

the walls were book-shelves likewise well filled, but with books in
tattery, ill-bound, or unbound condition. "Bad new literature
these will be," thought I; "the table ones are probably on hand!"
Five pair of candles were cheerfully burning, in the light of which
sate my famous little gentleman; laid aside his work, cheerfully
invited me to sit, and began talking in a perfectly human manner.
Our dialogue was perfectly human and successful; lasted for perhaps twenty minutes (for I could not consume a great man's time),
turned upon the usual topics, what I was doing, what I had published, "German Romance," translations my last thing; to which
I remember he said, kindly, "We must give you a lift," an offer
which in some complimentary way I managed to his satisfaction
to decline.—My feeling with him was that of embarrassment; a
reasonable veracious little man, I could perceive, with whom any
truth one felt good to utter would have a fair chance. Whether
much was said of German literature, whether anything at all on
my writing of it for him, I don't recollect; but certainly I took
my leave in a gratified successful kind of mood; and both those
topics, the latter in practical form, did soon abundantly spring up
between us, with formal return call by him (which gave a new
speed to intimacy), agreement for a little paper on "Jean Paul,"
and whatever could follow out of an acquaintanceship well begun.
The poor paper on Jean Paul, a study piece, not without humor
and substance of my own, appeared in (I suppose) the very next
"Edinburgh Review," and made what they call a sensation among
the Edinburgh buckrams, which was greatly heightened next number by the more elaborate and grave article on "German Literature"
generally, which set many tongues wagging, and some few brains
considering, *what* this strange monster could be that was come to
disturb their quiescence and the established order of Nature!
Some newspapers or newspaper took to denouncing the "Mystic
School," which my bright little woman declared to consist of me
alone, or of her and me, and for a long while after merrily used to
designate us by that title, "Mystic School" signifying *us*, in the
pretty coterie speech which she was always so ready to adopt, and
which lent such a charm to her talk and writing. She was beautifully gay and hopeful under these improved phenomena, the
darling soul! "Foreign Review," "Foreign Quarterly," etc., followed, to which I was eagerly invited. Articles for Jeffrey (about
parts of which I had always to dispute with him) appeared also
from time to time. In a word, I was now in a sort fairly launched
upon literature, and had even to sections of the public become a

"Mystic School;" not quite prematurely, being now of the age of thirty-two, and having had my bits of experiences, and gotten really something which I wished much to say—and have ever since been saying the best way I could.

After Jeffrey's call at Comley Bank, the intimacy rapidly increased. He was much taken with my little Jeannie, as he well might be: one of the brightest and cleverest creatures in the whole world; full of innocent rustic simplicity and veracity, yet with the gracefulest discernment, calmly natural deportment; instinct with beauty and intelligence to the finger-ends! He became, in a sort, her would-be openly declared friend and quasi-lover; as was his way in such cases. He had much the habit of flirting about with women, especially pretty women, much more the both pretty and clever; all in a weakish, mostly dramatic, and wholly theoretic way (his age now fifty gone); would daintily kiss their hands in bidding good-morning, offer his due *homage*, as he phrased it; trip about, half like a lap-dog, half like a human adorer, with speeches pretty and witty, always of trifling import. I have known some women (not the prettiest) take offense at it, and awkwardly draw themselves up, but without the least putting him out. The most took it quietly, kindly, and found an entertainment to themselves in cleverly answering it, as he did in pertly offering it; pertly, yet with something of real reverence, and always in a dexterous light way. Considerable jealousy attended the reigning queen of his circle among the now non-reigning: who soon detected her position, and gave her the triumph of their sometimes half-visible spleen. An airy environment of this kind was, wherever possible, a coveted charm in Jeffrey's way of life. I can fancy he had seldom made such a surprising and agreeable acquaintance as this new one at Comley Bank! My little woman perfectly understood all that sort of thing, the methods and the rules of it; and could lead her clever little gentleman a very pretty minuet, as far as she saw good. They discovered mutual old cousinships by the maternal side, soon had common topics enough: I believe he really entertained a sincere regard and affection for her, in the heart of his theoretic dangling; which latter continued unabated for several years to come, with not a little quizzing and light interest on her part, and without shadow of offense on mine, or on anybody's. Nay, I had my amusements in it too, so naïve, humorous, and pretty were her bits of narratives about it, all her procedures in it so dainty, delicate, and sure—the noble little soul! Suspicion of her nobleness would have been mad in me; and could I grudge her the little bit of entertainment she might be able to extract from this poor harmless sport in a life so grim as she cheerfully had with me? My Jeannie! oh, my bonny little Jeannie! how did I ever deserve so queen-like a heart from thee? Ah me!

Jeffrey's acquaintanceship seemed, and was for the time, an immense acquisition to me, and everybody regarded it as my highest good fortune; though in the end it did not practically amount to much. Meantime it was very pleasant, and made us feel as if no longer cut off and isolated, but fairly admitted, or like to be admitted, and taken in tow by the world and its actualities. Jeffrey had begun to feel some form of bad health at this time (some remains of disease in the trachea, caught on circuit somewhere, "successfully defending a murderess," it was said). He rode almost daily, in intervals of court business, a slow amble, easy to accompany on foot; and I had much walking with him, and many a pleasant sprightly dialogue, cheerful to my fancy (as speech with an important man), but less instructive than I might have hoped. To my regret, he would not talk of his experiences in the world, which I considered would have been so instructive to me, nor of things concrete and current, but was theoretic generally; and seemed bent on, first of all, converting me from what he called my "German mysticism," back merely, as I could perceive, into dead Edinburgh Whigism, skepticism, and materialism; which I felt to be a forever impossible enterprise. We had long discussions and argumentative parryings and thrustings, which I have known continue night after night till two or three in the morning (when I was his guest at Craigcrook, as once or twice happened in coming years): there we went on in brisk logical exercise with all the rest of the house asleep, and parted usually in good-humor, though after a game which was hardly worth the candle. I found him infinitely witty, ingenious, sharp of fence, but not in any sense deep; and used without difficulty to hold my own with him. A pleasant enough exercise, but at last not a very profitable one.

He was ready to have tried anything in practical help of me; and did, on hint given, try two things: vacant "Professorship of Moral Philosophy" at St. Andrews; ditto of something similar (perhaps it was "English Literature") in the new Gower Street University at London; but both (thank Heaven!) came summarily to nothing. Nor were his review articles any longer such an important employment to me, nor had they ever been my least troublesome undertakings—plenty of small discrepancy about details as we went along, though no serious disagreement ever, and his treatment throughout was liberal and handsome. Indeed, he had much patience with me, I must say; for there was throughout a singular freedom in my way of talk with him; and though far from wishing or intending to be disrespectful, I doubt there was at times an unembarrassment and frankness of hitting and repelling, which did not quite beseem our respective ages and positions. He never testified the least offense, but possibly enough remembered it afterward, being a thin-skinned sensitive man, with all his pretended pococurantism and real knowledge of what is called the "world." I remember pleasant strolls out to Craigcrook (one of the prettiest places in the world), where on a Sunday especially I might hope, what was itself a rarity with me, to find a really companionable human acquaintance, not to say one of such quality as this. He would wander about the woods with me, looking on the Firth and Fife Hills, on the Pentlands and Edinburgh Castle and city; nowhere was there such a view. Perhaps he would walk most of the way back with me; quietly sparkling and chatting, probably quizzing me in a kind of way if his wife were with us, as sometimes happened. If I met him in the streets, in the Parliament House, or accidentally anywhere, there ensued, unless he were engaged, a cheerful bit of talk and promenading. He frequently rode round by Comley Bank in returning home: and there I would see him, or hear something pleasant of him. He never rode fast, but at a walk, and his little horse was steady as machinery. He on horseback, I on foot, was a frequent form of our dialogues. I suppose we must have dined sometimes at Craigcrook or Moray Place in this incipient period, but don't recollect.

The incipient period was probably among the best, though for a long while afterwards there was no falling off in intimacy and good-will. But sunrise is often lovelier than noon. Much in this first stage was not yet fulfillment, and was enhanced by the colors of hope. There was the new feeling, too, of what a precious conquest and acquisition had fallen to us, which all the world might envy. Certainly in every sense the adventure was a flattering and cheering one, and did both of us good. I forget how long it had lasted before our resolution to remove to Craigenputtoch came to be fulfilled; it seems to me some six or eight months. The flitting to Craigenputtoch took place in May, 1828; we staid a week in Moray Place (Jeffrey's fine new house there) after our furniture was on the road, and we were waiting till it should arrive and render a new home possible amid the moors and mountains. Jeffrey promised to follow us thither with wife and daughter for three

days in vacation-time ensuing, to see what kind of a thing we were
making of it, which of course was great news.   Doubtless he, like
most of my Edinburgh acquaintances, had been strongly dissuasive
of the step we were taking; but his or other people's arguments
availed nothing, and I have forgotten them.   The step had been
well meditated, saw itself to be founded on irrefragable considerations of health, finance, etc., etc., unknown to by-standers, and could
not be forborne or altered.   "I will come and see you at any rate,"
said Jeffrey, and dismissed us with various expressions of interest,
and no doubt with something of real regret.

Of our history at Craigenputtoch there might a great deal be
written which might amuse the curious; for it was in fact a very
singular scene and arena for such a pair as my darling and me,
with such a life ahead; and bears some analogy to the settlement
of Robinson Crusoe in his desert isle, surrounded mostly by the
wild populations, not wholly helpful or even harmless; and re-
quiring for its equipment into habitability and convenience infinite contrivance, patient adjustment, and natural ingenuity in the
head of Robinson himself.   It is a history which I by no means
intend to write, with such or with any object.   To me there is a
sacredness of interest in it consistent only with *silence*.   It was the
field of endless nobleness and beautiful talent and virtue in her
who is now gone; also of good industry, and many loving and
blessed thoughts in myself, while living there by her side.   Poverty and mean obstruction had given origin to it, and continued
to preside over it, but were transformed by human valor of various sorts into a kind of victory and royalty.   Something of high
and great dwelt in it, though nothing could be smaller and lower
than many of the details.   How blessed might poor mortals be in
the straitest circumstances, if only their wisdom and fidelity to
Heaven and to one another were *adequately* great!   It looks to me
now like a kind of humble russet-coated *epic*, that seven years' settlement at Craigenputtoch, very poor in this world's goods, but
not without an intrinsic dignity greater and more important than
then appeared; thanks very mainly to her, and her faculties and
magnanimities, without whom it had not been possible.   I incline
to think it the poor *best* place that could have been selected for
the ripening into fixity and composure of anything useful which
there may have been in me against the years that were coming.
And it is certain that for living in and thinking in, I have never
since found in the world a place so favorable.   And we were driven
and pushed into it, as if by necessity, and its beneficent though

ugly little shocks and pushes, shock after shock, gradually com-
pelling us thither! "For a divinity doth shape our ends, rough
hew them how we may." Often in my life have I been brought
to think of this, as probably every considering person is; and looking before and after, have felt, though reluctant enough to believe
in the importance or significance of so infinitesimally small an
atom as oneself, that the doctrine of a special providence is in
some sort natural to man. All piety points that way, all logic
points the other; one has in one's darkness and limitation a trembling faith, and can at least with the *voices* say, " *Wir heissen euch
hoffen*," if it be the will of the Highest.

The Jeffreys failed not to appear at Craigenputtoch; their big
carriage climbed our rugged hill roads, landed the three guests—
Charlotte ("Sharlie") with pa and ma—and the clever old valet
maid that waited on them; stood three days under its glazed sheet-
ing in our little back court, nothing like a house got ready for it,
and indeed all the out-houses and appurtenances still in a much
unfinished state, and only the main house quite ready and habita-
ble. The visit was pleasant and successful, but I recollect few or
no particulars. Jeffrey and I rode one day (or perhaps this was
on another visit?) round by the flank of Dunscore Craig, the Shil-
lingland, and Craigenery, and took a view of Loch Gor and the
black moorlands round us, with the Granite mountains of Galloway overhanging in the distance; not a beautiful landscape, but
it answered as well as another. Our party, the head of it especially, was chatty and cheery; but I remember nothing so well as
the consummate art with which my dear one played the domestic
field-marshal, and spread out our exiguous resources, without fuss
or bustle; to cover everything a coat of hospitality and even elegance and abundance. I have been in houses ten times, nay, a
hundred times as rich, where things went not so well. Though
never bred to this, but brought up in opulent plenty by a mother
that could bear no partnership in housekeeping, she, finding it become necessary, loyally applied herself to it, and soon surpassed in
it all the women I have ever seen. My noble one, how beautiful
has our poverty made thee to me! She was so true and frank
withal; nothing of the skulking Balderstone in her. One day at
dinner, I remember, Jeffrey admired the fritters or bits of pancake
he was eating, and she let him know, not without some vestige
of shock to him, that she had made them. "What, you! twist up
the frying-pan and catch them in the air?" Even so, my high
friend, and you may turn it over in your mind! On the fourth or

third day the Jeffreys went, and "carried off our little temporary
paradise," as I sorrowfully expressed it to them, while shutting
their coach door in our back yard; to which bit of pathos Jeffrey
answered by a friendly little sniff of quasi-mockery or laughter
through the nose, and rolled prosperously away.

They paid at least one other visit, probably not just next year,
but the one following. We met them by appointment at Dumfries
(I think in the intervening year), and passed a night with them in
the King's Arms there, which I well enough recollect; huge ill-kept
"head inn," bed opulent in bugs, waiter a monstrous baggy unwieldy old figure, hebetated, dreary, as if parboiled; upon whom
Jeffrey quizzed his daughter at breakfast: "Comes all of eating
eggs, Sharlie; poor man as good as owned it to me." After breakfast he went across with my wife to visit a certain Mrs. Richardson,
authoress of some novels, really a superior kind of woman and much
a lady, who had been an old flame of his, perhaps twenty-five or
thirty years before. "These old loves don't do," said Mrs. Jeffrey,
with easy sarcasm, who was left behind with me. And accordingly there had been some embarrassment I after found, but on both
sides a gratifying of some good though melancholy feelings.

This Mrs. Jeffrey was the American Miss Wilkes, whose marriage
with Jeffrey, or at least his voyage across to marry her, had made
considerable noise in its time. She was mother of this "Sharlie"
(who is now the widow Mrs. Empson, a morbidly shy kind of creature, who lives withdrawn among her children at Harrogate and
such places). Jeffrey had no other child. His first wife, a Hunter
of St. Andrews, had died very soon. This second, the American
Miss Wilkes, was from Pennsylvania, actual brother's daughter
of our *demagogue* "Wilkes." She was sister of the "Commodore
Wilkes" who boarded the *Trent* some years ago, and almost involved
us in war with Yankee-land, during that beautiful Nigger agony
or "civil war" of theirs.* She was roundish-featured, not pretty
but comely, a sincere and hearty kind of woman, with a great deal
of clear natural insight, often sarcastically turned; to which a certain nervous tic or jerk of the head gave new emphasis or singularity; for her talk went roving about in a loose random way, and
hit down like a flail unexpectedly on this or that, with the jerk for

---

* Some years after these words were written, Carlyle read " The Harvard Memorial Biographies." He was greatly impressed by the account of the gallant young
men whose lives are there described, and said to me, " Perhaps there was more in
that matter, after all, than I was aware of."—J. A. F.

accompaniment, in a really genial fashion. She and I were mutual favorites. She liked my sincerity, as I hers. The daughter Charlotte had inherited her nervous infirmity, and indeed I think was partly lame of one arm; for the rest, an inferior specimen to either of her parents; abstruse, suspicious, timid, enthusiastic; and at length, on death of her parents and of her good old jargoning husband, Empson (a long-winded Edinburgh Reviewer, much an adorer of Macaulay, etc.), became quite a morbid, exclusive character, and lives withdrawn as above. Perhaps she was already rather jealous of us? She spoke very little, wore a half-pouting, half-mocking expression, and had the air of a prettyish spoiled child.

The "old love" business finished, our friends soon rolled away, and left us to go home at leisure in our good old gig (value £11), which I always look back upon with a kind of veneration, so sound and excellent was it, though so unfashionable; the conquest of good Alick, my ever shifty brother, which carried us many a pleasant mile till Craigenputtoch ended. Probably the Jeffreys were bound for Cumberland, on this occasion, to see Brougham; of whom, as I remember, Mrs. Jeffrey spoke to me with candor, not with enthusiasm, during that short "old love" absence. Next year, it must have been, they all came again to Craigenputtoch, and with more success than ever.

One of the nights there, on this occasion, encouraged possibly by the presence of poor James Anderson, an ingenuous, simple, youngish man, and our nearest gentleman neighbor, Jeffrey in the drawing-room was cleverer, brighter, and more amusing than I ever saw him elsewhere. We had got to talk of public speaking, of which Jeffrey had plenty to say, and found Anderson and all of us ready enough to hear. Before long he fell into mimicking of public speakers, men unknown, perhaps imaginary generic specimens; and did it with such a felicity, flowing readiness, ingenuity, and perfection of imitation as I never saw equalled, and had not given him credit for before. Our cozy little drawing-room, bright-shining, hidden in the lowly wilderness, how beautiful it looked to us, become suddenly as it were a Temple of the Muses! The little man strutted about full of electric fire, with attitudes, with gesticulations, still more with winged words, often broken-winged, amid our admiring laughter; gave us the windy grandiloquent specimen, the ponderous stupid, the airy ditto, various specimens, as the talk, chiefly his own, spontaneously suggested, of which there was a little preparatory interstice between each two. And the mimicry was so complete, you would have said not his mind only, but his very body became the specimens, his face filled with the expression represented, and his little figure seeming to grow gigantic if the personage required it. At length he gave us the abstruse costive specimen, which had a meaning and no utterance for it, but went about clambering, stumbling, as on a path of loose bowlders, and ended in total down-break, amid peals of the heartiest laughter from us all. This of the aerial little sprite standing there in fatal collapse, with the brightest of eyes sternly gazing into utter nothingness and dumbness, was one of the most tickling and genially ludicrous things I ever saw, and it prettily winded up our little drama. I often thought of it afterwards, and of what a part mimicry plays among human gifts. In its lowest phase no talent can be lower (for even the Papuans and monkeys have it); but in its highest, where it gives you *domicile* in the spiritual world of a Shakspeare or a Goethe, there are only some few that are higher. No clever man, I suppose, is originally without it. Dickens's essential faculty, I often say, is that of a first-rate play-actor. Had he been born twenty or forty years sooner, we should most probably have had a second and greater Mathews, Incledon, or the like, and no writing Dickens.

It was probably next morning after this (one of these mornings it certainly was) that we received, i. e. Jeffrey did (I think through my brother John, then vaguely trying for "medical practice" in London, and present on the scene referred to), a sternly brief letter from poor Hazlitt, to the effect and almost in the words, "Dear sir, I am dying; can you send me £10, and so consummate your many kindnesses to me? W. Hazlitt." This was for Jeffrey; my brother's letter to me, inclosing it, would of course elucidate the situation. Jeffrey, with true sympathy, at once wrote a check for £50, and poor Hazlitt died in peace, from duns at least. He seemed to have no *old* friends about, to have been left in his poor lodging to the humanity of medical people and transient recent acquaintances, and to have died in a grim stoical humor, like a worn-out soldier in hospital. The new doctor people reckoned that a certain Dr. Darling, the first called in, had fatally mistreated him. Hazlitt had just finished his toilsome, unrewarded (not quite worthless) "Life of Napoleon," which at least recorded his own loyal admiration and quasi-adoration of that questionable person; after which he felt excessively worn and low, and was by unlucky Dr. Darling recommended, not to port-wine, brown soup, and the like generous regimen, but to a course of purgatives and blue-pill, which irrecoverably wasted his last remnants of strength, and brought him to his end in this sad way. Poor Hazlitt! he was never admirable to me; but I had my estimation of him, my pity for him; a man recognizably of fine natural talents and aspirations, but of no sound culture whatever, and flung into the roaring caldron of stupid, prurient, anarchic London, there to try if he could find some culture for himself.

This was Jeffrey's last visit to Craigenputtoch. I forget when it was (probably next autumn late) that we made our fortnight's visit to Craigcrook and him. That was a shining sort of affair, but did not in effect accomplish much for any of us. Perhaps, for one thing, we staid too long; Jeffrey was beginning to be seriously incommoded in health, had bad sleep, cared not how late he sate, and we had now more than ever a series of sharp fencing bouts, night after night, which could decide nothing for either of us, except our radical incompatibility in respect of world theory, and the incurable divergence of our opinions on the most important matters. "You are so dreadfully in earnest!" said he to me once or oftener. Besides, I own now I was deficient in reverence to him, and had not then, nor, alas! have ever acquired in my solitary and mostly silent existence, the art of gently saying strong things, or of insinuating my dissent, instead of uttering it right out at the risk of offence or otherwise. At bottom I did not find his the highest kind of insight in regard to any province whatever. In literature he had a respectable range of reading, but discovered little serious study; and had no views which I could adopt in preference [to my own]. On all subjects I had to refuse him the title of deep, and secretly to acquiesce in much that the new opposition party (Wilson, Lockhart, etc., who had broken out so outrageously in "Blackwood" for the last ten years) were alleging against the old excessive Edinburgh hero-worship—an unpleasant fact, which probably was not quite hidden to so keen a pair of eyes. One thing struck me in sad elucidation of his forensic glories. I found that essentially he was always as if speaking to a jury; that the thing of which he could not convince fifteen clear-headed men was to him a nothing, good only to be flung over the lists, and left lying without notice farther. This seemed to me a very sad result of law! For "the highest cannot be spoken of in words," as Goethe truly says, as in fact all truly deep men say or know. I urged this on his consideration now and then, but without the least acceptance. These "stormy sittings," as Mrs. Jeffrey laughingly called them, did not improve our relation to one another. But these were the last we had of that nature. In other respects Edinburgh had been barren; effulgences of

"Edinburgh society," big dinners, parties, we in due measure had; but nothing there was very interesting either to *her* or to me, and all of it passed away as an obliging pageant merely. Well do I remember our return to Craigenputtoch, after night-fall, amid the clammy yellow leaves and desolate rains, with the clink of Alick's stithy alone audible of human, and have marked it elsewhere.

A great deal of correspondence there still was, and all along had been; many Jeffrey letters to me and many to her, which were all cheerfully answered. I know not what has become of all these papers;* by me they never were destroyed, though indeed neither hers nor mine were ever of much importance except for the passing moment. I ought to add that Jeffrey, about this time (next summer I should think), generously offered to confer on me an annuity of £100, which annual sum, had it fallen on me from the clouds, would have been of very high convenience at that time, but which I could not for a moment have dreamt of accepting as gift or subventionary help from any fellow-mortal. It was at once in my handsomest, gratefullest, but brief and conclusive way [declined] from Jeffrey: "Republican equality the silently fixed law of human society at present; each man to live on his own resources, and have an *equality* of economies with every other man; dangerous and not possible, except through cowardice or folly, to depart from said clear rule, till perhaps a better era rise on us again." Jeffrey returned to the charge twice over in handsome enough sort; but my new answer was in briefest words a repetition of the former, and the second time I answered nothing at all, but stood by other topics; upon which the matter dropped altogether. It was not mere pride of mine that frustrated this generous resolution, but sober calculation as well, and correct weighing of the results probable in so dangerous a copartnery as that proposed. In no condition well conceivable to me could such a proposal have been accepted, and though I could not doubt but Jeffrey had intended an act of real generosity, for which I was and am grateful, perhaps there was something in the manner of it that savored of consciousness and of screwing one's self up to the point; less of godlike pity for a fine fellow and his struggles, than of human determination to do a fine action of one's own, which might add to the promptitude of my refusal. He had abundance of money, but he was not of that opulence which could render such an "annuity," in case I should accept it, totally insensible to him; I therefore en-

---

* All preserved, and in my possession.—EDITOR.

deavored all the more to be thankful; and if the heart would not quite do (as was probably the case), forced the intellect to take part, which it does at this day. Jeffrey's beneficence was undoubted, and his gifts to poor people in distress were a known feature of his way of life. I once, some months after this, borrowed £100 from him, my pitiful bits of "periodical literature" incomings having gone awry (as they were too liable to do), but was able, I still remember with what satisfaction, to repay punctually within a few weeks; and this was all of pecuniary chivalry *we* two ever had between us.

Probably he was rather cooling in his feelings towards me, if they ever had been very warm, so obstinate and rugged had he found me, "so dreadfully in earnest!" And now the time of the Reform Bill was coming on; Jeffrey and all high Whigs getting summoned into an official career; and a scene opening which (in effect), instead of irradiating with new glory and value, completely clouded the remaining years of Jeffrey's life. His health had for some years been getting weaker, and proved now unequal to his new honors; that was the fatal circumstance which rendered all the others irredeemable. He was not what you could call ambitious, rather the reverse of that, though he relished public honors, especially if they could be interpreted to signify public love. I remember his great pleasure in having been elected Dean of Faculty, perhaps a year or so before this very thing of Reform agitation, and my surprise at the real delight he showed in this proof of general regard from his fellow-advocates. But now, ambitious or not, he found the career flung open, all barriers thrown down, and was forced to enter, all the world at his back crushing him in.

He was, naturally, appointed Lord Advocate (political president of Scotland), had to get shoved into Parliament—some vacancy created for him by the great Whigs—"Malton, in Yorkshire," the place, and was whirled away to London and public life; age now about fifty-six, and health bad. I remember in his correspondence considerable misgivings and gloomy forecastings about all this, which in my inexperience and the general exultation then prevalent I had treated with far less regard than they merited. He found them too true; and what I, as a by-stander, could not quite see till long after, that his worst expectations were realized. The exciting, agitated scene abroad and at home, the unwholesome hours, bad air, noisy hubbub of St. Stephen's, and at home the incessant press of crowds, and of business mostly new to him, rendered his life completely miserable, and gradually broke down his health altogether. He had some momentary glows of exulta-tion, and dashed off triumphant bits of *letters* to my wife, which I remember we both of us thought somewhat juvenile and idyllic (es-pecially one written in the House of Commons library, just after his "great speech," and "with the cheers of that House still ring-ing in my ears"), and which neither of us pitied withal to the due degree. For there was in the heart of all of them—even of that "great speech" one—a deep misery traceable; a feeling how blessed the old peace and rest would be, and that peace and rest were now fled far away! We laughed considerably at this huge hurly-burly, comparable in certain features to a huge Sorcerer's Sabbath, pros-perously dancing itself out in the distance; and little knew how lucky we were, instead of unlucky (as perhaps was sometimes one's idea in perverse moments), to have no concern with it except as spectators in the shilling gallery or the two-shilling!

About the middle of August, as elsewhere marked, I set off for London with "Sartor Resartus" in my pocket. I found Jeffrey much preoccupied and bothered, but willing to assist me with Book-seller Murray and the like, and studious to be cheerful. He lived in Jermyn Street, wife and daughter with him, in lodgings at £11 a week, in melancholy contrast to the beautiful tenements and perfect equipments they had left in the north. On the ground-floor, in a room of fair size, was a kind of secretary, a blear-eyed, tacit Scotch figure, standing or sitting at a desk with many papers. This room seemed also to be anteroom or waiting-room, into which I was once or twice shown if important company was upstairs. The secretary never spoke; hardly even answered if spoken to, ex-cept by an ambiguous smile or sardonic grin. He seemed a shrewd enough fellow, and to stick faithfully by his own trade. Upstairs on the first floor were the apartments of the family; Lord Advo-cate's bedroom the back portion of the sitting-room, shut off from it merely by a folding-door. If I called in the morning, in quest, perhaps, of letters (though I don't recollect much troubling him in that way), I would find the family still at breakfast, ten A.M. or later; and have seen poor Jeffrey emerge in flowered dressing-gown, with a most boiled and suffering expression of face, like one who had slept miserably, and now awoke mainly to paltry misery and bother; poor official man! "I am made a mere post-office of!" I heard him once grumble, after tearing up several packets, not one of which was internally for himself.

Later in the day you were apt to find certain Scotch people

dangling about, on business or otherwise, Rutherford, the advocate, a frequent figure—I never asked or guessed on what errand; he, florid, fat, and joyous, his old chieftain very lean and dreary. On the whole, I saw little of the latter in those first weeks, and might have recognized more than I did how to me he strove always to be cheerful and obliging, though himself so heavy laden and internally wretched. One day he did my brother John, for my sake (or perhaps for *hers* still more), an easy service which proved very important. A Dr. Baron, of Gloucester, had called one day, and incidentally noticed that "the Lady Clare" (a great though most unfortunate and at length professedly valetudinary lady) "wanted a travelling physician, being bound forthwith to Rome." Jeffrey, the same day, on my calling, asked, "Wouldn't it suit your brother?" and in a day or two the thing was completely settled, and John, to his and our great satisfaction (I still remember him on the coach-box in Regent Circus), under way into his new Roman locality, and what proved his new career. My darling had arrived before this last step of the process, and was much obliged by what her little "Duke" had done. Duke was the name we called him by; for a foolish reason connected with one of Macaulay's swaggering articles in the "Edinburgh Review," and an insolent response to it in "Blackwood." "Horsewhipped by a duke," had said Macaulay of his victim in the article. "Duke! quotha!" answered "Blackwood;" "such a set of dukes!" and hinted that "Duke Macaulay" and "the Duke of Craigcrook" were extremely unheraldic dignitaries, both of them.

By my Jeannie too had come for John and me the last note we ever had from our father. It was full of the profoundest sorrow (now that I recall it), "drawing nigh to the gates of death," which none of us regarded as other than common dispiritment, and the weak chagrin of old age. Ah me, how blind, how indifferent are all of us to sorrows that lie remote from us, and in a sphere not ours! In vain did our brave old father, sinking in the black gulfs of eternity, seek even to convince us that he was sinking. Alone, left alone, with only a tremulous and fitful though eternal star of hope, he had to front that adventure for himself—with an awestruck imagination of it such as few or none of men now know. More valiant soul I have never seen; nor one to whom death was more unspeakably "the King of Terrors." Death, and the Judgment Bar of the Almighty following it, may well be terrible to the bravest. Death with *nothing* of that kind following it, one readily enough finds cases where that is insignificant to very mean and silly natures. Within three months my father was suddenly gone. I might have noticed something of what the old Scotch people used to call *fey* in his last parting with me (though I did not then so read it, nor do superstitiously now, but only *understand* it and the superstition): it is visible in Frederick Wilhelm's Ultimatum too. But nothing of all that belongs to this place!

My Jeannie had brought us *silhouettes* of all the faces she had found at Scotsbrig; one of them (and I find they are all still at Chelsea) is the only outward shadow of my father's face now left me.* Thanks to her for this also, the dear and ever helpful one!

After her arrival, and our settlement in the Miles's lodgings (Ampton Street, Gray's Inn Lane—a place I will go to see if I return), Jeffrey's appearances were more frequent and satisfactory. Very often in the afternoon he came to call, for her sake mainly, I believe, though mostly I was there too; I perceive now his little visits to that unfashionable place were probably the golden item of his bad and troublous day; poor official man, begirt with empty botheration! I heard gradually that he was not reckoned "successful" in public life; that as Lord Advocate the Scotch, with their multifarious business, found him irritable, impatient (which I don't wonder at); that his "great speech" with "the cheers of that House," etc., etc., had been a Parliamentary failure, rather unadapted to the place, and what was itself very mortifying, that the reporters had complained of his "Scotch accent" to excuse themselves for various omissions they had made! His accent was, indeed, singular, but it was by no means Scotch: at his first going to Oxford (where he did not stay long) he had peremptorily crushed down his Scotch (which he privately had in store in excellent condition to the very end of his life, producible with highly ludicrous effect on occasion), and adopted instead a strange, swift, sharp-sounding, fitful modulation, part of it pungent, quasi-latrant, other parts of it cooing, bantery, lovingly quizzical, which no charms of his fine ringing voice (metallic tenor of sweet tone), and of his vivacious rapid looks, and pretty little attitudes and gestures, could altogether reconcile you to, but in which he persisted through good report and bad. Old Braxey (Macqueen, Lord Braxfield), a sad old cynic, on whom Jeffrey used to set me laughing often enough, was commonly reported to have said, on hearing Jeffrey again after that Oxford sojourn, "The laddie has clean tint his Scotch, and found nae English!" which was an exaggerative

---

* Engraved and inserted in this volume.

reading of the fact, his vowels and syllables being elaborately English (or English and *more*, e. g. "heppy," "my lud," etc., etc.), while the tune which he sang them to was all his own.

There was not much of interest in what the Lord Advocate brought to us in Ampton Street; but there was something friendly and home-like in his manners there; and a kind of interest and sympathy in the extra-official fact of his seeking temporary shelter in that obscure retreat. How he found his way thither I know not (perhaps in a cab, if quite lost in his azimuth); but I have more than once led him back through Lincoln's Inn Fields, launched him safe in Long Acre, with nothing but Leicester Square and Piccadilly ahead; and he never once could find his way home; wandered about, and would discover at last that he had got into Lincoln's Inn Fields *again*. He used to tell us sometimes of ministerial things, not often, nor ever to the kindling of any admiration in either of us; how Lord Althorp would bluffly say, etc., etc. (some very dull piece of bluff candor); more sparingly what the aspects and likelihoods were, in which my too Radical humor but little sympathized. He was often unwell, hidden for a week at Wimbledon Park (Lord Althorp's, and then a beautiful secluded place), for quiet and rural air. We seldom called at Jermyn Street; but did once in a damp clammy evening, which I still fondly recollect; ah me! Another ditto evening I recollect being there myself. We were sitting in homely ease by the fire, ourselves four, I the only visitor, when the house-bell rang, and something that sounded like "Mr. Fisher" (Wishaw it should have been) was announced as waiting down stairs; the emotion about whom, on Mrs. Jeffrey's part, and her agitated industry in sorting the apartment in the few seconds still available, struck me somewhat all the more when "Mr. Fisher" himself waddled in, a puffy, thickset, vulgar little dump of an old man, whose manners and talk (talk was of cholera then, threatened as imminent or almost come) struck me as very cool, but far enough from admirable. By the first good chance I took myself away; learned by-and-by that this had been a "Mr. Wishaw," whose name I had sometimes heard of (in connection with Mungo Park's Travels or the like); and long afterwards, on asking old Sterling who or what this Wishaw specially was, "He's a damned old humbug; dines at Holland House," answered Sterling, readily. Nothing real in him but the stomach and the effrontery to fill it, according to his version: which was all the history I ever had of the poor man, whom I never heard of more, nor saw, except that one time.

9 -

We were at first rather surprised that Jeffrey did not introduce me to some of his grand literary figures, or try in some way to be of help to one for whom he evidently had a value. The explanation I think partly was that I myself expressed no trace of aspiration that way; that his grand literary or other figures were clearly by no means so adorable to the rustic, hopelessly Germanized soul as an introducer of one might have wished; and chiefly that in fact Jeffrey did not consort with literary or other grand people, but only with Wishaws and bores in this bad time; that it was practically the very worst of times for him, and that he was himself so heartily miserable as to think me and his other fellow-creatures happy in comparison, and to have no care left to bestow on us. I never doubted his real wish to help me should an opportunity offer, and while it did not, we had no want of him, but plenty of society, of resources, outlooks, and interests otherwise. Truly one might have pitied him this his influx of unexpected dignities, as I hope I in silence loyally sometimes did. So beautiful and radiant a little soul, plunged on the sudden into such a mother of (gilt) dead dogs! But it is often so; and many an envied man fares like that mythic Irishman who had resolved on treating himself to a Sedan-chair, and on whom the mischievous chairmen, giving one another the wink, *left the bottom open* and ran away with him, to the sorrow of his poor shins. "And that's your Sedan-chairs!" said the Irish gentleman, paying his shilling, and satisfied to finish the experiment.

In March or the end of February I set to writing "Johnson;" and having found a steady table (what fettling in that poor room, and how kind and beautiful she was to me!), I wrote it by her side for most part, pushing my way through the mud elements, with a certain glow of victory now and then. This finished, this and other objects and arrangements (Jeffrey much in abeyance, to judge by my memory now so blank), we made our adieus (Irving, Badams, Mill, Leigh Hunt, who was a new acquaintance, but an interesting), and by Birmingham, Liverpool, Scotsbrig, with incidents all fresh in mind to me just now, arrived safely home, well pleased with our London sojourn, and feeling our poor life to a certain degree made richer by it. Ah me! "so strange, so sad, the days that are no more!"

Jeffrey's correspondence continued brisk as ever, but it was now chiefly to her address; and I regarded it little, feeling, as she too did, that it greatly wanted practicality, and amounted mainly to a flourish of fine words, and the pleasant expenditure now and

then of an idle hour in intervals of worry. My time, with little
"Goethe" papers and excerptings (Das Mährchen, etc., etc.), printing of "Sartor" piecemeal in "Fraser," and London correspondings,
went more prosperously than heretofore. Had there been *good
servants* procurable, as there were *not*, one might almost have called
it a happy time, this at Craigenputtoch, and it might have lasted
longer; but permanent we both silently felt it could not be, nor
even very lasting, as matters stood. I think it must have been the
latter part of next year, 1833, when Jeffrey's correspondence with
me sputtered out into something of sudden life again; and something so unlucky that it proved to be essentially death instead!
The case was this: we heard copiously in the newspapers that the
Edinburgh people, in a meritorious scientific spirit, were about re-
modelling their old Astronomical Observatory; and at length that
they had brought it to the proper pitch of real equipment, and that
nothing now was wanting but a fit observer to make it scientific-
ally useful and notable. I had hardly even looked through a telescope, but I had good strength in mathematics, in astronomy, and
did not doubt but I could soon be at home in such an enterprise
if I fairly entered on it. My old enthusiasms, I felt too, were not
dead, though so long asleep. We were eagerly desirous of some
humblest anchorage, in the finance way, among our fellow-creatures; my heart's desire, for many years past and coming, was always to find *any* honest employment by which one might regularly
gain one's daily bread. Often long after this (while hopelessly
writing the "French Revolution," for example, hopelessly of money
or any other success from it), I thought my case so tragically hard:
"could learn to do honestly so many things, nearly all the things I
have ever seen done, from the making of shoes up to the engineer-
ing of canals, architecture of mansions as palatial as you liked, and
perhaps to still higher things of the physical or spiritual kind;
would moreover toil so loyally to do my task right, not wrong, and
am forbidden to try any of them; see the practical world closed
against me as with brazen doors, and must stand here and perish
idle!"

In a word, I had got into considerable spirits about that astronomical employment, fancied myself in the silent midnight inter-
rogating the eternal stars, etc., with something of real geniality—
in addition to financial considerations; and, after a few days, in
the light friendly tone, with modesty and brevity, applying to
my Lord Advocate for his countenance as the first or preliminary
step of procedure, or perhaps it was virtually in his own appoint-

ment—or perhaps, again (for I quite forget), I wrote rather as
inquiring what he would think of me in reference to it? The
poor bit of letter still seems to me unexceptionable, and the answer was prompt and surprising! Almost or quite by return of
post I got not a flat refusal only, but an angry, vehement, almost
shrill-sounding and scolding one, as if it had been a crime and an
insolence in the like of me to think of such a thing. Thing was
intended, as I soon found, for his old Jermyn Street secretary (my
taciturn friend with the blear eyes); and it was indeed a plain in-
convenience that the like of me should apply for it, but not a crime
or an insolence by any means. "The like of me?" thought I, and
my provocation quickly subsided into contempt. For I had in
Edinburgh a kind of mathematical reputation withal, and could
have expected votes far stronger than Jeffrey's on that subject.
But I perceived the thing to be settled, believed withal that the
poor secretary, though blear-eyed when I last saw him, would do
well enough, as in effect I understood he did; that his master
might have reasons of his own for wishing a provisionary settlement to the poor man; and that, in short, I was an outsider, and
had nothing to say to all that. By the first post I accordingly
answered, in the old light style, thanking briefly for at least the
swift dispatch, affirming the maxim *bis dat qui cito dat* even in case
of *refusal*, and good-humoredly enough leaving the matter to rest
on its own basis. Jeffrey returned to it, evidently somewhat in
repentant mood (his tone had really been splenetic, sputtery, and
improper, poor worried man); but I took no notice, and only marked for my own private behoof what exiguous resource of practical
help for me lay in that quarter, and how the economical and useful,
there as elsewhere, would always override the sentimental and or-
namental.

I had internally no kind of anger against my would-be generous
friend. Had not he after all a kind of gratuitous regard for me;
perhaps as much as I for him? Nor was there a diminution of
respect, perhaps only a clearer view how little respect there had
been! My own poor task was abundantly serious, my posture in
it solitary; and I felt that silence would be fittest. Then and subsequently I exchanged one or two little notes of business with Jeffrey, but this of late autumn, 1833, was the last of our sentimental
passages, and may be said to have closed what of correspondence
we had in the friendly or effusive strain. For several years more
he continued corresponding with my wife, and had, I think, to the
end a kind of lurking regard to us, willing to show itself; but our

own struggle with the world was now become stern and grim, not fitly to be interrupted by these theoretic flourishes of epistolary trumpeting: and (toward the finale of "French Revolution," if I recollect) my dearest also gave him up, and nearly altogether ceased corresponding.

What a finger of Providence once more was this of the Edinburgh Observatory; to which, had Jeffrey assented, I should certainly have gone rejoicing. These things really strike one's heart. The good Lord Advocate, who really was pitiable and miserably ill off in his eminent position, showed visible embarrassment at sight of me (in 1834), come to settle in London without furtherance asked or given; and, indeed, on other occasions, seemed to recollect the Astronomical catastrophe in a way which touched me, and was of generous origin or indication. He was quitting his Lord Advocateship, and returning home to old courses and habits, a solidly wise resolution. He always assiduously called on us in his subsequent visits to London; and we had our kind thoughts, our pleasant reminiscences, and loyal pities of the once brilliant man and friend; but he was now practically become little or nothing to us, and had withdrawn as it were to the sphere of the past. I have chanced to meet him in a London party; found him curiously exotic. I used punctually to call if passing through Edinburgh; some recollection I have of an evening, perhaps a night, at Craigcrook, pleasantly hospitable, with Empson (son-in-law) there, and talk about Dickens, etc. Jeffrey was now a judge, and giving great satisfaction in that office; "seldom a better judge," said everybody. His health was weak, and age advancing, but he had escaped his old London miseries, like a sailor from shipwreck, and might now be accounted a lucky man again. The last time I saw him was on my return from Glen Truin in Inverness-shire or Perthshire, and my Ashburton visit there (in 1849 or '50). He was then at least for the time withdrawn from judging, and was reported very weak in health. His wife and he, sauntering for a little exercise on the shore at Newhaven, had stumbled over some cable, and both of them fallen and hurt themselves, his wife so ill that I did not see her at all. Jeffrey I did see after some delay, and we talked and strolled slowly some hours together; but there was no longer stay possible, such the evident distress and embarrassment Craigcrook was in. I had got breakfast on very kind terms from Mrs. Empson, with husband and three or four children (of strange Edinburgh type). Jeffrey himself on coming down was very kind to me, but sadly weak; much worn

away in body, and in mind more thin and sensitive than ever. He
talked a good deal, distantly alluding once to our *changed* courses,
in a friendly (not a very dexterous way), was throughout friendly,
good, but tremulous, thin, almost affecting, in contrast with old
times; grown Lunar now, not Solar any more! He took me, bag-
gage and all, in his carriage to the railway station, Mrs. Empson
escorting, and there said farewell, for the last time as it proved.
Going to the Grange some three or four months after this, I accidentally heard from some newspaper or miscellaneous fellow-pas-
senger, as the news of the morning, that Lord Jeffrey in Edinburgh
was dead. Dull and heavy, somewhere in the Basingstoke localities, the tidings fell on me, awakening frozen memories not a few.
He had died, I afterward heard, with great constancy and firmness;
lifted his finger as if in cheerful encouragement amid the lamenting loved ones, and silently passed away. After that autumn
morning at Craigcrook I have never seen one of those friendly
souls, not even the place itself again. A few months afterwards
Mrs. Jeffrey followed her husband; in a year or two, at Haileybury
(some East India college where he had an office or presidency),
Empson died, " correcting proof-sheets of the ' Edinburgh Review,' "
as appears, " while waiting daily for death "—a most quiet editorial
procedure, which I have often thought of! Craigcrook was sold;
Mrs. Empson with her children vanished mournfully into the dumb
distance; and all was over there, and a life scene once so bright
for us and others had ended, and was gone like a dream.

Jeffrey was perhaps at the height of his reputation about 1816;
his "Edinburgh Review" a kind of Delphic oracle and voice of the
inspired for great majorities of what is called the "intelligent public," and himself regarded universally as a man of consummate
penetration and the *facile princeps* in the department he had chosen
to cultivate and practice. In the half-century that has followed,
what a change in all this! the fine gold become dim to such a degree, and the Trismegistus hardly now regarded as a *Megas* by any
one, or by the generality remembered at all. He may be said to
have begun the rash, reckless style of criticising everything in heaven and earth by appeal to *Molière's maid;* " Do *you* like it ?" " *Don't*
you like it ?" a style which in hands more and more inferior to that
sound-hearted old lady and him, has since grown gradually to such
immeasurable length among us; and he himself is one of the first
that suffers by it. If praise and blame are to be perfected, not in
the mouth of Molière's maid only, but in that of mischievous pre-
cocious babes and sucklings, you will arrive at singular judgments

by degrees! Jeffrey was by no means the supreme in criticism or in anything else; but it is certain there has no critic appeared among us since who was worth naming beside him; and his influence for good and for evil in literature and otherwise has been very great. Democracy, the gradual uprise and rule in all things of roaring million-headed unreflecting, darkly suffering, darkly sinning "Demos," come to call its old superiors to account at its maddest of tribunals; nothing in my time has so forwarded all this as Jeffrey and his once famous "Edinburgh Review."

He was not deep enough, pious or reverent enough, to have been great in literature; but he was a man intrinsically of veracity; said nothing without meaning it to some considerable degree, had the quickest perceptions, excellent practical discernment of what lay before him; was in earnest, too, though not "dreadfully in earnest;" in short, was well fitted to set forth that "Edinburgh Review" (at the dull opening of our now so tumultuous century, and become coryphæus of his generation in the waste, wide-spreading, and incalculable course appointed *it* among the centuries. I used to find in him a finer talent than any he has evidenced in writing. This was chiefly when he got to speak Scotch, and gave me anecdotes of old Scotch Braxfields and vernacular (often enough but not always cynical) curiosities of that type, which he did with a greatness of gusto quite peculiar to the topic, with a fine and deep sense of humor, of real comic mirth, much beyond what was noticeable in him otherwise; not to speak of the perfection of the mimicry, which itself was something. I used to think to myself, "Here is a man whom they have kneaded into the shape of an Edinburgh reviewer, and clothed the soul of in Whig formulas and blue and yellow; but he might have been a beautiful Goldoni too, or something better in that kind, and have given us *comedies* and aerial pictures true and poetic of human life in a far other way." There was something of Voltaire in him, something even in bodily features; those bright-beaming, swift, and piercing hazel eyes, with their accompaniment of rapid keen expression in the other lineaments of face, resembled one's notion of Voltaire; and in the voice, too, there was a fine half-plangent kind of metallic ringing tone which used to remind me of what I fancied Voltaire's voice might have been: "voix sombre et majestueuse," Duvernet calls it. The culture and respective natal scenery of the two men had been very different; nor was their *magnitude* of faculty anything like the same, had their respective kinds of it been much more identical than they were. You could not define Jeffrey to have been more than a potential Voltaire; say "Scotch Voltaire;" with about as much reason (which was not very much) as they used in Edinburgh to call old Playfair the "Scotch D'Alembert." Our Voltaire, too, whatever else might be said of him, was at least worth a large multiple of our D'Alembert. A beautiful little man the former of these, and a bright island to me and to mine in the sea of things, of whom it is now again mournful and painful to take farewell.

[Finished at Mentone, this Saturday, January 19, 1867; day bright as June (while all from London to Avignon seems to be choked under snow and frost); other conditions, especially the internal, not good, but baddish or bad.]

JANE WELSH CARLYLE

JANE WELSH CARLYLE.

" IN the ancient county town of Haddington, July 14, 1801, there was born to a lately wedded pair, not natives of the place, but already reckoned among the best class of people there, a little daughter, whom they named Jane Baillie Welsh, and whose subsequent and final name (her own common signature for many years) was *Jane Welsh Carlyle,* and now so stands, now that she is mine in death only, on her and her father's tombstone in the Abbey Kirk of that town. July 14, 1801; I was then in my sixth year, far away in every sense, now near and infinitely concerned, trying doubtfully after some three years' sad cunctation, if there is anything that I can profitably put on record of her altogether bright, beneficent, and modest little life, and *her,* as my final task in this world."

These are the words in which Mr. Carlyle commenced an intended sketch of his wife's history, three years after she had been taken from him; but finding the effort too distressing, he passed over her own letters, with notes and recollections which he had written down immediately after her death, directing me, as I have already stated,* either to destroy them, or arrange and publish them, as I might think good. I told him afterwards that before I could write any biography either of Mrs. Carlyle or himself, I thought that these notes ought to be printed in the shape in which he had left them, being adjusted merely into some kind of order. He still left me to my own discretion; on myself, therefore, the responsibility rests entirely for their publication. The latter part of the narrative flows on consecutively; the beginning is irregular from the conditions under which Mr. Carlyle was writing. He had requested Miss Geraldine Jewsbury, who had been his wife's most intimate friend, to tell him any biographical anecdotes which she could remember to have heard from Mrs. Carlyle's

---

* See Preface.

lips. On these anecdotes, when Miss Jewsbury gave him as much as she was able to give, Mr. Carlyle made his own observations, but he left them undigested, still for the most part remaining in Miss Jewsbury's words; and in the same words I think it best that they shall appear here, as material which may be used hereafter in some record more completely organized, but for the present serving to make intelligible what Mr. Carlyle has to say about them.

IN MEMORIAM JANE WELSH CARLYLE.*
Ob. April 21, 1866.

She told me that once, when she was a very little girl, there was going to be a dinner party at home, and she was left alone with some tempting custards, ranged in their glasses upon a stand. She stood looking at them, and the thought, "What *would* be the consequence if I should eat one of them?" came into her mind. A whimsical sense of the dismay it would cause took hold of her; she thought of it again, and scarcely knowing what she was about, she put forth her hand, and—took a little from the top of each! She was discovered; the sentence upon her was to eat *all* the remaining custards, and to hear the company told the reason why there were none for them! The poor child hated custards for a long time afterwards.

THE BUBBLY JOCK.

On her road to school, when a very small child, she had to pass a gate where a horrid turkey-cock was generally standing. He always ran up to her, gobbling, and looking very hideous and alarming. It frightened her at first a good deal, and she dreaded having to pass the place; but after a little time she hated the thought of living in fear. The next time she passed the gate, several laborers and boys were near, who seemed to enjoy the thought of the turkey running at her. She gathered herself together, and made up her mind. The turkey ran at her as usual, gobbling and swelling; she suddenly darted at him, and seized him by the throat, and swung him round. The men clapped their hands, and shouted, "Well done, little Jeannie Welsh!" and the Bubbly Jock never molested her again.

LEARNING LATIN.

She was anxious to learn lessons like a boy; and, when a very little thing, she asked her father to let her "learn Latin like a boy." Her mother did not wish her to learn so much; her father always tried to push her forwards; there was a division of opinion on the subject. Jeannie

---

* Described by Mr. Carlyle as Geraldine's Mythic Jottings.

MRS. THOMAS CARLYLE.

went to one of the town scholars in Haddington, and made him teach her a noun of the first declension (" *Penna,* a pen," I think it was). Armed with this, she watched her opportunity; instead of going to bed, she crept under the table, and was concealed by the cover. In a pause of conversation, a little voice was heard, " *Penna,* a pen; *pennæ,* of a pen," etc., and as there was a pause of surprise, she crept out, and went up to her father, saying, " I want to learn Latin; please let me be a boy." Of course she had her own way in the matter.

SCHOOL AT HADDINGTON.

Boys and girls went to the same school; they were in separate rooms, except for Arithmetic and Algebra. Jeannie was the best of the girls at Algebra. Of course she had many devoted slaves among the boys; one of them especially taught her, and helped her all he knew; but he was quite a poor boy, whilst Jeannie was one of the gentry of the place; but she felt no difficulty, and they were great friends. She was fond of doing everything difficult that boys did. There was one particularly dangerous feat to which the boys dared each other; it was to walk on a *very* narrow ledge on the parapet of the bridge overhanging the water; the ledge went in an arch, and the height was considerable. One fine morning Jeannie got up early and went to the Nungate Bridge; she lay down on her face, and crawled from one end of the bridge to the other, to the imminent risk of either breaking her neck or drowning.

One day, in the boys' school-room, one of the boys said something to displease her. She lifted her hand, doubled it, and hit him hard; his nose began to bleed, and in the midst of the scuffle the master came in. He saw the traces of the fray, and said, in an angry voice, " You know, boys, I have forbidden you to fight in school, and have promised that I would flog the next. Who has been fighting this time ?" Nobody spoke, and the master grew angry, and threatened *tawse* all round unless the culprit were given up. Of course no boy would tell of a girl, so there was a pause: in the midst of it Jeannie looked up and said, " Please, I gave that black eye." The master tried to look grave, and pursed up his mouth; but the boy was big, and Jeannie was little, so, instead of the *tawse,* he burst out laughing, and told her she was " a little deevil," and had no business there, and to go her ways back to the girls.

Her friendship with her school-fellow teacher came to an untimely end. An aunt who came on a visit saw her standing by a stile with him, and a book between them. She was scolded, and desired not to keep his company. This made her very sorry, for she knew how good he was to her; but she never had a notion of disobedience in any matter, small or great. She did not know how to tell him or to explain; she thought it shame to tell him he was not thought good enough, so she determined he should imagine it a fit of caprice, and from that day she never spoke to him, or took the least notice; she thought a sudden cessation would pain him less than a gradual coldness. Years and years afterwards, going back on a visit to Haddington, when she was a middle-aged woman, and he was a man married and doing well in the world, she saw him again, and then, for the first time, told him the explanation.

She was always anxious to work hard, and would sit up half the night over her lessons. One day she had been greatly perplexed by a problem in Euclid; she *could not* solve it. At last she went to bed; and in a dream got up and did it, and went to bed again. In the morning she had no consciousness of her dream; but on looking at her slate, there was the problem solved.

She was afraid of sleeping too much, and used to tie a weight to one of her ankles that she might awake. Her mother discovered it; and her father forbade her to rise before five o'clock. She was a most healthy little thing then; only she did her best to ruin her health, not knowing what she did. She always would push everything to its extreme to find out if possible the ultimate consequence. One day her mother was ill, and a bag of ice had to be applied to her head. Jeannie wanted to know the sensation, and took an opportunity when no one saw her to get hold of the bag, and put it on her own head, and kept it on till she was found lying on the ground insensible.

She made great progress in Latin, and was in Virgil when nine years old. She always loved her doll ; but when she got into Virgil she thought it shame to care for a doll. On her tenth birthday she built a funeral pile of lead-pencils and sticks of cinnamon, and poured some sort of perfume over all, to represent a funeral pile. She then recited the speech of Dido, stabbed her doll, and let out all the sawdust; after which she consumed her to ashes, and then burst into a passion of tears.

HER APPEARANCE IN GIRLHOOD.

As a child she was remarkable for her large black eyes with their long curved lashes. As a girl she was extremely pretty—a graceful and beautifully formed figure, upright and supple—a delicate complexion of creamy white with a pale rose tint in the cheeks, lovely eyes full of fire and softness, and with great depths of meaning. Her head was finely formed, with a noble arch, and a broad forehead. Her other features were not regular ; but they did not prevent her conveying all the impression of being beautiful. Her voice was clear, and full of subtle intonations, and capable of great variety of expression. She had it under full control. She danced with much grace ; and she was a good musician. She was ingenious in all works that required dexterity of hand ; she could draw and paint, and she was a good carpenter. She could do anything well to which she chose to give herself. She was fond of logic—too much so; and she had a keen, clear, incisive faculty of seeing through things, and hating all that was make-believe or pretentious. She had good sense that amounted to genius. She loved to learn, and she cultivated all her faculties to the utmost of her power. She was always witty, with a gift for narration; in a word, she was fascinating, and everybody fell in love with her. A relative of hers told me that every man who spoke to her for five minutes felt impelled to make her an offer of marriage! From which it resulted that a great many men were made unhappy. She seemed born "for the destruction of mankind." Another person told me that she was "the most beautiful starry-looking creature that could be imagined," with a peculiar grace of manner and motion that was more charming than beauty. She had a great quantity of very fine silky black hair, and she always had a natural taste for dress. The first thing I ever heard about her was that she dressed well—an excellent gift for a woman.

Her mother was a beautiful woman, and as charming as her daughter, though not so clever. She had the gift of dressing well also. Genius is profitable for all things, and it saves expense. Once her mother was going to some grand fête, and she wanted her dress to be something specially beautiful. She did not want to spend money. Jeannie was intrusted with a secret mission to gather ivy leaves and trails of ivy of different kinds and sizes, also mosses of various kinds, and was enjoined to silence. Mrs. Welsh arranged these round her dress, and the moss formed a beautiful embossed trimming, and the ivy made a graceful scroll-work; the effect was lovely; nobody could imagine of what the trimming was composed, but it was generally supposed to be a French trimming of the latest fashion and of fabulous expense.

She always spoke of her mother with deep affection and great admiration. She said she was so noble and generous that no one ever came near her without being the better. She used to make beautiful presents by saving upon herself—she economized upon herself to be generous to others; and no one ever served her in the least without experiencing her generosity. She was almost as charming and as much adored as her daughter.

Of her *father* she always spoke with reverence; he was the only person who had any real influence over her. But however willful or indulged she might be, *obedience* to her parents—unquestioning and absolute—lay at the foundation of her life. She was accustomed to say that this habit of obedience to her parents was her salvation through life—that she owed all that was of value in her character to this habit as the foundation. Her father, from what she told me, was a man of strong and noble character—very true, and hating all that was false. She always spoke of any praise he gave her as of a precious possession. She loved him with a deep reverence; and she never spoke of him except to friends whom she valued. It was the highest token of her regard when she told any one about her father. She told me that once he was summoned to go a sudden journey to see a patient, and he took her with him. It was the greatest favor and pleasure she had ever had. They travelled at night, and were to start for their return by a very early hour in the morning. She used to speak of this journey as something that made her perfectly happy; and during that journey her father told her that her conduct and character satisfied him. It was not often he praised her; and this unreserved flow of communication was very precious to her. Whilst he went to the sick person, she was sent to bed until it should be time to return. She had his watch that she might know the time. When the chaise came round, the landlady brought her some tea; but she was in such haste not to keep him waiting that she forgot the *watch*, and they had to return several miles to fetch it. This was the last time she was with her father; a few days afterwards he fell ill of typhus fever, and would not allow her to come into the room. She made her way once to him, and he sent her away. He died of this illness, and it was the very greatest sorrow she ever experienced. She always relapsed into a deep silence for some time after speaking of her father. [*Not very correct.* T. C.]

After her father's death they ["*they,*" *no!*] left Haddington, and went to live at *Templand*, near Thornhill, in Dumfries-shire. It was a country house, standing in its own grounds, prettily laid out. The house has been described to me as furnished with a certain elegant thrift which gave it a great charm. I do not know how old she was when her father died,* but she was one with whom years did not signify, they conveyed no meaning as to what she was. Before she was fourteen she wrote a *tragedy* in five acts, which was greatly admired and wondered at; but she never wrote another. She used to speak of it "as just an explosion." I don't know what the title was; she never told me.

She had many ardent lovers, and she owned that some of them had reason to complain. I think it highly probable that if *flirting* were a capital crime, she would have been in danger of being hanged many times over. She told me one story that showed a good deal of character: There was a young man who was very much in love, and I am afraid he had had reason to hope she cared for him: and she only liked him. She refused him decidedly when he proposed; but he tried to turn her from her decision, which showed how little he understood her; for her *will* was very steadfast through life. She refused him peremptorily this time. He then fell ill, and took to his bed, and his mother was very miserable about her son. She was a widow, and had but the one. At last he wrote her another letter, in which he declared that unless she would marry him, he would kill himself. He was in such distraction that it was a very likely thing for him to do. Her mother was very angry indeed, and reproached her bitterly. She was very sorry for the mischief she had done, and took to her bed, and made herself ill with crying. The old servant, Betty, kept imploring her to say just one word to save the young man's mother from her misery. But though she felt horribly guilty, she was not going to be forced or frightened into anything. She took up the letter once more, which she

---

* Eighteen, just gone.

said was very moving, but a slight point struck her; and she put down the letter, saying to her mother: "You need not be frightened; he won't kill himself at all; look here, he has scratched out one word to substitute another. A man intending anything desperate would not have stopped to scratch out a word; he would have put his pen through it, or left it." That was very sagacious, but the poor young man was very ill, and the doctor brought a bad report of him to the house. She suddenly said, "We must go away, go away for some time; he will get well when we are gone." It was as she had said it would be; her going away set his mind at rest, and he began to recover. In the end he married somebody else, and what became of him I forget, though I think she told me more about him.

There was another man whom she had allowed to fall in love, and never tried to hinder him, though she refused to marry him. After many years she saw him again. He was then an elderly man; had made a fortune, and stood high as a county gentleman. He was happily married, and the father of a family. But one day he was driving her somewhere, and he slackened the pace to a walk, and said: "I once thought I would have broken my heart about you, but I think my attachment to you was the best thing that ever happened to me: it made me a better man. It is a part of my life that stands out by itself, and belongs to nothing else. I have heard of you from time to time, and I know what a brilliant lot yours has been, and I have felt glad that you were in your rightful place, and I felt glad that I had suffered for your sake, and I have sometimes thought that if I had known, I would not have tried to turn you into any other path." This, as well as I can render it, is the sense of what he said, gravely and gently, and I admired it very much when she told me: but it seems to me that it was *much* better as she told it to me. Nobody could help loving her, and nobody but was the better for doing so. She had the gift of calling forth the best qualities that were in people.

I don't know at what period she knew Irving, but he loved her, and wrote letters and poetry (very true and touching); but there had been some vague understanding with another person, not a definite engagement, and she insisted that he must keep to it, and not go back from what had once been spoken. There had been just then some trial and a great scandal about a Scotch minister who had broken an engagement of marriage, and she could not bear that the shadow of any similar reproach should be cast on him. Whether, if she had cared for him very much, she could or would have insisted on such punctilious honor, she did not know herself; but anyhow that is what she did. After Irving's marriage, years afterwards, there was not much intercourse between them; the whole course of his life had changed.

I do not know in what year she married, nor anything connected with her marriage. I believe that she brought no money, or very little, at her marriage. Her father had left everything to her, but she made it over to her mother, and only had what her mother gave her. Of course people thought she was making a dreadfully bad match; they only saw the outside of the thing; but she had faith in her own insight. Long afterwards, when the world began to admire her husband, at the time he delivered the "Lectures on Hero-Worship," she gave a little half-scornful laugh, and said, "They tell me things as if they were new that I found out years ago." She knew the power of help and sympathy that lay in her, and she knew she had strength to stand the struggle and pause before he was recognized. She told me that she resolved that he should never write for money, only when he wished it, when he had a message in his heart to deliver, and she determined that she would make whatever money he gave her answer for all needful purposes; and she was ever faithful to this resolve. She bent her faculties to economical problems, and she managed so well that comfort was never absent from her house, and no one looking on could have guessed whether they were rich or poor. Until she married, she had never minded household things; but she took them up when necessary, and accomplished them, as she accomplished everything else she undertook, well and gracefully. Whatever she had to do, she did it with a peculiar personal grace that gave a charm to the most prosaic details. No one who in later years saw her lying on the sofa in broken health, and languor, would guess the amount of energetic hard work she had done in her life. She could do everything and anything, from mending the Venetian blinds to making picture-frames or trimming a dress. Her judgment in all literary matters was thoroughly good; she could get to the very core of a thing, and her insight was like witchcraft.

Some of her stories about her servants in the early times were very amusing, but she could make a story about a broom-handle, and make it entertaining. Here are some things she told me about their residence at Craigenputtoch.

At first on their marriage they lived in a small pretty house in Edinburgh called "Comley Bank." Whilst there her first experience of the difficulties of housekeeping began. She had never been accustomed to anything of the kind; but Mr. Carlyle was obliged to be very careful in diet. She learned to make bread, partly from recollecting how she had seen an old servant set to work; and she used to say that the first time she attempted brown-bread it was with awe. She mixed the dough, and saw it rise; and then she put it into the oven, and sat down to watch the oven door, with feelings like Benvenuto Cellini's when he watched his Perseus put into the furnace. She did not feel too sure what it would come out. But it came out a beautiful crusty loaf, very light and sweet; and proud of it she was. The first time she tried a pudding she went into the kitchen and locked the door on herself, having got the servant out of the road. It was to be a suet pudding—not just a common suet pudding, but something special— and it was good, being made with care by weight and measure with exact-

ness. Whilst they were in Edinburgh they knew everybody worth knowing; Lord Jeffrey was a great admirer of hers, and an old friend; Chalmers,
Guthrie, and many others. But Mr. Carlyle's health and work needed
perfect quietness and absolute solitude. They went to live at the end of
two years at Craigenputtoch—a lonely farm-house belonging to Mrs. Welsh,
her mother. A house was attached to the farm, beside the regular farm-
house. The farm was let; and Mr. and Mrs. Carlyle lived in the house,
which was separated from the farm-yard and buildings by a yard. A garden and out-buildings were attached to it. They had a cow, and a horse,
and poultry. They were fourteen miles from Dumfries, which was the
nearest town. The country was uninhabited for miles round, being all
moor-land, with rocks, and a high steep green hill behind the house. She
used to say that the stillness was almost awful, and that when she walked
out she could hear the sheep nibbling the grass, and they used to look at
her with innocent wonder. The letters came in once a week, which was
as often as they sent into Dumfries. All she needed had to be sent for
there or done without. One day she had desired the farm-servant to bring
her a bottle of yeast. The weather was very hot. The man came back
looking scared, and without the yeast. He said doggedly that he would
do anything lawful for her; but he begged she would never ask him to
fetch such an uncanny thing again, for it had just worked and worked till
it flew away with the bottle! When asked where it was, he replied "it
had a' gane into the ditch, and he had left it there."

Lord Jeffrey and his family came out twice to visit her, expecting, as
he said, to find that she had hanged herself upon a door-nail. But she
did no such thing. It was undoubtedly a great strain upon her nerves,
from which she never entirely recovered; but she lived in the solitude
cheerfully and willingly for six years. It was a much greater trial than it
sounds at first; for Mr. Carlyle was engrossed in his work, and had to
give himself up to it entirely. It was work and thought with which he
had to wrestle with all his might to bring out the truths he felt, and to
give them due utterance. It was his life that his work required, and it
was his life that he gave, and she gave her life too, which alone made such
life possible for him. All those who have been strengthened by Mr. Carlyle's written words—and they have been wells of life to more than have
been numbered—owe to her a debt of gratitude no less than to him. If
she had not devoted her life to him, he could not have worked; and if she
had let the care for money weigh on him, he could not have given his best
strength to teach. Hers was no holiday task of pleasant companionship;
she had to live beside him in silence that the people in the world might
profit by his full strength and receive his message. She lived to see his
work completed, and to see him recognized in full for what he is, and for
what he has done.

Sometimes she could not send to Dumfries for butcher's-meat; and then
she was reduced to her poultry. She had a peculiar breed of very long-

legged hens, and she used to go into the yard amongst them with a long stick, and point out those that were to be killed, feeling, she said, like Fouquier Tinville pricking down his victims.

One winter her servant Grace asked leave to go home to see her parents; there was some sort of a fair held in her village. She went, and was to return at night. The weather was bad, and she did not return. The next morning there was nothing for it but for her to get up to light the fires and prepare breakfast. The house had beautiful and rather elaborate steel grates; it seemed a pity to let them rust, so she cleaned them carefully, and then looked round for wood to kindle the fire. There was none in the house; it all lay in a little out-house across the yard. On trying to open the door, she found it was frozen beyond her power to open it, so Mr. Carlyle had to be roused; it took all his strength, and when opened, a drift of snow six-feet high fell into the hall. Mr. Carlyle had to make a path to the wood-house, and bring over a supply of wood and coal; after which he left her to her own resources.

The fire at length made, the breakfast had to be prepared; but it had to be raised from the foundation. The bread had to be made, the butter to be churned, and the coffee ground. All was at last accomplished, and the breakfast was successful. After breakfast she went about the work of the house, as there was no chance of the servant being able to return. The work fell into its natural routine. Mr. Carlyle always kept a supply of wood ready; he cut it, and piled it ready for her use inside the house; and he fetched the water, and did things she had not the strength to do. The poor cow was her greatest perplexity. She could continue to get hay down to feed it, but she had never in her life milked a cow. The first day the servant of the farmer's wife who lived at the end of the yard milked it for her willingly, but the next day Mrs. Carlyle heard the poor cow making an uncomfortable noise; it had not been milked. She went herself to the byre, and took the pail and sat down on the milking-stool and began to try to milk the cow. It was not at first easy; but at last she had the delight of hearing the milk trickle into the can. She said she felt quite proud of her success; and talked to the cow as though it were a human creature. The snow continued to lie thick and heavy on the ground, and it was impossible for her maid to return. Mrs. Carlyle got on easily with all the house-work, and kept the whole place bright and clean except the large kitchen or house place, which grew to need scouring very much. At length she took courage to attack it. Filling up two large pans of hot water, she knelt down and began to scrub; having made a clean space round the large arm-chair by the fireside, she called Mr. Carlyle and installed him with his pipe to watch her progress. He regarded her beneficently, and gave her from time to time words of encouragement. Half the large floor had been successfully cleansed, and she felt anxious of making a good ending, when she heard a gurgling sound. For a moment or two she took no notice, but it increased, and there was a sound of something falling upon the fire, and instantly a great black thick stream came down the chimney, pouring like a flood along the floor, taking precisely the lately cleaned portion first in its course, and extinguishing the fire. It was too much; she burst into tears. The large fire, made up to heat the water, had melted the snow on the top of the chimney, it came down mingling with the soot, and worked destruction to the kitchen floor. All that could be done was to dry up the flood. She had no heart to recommence her task. She rekindled the fire and got tea ready. That same night her maid came back, having done the impossible to get home. She clasped Mrs. Carlyle in her arms, crying and laughing, saying, "Oh, my dear mistress, my dear mistress, I dreamed ye were deed!"

During their residence at Craigenputtoch she had a good little horse, called "Harry," on which she sometimes rode long distances. She was an excellent and fearless horsewoman, and went about like the women used to do before carriages were invented. One day she received news that Lord Jeffrey and his family, with some visitors, were coming. The letter only arrived the day they were expected (for letters only came in one day in the week). She mounted "Harry" and galloped off to Dumfries to get what was needed, and galloped back, and was all ready and dressed to receive her visitors, with no trace of her thirty-mile ride except the charming history she made of it. She said that "Harry" understood all was needed of him.

She had a long and somewhat anxious ride at another time. Mr. Carlyle had gone to London, leaving her to finish winding up affairs at Craigenputtoch and to follow him. The last day came. She got the money out of the bank at Dumfries, dined with a friend, and mounted her horse to ride to Ecclefechan, where she was to stay for a day or two. Whether she paid no attention to the road or did not know it I don't know; but she *lost* her way: and at dusk found herself entering Dumfries from the *other side*, having made a circuit. She alighted at the friend's house where she had dined, to give her horse a rest. She had some tea herself, and then mounted again to proceed on her journey, fearing that those to whom she was going would be alarmed if she did not appear. This time she made sure she was on the right tack. It was growing dusk, and at a joining of two roads she came upon a party of men half-tipsy, coming from a fair. They accosted her, and asked where she was going, and would she come along with them? She was rather frightened, for she had a good deal of money about her, so she imitated a broad country dialect, and said their road was not hers, and that she had "a gey piece to ride before she got to Annan." She whipped her horse, and took the other road, thinking she could easily return to the right track; but she had again lost her way, and seeing a house with a light in the lower story, she rode up the avenue which led to it. Some women-servants had got up early, or rather late at night, to begin their washing. She knocked at the window. At first they thought it was one of their sweethearts; but when they saw a lady on a horse they thought it a ghost. After a while she got them to listen to her, and when she told them her tale they were vehement in their sympathy, and would have had her come in to refresh herself. They gave her a cup of their tea, and one of them came with her to the gate, and set her face towards the right road. She had actually come back to within a mile of Dumfries once more! The church clocks struck twelve as she set out a third time, and it was after two o'clock in the morning before she arrived, dead tired, she and her horse too, at Ecclefechan, where, however, she had long since been given up. The inmates had gone to bed, and it was long before she could make them hear. After a day or two of repose, she proceeded to join Mr. Carlyle in London. At first they lived in lodgings with some people who were very kind to them, and became much attached to her. They looked upon her as a superior being, of another order, to themselves. The children were brought up to think of her as a sort of fairy lady. One day, a great many years afterwards, when I had come to live in London, it was my birthday, and we resolved to celebrate it "by doing something;" and at last we settled that she should take me to see the daughter of the people she used to lodge with, who had been an affectionate attendant upon her, and who was now very well married, and an extremely happy woman. Mrs. Carlyle said it was a good omen to go and see "a happy woman" on such a day. So she and I, and her dog "Nero," who accompanied her wherever she went, set off to Dalston, where the "happy woman" lived. I forget her name, except that she was called "*Eliza.*" It was washing-day, and the husband was absent; but I remember a pleasant-looking kind woman, who gave us a nice tea, and rejoiced over Mrs. Carlyle, and said she had brought up her children in the hope of seeing her some day. She lived in a house in a row, with little gardens before them. We saw the children, who were like others; and we went home by omnibus; and we had enjoyed our little outing; and Mrs. Carlyle gave me a pretty lace collar, and Bohemian-glass vase, which is still unbroken.

I end these "stories told by herself," not because there are no more. They give some slight indication of the courage and nobleness and fine qualities which lay in her who is gone. Very few women so truly great come into the world at all; and no two like her at the same time. Those who were her friends will only go on feeling their loss and their sorrow more and more every day of their own lives.   G. E. J.

CHELSEA, *May* 20, 1866.

So far Miss Jewsbury. Mr. Carlyle now continues:
Few or none of these narratives are correct in details, but there is a certain mythical truth in all or most of them. That of young

lovers, especially that of flirting, is much exaggerated.   If "flirt" means one who tries to inspire love without feeling it, I do not think she ever was a flirt; but she was very charming, full of grave clear insight, playful humor, and also of honest dignity and pride; and not a few young fools of her own, and perhaps a slightly better station, made offers to her which sometimes to their high temporary grief and astonishment were decisively rejected.   The most serious-looking of those affairs was that of George Rennie, nephew of the first Engineer Rennie, a clever, decisive, ambitious, but quite *un*melodious young fellow, whom we knew afterwards here as sculptor, as M.P. for a while, finally as retired Governor of the Falkland Islands, in which latter character he died here seven or eight years ago.   She knew him thoroughly, had never loved him, but respected various qualities in him, and naturally had some peculiar interest in him to the last.   In his final time he used to come pretty often down to us here, and was well worth talking to on his Falkland or other experiences; a man of sternly sound common-sense (so called), of strict veracity, who much contemned imbecility, falsity, or nonsense wherever met with; had swallowed manfully his many bitter disappointments, and silently awaited death itself for the last year or more (as I could notice), with a fine honest stoicism always complete.   My poor Jane hurried to his house, and was there for three days zealously assisting the widow.

The wooer who would needs die for want of success, was a Fyfe M.D., an extremely conceited, limited, strutting little creature, who well deserved all he got or more.   The end of him had something of tragedy in it, but is not worth recording.

Dods is the "peasant school-fellow's" name, about seven or eight years her senior, son of a nurseryman, now rich abundantly, banker, etc., etc., and an honest, kindly, though clumsy prosaic man.

The story of her being taken as a child to drive with her father has some truth in it, but consists of two stories rolled into one. Child of seven or eight "with watch forgotten," was to the Press Inn (then a noted place, and to her an ever-memorable expedition beside a father almost her divinity); but drive second, almost still more memorable, was for an afternoon of several hours as a young girl of eighteen, over some district of her father's duties.   She waiting in the carriage unnoticed, while he made his visits.   The usually tacit man, tacit especially about his bright daughter's gifts and merits, took to talking with her that day in a style quite new; told her she was a good girl, capable of being useful and precious to him and the circle she would live in; that she must summon her utmost judgment and seriousness to choose her path, and be what he expected of her; that he did not think she had yet seen the life partner that would be worthy of her—in short, that he expected her to be wise as well as good-looking and good; all this in a tone and manner which filled her poor little heart with surprise, and a kind of sacred joy, coming from the man she of all men revered.

Often she told me about this, for it was her last talk with him. On the morrow, perhaps that evening, certainly within a day or two, he caught from some poor old woman patient a typhus fever, which under injudicious treatment killed him in three or four days (September, 1819), and drowned the world for her in the very blackness of darkness. In effect it was her first sorrow, and her greatest of all. It broke her health for the next two or three years, and in a sense almost broke her heart. A father so mourned and loved I have never seen; to the end of her life his title even to me was "he" and "him;" not above twice or thrice, quite in late years, did she ever mention (and then in a quite slow tone), "my father;" nay, I have a kind of notion (beautiful to me and sad exceedingly), she was never as happy again, after that sunniest youth of hers, as in the last eighteen months, and especially the last two weeks of her life, when after wild rain deluges and black tempests many, the sun shone forth again for another's sake with full mild brightness, taking sweet farewell. Oh, it is beautiful to me, and oh, it is humbling and it is sad! Where was my Jeannie's peer in this world? and she fell to me, and I could not screen her from the bitterest distresses! God pity and forgive me! My own burden, too, might have broken a stronger back, had not she been so loyal and loving.

The Geraldine accounts of her childhood are substantially correct, but without the light melodious clearness and charm of a fairy tale all true, which my lost one used to give them in talking to me. She was fond of talking about her childhood; nowhere in the world did I ever hear of one more beautiful, all sunny to her and to me, to our last years together.

That of running on the parapet of the Nungate Bridge (John Knox's old suburb), I recollect well; that of the boy with the bloody nose; many adventures skating and leaping; that of penna, pennæ, from below the table is already in print through Mrs. Oliphant's "Life of Irving." In all things she strove to "be a boy" in education; and yet by natural guidance never ceased to be the prettiest and gracefullest of little girls, full of intelligence, of veracity, vivacity, and bright curiosity; she went into all manner of shops and workshops that were accessible, eager to see and understand what was going on. One morning, perhaps in her third or fourth year, she went into the shop of a barber on the opposite side of the street, back from which by a narrow entrance was her own nice, elegant, quiet home. Barber's shop was empty; my Jeannie went in silently, sate down on a bench at the wall, old barber giving her a kind glance, but no word. Presently a customer came in, was soaped and lathered in silence mainly or altogether, was getting diligently shaved, my bonny little bird as attentive as possible, and all in perfect silence. Customer at length said in a pause of the razor, "How is John so and so now?" "He's deed" (dead), replied barber, in a rough hollow voice, and instantly pushed on with business again. The bright little child burst into tears and hurried out. This she told me not half a year ago.

Her first school-teacher was Edward Irving, who also gave her private lessons in Latin, etc., and became an intimate of her family. It was from him (probably in 1818) that I first heard of her father and her, some casual mention, the loving and reverential tone of which had struck me. Of the father he spoke always as of one of the wisest, truest, and most dignified of men. Of her as a paragon of gifted young girls, far enough from me both, and objects of distant reverence and unattainable longing at that time! The father, whom I never saw, died next year. Her I must have seen first, I think, in June, 1821. Sight forever memorable to me. I looked up at the windows of the old room, in the desolate moonlight of my last visit to Haddington,* five weeks ago come Wednesday next: and the old summer dusk, and that bright pair of eyes inquiringly fixed on me (as I noticed for a moment), came up clear as yesterday, all drowned in woes and death. Her second teacher (Irving's successor) was a Rev. James Brown, who died in India, whom also I slightly knew. The school, I believe, was, and is, at the western end of the Nungate Bridge, and grew famed in the neighborhood by Irving's new methods and managements (adopted as far as might be by Brown), a short furlong or so along paved streets from her father's house. Thither daily at an early hour (perhaps eight A.M. in summer) might be seen my little Jeannie tripping nimbly and daintily along, her little satchel in hand, dressed by her mother (who had a great talent that way) in tasteful simplicity; neat bit of pelisse (light blue sometimes), fastened

---

* Mrs. Carlyle's funeral.

with black belt, dainty little cap, perhaps little beaverkin, with
flap turned up, and, I think, one at least with modest little plume
in it. Fill that figure with electric intellect, ditto love and generous vivacity of all kinds, where in nature will you find a prettier?

At home was opulence without waste, elegance, good sense, silent practical affection, and manly wisdom, from threshold to roof-
tree; no paltriness or unveracity admitted into it. I often told her
how very beautiful her childhood was to me, so authentic-looking
actual, in her charming naïve and humorous way of telling, and
that she must have been the prettiest little Jenny Spinner (Scotch
name for a long-winged, long-legged, extremely bright and airy in-
sect) that was dancing in the summer rays in her time. More enviable lot than all this was I cannot imagine to myself in any
house high or low, in the higher and highest still less than in the
other kind.

Three or four child anecdotes I will mark as ready at this time.

Father and mother returning from some visit (probably to
Nithsdale) along with her (age say four), at the Black Bull, Edinburgh, and were ordering dinner. Waiter, rather solemn personage, inquired, "And what will little missy eat?" " A roasted bumm-
bee" (humming or field bee), answered little missy.

"Mamma, wine makes cozy!" said the little naturalist once at
home (year before, perhaps), while sipping a drop of wine mamma
had given her.

One of the prettiest stories was of the child's first ball, "Dan-
cing-school Ball," her first public appearance, as it were, on the
theatre of the world. Of this, in the daintiest style of kind mockery, I often heard, and have the general image still vivid; but
have lost the express details, or rather, in my ignorance of such
things, never completely understood the details. How the evening was so great; all the higher public, especially the maternal
or paternal sections of it, to see the children dance; and Jeannie
Welsh, then about six, had been selected to perform some *pas seul*
beautiful and difficult, the jewel of the evening, and was privately anxious in her little heart to do it well; how she was dressed to
perfection, with elegance, with simplicity, and at the due hour was
carried over in a clothes-basket (streets being muddy, and no carriage), and landed safe, pretty silks and pumps uninjured.
Through the ball everything went well and smoothly, nothing to
be noted till the *pas seul* came. My little woman (with a look that
I can still fancy) appeared upon the scene, stood waiting for the
music; music began, but also, alas! it was the wrong music, im-

possible to dance that *pas seul* to it. She shook her little head, looked or made some sign of distress. Music ceased, took counsel, scraped; began again; again wrong; hopelessly, flatly impossible. Beautiful little Jane, alone against the world, forsaken by the music, but not by her presence of mind, plucked up her little skirt, flung it over her head, and courtesying in that veiled manner, withdrew from the adventure amidst general applause.

The last of my anecdotes is not easily intelligible except to myself. Old Walter Welsh, her maternal grandfather, was a most picturesque, peculiar, generous-hearted, hot-tempered, abrupt, and impatient old man. I guess she might be about six, and was with her mother on a visit; I know not whether at Capelgill (Moffat Water) or at Strathmilligan. Old Walter, who was of few words, though of very lively thought and insight, had a *burr* in pronouncing his *r*, and spoke in the old style generally. He had taken little Jeannie out to ride on a quiet pony; very pleasant winding ride, and at length, when far enough, old Walter said, "Now we will go back by so and so, etc., to vary the scene." Home at dinner, the company asked her, "Where did you ride to, Pen?" (Pen was her little name there, from paternal grandfather's house, Penfillan, to distinguish her from the other Welshes of Walter's household.) "We rode to *so*, then to *so*," answered she, punctually; "then from *so* returned by *so*, to vah-chry the shane!" At which I suppose the old man himself burst into his cheeriest laugh at the mimicry of tiny little Pen. "Mamma, oh, mamma, don't exposie me," exclaimed she once, not yet got quite the length of speaking, when her mother for some kind purpose was searching under her clothes.

But I intend to put down something about her parentage now, and what of reminiscence must live with me on that head.

John Welsh, farmer, of Penfillan, near Thornhill, Nithsdale, for the greater part of his life, was born, I believe, at Craigenputtoch, December 9, 1757, and was sole heir of that place, and of many ancestors there; my wife's paternal grandfather, of whom she had many pretty things to report, in her pleasant, interesting way; genuine affection blending so beautifully with perfect candor, and with arch recognition of whatever was, comically or otherwise, singular in the subject-matter. Her father's name was also John; which from of old had specially been that of the laird, or of his first-born, as her father was. This is one of the probabilities they used to quote in claiming to come from John Knox's youngest daughter and her husband, the once famous John Welsh, minister of Ayr, etc. A better probability, perhaps, is the topographical one that Craigenputtoch, which by site and water-shed would belong to Galloway, is still part of Dumfries-shire, and did apparently form part of Collieston, fertile little farm still extant, which probably was an important estate when the antique "John Welsh's father" had it in Knox's day: to which Collieston, Craigenputtoch, as moorland, extending from the head of the Glenessland valley, and a two miles farther southward (quite over the slope and down to Orr, the next river), does seem to have been an appendage. My Jeannie cared little or nothing about these genealogies, but seeing them interest me, took some interest in them. Within the last three months (*à propos* of a new life of the famed John Welsh) she mentioned to me some to me new, and still livelier spark of likelihood, which her "Uncle Robert" (an expert Edinburgh lawyer) had derived from reading the old Craigenputtoch law-papers. What this new "spark" of light on the matter was (quite forgotten by me at the time, and looking "new") I in vain strive to recall, and have again forgotten it (swallowed in the sad Edinburgh hurly-burlies of "three months ago," which have now had such an issue!). To my present judgment there is really good likelihood of the genealogy, and likelihood all going that way, but no certainty attained, or perhaps ever attainable. That "famed John Welsh" lies buried (since the end of James I.'s reign) in some church-yard of Eastern London, name of it known, but nothing more. His grandson was minister of Erncray ("Irongray" they please to spell it), near by, in Clavers's bloody time; and there all certainty ends. . . . By her mother's mother, who was a Baillie, of somewhat noted kindred in Biggar country, my Jeannie was further said to be descended from "Sir William Wallace" (the great); but this seemed to rest on nothing but air and vague fireside rumor of obsolete date, and she herself, I think, except perhaps in quizzical allusion, never spoke of it to me at all. Edward Irving once did (1822 or so) in his half-laughing Grandison way, as we three sat together talking. "From Wallace and from Knox," said he, with a wave of the hands: "there's a Scottish pedigree for you!" The good Irving: so guileless, loyal always, and so hoping and so generous.

My wife's grandfather, I can still recollect, died September 20, 1823, aged near sixty-six; I was at Kinnaird (Buller's in Perthshire), and had it in a letter from her: letters from her were almost the sole light-points in my dreary miseries there (fruit of miserable health mainly, and of a future blank and barred to me, as I felt).

Trustfully she gave me details; how he was sixty-three;* hair still raven black, only within a year eyebrows had grown quite white; which had so softened and sweetened the look of his bright glancing black eyes, etc., etc. A still grief lay in the dear letter, too, and much affection and respect for her old grandfather just gone. Sweet and soft to me to look back upon; and very sad now, from the threshold of our own grave. My bonnie darling! I shall follow thee very soon, and then—!

Grandfather's youngest years had been passed at Craigenputtoch; mother had been left a widow there, and could not bear to part with him; elder sisters there were, he the only boy. Jane always thought him to have fine faculty, a beautiful clearness, decision, and integrity of character; but all this had grown up in solitude and vacancy, under the silent skies on the wild moors for most part. She sometimes spoke of his (and her) ulterior ancestors; "several blackguards among them," her old grandfather used to say, "but not one blockhead that I heard of!" Of one, flourishing in 1745, there is a story still current among the country people thereabouts; how, though this laird of Craigenputtoch had not himself gone at all into the Rebellion, he received with his best welcome certain other lairds or gentlemen of his acquaintance who had, and who were now flying for their life; kept them there, as in a seclusion lonelier almost than any other in Scotland; heard timefully that dragoons were coming for them; shot them thereupon instantly away by various well-contrived routes and equipments, and waited his dragoon guests as if nothing were wrong. "Such and such men here with you, aren't they, you—!" said they. "Truly they were, till three hours ago; and they are rebels, say you? Fie, the villains, had I but known or dreamt of that! But come, let us chase immediately; once across the Orr yonder (and the swamps on this side, which look green enough from here), you find firm road, and will soon catch the dogs!" Welsh mounted his galloway, undertook to guide the dragoons through that swamp or "bottom" (still a place that needed guiding in our time, though there did come at last a "solid road and bridge)". Welsh, trotting along on his light galloway, guided the dragoons in such way that their heavy animals sank mostly or altogether in the treacherous element, safe only for a native galloway and man; and with much pretended lamentation, seeing them provided with work that would last till darkness had fallen, rode his ways again. I believe this

* Near sixty-six in fact.

was true in substance, but never heard any of the saved rebels named. Maxwells, etc., who are of Roman-Catholic Jacobite type, abound in those parts : a Maxwell, I think, is feudal superior of Craigen-puttoch. This Welsh, I gather, must have been grandfather of my wife's grandfather. She had strange stories of his wives (three in succession, married perhaps all, especially the second and third, for money), and how he kept the last of them, a decrepit, ill-natured creature, invisible in some corner of his house, and used gravely to introduce visitors to her "gown and bonnet" hanging on a stick as "Mrs. Welsh III." Him his grandson doubtless ranked among the "blackguard" section of ancestry; I suppose his immediate heir may have died shortly after him, and was an unexceptionable man.

In about 1773, friends persuaded the widow of this latter that she absolutely must send her boy away for some kind of schooling, his age now fourteen, to which she sorrowfully consenting, he was despatched to Tynron school (notable at that time), about twelve miles over the hills Nithsdale way, and consigned to a farmer named Hunter, whose kin are now well risen in the world there-abouts, and who was thought to be a safe person for boarding and supervising the young moor-land laird. The young laird must have learned well at school, for he wrote a fine hand (which I have seen), and had acquired the ordinary elements of country education in a respectable way in the course of one year, as turned out. Within one year, February 16, 1774, these Hunters had married him to their eldest girl (about sixteen, four months younger than himself), and his school-days were suddenly completed. This young girl was my Jeannie's grandmother; had, I think, some fourteen chil-dren, mostly men (of whom, or of whose male posterity, none now survive, except the three Edinburgh aunts, youngest of them a month younger than my Jane was); and thus held the poor laird's face considerably to the grindstone all his days. I have seen the grandmother, in her old age and widowhood, a respectable-looking old person (lived then with her three daughters in a house they had purchased at Dumfries); silently my woman never much liked her or hers (a palpably rather tricky, cunning set these, with a turn for ostentation and hypocrisy in them); and was accustomed to divide her uncles (not without some ground, as I could see) into "Welshes," and "Welshes with a cross of Hunter," traceable often-est (not always, though) in their very physiognomy and complex-ion. They are now all gone; the kindred as good as out, only their works following them, *talia, qualia !*

This imprudent marriage reduced the poor young man to pecuniary straits (had to sell first Nether Craigenputtoch, a minor part, in order to pay his sisters' portion, then long years afterwards, in the multitude of his children, Upper Craigenputtoch, or Craigen- puttoch Proper; to my wife's father this latter sale), and though, being a thrifty, vigorous, and solid manager, he prospered hand- somely in his farming, first of Milton, then ditto of Penfillan, the best thing he could try in the circumstances, and got completely above all money difficulties, the same "circumstances" kept him all his days a mere "*terræ filius*," restricted to Nithsdale and his own eyesight (which indeed was excellent) for all the knowledge he could get of this universe; and on the whole had made him—such the contrast between native vigor of faculty and accidental con- traction of arena—a singular and even interesting man, a Scottish Nithsdale son of nature; highly interesting to his bright young granddaughter, with the clear eyesight and valiant true heart like his own, when she came to look into him in her childhood and girl- hood. He was solidly devout, truth's own self in what he said and did, had dignity of manners too; in fact, a really brave, sincere, and honorable soul (reverent of talent, honesty, and sound sense beyond all things), and was silently a good deal respected and honorably es- teemed (though with a grin here and there) in the district where he lived. For chief or almost sole intimate he had the neighbor- ing (biggish) laird, "old Hoggan of Waterside," almost close by Penfillan, whose peremptory ways and angularities of mind and conduct are still remembered in that region sorrowfully and strangely, as his sons, grandsons, and now great-grandson, have distinguished themselves in the other direction there. It was de- lightful to hear my bright one talk of this old grandfather; so kindly yet so playfully, with a vein of fond affection, yet with the justest insight. In his last will (owing to Hunterian artifices and unkind whisperings, as she thought) he had omitted her, though her father had been such a second father to all the rest:—£1000 apiece might be the share of each son and each daughter in this deed of the old man's; and my Jane's name was not found there, as if she too had been dead like her beneficent father. Less care for the money no creature in the world could have had; but the neglect had sensibly grieved her, though she never at all blamed the old man himself, and before long, as was visible, had forgiven the suspected Hunterian parties themselves, "poor souls, so earnest about their paltry bits of interests, which are the vitallest and highest they have! or perhaps it was some whim of the old man himself? Never mind, never mind!" And so, as I could perceive it actually was abolished in that generous heart, and not there any longer before much time had passed. Here are two pictures, a wise and an absurd, two of very many she used to give me of loved old grandfather, with which surely I may end:

1. "Never hire as servant a very poor person's daughter or son; they have seen nothing but confusion, waste, and hugger-mugger, mere want of thrift or method." This was a very wise opinion surely. On the other hand—

He was himself a tall man, perhaps six feet or more, and stood erect as a column. And he had got gradually into his head, supported by such observation as the arena of Kier parish and neighboring localities afforded, the astonishing opinion—

2. That small people, especially short people, were good for nothing; and, in fine, that a man's bodily stature was a correctish sign of his spiritual! Actually so, and would often make new people, aspiring to be acquaintances, stand up and be measured, that he might have their inches first of all. Nothing could drive this out of him; nothing till he went down once to sit on a jury at Dumfries, and for pleader to him had Francis Jeffrey, a man little above five feet, and evidently the cleverest advocate one had ever heard or dreamed of! Ah me! these were such histories and portrayings as I shall never hear again, nor I think did ever hear, for some of the qualities they had.

John Welsh, my wife's father, was born at Craigenputtoch (I now find, which gives the place a new interest to me), April 4, 1776, little more than eighteen years younger than his father or than his mother. His first three years or so (probably till May 26, 1779, when the parents may have moved to Milton in Tynron) must have been passed in those solitudes. At Milton he would see his poor young sister die—wonted playmate sadly vanish from the new hearth—and would no doubt have his thoughts about it (my own little sister Jenny in a similar stage, and my dear mother's tears about her, I can vividly remember; the strangely silent white-sheeted room, white-sheeted linen-curtained bed, and small piece of elevation there, which the joiner was about measuring; and my own outburst into weeping thereupon, I hardly knew why, my first passing glance at the spectre Death). More we know not of the boy's biography there, except that it seems to have lasted about seven years at Milton, and that, no doubt, he had been for three or four years at school there (Tynron school, we may well guess) when (1785 or 6) the family shifted with him to Penfillan. There probably he spent some four or five years more;

Tynron was still his school, to which he could walk, and where I conclude he must have got what Latin and other education he had. Very imperfect he himself, as I have evidence, considered it; and in his busiest time he never ceased to struggle for improvement of it. Touching to know, and how superlatively well, in other far more important respects, nature and his own reflections and inspirations had "educated" him. Better than one of many thousands, as I do perceive! Closeburn (a school still of fame) lay on the other side of Nith River, and would be inaccessible to him, though daily visible.

What year he first went to Edinburgh or entered the University I do not know; I think he was first a kind of apprentice to a famous Joseph or Charles Bell (father of a surgeon still in great practice and renown, though intrinsically stupid, reckoned a sad falling off from his father, in my own time); and with this famed Bell he was a favorite, probably, I think, attending the classes, etc., while still learning from Bell. I rather believe he never took an M.D. degree; but was, and had to be, content with his diploma as surgeon; very necessary to get out of his father's way, and shift for himself in some honest form! Went, I should dimly guess, as assistant to some old doctor at Haddington on Bell's recommendation. Went first, I clearly find, as Regimental Surgeon, August 16, 1796, into the "Perthshire Fencible Cavalry," and served there some three years. Carefully tied up and reposited by pious hands (seemingly in 1819), I find three old "commissions" on parchment, with their stamps, seals, signatures, etc. (Surgeon, August 10, 1796; Cornet, September 15, 1796; and Lieutenant, April 5, 1799), which testify to this; after which there could have been no "assistant-ship" with Somers, but purchase and full practice at once, marriage itself having followed in 1800, the next year after that "Lieutenancy" promotion. I know not in what year (say about 1796, his twentieth year, my first in this world) Somers, finding his assistant able for everything, a man fast gaining knowledge, and acceptable to all the better public, or to the public altogether, agreed in a year or two to demit, withdraw to country retirement, and declare his assistant successor, on condition, which soon proved easy and easier, of being paid (I know not for how long, possibly for life of self and wife, but it did not last long) an annuity of £200. Of which I find trace in that poor account-book (year ——) of his; piously preserved, poor solitary relic [no; several more, "commissions," lancet, etc., found by me since (July 28, '66)], by his daughter ever since his death.

Dr. Welsh's success appears to have been, henceforth and former-ly, swift and constant; till, before long, the whole sphere or sec-tion of life he was placed in had in all senses, pecuniary and other, become his own, and there remained nothing more to conquer in it, only very much to retain by the methods that had acquired it, and to be extremely thankful for as an allotment in this world. A truly superior man, according to all the evidence I from all quar-ters have. A very valiant man, Edward Irving once called him in my hearing. His medical sagacity was reckoned at a higher and higher rate, medical and other honesty as well; for it was by no means as a wise physician only, but as an honorable, exact, and quietly dignified man, punctual, faithful in all points, that he was esteemed over the country. It was three years after his death when I first came into the circle which had been his; and nowhere have I met with a posthumous reputation that seemed to be more unanimous or higher among all ranks of men. The brave man himself I never saw, but my poor Jeannie, in her best moments, often said to me about this or that, "Yes, he would have done it so!" "Ah, he would have liked you!" as her highest praise. "Punctuality" Irving described as a thing he much insisted on. Many miles daily of riding (three strong horses in saddle always, with inventions against frost, etc.); he had appointed the minute everywhere; and insisted calmly on having it kept by all interest-ed parties, high or low. Gravely inflexible where right was con-cerned, and "very independent" where mere rank, etc., attempted to avail upon him. Story of some old valetudinarian Nabal of eminence (Nisbet of Dirleton, immensely rich, continually cocker-ing himself, and suffering); grudging audibly once at the many fees he had to pay (from his annual £30,000): "Dare say I have to pay you £300 a year, Dr. Welsh?" "Nearly or fully that, I should say; all of it accurately for work done." "It's a great deal of money, though!" "Work not demanded, drain of payment will cease of course; not otherwise," answered the doctor, and came home with the full understanding that his Dirleton practice and connection had ended. My Jeannie recollected his quiet report of it to mamma and her, with that corollary; however, after some short experience (or re-experience of London doctors) Nabal Nisbet (who had "butter churned daily for breakfast," as one item of ex-penditure) came back, with the necessary *Peccavi* expressed or un-derstood.

One anecdote I always remember, of the *per contra* kind. Rid-ing along one day on his multifarious business, he noticed a poor wounded partridge fluttering and struggling about, wing or leg, or both, broken by some sportsman's lead. He alighted in his haste, or made the groom alight if he had one, gathered up the poor partridge, looped it gently in his handkerchief, brought it home, and by careful splint and salve and other treatment, had it soon on wing again, and sent it forth healed. This in so grave and practical a man had always in it a fine expressiveness to me; she never told it me but once, long ago; and perhaps we never spoke of it again.

Some time in autumn, 1800 (I think), the young Haddington doctor married; my wife, his first and only child, was born July 14 (Bastile-day, as we often called it), 1801; 64½ years old when she died. The bride was Grace Welsh, of Capelgill (head of Moffat Water in Annandale); her father an opulent store-farmer up there, native of Nithsdale; her mother a Baillie from Biggar region, already deceased. Grace was beautiful, must have been: she continued what might be called beautiful till the very end, in or beyond her sixtieth year. Her Welshes were Nithsdale people of good condition, though beyond her grandfather and uncles, big farmers in Thornhill Parish (the Welshes of Morton Mains for I know not for what length of time before, nor exactly what after, only that it ceased some thirty or perhaps almost fifty years ago, in a tragic kind of way); I can learn nothing certain of them from Rev. Walter of Auchtertool, nor from his sister Maggie here, who are of that genealogy, children of my mother-in-law's brother John; concerning whom perhaps a word afterwards. When the young Haddington doctor and his beautiful Grace had first made acquaintance I know not; probably on visits of hers to Morton Mains, which is but a short step from Penfillan. Acquainted they evidently were, to the degree of mutually saying, "Be it for life, then;" and, I believe, were and continued deeply attached to one another. Sadder widow than my mother-in-law, modestly, delicately, yet discernibly was, I have seldom or never seen, and my poor Jeannie has told me he had great love of her, though obliged to keep it rather secret or undemonstrative, being well aware of her too sensitive, fanciful, and capricious ways.

Mrs. Welsh when I first saw her (1822, as dimly appears) must have been in the third year of her widowhood. I think, when Irving and I entered, she was sitting in the room with Benjamin[*] and my Jane, but soon went away. An air of deep sadness lay on

---

[*] Brother of Dr. Welsh.

her, and on everybody, except on poor dying Benjamin, who affected to be very sprightly, though overwhelmed as he must have felt
himself. His spirit, as I afterwards learned from his niece, who did
not love him or feel grateful to him, was extraordinary, in the
worldly-wise kind. Mrs. Welsh, though beautiful, a tall aquiline
figure, of elegant carriage and air, was not of an intellectual or
specially distinguished physiognomy; and, in her severe costume
and air, rather repelled me than otherwise at that time. A day or
so after, next evening perhaps, both Irving and I were in her drawing-room, with her daughter and her, both very humane to me,
especially the former, which I noticed with true joy for the moment. I was miserably ill in health; miserable every way more
than enough, in my lonely imprisonment, such as it was, which
lasted many years. The drawing-room seemed to me the finest
apartment I had ever sate or stood in; in fact, it was a room of large
and fine proportions, looking out on a garden, on more gardens or
garden walls and sprinkling of trees, across the valley or plain of
the Tyne (which lay hidden), house quite at the back of the town,
facing towards Lethington, etc., the best rooms of it; and everywhere bearing stamp of the late owner's solid temper. Clean, all
of it, as spring-water; solid and correct as well as pertinently ornamented; in the drawing-room, on the tables there, perhaps rather a superfluity of elegant whimwhams. The summer twilight, I
remember, was pouring in rich and soft; I felt as one walking
transiently in upper spheres, where I had little right even to make
transit. Ah me! they did not know of its former tenants when I
went to the house again in April last. I remember our all sitting,
another evening, in a little parlor off the dining-room (down-
stairs), and talking a long time; Irving mainly, and bringing out
me, the two ladies benevolently listening with not much of speech,
but the younger with a lively apprehension of all meanings and
shades of meaning. Above this parlor I used to sleep, in my visits
in after years, while the house was still unsold. Mrs. W. left it at
once, autumn 1826, the instant her Jeannie had gone with me; went
to Templand, Nithsdale, to her father; and turned out to have decided never to behold Haddington more.

  She was of a most generous, honorable, affectionate turn of mind;
had consummate skill in administering a household; a goodish well-
tending intellect—something of real drollery in it, from which my
Jeannie, I thought, might have inherited that beautiful lambency
and brilliancy of soft genial humor, which illuminated her perceptions and discoursings so often to a singular degree, like pure soft

morning radiance falling upon a perfect picture, true to the facts. Indeed, I once said, "Your mother, my dear, has narrowly missed being a woman of genius." Which doubtless was reported by-and-by, in a quizzical manner, and received with pleasure. For the rest, Mrs. W., as above said, was far too sensitive; her beauty, too, had brought flatteries, conceits perhaps ; she was very variable of humor, flew off or on upon slight reasons, and, as already said, was not easy to live with for one wiser than herself, though very easy for one more foolish, if especially a touch of hypocrisy and perfect admiration were superadded. The married life at Haddington, I always understood, was loyal and happy, sunnier than most, but it was so by the husband's softly and steadily taking the command, I fancy, and knowing how to keep it in a silent and noble manner. Old Penfillan (I have heard the three aunts say) reported once, on returning from a visit at Haddington, "He had seen her one evening in fifteen different humors" as the night wore on. This, probably, was in his own youngish years (as well as hers and his son's), and might have a good deal of satirical exaggeration in it. She was the most exemplary nurse to her husband's brother William, and to other of the Penfillan sons who were brought there for help or furtherance. William's stay lasted five years, three of them involving two hours daily upon the spring deal (a stout elastic plank of twenty or thirty feet long, on which the weak patient gets himself shaken, and secures exercise), she herself, day after day, doing the part of trampler, which perhaps was judged useful or as good as necessary for her own health. William was not in all points a patient one could not have quarrelled with, and my mother-in-law's quiet obedience I cannot reckon other than exemplary—even supposing it was partly for her own health too. This I suppose was actually the case ; she had much weak health, more and more towards the end of life. Her husband had often signally helped her by his skill and zeal; once, for six months long, he, and visibly he alone, had been the means of keeping her alive. It was a bad inflammation or other disorder of the liver; liver disorder was cured, but power of digestion had ceased. Doctors from Edinburgh, etc., unanimously gave her up; food of no kind would stay a moment on the stomach; what can any mortal of us do ? Husband persisted; found food that would stay (arrowroot perfectly pure ; if by chance, your pure stock being out, you tried shop arrowroot, the least of starch in it declared it futile), for six months kept her alive and gathering strength on those terms, till she rose again to her feet. "He much loved her,"

said my Jeannie, "but none could less love what of follies she had."
Not a few, though none of them deep at all, the good and even noble soul! How sadly I remember now, and often before now, the
time when she vanished from her kind Jane's sight and mine, never more to meet us in this world! It must have been in autumn,
1841; she had attended Jane down from Templand* to Dumfries,
probably I was up from Scotsbrig (but don't remember); I was, at
any rate, to conduct my wife to Scotsbrig that night, and on the
morrow or so thence for London. Mrs. W. was unusually beautiful,
but strangely sad too, eyes bright, and as if with many tears behind them. Her daughter too was sad, so was I at the sadness of
both, and at the evidently boundless feeling of affection which
knew not how to be kind enough. Into shops, etc., for last gifts
and later than last; at length we had got all done, and withdrew
to sister Jean's to order the gig and go. She went with us still,
but feeling what would now be the kindest, heroically rose (still
not weeping), and said Adieu there. We watched her, sorrowful both of us, from the end window, stepping, tall and graceful,
feather in bonnet, etc., down Lochmaben gate, casting no glance
back, then vanishing to rightward, into High Street (bonnet feather, perhaps, the last thing), and she was gone forever. *Ay de mi!*
Ay de mi! What a thing is life, bounded thus by death! I do
not think we ever spoke of this, but how could either of us ever
forget it at all?

Old Walter Welsh, my wife's maternal grandfather, I had seen
twice or thrice at Templand before our marriage, and for the next
six or seven years, especially after our removal to Craigenputtoch,
he was naturally a principal figure in our small circle. He liked
his granddaughter cordially well; she had been much about him on
visits and so forth from her early childhood, a bright merry little
grig, always pleasant in the troubled atmosphere of the old grandfather. "Pen" (Penfillan Jeannie, for there was another) he used
to call her to the last; mother's name in the family was "Grizzie"
(Grace). A perfect true affection ran through all branches, my poor
little "Pen" well included and returning it well. She was very
fond of old Walter (as he privately was of her), and got a great
deal of affectionate amusement out of him. Me, too, he found much
to like in, though practically we discorded commonly on two points:
1°, that I did and would smoke tobacco; 2°, that I could not and
would not drink with any freedom whiskey punch, or other liquid

---

* House in Nithsdale, where Mrs. Welsh's father lived.

stimulants, a thing breathing the utmost poltroonery in some section of one's mind, thought Walter always. He for himself cared nothing about drink, but had the rooted idea (common in his old circles) that it belonged in some indissoluble way to good-fellowship. We used to presently knit up the peace again, but tiffs of reproach from him on this score would always arise from time to time, and had always to be laughed away by me, which was very easy, for I really liked old Walter heartily, and he was a continual genial study to me over and above; microcosm of old Scottish life as it had been, and man of much singularity and real worth of character, and even of intellect too if you saw well. He abounded in contrasts; glaring oppositions, contradictions, you would have said, in every element of him, yet all springing from a single centre (you might observe), and honestly uniting themselves there. No better-natured man (sympathy, sociality, honest loving-kindness towards all innocent people), and yet of men I have hardly seen one of hotter, more impatient temper. Sudden, vehement, break-ing out into fierce flashes of lightning when you touched him the wrong way. Yet they were flashes only, never bolts, and were gone again in a moment, and the fine old face beaming quietly on you as before. Face uncommonly fine, serious, yet laughing eyes, as if inviting you in, bushy eyebrows, face which you might have called picturesquely shaggy, under its plenty of gray hair, beard itself imperfectly shaved here and there; features mas-sive yet soft (almost with a tendency to pendulous or flabby in parts), and nothing but honesty, quick ingenuity, kindliness, and frank manhood as the general expression. He was a most simple man, of stunted utterance, burred with his r, and had a chewing kind of way with his words, which, rapid and few, seemed to be forcing their way through laziness or phlegm, and were not ex-tremely distinct till you attended a little (and then, aided by the face, etc., they were extremely and memorably brave, old Walter's words, so true, too, as honest almost as my own father's, though in a strain so different). Clever things Walter never said or attempt-ed to say, not wise things either in any shape beyond that of sin-cerely accepted commonplace; but he very well knew when such were said by others, and glanced with a bright look on them, a bright dimpling chuckle sometimes (smudge of laughter, the Scotch call it, one of the prettiest words and ditto things), and on the whole hated no kind of talk but the unwise kind. He was seri-ous, pensive, not more, or sad, in those old times. He had the prettiest laugh (once, or at most twice, in my presence) that I can

remember to have seen, not the loudest, my own father's still rarer
laugh was louder far, though perhaps not more complete, but his
was all of artillery-thunder, *feu de joie* from all guns as the main
element, while in Walter's there was audible something as of infinite flutes and harps, as if the vanquished themselves were invited or compelled to partake in the triumph. I remember one
such laugh (quite forget about what), and how the old face looked
suddenly so beautiful and young again. "Radiant ever young
Apollo," etc., of Teufelsdröckh's laugh is a reminiscence of that.
Now when I think of it, Walter must have had an immense fund
of inarticulate gayety in his composition, a truly fine sense of the
ridiculous (excellent sense in a man, especially if he never cultivate it, or be conscious of it, as was Walter's case); and it must
have been from him that my Jane derived that beautiful light of
humor, never going into folly, yet full of tacit fun, which spontaneously illuminated all her best hours. Thanks to Walter, she was
of him in this respect; my father's laugh, too, is mainly mine, a
grimmer and inferior kind; of my mother's beautifully sportive
vein, which was a third kind, also hereditary I am told, I seem to
have inherited less, though not nothing either, nay, perhaps at
bottom not even less, had my life chanced to be easier or joyfuller.
"Sense of the ridiculous" (worth calling such; i. e. "brotherly
sympathy with the downward side") is withal very indispensable
to a man; Hebrews have it not, hardly any Jew creature, not even
blackguard Heine, to any real length—hence various misqualities
of theirs, perhaps most of their qualities, too, which have become
historical. This is an old remark of mine, though not yet written
anywhere.

Walter had been a buck in his youth, a high-prancing horseman,
etc.; I forget what image there was of him, in buckskins, pipe
hair-dressings, grand equipments, riding somewhither (with John
Welsh of Penfillan, I almost think ?), bright air image, from some
transient discourse I need not say of whom. He had married a
good and beautiful Miss Baillie (of whom already), and settled with
her at Capelgill, in the Moffat region, where all his children were
born, and left with him young, the mother having died, still in the
flower of her age, ever tenderly remembered by Walter to his last
day (as was well understood, though mention was avoided). From
her my Jeannie was called "Jane Baillie Welsh" at the time of our
marriage, but after a good few years, when she took to signing
"Jane Welsh Carlyle," in which I never hindered her, she dropped
the "Baillie," I suppose as too long. I have heard her quiz about

the "unfortunate Miss Baillie" of the song at a still earlier time. Whether Grace Welsh was married from Capelgill I do not know. Walter had been altogether prosperous in Capelgill, and all of the family that I knew (John, a merchant in Liverpool, the one remaining of the sons, and Jeannie, the one other daughter, a beautiful "Aunt Jeannie," of whom a word by-and-by) continued warmly attached to it as their real home in this earth, but at the renewal of leases (1801 or so) had lost it in a quite provoking way. By the treachery of a so-called friend, namely : friend a neighboring farmer, perhaps, but with an inferior farm, came to advise with Walter about rents, probably his own rent first, in this general time of leasing. "I am thinking to offer so-and-so, what say you? what are you going to offer, by-the-bye ?" Walter, the very soul of fidelity himself, made no scruple to answer, found by-and-by that this precious individual had thereupon himself gone and offered for Capelgill the requisite few pounds more, and that, according to fixed customs of the estate, he and not Walter was declared tenant of Capelgill henceforth. Disdain of such scandalous conduct, astonishment and quasi-horror at it, could have been stronger in few men than in Walter, a feeling shared in heartily and irrevocably by all the family, who, for the rest, seldom spoke of it, or hardly ever, in my time, and did not seem to hate the man at all, but to have cut him off as non-extant, and left him unmentioned. Perhaps some Welsh he too, of a different stock? There were Moffat country Welshes, I observed, with whom they rather eagerly (John of Liverpool eagerly) disclaimed all kinship, but it might be on other grounds. This individual's name I never once heard, nor was the story touched upon except by rare chance and in the lightest way.

After Capelgill, Walter had no more farming prosperity ; I believe he was unskilful in the arable kind of business, certainly he was unlucky, shifted about to various places (all in Nithsdale, and I think on a smaller and smaller scale, Castlehill in Durisdeer, Strathmilligan in Tynron, ultimately Templand), and had gradually lost nearly all his capital, which at one time was of an opulent extent (actual number of thousands quite unknown to me), and felt himself becoming old and frail, and as it were thrown out of the game. His family meanwhile had been scattered abroad, seeking their various fortune ; son John to Liverpool (where he had one or perhaps more uncles of mercantile distinction), son William to the West Indies (?) and to early death, whom I often heard lamented by my mother-in-law ; these and possibly others who were not known to me. John by this time had, recovering out of one bit of very bad luck, got into a solid way of business, and was, he alone of the brothers, capable of helping his father a little on the pecuniary side. Right willing to do it, to the utmost of his power or farther. A most munificent, affectionate, and nobly honorable kind of man, much esteemed by both Jane and me, foreign as his way of life was to us.

Besides these there was the youngest daughter, now a woman of thirty or so, the excellent "Aunt Jeannie," so lovable to both of us, who was said to resemble her mother ("nearly as beautiful, all but the golden hair"—Jeannie's was fine flaxen, complexion of the fairest), who had watched over and waited on her father through all his vicissitudes, and everywhere kept a comfortable, frugally effective, and even elegant house round him, and in fact let no wind visit him too roughly. She was a beautifully, patient, ingenious, and practically thoughtful creature, always cheerful of face, suppressing herself and her sorrows, of which I understood there had been enough, in order to screen her father, and make life still soft to him. By aid of John, perhaps slightly of my mo- ther-in-law, the little farm of Templand (Queensberry farm, with a strong but gaunt and inconvenient old stone house on it) was leased and equipped for the old man. House thoroughly repaired, garden, etc., that he might still feel himself an active citizen, and have a civilized habitation in his weak years. Nothing could be neater, trimmer, in all essential particulars more complete than house and environment, under Aunt Jeannie's fine managing, had in a year or two grown to be. Fine sheltered, beautifully useful, garden in front, with trellises, flower-work, and stripe of the clean- est river shingle between porch and it. House all clean and com- plete like a new coin, steadily kept dry (by industry), bedroom and every part; old furniture (of Capelgill) really interesting to the eye, as well as perfect for its duties. Dairy, kitchen, etc., nothing that was fairly needful or useful could you find to be wanting; the whole had the air, to a visitor like myself, as of a rustic idyl, (the seamy side of it all strictly hidden by clever Aunt Jeannie ; I think she must have been, what I often heard, one of the best house- keepers in the world). Dear, good little beauty ; it appears, too, she had met with her tragedies in life ; one tragedy hardest of all upon a woman, betrothed lover flying off into infamous treason, not against her specially, but against her brother and his own hon- or and conscience (brother's partner he was, if I recollect rightly, and fled with all the funds, leaving £12,000 of minus), which anni-

hilated him for her, and closed her poor heart against hopes of
that kind at an early period of her life. Much lying on her mind,
I always understood, while she was so cheery, diligent, and helpful
to everybody round her. I forget, or never knew, what time they
had come to Templand, but guess it may have been in 1822 or
shortly after; dates of Castlehill and Strathmilligan I never knew,
even order of dates; last summer I could so easily have known
(deaf-and-dumb "Mr. Turner," an old Strathmilligan acquaintance,
recognized by her in the Dumfries Railway Station, and made to
speak by paper and pencil, I writing for her because she could
not). Oh me! oh me! where is now that summer evening, so beautiful, so infinitely sad and strange! The train rolled off with her
to Thornhill [Holmhill], and that too, with its setting sun, is gone.
I almost think Durisdeer (Castlehill) must have been last before
Templand; I remember passing that quaint old kirk (with village
hidden) on my left one April evening, on the top of a Dumfries
coach from Edinburgh, with reveries and pensive reflections which
must have belonged to 1822 or 1823. Once, long after, on one of
our London visits, I drove thither sitting by her, in an afternoon,
and saw the gypsy village for the first time, and looked in with
her at the fine Italian sculptures on the Queensberry tomb through
a gap in the old kirk wall. Again a pensive evening, now so beautiful and sad.

From childhood upwards she seemed to have been much about
these homes of old Walter, summer visits almost yearly, and after
her father's death, like to be of longer continuance. They must
have been a quiet, welcome, and right wholesome element for her
young heart and vividly growing mind; beautiful simplicity and
rural Scottish nature in its very finest form, frugal, elegant, true,
and kindly; *simplex munditiis* nowhere more descriptive both for
men and things. To myself, summoning up what I experienced
of them, there was a real gain from them as well as pleasure.
Rough nature I knew well already, or perhaps too well, but here
it was reduced to cosmic, and had a victorious character which was
new and grateful to me, well-nigh poetical. The old Norse kings,
the Homeric grazier sovereigns of men, I have felt in reading of
them as if their ways had a kinship with these (unsung) Nithsdale
ones. Poor "Aunt Jeannie" sickened visibly the summer after our
marriage (summer, 1827), while we were there on visit. My own
little Jeannie, whom nothing could escape that she had the interest to fix her lynx-eyed scrutiny upon, discovered just before our
leaving that her dear aunt was dangerously ill, and indeed had

long been, a cancer—tumor, now evidently cancerous—growing on
her breast for twelve years past, which, after effort, she at last
made the poor aunt confess to. We were all (I myself by sympathy, had there been nothing more) thrown into consternation, made
the matter known at Liverpool, etc., to everybody but old Walter,
and had no need to insist on immediate steps being taken. My
mother-in-law was an inmate there, and probably in chief command (had moved thither, quitting Haddington for good, directly
on our marriage); she at once took measures, having, indeed, a
turn herself for medicining and some skill withal. That autumn
Aunt Jeannie and she came to Edinburgh, had a furnished house
close by us, in Comley Bank, and there the dismal operation was
performed, successfully the doctors all said; but alas! Dim sorrow rests on those weeks to me. Aunt Jeannie showed her old
heroism, and my wife herself strove to hope, but it was painful,
oppressive, sad; twice or so I recollect being in the sick-room, and
the pale yet smiling face, more excitation in the eyes than usual;
one of the times she was giving us the earnest counsel (my Jane
having been consulting) "to go to London, clearly, if I could—if
they would give me the professorship there." (Some professorship
in Gower Street, perhaps of Literature, which I had hoped vaguely, not strongly at all, nor ever formally declaring myself, through
Jeffrey, from his friend Brougham and consorts, which they were
kind enough to dispose of otherwise.) My own poor little Jeannie!
my poor pair of kind little Jeannies! Poor Templand Jeannie
went home again, striving to hope, but sickened in winter, worsened
when the spring came, and summer, 1838, was still some weeks off
when she had departed. It must have been in April or March of
1828. The funeral at Crawfurd I remember sadly well; old Walter,
John, and two sons (Walter of Auchtertool, and Alick now successor in Liverpool), with various old Moffat people, etc., etc., at
the inn at Crawfurd; pass of Dalveen with Dr. Russell in the dark
(holding candles, both of us, inside the chaise), and old Walter's
silent sorrow and my own as we sat together in the vacant parlor
after getting home. "Hah, w'll no see her nae mair!" murmured
the old man, and that was all I heard from him. I think.

Old Walter now fell entirely to the care of daughter "Grizzie,"
who was unweariedly attentive to him, a most affectionate daughter, an excellent housewife too, and had money enough to support
herself and him in their quiet, neat, and frugal way. Templand
continued in all points as trim and beautiful as ever; the old man
made no kind of complaint, and in economics there was even an

improvement. But the old cheery patience of daughter "Jeannie," magnanimously effacing herself, and returning all his little spirits of smoke in the form of lambent kindly flame and radiant light upon him, was no longer there; and we did not doubt but he sometimes felt the change. Templand has a very fine situation; old Walter's walk, at the south end of the house, was one of the most picturesque and pretty to be found in the world. Nith valley (river half a mile off, winding through green holms, now in its borders of clean shingle, now lost in pleasant woods and rushes) lay patent to the S., the country sinking perhaps 100 feet rather suddenly; just beyond Templand, Kier, Penpont, Tynron, lying spread across the river, all as in a map, full of cheerful habitations, gentlemen's mansions, well-cultivated farms and their cottages and appendages, spreading up in irregular slopes and gorges against the finest range of hills; Barjarg with its trees and mansion atop; to your left hand Tynron Down, a grand massive lowland mountain (you might call it), with its white village at the base (behind which in summer-time was the setting of the sun for you); one big pass (Glen-shinnel, with the clearest river-water I ever saw out of Cumberland) bisecting this expanse of heights, and leading you by the Clove ("cloven?") of Maxwellton, into Glencairn valley, and over the Black Craig of Dunscore (Dun-scoir= Black hill), and to Craigenputtoch if you chose. Westward of Tynron rose Drumlanrig Castle and woods, and the view, if you quite turned your back to Dumfries, ended in the Lothers, Leadhills, and other lofty mountains, water-shed and boundary of Lanarkshire and Dumfriesshire, rugged, beautifully piled sierra, winding round into the eastern heights (very pretty too), which part Annandale from Nithsdale. [Alas! what is the use of all this, here and now?] Closeburn, mansion, woods, greeneries, backed by brown steep masses, was on the southeastern side, house, etc., hiding it from Walter's walk. Walk where you liked, the view you could reckon unsurpassable, not the least needing to be "surpassed." Walter's walk special (it never had any name of that kind; but from the garden he glided mostly into it, in fine days, a small green seat at each end of it, and a small ditto gate, easy to open and shut) was not above 150 yards long; but he sauntered and walked in it as fancy bade him (not with an eye to "regimen," except so far as "fancy" herself might unconsciously point that way); took his newspapers (Liverpool, sent by John) to read there in the sunny seasons; or sat silent, but with a quietly alert look, contemplating the glorious panorama of "sky-covered earth" in that part, and mildly reaping his poor bit of harvest from it without needing to pay rent!

We went over often from Craigenputtoch: were always a most welcome arrival, surprise oftenest, and our bits of visits, which could never be prolonged, were uniformly pleasant on both sides. One of our chief pleasures, I think almost our chief, during those moor-land years. Oh, those pleasant gig-drives, in fine leafy twilight, or deep in the night sometimes, ourselves two alone in the world, the good "Larry" faring us (rather too light for the job, but always soft and willing), how they rise on me now, benignantly luminous from the bosom of the grim dead night! Night! what would I give for one, the very worst of them, at this moment! Once we had gone to Dumfries, in a soft misty December day (for a portrait which my darling wanted, not of herself!); a bridge was found broken as we went down, brook unsafe by night; we had to try "Cluden (Lower Cairn) Water" road, as all was mist and pitch-dark-ness, on our return, road unknown except in general, and drive like no other in my memory. Cairn hoarsely roaring on the left (my darling's side); "Larry," with but one lamp-candle (for we had put out the other, lest both might fall done), bending always to be straight in the light of that; I really anxious, though speaking only hopefully; my darling so full of trust in me, really happy and opulently interested in these equipments; in these poor and dan-gerous circumstances how opulent is a nobly royal heart! She had the worthless "portrait" (pencil sketch by a wandering Ger-man, announced to us by poor and hospitable Mrs. Richardson, once a "novelist" of mark, much of a gentlewoman, and well loved by us both) safe in her reticule; "better far than none," she cheerful-ly said of it, and the price, I think, had been 5s., fruit of her thrift too:—well, could California have made me and her so rich, had I known it (sorry gloomy mortal) just as she did? To noble hearts such wealth is there in poverty itself, and impossible without pov-erty! I saw ahead, high in the mist, the minarets of Dunscore Kirk, at last, glad sight; at Mrs. Broatch's cozy rough inn we got "Larry" fed, ourselves dried and refreshed (still seven miles to do, but road all plain); and got home safe, after a pleasant day in spite of all. Then the drive to Boreland once (George Welsh's, "Uncle George," youngest of the Penfillans); heart of winter, intense calm frost, and through Dumfries, at least 35 miles for poor "Larry" and us; very beautiful that too, and very strange, past the base of towering New Abbey, huge ruins, piercing grandly into the silent frosty sunset, on this hand, despicable cow-house of

Presbyterian kirk on that hand (sad new contrast to Devorgilla's old bounty), etc., etc. Of our drive home again I recollect only her invincible contentment, and the poor old cotter woman offering to warm us with a flame of dry broom, "A'll licht a bruim couev, if ye'll please to come in!" Another time we had gone to "Dumfries Cattle Show" (first of its race, which are many since); a kind of lark on our part, and really entertaining, though the day proved shockingly wet and muddy; saw various notabilities there, Sir James Grahame (baddish, proud man, we both thought by physiognomy, and did not afterwards alter our opinion much), Ramsay Macculloch (in sky-blue coat, shiningly on visit from London), etc., etc., with none of whom, or few, had we right (or wish) to speak, abundantly occupied with seeing so many fine specimens, biped and quadruped. In afternoon we suddenly determined to take Templand for the night (nearer by some miles, and weather still so wet and muddy); and did so, with the best success, a right glad surprise there. Poor Huskisson had perished near Liverpool, in first trial of the railway, I think, the very day before; at any rate we heard the news, or at least the full particulars there, the tragedy (spectacular mostly, but not quite, or inhumanly in any sense) of our bright glad evening there.

The Liverpool children first, then "Uncle John" himself for a fortnight or so, used to come every summer, and stir up Templand's quietude to us by-standers in a purely agreeable way. Of the children I recollect nothing almost; nothing that was not cheerful and auroral matutinal. The two boys, Walter and Alick, came once on visit to us, perhaps oftener; but once I recollect their lying quiet in their big bed till eleven A.M., with exemplary politeness, for fear of awakening me who had been up for two hours, though everybody had forgotten to announce it to them. We ran across to Templand rather oftener than usual on these occasions, and I suppose staid a shorter time.

My Jeannie had a great love and regard for her "Uncle John," whose faults she knew well enough, but knew to be of the surface all, while his worth of many fine kinds ran in the blood, and never once failed to show in the conduct when called for. He had all his father's veracity, integrity, abhorrence of dishonorable behavior; was kind, munificent, frank, and had more than his father's impetuosity, vehemence, and violence, or perhaps was only more provoked (in his way of life), to exhibit these qualities now and then. He was cheerful, musical, politely conversible; truly a genial, harmonious, loving nature; but there was a roar in him

too like a lion's. He had had great misfortunes and provocations;
his way of life in dusty, sooty, ever noisy Liverpool, with its din-
nerings, wine-drinkings, dull evening parties issuing in whist, was
not his element, few men's less, though he made not the least complaint of it (even to himself, I think): but his heart, and all his
pleasant memories and thoughts, were in the breezy hills of Moffat-
dale, with the rustic natives there, and their shepherdings, hunt-
ings (brock and fox), and solitary fishings in the clear streams. It
was beautiful to see how he made some pilgriming into those or the
kindred localities; never failed to search out all his father's old
herdsmen (with a sovereign or two for each, punctual as fate), and
had a few days' fishing as one item. He had got his schooling at
Closeburn ; was, if not very learned, a very intelligent, inquiring
kind of man ; could talk to you instructively about all manner of
practical things, and loved to talk with the intelligent, though
nearly all his life was doomed to pass itself with the stupid or
commonplace sort, who were intent upon nothing but "getting on,"
and giving dinners or getting them. Rarely did he burst out into
brief fiery recognition of all this; yet, once at least, before my
time, I heard of his doing so in his own drawing-room, with brevity, but with memorable emphasis and fury. He was studiously
polite in general, always so to those who deserved it, not quite always to those who did not.

His demeanor in his bankruptcy, his and his wife's (who, for the
rest, though a worthy, well-intending, was little of an amiable
woman), when the villain of a partner eloped, and left him pos-
sessor of a minus £12,000, with other still painfuller items (sister
Jeannie's incurable heart, for example), was admitted to be beautiful. Creditors had been handsome and gentle, aware how the
case stood; household with all its properties and ornaments left
intact, etc. Wife rigorously locked all her plate away ; husband
laboriously looked out for a new course of business; ingeniously
found or created one, prospered in it, saving every penny possible ;
thus, after perhaps seven or eight years, had a great dinner: all
the plate out again, all the creditors there, and under every man's
cover punctual sum due, payment complete to every creditor;
"Pocket your checks, gentlemen, with our poor warmest thanks,
and let us drink better luck for time coming!" He prospered always afterwards, but never saved much money; too hospitable, far
too open-handed, for that; all his dinners, ever since I knew him,
were given (never dined out, he), and in more than one instance, to
our knowledge, ruined people were lifted up by him (one widow

cousin, one orphan, youngest daughter of an acquaintance, e. g.) as if they had been his own; sunk possibly enough mainly or altogether into his hands, and were triumphantly (with patience and in silence) brought through. No wonder my darling liked this uncle, nor had I the least difficulty in liking him.

Once I remember mounting early, almost with the sun (a kind hand expediting, perhaps sending me), to breakfast at Templand, and spend the day with him there. I rode by the shoulder of the Black Craig (Dunscore Hill), might see Dumfries with its cap of early kitchen smoke, all shrunk to the size of one's hat, though there were 11,000 souls in it, far away to the right; descended then by Cairn, by the Clove of Maxwellton (where at length came roads), through fragrant grassy or bushy solitudes; at the Bridge of Shinnel, looked down into the pellucid glassy pool, rushing through its rock chasms, and at a young peasant woman, pulling potatoes by the brink, chubby infant at her knee—one of the finest mornings, one of the pleasantest rides; and arrived at Templand in good time and trim for my hosts. The day I forget; would be spent wholesomely wandering about, in rational talk on indifferent matters. Another time, long after, new from London then, I had wandered out with him, his two pretty daughters, and a poor good cousin called Robert Macqueen attending. We gradually strolled into Crichop Linn (a strange high-lying chasmy place, near Closeburn); there pausing, well aloft, and shaded from the noon sun, the two girls, with their father for octave accompaniment, sang us "The Birks of Aberfeldy" so as I have seldom heard a song; voices excellent and true, especially his voice and native expression given; which stirred my poor London-fevered heart almost to tears. One earlier visit from London, I had driven up, latish, from Dumfries, to see my own little woman, who was there among them all. No wink could I sleep; at length about three A.M., reflecting how miserable I should be all day, and cause only misery to the others, I (with leave had) rose, yoked my gig, and drove away the road I had come. Morning cold and surly, all mortals still quiet, except unhappy self; I remember seeing towards Auldgarth, within a few yards of my road, a vigilant industrious heron, mid-leg deep in the Nith stream, diligently fishing, dabbing its long bill and hungry eyes down into the rushing water (tail up stream), and paying no regard to my wheels or me. The only time I ever saw a hernshaw ("herrin'shouw" the Annandalers call it) actually fishing. *Cætera desunt;* of Dumfries, of the day there, and its sequences, all trace is gone. It must have been soon after French Revolution Book;

nerves all inflamed and torn up, body and mind in a most hag-rid-den condition (too much their normal one those many London years).

Of visits from Templand there were not so many; but my darling (hampered and gyved as we were by the *genius loci* and its difficulties) always triumphantly made them do. She had the genius of a field-marshal, not to be taken by surprise, or weight of odds, in these cases! Oh, my beautiful little guardian spirit! Twice at least there was visit from Uncle John in person and the Liverpool strangers, escorted by mother; my mother, too, was there one of the times. Warning I suppose had been given; night-quarters, etc., all arranged. Uncle John and boys went down to Orr Water, I attending without rod, to fish. Tramping about on the mossy brink, uncle and I awoke an adder; we had just passed its under-ground hole; alarm rose, looking round, we saw the vile, sooty-looking, fatal, abominable wretch, towering up above a yard high (the only time I ever saw an adder); one of the boys snatched a stray branch, hurried up from behind, and with a good hearty switch or two broke the creature's back.

Another of these dinner days, I was in the throes of a review article ("Characteristics," was it ?), and could not attend the sport; but sauntered about, much on the strain, to small purpose; dinner all the time that I could afford. Smoking outside at the dining-room window, "Is not every day the conflux of two eternities," thought I, "for every man ?" Lines of influence from all the past and stretching onwards into all the future, do intersect there. That little thoughtkin stands in some of my books; I recollect being thankful (scraggily thankful) for the day of small things.

We must have gone to Craigenputtoch early in May, 1828. I remember passing our furniture carts (my father's carts from Scotsbrig, conducted by my two farming brothers) somewhere about Elvanfoot, as the coach brought us two along. I don't remember our going up to Craigenputtoch, a day or two after, but do well remember what a bewildering heap it all was for some time after.

Geraldine's Craigenputtoch stories are more mythical than any of the rest. Each consists of two or three, in confused exaggerated state, rolled with new confusion into one, and given wholly to her, when perhaps they were mainly some servant's in whom she was concerned. That of the kitchen door, which could not be closed again on the snowy morning, etc., that is a fact very visible to me yet; and how I, coming down for a light to my pipe, found Grace Macdonald (our Edinburgh servant, and a most clever and complete one) in tears and despair, with a stupid farm-servant endeavoring vainly by main force to pull the door to, which, as it had a frame round it, sill and all, for keeping out the wind, could not be shut except by somebody from within (me, e. g.) who would first clear out the snow at the sill, and then, with his best speed, shut; which I easily did. The washing of the kitchen floor, etc. (of which I can remember nothing), must have been years distant, under some quite other servant, and was probably as much of a joyous half frolic as of anything else. I can remember very well her coming in to me, late at night (eleven or so), with her first loaf, looking mere triumph and quizzical gayety: "See!" The loaf was excellent, only the crust a little burnt; and she compared herself to Cellini and his Perseus, of whom we had been reading. From that hour we never wanted excellent bread. In fact, the saving charm of her life at Craigenputtoch, which to another young lady of her years might have been so gloomy and vacant, was that of conquering the innumerable practical problems that had arisen for her there; all of which, I think all, she triumphantly mastered. Dairy, poultry-yard, piggery; I remember one exquisite pig, which we called Fixie ("Quintus Fixlein" of Jean Paul), and such a little ham of it as could not be equalled. Her cow gave twenty-four quarts of milk daily in the two or three best months of summer; and such cream, and such butter (though, oh! she had such a problem with that; owing to a bitter herb among the grass, not known of till long after by my heroic darling, and she triumphed over that too)! That of milking with her own little hand, I think, could never have been necessary, even by accident (plenty of milk-maids within call), and I conclude must have had a spice of frolic or adventure in it, for which she had abundant spirit. Perfection of housekeeping was her clear and speedy attainment in that new scene. Strange how she made the desert blossom for herself and me there; what a fairy palace she had made of that wild moor-land home of the poor man! In my life I have seen no human intelligence that so genuinely pervaded every fibre of the human existence it belonged to. From the baking of a loaf, or the darning of a stocking, up to comporting herself in the highest scenes or most intricate emergencies, all was insight, veracity, graceful success (if you could judge it), fidelity to insight of the fact given.

We had trouble with servants, with many paltry elements and objects, and were very poor; but I do not think our days there were sad, and certainly not hers in especial, but mine rather. We read together at night, one winter, through "Don Quixote" in the original; Tasso in ditto had come before; but that did not last very long. I was diligently writing and reading there; wrote most of the "Miscellanies" there, for Foreign, Edinburgh, etc., Reviews (obliged to keep several strings to my bow), and took serious thought about every part of every one of them. After finishing an article, we used to get on horseback, or mount into our soft old gig, and drive away, either to her mother's (Templand, fourteen miles off) or to my father and mother's (Scotsbrig, seven or six and thirty miles)—the pleasantest journeys I ever made, and the pleasantest visits. Stay perhaps three days; hardly ever more than four; then back to work and silence. My father she particularly loved, and recognized all the grand rude worth and immense originality that lay in him. Her demeanor at Scotsbrig, throughout in fact, was like herself, unsurpassable; and took captive all those true souls, from oldest to youngest, who by habit and type might have been so utterly foreign to her. At Templand or there, our presence always made a sunshiny time. To Templand we sometimes rode on an evening, to return next day early enough for something of work; this was charming generally. Once I remember we had come by Barjarg, not by Auldgarth (Bridge), and were riding, the Nith then in flood, from Penfillan or Penpont neighborhood; she was fearlessly following or accompanying me, and there remained only one little arm to cross, which did look a thought uglier, but gave me no disturbance, when a farmer figure was seen on the farther bank or fields, earnestly waving and signalling (could not be heard for the floods); but for whom we should surely have had some accident, who knows how bad! Never rode that water again, at least never in flood, I am sure.

We were not unhappy at Craigenputtoch; perhaps these were our happiest days. Useful, continual labor, essentially successful; that makes even the moor green. I found I could do fully twice as much work in a given time there as with my best effort was possible in London, such the interruptions, etc. Once, in the winter-time, I remember counting that for three months there had not been any stranger, not even a beggar, called at Craigenputtoch door. In summer we had sparsely visitors, now and then her mother, or my own, once my father, who never before had been so far from his birth-place as when here (and yet "knew the world" as few of his time did, so well had he looked at what he did see). At Auldgarth Brig, which he had assisted to build when a lad of fifteen, and which was the beginning of all good to him, and to all his brothers (and to me), his emotion, after fifty-five years, was described to me as strong, conspicuous, and silent. He delighted us, especially her, at Craigenputtoch, himself evidently thinking of his latter end, in a most intense, awe-stricken, but also quiet and altogether human way. Since my sister Margaret's death he had been steadily sinking in strength, though we did not then notice it. On August 12 (for the grouse's sake) Robert Welsh, her uncle, was pretty certain to be there, with a tag-raggery of Dumfries Writers, dogs, etc., etc., whom, though we liked him very well, even I, and much more she, who had to provide, find beds, etc., felt to be a nuisance. I got at last into the way of riding off, for some visit or the like, on August 12, and unless "Uncle Robert" came in person, she also would answer, "Not at home."

An interesting relation to Goethe had likewise begun in Comley Bank first, and now went on increasing; "boxes from Weimar" (and "to," at least once or twice) were from time to time a most sunny event; I remember her making for Ottilie a beautiful Highland bonnet (bright blue velvet, with silvered thistle, etc.), which gave plenty of pleasure on both hands. The sketch of Craigenputtoch* was taken by G. Moir, advocate (ultimately sheriff, professor, etc., "little Geordie Moir," as we called him), who was once and no more with us. The visit of Emerson from Concord, and our quiet night of clear fine talk, was also very pretty to both of us. The Jeffreys came twice, expressly, and once we went to Dumfries by appointment to meet them in passing. Their correspondence was there a steadily enlivening element. One of the visits (I forget whether first or last, but from Hazlitt, London, there came to Jeffrey a death-bed letter one of the days, and instead of "£10," £50 went by return); Jeffrey, one of the nights, young laird of Stroquhan present, was, what with mimicry of speakers, what with other cleverness and sprightliness, the most brilliantly amusing creature I have ever chanced to see. One time we went to Craigcrook, and returned their visit, and, as I can now see, staid at least a week too long. His health was beginning to break; he and I had, nightly, long arguments (far too frank and equal on my side, I can now see with penitence) about moral matters, perhaps till two or three A.M. He was a most gifted, prompt, ingenious little man (essentially a dramatic genius, say a melodious Goldoni or more, but made into a Scotch advocate and Whig); never a

* Sent to Goethe, and engraved under Goethe's direction for the German translation of Carlyle's "Life of Schiller."

deeply serious man. He discovered here, I think, that I could not
be "converted," and that I was of thoughtlessly rugged rustic
ways, and faultily irreverent of him (which, alas, I was). The correspondence became mainly hers by degrees, but was, for years
after, a cheerful, lively element, in spite of Reform Bills and officialities (ruinous to poor Jeffrey's health and comfort) which, before
long, supervened. We were at Haddington on that Craigcrook
occasion, staid with the Donaldsons at Sunnybank (*hodie* Tenter-
field), who were her oldest and dearest friends (hereditarily and
otherwise) in that region. I well remember the gloom of our arrival back to Craigenputtoch, a miserable, wet, windy November
evening, with the yellow leaves all flying about, and the sound of
brother Alick's stithy (who sometimes amused himself with smith-
work, to small purpose), clink, clinking solitary through the blus-
tering element. I said nothing, far was she from ever, in the like
case, saying anything. Indeed, I think we at once re-adjusted ourselves, and went on diligently with the old degree of industry and
satisfaction.

"Old Esther," whose death came one of our early winters, was a
bit of memorability in that altogether vacant scene. I forget the
old woman's surname (perhaps McGeorge?), but well recall her
lumpish heavy figure (lame of a foot), and her honest, quiet, not
stupid countenance of mixed ugliness and stoicism. She lived
about a mile from us in a poor cottage of the next farm (Corson's,
of Nether Craigenputtoch; very stupid young brother, now minister in Ayrshire, used to come and bore me at rare intervals); Esther had been a laird's daughter riding her palfrey at one time, but
had gone to wreck, father and self—a special "misfortune" (so
they delicately name it), being of Esther's own producing. "Misfortune" in the shape ultimately of a solid tall ditcher, very good
to his old mother Esther, had, just before our coming, perished
miserably one night on the shoulder of Dunscore Hill (found dead
there next morning), which had driven his poor old mother up to
this thriftier hut, and silent mode of living, in our moor-land part
of the parish. She did not beg, nor had my Jeannie much to have
given her of help (perhaps on occasion milk, old warm clothes, etc.),
though always very sorry for her last sad bereavement of the stalwart affectionate son. I remember one frosty kind of forenoon,
while walking meditative to the top of our hill (now a mass of
bare or moor-land whinstone crag, once a woody wilderness, with
woody mountain in the middle of it, "Craigenputtick, or the stone
mountain," "Craig" of the "Puttick," puttick being a sort of

hawk, both in Galloway speech and in Shakspeare's old English ; " Hill forest of the Putticks," now a very bare place), the universal silence was complete, all but one click-clack, heard regularly like a far-off spondee or iambus rather, " click-clack," at regular intervals, a great way to my right. No other sound in nature ; on looking sharply I discovered it to be old Esther on the highway, crippling along towards our house most probably. Poor old soul, thought I, what a desolation! but you will meet a kind face too, perhaps! heaven is over all.

Not long afterwards, poor old Esther sank to bed ; death-bed, as my Jane (who had a quick and sure eye in these things) well judged it would be. Sickness did not last above a ten days ; my poor wife zealously assiduous, and with a minimum of fuss or noise. I remember those few poor days ; as full of human interest to her (and through her to me), and of a human pity, not painful, but sweet and genuine. She went walking every morning, especially every night, to arrange the poor bed, etc. (nothing but rudish hands, rude though kind enough, being about), the poor old woman evidently gratified by it, and heart-thankful, and almost to the very end giving clear sign of that. Something pathetic in poor old Esther and her exit—nay, if I rightly bethink me, that " click-clack " pilgrimage had in fact been a last visit to Craigenputtoch with some poor bit of crockery (small gray-lettered butter plate, which I used to see) " as a wee memorandum o' me, mem, when I am gane!" "Memorandum" was her word; and I remember the poor little platter for years after. Poor old Esther had awoke, that frosty morning, with a feeling that she would soon die, that " the bonny leddy" had been "unco' guid" to her, and that there was still that "wee bit memorandum." Nay, I think she had, or had once had, the remains or complete ghost of a "fine old riding-habit," once her own, which the curious had seen : but she had judged it more polite to leave to the parish. Ah me!

The gallop to Dumfries and back on "Larry," an excellent, well-paced, well-broken, loyal little horse of hers (thirteen hands or so, an exceeding favorite, and her last), thirty good miles of swift canter at the least, is a fact which I well remember, though from home at the moment. Word had come (to her virtually, or properly perhaps) that the Jeffreys, three and a servant, were to be there day after to-morrow, perhaps to-morrow itself; I was at Scotsbrig, nothing ready at all (and such narrow means to get ready anything, my darling heroine!). She directly mounted "Larry," who "seemed to know that he must gallop, and faithfully did it;" laid her plans while galloping; ordered everything at Dumfries; sent word to me express; and galloped home, and stood victoriously prepared at all points to receive the Jeffreys, who, I think, were all there on my arrival. The night of her express is to me very memorable for its own sake. I had been to Burnswark (visit to good old Grahame, and walk of three miles to and three from); it was ten P.M. of a most still and fine night when I arrived at my father's door, heard him making worship, and stood meditative, gratefully, lovingly, till he had ended; thinking to myself how good and innocently beautiful and peaceful on the earth is all this, and it was the last time I was ever to hear it. I must have been there twice or oftener in my father's time, but the sound of his pious Coleshill (that was always his tune), pious psalm and prayer, I never heard again. With a noble politeness, very noble when I consider they kept all that in a fine kind of remoteness from us, knowing (and somehow forgiving us completely) that we did not think of it quite as they. My Jane's express would come next morning; and of course I made "Larry" ply his hoofs.

The second ride, in Geraldine, is nearly altogether mythical, being in reality a ride from Dumfries to Scotsbrig (two and a half miles beyond "Ecclefechan," where none of us ever passed), with some loss of road within the last five miles (wrong turn at Hodden Brig, I guessed), darkness (night-time in May), money, etc., and "terror" enough for a commonplace young lady, but little or nothing of real danger, and terror not an element at all, I fancy, in her courageous mind. "Larry," I think, cannot have been her horse (half-blind two years before in an epidemic, through which she nursed him fondly, she once "kissing her cheek" in gratitude, she always thought), or "Larry" would have known the road, for we had often ridden and driven it. I was at that time gone to London in quest of houses.

My last considerable bit of writing at Craigenputtoch was "Sartor Resartus;" done, I think, between January and August, 1830; my sister Margaret had died while it was going on. I well remember when and how (at Templand one morning) the germ of it rose above ground. "Nine months," I used to say, it had cost me in writing. Had the perpetual fluctuation, the uncertainty and unintelligible whimsicality, of Review Editors not proved so intolerable, we might have lingered longer at Craigenputtoch, "perfectly left alone, and able to do more work, beyond doubt, than elsewhere." But a book did seem to promise some respite from that, and perhaps further advantages. Teufelsdröckh was ready; and (first days of August) I decided to make for London. Night before going, how I still remember it! I was lying on my back on the sofa in the drawing-room, she sitting by the table (late at night, packing all done, I suppose): her words had a guise of sport, but were profoundly plaintive in meaning. "About to depart, who knows for how long, and what may have come in the interim!" this was her thought, and she was evidently much out of spirits. "Courage, dearie, only for a month!" I would say to her in some form or other. I went, next morning early, Alick driving: embarked at Glencaple Quay; voyage as far as Liverpool still vivid to me; the rest, till arrival in London, gone mostly extinct: let it! The beggarly history of poor "Sartor" among the blockheadisms is not worth recording or remembering—least of all here! In short, finding that whereas I had got £100 (if memory serve) for "Schiller" six or seven years before, and for "Sartor" at least thrice as good, I could not only not "get £200" but even get no "Murray" or the like to publish it on "half profits" (Murray a most stupendous object to me; tumbling about, eyeless, with the evidently strong wish to say "yes and no;" my first signal experience of that sad human predicament); I said, "We will make it no, then; wrap up our MS.; wait till this Reform Bill uproar abate; and see, and give our brave little Jeannie a sight of this big Babel, which is so altered since I saw it last (in 1824–25)." She came right willingly, and had, in spite of her ill-health, which did not abate, but the contrary, an interesting, cheery, and, in spite of our poor arrangements, really pleasant winter here. We lodged in Ampton Street, Gray's Inn Lane, clean and decent pair of rooms, and quiet, decent people (the daughter is she whom Geraldine speaks of as having, I might say, fallen in love with her, wanted to be our servant at Craigenputtoch, etc.), reduced from wealth to keeping lodgings, and prettily resigned to it; really good people. Visitors, etc., she had in plenty; John Mill one of the most interesting, so modest, ardent, ingenuous, ingenious, and so very fond of me at that time! Mrs. Basil Montague (already a correspondent of hers), now accurately seen, was another of the distinguished. Jeffrey, Lord Advocate, often came on an afternoon; never could learn his road to and from the end of Piccadilly, though I showed it him again and again. In the evening, miscellany of hers and mine, often dullish had it not been for her, and the light she had shed on everything. I wrote "Johnson" here, just before going. News of my father's death came here: oh, how good and tender she was, and consolatory by every kind of art, in those black days! I remember our walk along Holborn forward

11*

into the City, and the bleeding mood I was in, she wrapping me
like the softest of bandages:—in the City somewhere, two boys
fighting, with a ring of grinning blackguards round them; I rushed passionately through, tore the fighters asunder, with some passionate rebuke (" in this world full of death"), she on my arm, and
everybody silently complied. Nothing was wanting in her sympathy, or in the manner of it, as even from sincere people there
often is. How poor we were, and yet how rich! I remember
once taking her to Drury Lane Theatre (ticket from Playwright
Kenny belike) along sloppy streets, in a November night (this was
before my father's sudden death); and how paltry the equipment
looked to me, how perfectly unobjectionable to her, who was far
above equipments and outer garnitures! Of the theatricality itself that night I can remember absolutely nothing. Badams, my
old Birmingham friend and physician, a most inventive, light-
hearted, and genially gallant kind of man, sadly eclipsed within
the last five years, ill married, plunged amid grand mining speculations (which were and showed themselves sound, but not till
they had driven him to drink brandy instead of water, and next
year to die miserably overwhelmed). Badams with his wife was
living out at Enfield, in a big old rambling sherd of a house
among waste gardens; thither I twice or thrice went, much liking
the man, but never now getting any good of him; she once for
three or four days went with me; sorry enough days, had not we,
and especially she, illumined them a little. Charles Lamb and his
sister came daily once or oftener; a very sorry pair of phenomena.
Insuperable proclivity to gin in poor old Lamb. His talk con-
temptibly small, indicating wondrous ignorance and shallowness,
even when it was serious and good-mannered, which it seldom
was, usually ill-mannered (to a degree), screwed into frosty artifi-
cialities, ghastly make-believe of wit; in fact, more like "diluted
insanity" (as I defined it) than anything of real jocosity, humor,
or geniality. A most slender fibre of actual worth in that poor
Charles, abundantly recognizable to me as to others, in his better
times and moods; but he was cockney to the marrow; and cockneydom, shouting, "glorious, marvellous, unparalleled in nature!"
all his days had quite bewildered his poor head, and churned
nearly all the sense out of the poor man. He was the leanest of
mankind, tiny black breeches buttoned to the knee-cap, and no
further, surmounting spindle-legs, also in black, face and head fine-
ish, black, bony, lean, and of a Jew type rather; in the eyes a kind
of smoky brightness or confused sharpness; spoke with a stutter;

CHARLES LAMB.

in walking tottered and shuffled; emblem of imbecility bodily and spiritual (something of real insanity I have understood), and yet something too of human, ingenuous, pathetic, sportfully much enduring. Poor Lamb! he was infinitely astonished at my wife, and her quiet encounter of his too ghastly London wit by a cheerful native ditto. Adieu, poor Lamb! He soon after died, as did Badams, much more to the sorrow of us both. Badams at our last parting (in Ampton Street, four or more months after this) burst into tears. "Pressed down like putty under feet," we heard him murmuring, "and no strength more in me to rise!" We invited him to Craigenputtoch with our best temptations next summer, but it was too late; he answered, almost as with tears, "No, alas!" and shortly died.

We had come home, last days of previous March: wild journey by heavy coach, I outside, to Liverpool; to Birmingham it was good, and inn there good, but next day (a Sunday, I think) we were quite overloaded; and had our adventures, especially on the street in Liverpool, rescuing our luggage after dark. But at Uncle John's again, in Maryland Street, all became so bright. At mid-day, somewhere, we dined pleasantly *tête-à-tête*, in the belly of the coach, from my dear one's stores (to save expense doubtless, but the rest of the day had been unpleasantly chaotic) even to me, though from her, as usual, there was nothing but patient goodness. Our dinners at Maryland Street I still remember, our days generally as pleasant, our departure in the Annan steamer, one bright sunshiny forenoon, uncle, etc., zealously helping and escorting; sick, sick my poor woman must have been; but she retired out of sight, and would suffer with her best grace in silence:—ah me, I recollect now a tight, clean brandy barrel she had bought; to "hold such quantities of luggage, and be a water barrel for the rain at Craigenputtoch!" how touching to me at this moment! And an excellent water barrel it proved; the purest tea I ever tasted made from the rain it stored for us. At Whinniery, I remember, brother Alick and others of them were waiting to receive us; there were tears among us (my father gone, when we returned); she wept bitterly, I recollect, her sympathetic heart girdled in much sickness and dispiritment of her own withal; but my mother was very kind and cordially good and respectful to her always. We returned in some days to Craigenputtoch, and were again at peace there. Alick, I think, had by this time left, and a new tenant was there (a peaceable but dull stupid fellow); and our summers and winters for the future (1832–34) were lonelier than ever. Good servants, too, were hardly procurable; difficult anywhere, still more so at Craigenputtoch, where the choice was so limited. However, we pushed along; writing still brisk; "Sartor" getting published in Frazer, etc., etc. We had not at first any thought of leaving. And, indeed, would the Review Editors but have stood steady (instead of forever changeful), and domestic service gone on comfortably, perhaps we might have continued still a good while. We went one winter (1833? or '32?) to Edinburgh; the Jeffreys absent in official regions. A most dreary, contemptible kind of element we found Edinburgh to be (partly by accident, or baddish behavior of two individuals, Dr. Irving one of them, in reference to his poor kinswoman's furnished house); a locality and life-element never to be spoken of in comparison with London, and the frank friends there. To London, accordingly, in the course of next winter, and its new paltry experiences of house-service, etc., we determined to go. Edinburgh must have been in 1833–32 after all? Our home-coming I remember; missed the coach in Princes Street, waited perdue till following morning; bright weather, but my poor Jeannie so ill by the ride that she could not drive from Thornhill to Templand (half a mile), but had to go or stagger hanging on my arm, and instantly took to bed with one of her terrible headaches. Such headaches I never witnessed in my life; agony of retching (never anything but phlegm) and of spasmodic writhing, that would last from twenty-four to sixty hours, never the smallest help affordable. Oh, what of pain, pain, my poor Jeannie had to bear in this thorny pilgrimage of life; the unwitnessed heroine, or witnessed only by me, who never till now see it wholly!

She was very hearty for London, when I spoke of it, though till then her voice on the subject had never been heard. "Burn our ships!" she gayly said, one day—i. e., dismantle our house; carry all our furniture with us. And accordingly here it still is (mostly all of it her father's furniture: whose character of solidly noble is visibly written on it: "respect what is truly made to its purpose; detest what is falsely, and have no concern with it!"). My own heart could not have been more emphatic on that subject; honor to him for its worth to me, not as furniture alone. My writing-table, solid mahogany well devised, always handy, yet steady as the rocks, is the best I ever saw; "no book could be too good for being written here," it has often mutely told me. His watch, commissioned by him in Clerkenwell, has measured my time for forty years, and would still guide you to the longitude, could anybody now take the trouble of completely regulating it (old White-law in Edinburgh, perhaps thirty-five years ago, was the last that did). Repeatedly have upholsterers asked, "Who made these chairs, ma'am?" In cockneydom, nobody in our day; "unexampled prosperity" makes another kind. Abhorrence, quite equal to my own, of cheap and nasty, I have nowhere seen, certainly nowhere else seen completely accomplished, as poor mine could never manage almost in the least degree to be. My pride, fierce and sore as it might be, was never hurt by that furniture of his in the house called mine; on the contrary, my piety was touched, and ever and anon have this table, etc., been a silent, solemn sermon to me. Oh, shall not victory at last be to the handful of brave, in spite of the rotten multitudinous canaille, who seem to inherit all the world and its forces and steel weapons and culinary and stage properties? Courage; and be true to one another!

I remember well my departure (middle of May, 1834), she staying to superintend packing and settling; in gig, I, for the last time; with many thoughts (forgotten there); brother Alick voluntarily waiting at Shillahill Bridge with a fresh horse for me; night at Scotsbrig, ride to Annan (through a kind of May series of slight showers), pretty breakfast waiting us in poor good Mary's (ah me! how strange is all that now! "Mother, you shall see me once yearly, and regularly hear from me while we live," etc., etc.); embarkation at Annan foot; Ben Nelson and James Stuart; our lifting . . . . . * and steaming off, my two dear brothers (Alick and Jamie) standing silent, apart, feeling I well knew what—self-resolute enough, and striving (not quite honestly) to feel more so. Ride to London all night and all day (I think). Trades-Union people out processioning ("Help us; what is your Reform Bill else?" thought they, and I gravely saluting one body of them, I remember, and getting grave response from the leader of them). At sight of London I remember humming to myself a ballad stanza of "Johnnie o' Braidislea" which my dear old mother used to sing.

> "For there's seven foresters in yon forest;
> And them I want to see, see,
> And them I want to see (and shoot down)!"

Lodged at Ampton Street again; immense stretches of walking in search of houses. Camden Town once; Primrose Hill and its bright . . . . . † population in the distance; Chelsea; Leigh Hunt's huggermugger, etc., etc.—what is the use of recollecting all that?

---

* Word omitted in MS.   † Word omitted in MS.

Her arrival I best of all remember: ah me! She was clear for this poor house (which she gradually, as poverty a little withdrew after long years' pushing, has made so beautiful and comfortable) in preference to all my other samples: and here we spent our two-and-thirty years of hard battle against fate; hard but not quite unvictorious, when she left me, as in her car of heaven's fire. My noble one! I say deliberately her part in the stern battle, and except myself none knows how stern, was brighter and braver than my own. Thanks, darling, for your shining words and acts, which were continual in my eyes, and in no other mortal's. Worthless I was your divinity, wrapt in your perpetual love of me and pride in me, in defiance of all men and things. Oh, was it not beautiful, all this that I have lost forever! And I was Thomas the Doubter, the unhoping; till now the only half-believing, in myself and my priceless opulences! At my return from Annandale, after "French Revolution," she so cheerily recounted to me all the good "items;" item after item. "Oh, it has had a great success, dear!"—to no purpose; and at length beautifully lost patience with me for my incredulous humor. My life has not wanted at any time what I used to call "desperate hope" to all lengths; but of common "hoping hope" it has had but little; and has been shrouded since youth-hood (almost since boyhood, for my school-years, at Annan, were very miserable, harsh, barren, and worse) in continual gloom and grimness, as of a man set too nakedly *versus* the devil and all men. Could I be easy to live with? She flickered round me like perpetual radiance, and in spite of my glooms and my misdoings would at no moment cease to love me and help me. What of bounty, too, is in heaven!

We proceeded all through Belgrave Square hither, with our servant, our looser luggage, ourselves, and a little canary-bird ("Chico," which she had brought with her from Craigenputtoch), one hackney-coach rumbling on with us all. Chico, in Belgrave Square, burst into singing, which we took as a good omen. We were all of us striving to be cheerful (she needed no effort of striving); but we "had burnt our ships," and at bottom the case was grave. I do not remember our arriving at this door, but I do the cheerful gypsy life we had here among the litter and carpenters for three incipient days. Leigh Hunt was in the next street, sending kind *un*practical messages; in the evenings, I think, personally coming in; we had made acquaintance with him (properly he with us), just before leaving in spring 1832. Huggermugger was the type of his economics, in all respects, financial and other; but he was himself a pretty man, in clean cotton night-gown, and with the airiest kind-ly style of sparkling talk, wanting only wisdom of a sound kind, and true insight into fact. A great want!

I remember going with my dear one (and Eliza Miles, the "daugh-ter" of Ampton Street, as escort) to some dim iron-monger's shop, to buy kettles and pans on the thriftiest of fair terms. How noble and more than royal is the look of that to me now, and of my roy-al one then! California is dross and dirt to the experiences I have had. A tinder-box with steel and flint was part of our outfit (in-credible as it may seem at this date); I could myself burn rags into tinder, and I have groped my way to the kitchen, in sleepless nights, to strike a light for my pipe in that manner. Chico got a wife by-and-by (oh, the wit there was about that and its sequels), produced two bright yellow young ones, who, as soon as they were fledged, got out into the trees of the garden, and vanished towards swift de-struction; upon which, villain Chico finding his poor wife fallen so tattery and ugly, took to pecking a hole in her head, pecked it and killed her, by-and-by ending his own disreputable life. I had be-gun "The French Revolution" (trees at that time before our win-dow—a tale by these too on her part): infinitesimal little matters of that kind hovered round me like bright fire-flies, irradiated by her light! Breakfast early, was in the back part of this ground-floor room, details of gradual intentions, etc., as to " French Revo-lution," advices, approval, or criticism, always beautifully wise, and so soft and loving, had they even been foolish!

We were not at all unhappy during those three years of "French Revolution;" at least she was not; her health perhaps being bet-ter than mine, which latter was in a strangely painful, and as if conflagrated condition towards the end. She had made the house "a little Eden round her" (so neat and graceful in its simplicity and thrifty poverty); "little Paradise round you," those were Edward Irving's words to her, on his visit to us; short, affectionate visit, the first and the last (October, 1834); on horseback, just about set-ting off for Glasgow, where he died December following. I watch-ed him till at the corner of Cook's Grounds he vanished, and we never saw him more. Much consulting about him we had always had; a letter to Henry Drummond (about delivering him from the fools and fanatics that were agitating him to death, as I clearly saw) lay on the mantel-piece here for some days in doubt, and was then burnt. Brother, father, rational friend, I could not think of, except Henry; and him I had seen only once, not without clear view of his unsoundness too. Practically we had long ago had to take leave of poor Irving, but we both knew him well, and all his brotherhoods to us first and last, and mourned him in our hearts as a lost hero. Nobler man I have seen few if any, till the foul gulfs of London pulpit-popularity sucked him in, and tragically swallowed him.

We were beginning to find a friend or two here; that is, an eligible acquaintance, none as yet very dear to us, though several brought a certain pleasure. Leigh Hunt was here almost nightly, three or four times a week, I should reckon; he came always neatly dressed, was thoroughly courteous, friendly of spirit, and talked like a singing-bird. Good insight, plenty of a kind of humor too; I remember little warbles in the tones of his fine voice which were full of fun and charm. We gave him Scotch porridge to supper ("nothing in nature so interesting and delightful"); she played him Scotch tunes; a man he to understand and feel them well. His talk was often enough (perhaps at first oftenest), literary, biographical, autobiographical, wandering into criticism, reform of society, progress, etc., etc., on which latter points he gradually found me very shocking (I believe—so fatal to his rose-colored visions on the subject). An innocent-hearted, but misguided, in fact rather foolish, unpractical, and often much-suffering man. John Mill was another steady visitor (had by this time introduced his Mrs. Taylor too, a very will-o'-wispish "iridescence" of a creature; meaning nothing bad either). She at first considered my Jane to be a rustic spirit fit for rather tutoring and twirling about when the humor took her, but got taught better (to her lasting memory) before long. Mill was very useful about "French Revolution;" lent me all his books, which were quite a collection on that subject; gave me, frankly, clearly, and with zeal, all his better knowledge than my own (which was pretty frequently of use in this or the other detail), being full of eagerness for such an advocate in that cause as he felt I should be. His evenings here were sensibly agreeable for most part. Talk rather wintry ("sawdustish," as old Sterling once called it), but always well-informed and sincere. The Mrs. Taylor business was becoming more and more of questionable benefit to him (we could see), but on that subject we were strictly silent, and he was pretty still. For several years he came hither, and walked with me every Sunday. Dialogues fallen all dim, except that they were never in the least genial to me, and that I took them as one would wine where no nectar is to be had, or even thin ale where no wine. Her view of him was very kindly, though precisely to the same effect. How well do I still remember that night when he came to tell us, pale as Hector's ghost, that my unfortunate first volume was burnt. It was like half sentence of death to us both, and we had to pretend to take it lightly, so dismal and ghastly was his horror at it, and try to talk of other matters. He staid three mortal hours or so; his departure quite a relief to us. Oh, the burst of sympathy my poor darling then gave me, flinging her arms round my neck, and openly lamenting, condoling, and encouraging like a nobler second self! Under heaven is nothing beautifuller. We sat talking till late; "shall be written again," my fixed word and resolution to her. Which proved to be such a task as I never tried before or since. I wrote out "Feast of Pikes" (vol. ii.), and then went at it. Found it fairly impossible for about a fortnight; passed three weeks (reading Marryat's novels), tried, cautious-cautiously, as on ice paper-thin, once more; and in short had a job more like breaking my heart than any other in my experience. Jeannie, alone of beings, burnt like a steady lamp beside me. I forget how much of money we still had. I think there was at first something like £300, perhaps £280, to front London with. Nor can I in the least remember where we had gathered such a sum, except that it was our own, no part of it borrowed or given us by anybody. "Fit to last till 'French Revolution' is ready!" and she had no misgivings at all. Mill was penitently liberal; sent me £200 (in a day or two), of which I kept £100 (actual cost of house while I had written burnt volume); upon which he bought me "Biographie Universelle," which I got bound, and still have. Wish I could find a way of getting the now much macerated, changed, and fanaticized "John Stuart Mill" to take that £100 back; but I fear there is no way.

How my incomparable one contrived to beat out these exiguous resources into covering the appointed space I cannot now see, nor did I then know; but in the like of that, as in her other tasks, she was silently successful always, and never, that I saw, had a misgiving about success. There would be some trifling increments from "Fraser's Magazine," perhaps ("Diamond Necklace," etc., were probably of those years); but the guess stated above is the nearest I can now come to, and I don't think is in defect of the actuality. I was very diligent, very desperate ("desperate hope"); wrote my two (folio) pages (perhaps four or five of print) day by day; then about two P.M. walked out; always heavy laden, grim of mood, sometimes with a feeling (not rebellious or impious against God Most High), but otherwise too similar to Satan's stepping the burning marle. Some conviction I had that the book was worth something, and pretty constant persuasion that it was not I that could make it better. Once or twice among the flood of equipages at Hyde Park Corner I recollect sternly thinking, "Yes; and perhaps none of you could do what I am at!" But generally my feeling was, "I shall finish this book, throw it at your feet, buy a rifle and spade, and withdraw to the Transatlantic Wilderness, far from human beggaries and basenesses!" This had a kind of comfort to me; yet I always knew, too, in the background, that this would not practically do. In short, my nervous system had got dreadfully irritated and inflamed before I quite ended, and my desire was intense, beyond words, to have done with it. The last paragraph I well remember writing up stairs in the drawing-room that now is, which was then my writing-room; beside her there and in a gray evening (summer, I suppose), soon after tea (perhaps) thereupon, with her dear blessing on me, going out to walk. I had said before going out, "What they will do with this book, none knows, my Jeannie, lass; but they have not had, for a two hundred years, any book that came more truly from a man's very heart, and so let them trample it under foot and hoof as they see best!" "Pooh, pooh! they cannot trample that!" she would cheerily answer; for her own approval (I think she had read always regularly behind me), especially in vol. iii., was strong and decided.

We knew the Sterlings by this time, John, and all of them; old Sterling very often here. Knew Henry Taylor, etc., the Wilsons of Eccleston Street, Rev. Mr. Dunn, etc., etc.; and the waste wilderness of London was becoming a peopled garden to us, in some measure, especially to her, who had a frank welcome to every sort of worth and even kindly singularity in her fellow-creatures, such as I could at no time rival.

Sprinklings of foreigners, "political refugees," had already begun to come about us; to me seldom of any interest, except for the foreign instruction to be gathered from them (if any), and the curiosity attached to their foreign ways. Only two of them had the least charm to me as men: Mazzini, whom I remember, Mr. Taylor, Mrs. Taylor's (ultimately Mrs. Mill's) then husband, an innocent dull good man, brought in to me one evening; and Godefroi Cavaignac, whom my Jane had met somewhere, and thought worth inviting. Mazzini I once or twice talked with; recognizably a most valiant, faithful, considerably gifted and noble soul, but hopelessly given up to his republicanisms, his "Progress," and other Rousseau fanaticism, for which I had at no time the least credence, or any considerable respect amid my pity. We soon tired of one another,

Mazzini and I, and he fell mainly to her share; off and on, for a good many years, yielding her the charm of a sincere mutual esteem, and withal a good deal of occasional amusement from Mazzini's curious bits of exile London and foreign life, and his singular Italian-English modes of locution now and then. For example, Petrucci, having quenched his own fiery chimney one day, and escaped the fine (as he hoped), "there came to pass a sweep" with finer nose in the solitary street, who involved him again. Or, "*Ma, mio caro, non v'è ci un morto!*" which, I see, she has copied into her poor little book of notabilia.* Her reports of these things to me, as we sate at breakfast or otherwise, had a tinkle of the finest mirth in them, and in short a beauty and felicity I have never seen surpassed. Ah me! ah me! whither fled?

Cavaignac was considerably more interesting to both of us. A fine Bayard soul (with figure to correspond), a man full of seriousness and of genial gayety withal; of really fine faculties, and of a politeness (especially toward women) which was curiously elaborated into punctiliousness, yet sprang everywhere from frank nature. A man very pleasant to converse with, walk with, or see drop in on an evening, and lead you or follow you far and wide on the world of intellect and humanly recorded fact. A Republican to the bone, but a "Bayard" in that vesture (if only Bayard had wit and fancy at command). We had many dialogues while "French Revolution" struggled through its last two volumes; Cavaignac freely discussing with me, accepting kindly my innumerable dissents from him, and on the whole elucidating many little points to me. Punctually on the *jour de l'an* came some little gift to her, frugal yet elegant; and I have heard him say, with mantling joyous humor overspreading that sternly sad French face, "*Vous n'êtes pas Écossaise, Madame; désormais vous serez Française!*" I think he must have left us in 1843; he and I rode, one summer forenoon, to Richmond and back (some old Bonapartist colonel married out there, dull, ignorant, loud fellow, to my feeling): country was beautiful, air balmy, ride altogether ditto, ditto. I don't remember speaking with him again; "going to Paris this week" or so, he (on unconditional amnesty, not on conditional like all the others). He returned once, or indeed twice, during the

---

* Explained in this book. An undertaker came one dark winter morning by mistake to Mazzini's house to inquire for the corpse. Mazzini, who answered the bell himself, said, " But, my dear " (an Italian would say " my dear " to a hangman), " there is not here a dead."

three years he still lived; but I was from home the last time, both of us the first (at Newby Cottage, Annan, oh dear!), and I saw him no more. The younger brother ("President" in 1849, etc.) I had often heard of from him, and learned to esteem on evidence given, but never saw. I take him to have been a second Godefroi probably, with less gift of social utterance, but with a soldier's breeding in return.

One autumn, and perhaps another, I recollect her making a tour with the elder Sterling (Thunderer) and wife, which, in spite of the hardships to one so delicate, she rather enjoyed. Thunderer she had at her apron-string, and brought many a comical pirouette out of him from time to time. Good Mrs. S. really loved her, and *vice versa;* a luminous household circle that to us: as may be seen in "Life of Sterling," more at large.

Of money from "French Revolution" I had here as yet got absolutely nothing; Emerson in America, by an edition of his there, sent me £150 ("pathetic!" was her fine word about it, "but never mind, dear"); after some three years grateful England (through poor scrubby but correctly arithmetical Fraser) £100; and I don't remember when, some similar munificence; but I now (and indeed not till recent years do I) see it had been, as she called it, "a great success," and greatish of its kind. Money I did get somewhere honestly, articles in "Fraser," in poor Mill's (considerably hidebound) "London Review;" "Edinburgh" I think was out for me before this time. "London Review" was at last due to the charitable faith of young Sir William Molesworth, a poorish narrow creature, but an ardent believer in Mill Père (James) and Mill Fils. "How much will your Review take to launch it, then?" asked he (all other Radical believers being so close of fist). "Say £4000," answered Mill. "Here, then," writing a check for that amount, rejoined the other. My private (altogether private) feeling, I remember, was, that they could, with profit, have employed me much more extensively in it; perhaps even (though of this I was candid enough to doubt) made me editor of it; let me try it for a couple of years; worse I could not have succeeded than poor Mill himself did as editor (sawdust to the mast-head, and a croakery of crawling things, instead of a speaking by men); but I whispered to none but her the least hint of all this; and oh, how glad am I now, and for long years back, that apparently nothing of it ever came to the thoughts or the dreams of Mill and Co.! For I should surely have accepted of it, had the terms been at all tolerable. I had plenty of Radicalism, and have, and to all appearance shall have; but the opposite hemisphere (which never was wanting either, nor will be, as it miserably is in Mill and Co.) had not yet found itself summoned by the trumpet of time and his events (1848; study of Oliver, etc.) into practical emergence and emphasis and prominence as now. "Ill-luck," take it quietly; you never are sure but it may be good and the best.

Our main revenue three or four (?) years now was lectures; in Edward Street, Portman Square, the only free room there was; earnestly forwarded by Miss and Thomas Wilson, of Eccleston Street (who still live and are good), by Miss Martineau, by Henry Taylor, Frederick Elliot, etc., etc. Brought in, on the average, perhaps £200, for a month's labor; first of them must have been in 1838, I think; Willis's rooms, this. "Detestable mixture of prophecy and play-actorism," as I sorrowfully defined it; nothing could well be hatefuller to me; but I was obliged. And she, oh, she was my angel, and unwearied helper and comforter in all that; how we drove together, we poor two, to our place of execution; she with a little drop of brandy to give me at the very last, and shone round me like a bright aureola, when all else was black and chaos! God reward thee, dear one! now when I cannot even own my debt. Oh, why do we delay so much, till death makes it impossible? And don't I continue it still with others? Fools, fools! we forget that it has to end; so this has ended, and it is such an astonishment to me; so sternly undeniable, yet as it were incredible!

It must have been in this 1838 that her mother first came to see us here. I remember giving each of them a sovereign, from a pocketful of odd which I had brought home,—greatly to satisfaction especially of Mrs. Welsh, who I doubt not bought something pretty and symbolic with it. She came perhaps three times; on one of the later times was that of the "one soirée," with the wax candles on mother's part—and subsequent remorse on daughter's! "Burn these last two on the night when I lie dead!" Like a stroke of lightning this has gone through my heart, cutting and yet healing. Sacred be the name of it; its praise silent. Did I elsewhere meet in the world a soul so direct from the Empyrean? My dear old mother was perhaps equally pious, in the Roman sense; in the British she was much more so; but starry flashes of this kind she had not—from her education, etc., could not.

By this time we were getting noticed by select individuals of the Aristocracy; and were what is called "rather rising in society." Ambition that way my Jane never had; but she took it always as a something of honor done to me, and had her various bits of satisfaction in it. The Spring-Rices (Lords Monteagle afterwards) were probably the first of their class that ever asked me out as a distinguished thing. I remember their flunkey arriving here with an express while we were at dinner; I remember, too, their soirée itself in Downing Street, and the καλοὶ and καλαὶ (as I called them) with their state and their effulgences, as something new and entertaining to me. The Stanleys (of Alderley), through the Bullers, we had long since known, and still know; but that I suppose was still mostly theoretic,—or perhaps I had dined there, and seen the Hollands (Lord and Lady), the etc. (as I certainly did ultimately), but not been judged eligible, or both catchable and eligible ? To me I can recollect (except what of snob ambition there might be in me, which I hope was not very much, though for certain it was not quite wanting either) there was nothing of charm in any of them; old Lady Holland I viewed even with aversion, as a kind of hungry "ornamented witch," looking over at me with merely carnivorous views (and always questioning her Dr. Allen when I said anything); nor was it till years after (husband, Allen, etc., all dead) that I discovered remains of beauty in her, a pathetic situation, and distinguished qualities. My Jane I think knew still less of her; in her house neither my Jane nor I ever was. At Marshall's (millionaire of Leeds, and an excellent man, who much esteemed me, and once gave me a horse for health's sake) we had ample assemblages, shining enough in their kind; but she, I somehow think, probably for saving the cost of "fly" (oh my queen, mine and a true one!), was not so often there as I. On the whole, that too was a thing to be gone through in our career; and it had its bits of benefits, bits of instructions, etc., etc.; but also its temptations, intricacies, tendencies to vanity, etc., to waste of time and faculty; and in a better sphere of arrangement would have been a "game not worth the candle." Certain of the Aristocracy, however, did seem to me still very noble; and, with due limitation of the grossly worthless (none of whom had we to do with), I should vote at present that, of classes known to me in England, the Aristocracy (with its perfection of human politeness, its continual grace of bearing and of acting, steadfast "honor," light address, and cheery stoicism), if you see well into it, is actually yet the best of English classes. Deep in it we never were, promenaders on the shore rather; but I have known it too, and formed deliberate judgment as above. My dear one in theory did not go so far (I think) in that direction —in fact, was not at the pains to form much "theory;" but no eye in the world was quicker than hers for individual specimens; and to the last she had a great pleasure in consorting more or less with the select of these—Lady William Russell, Dowager Lady Sandwich, Lady etc., etc. (and not in over-quantity). I remember at first sight of the first Lady Ashburton (who was far from regularly beautiful, but was probably the chief of all these great ladies), she said of her to me, "Something in her like a heathen goddess!" which was a true reading, and in a case not plain at all, but oftener mistaken than rightly taken.

Our first visit to Addiscombe together, a bright summer Sunday, we walked (thrift, I dare say, ah me! from the near railway station; and my poor Jeannie grew very tired and disheartened, though nothing ill came); I had been there several times, and she had seen the lady here (and called her "heathen goddess" to me). This time I had at once joined the company under the shady trees, on their beautiful lawn; and my little woman, in few minutes, her dress all adjusted, came stepping out, round the corner of the house, with such a look of lovely innocency, modesty, ingenuousness, gracefully suppressed timidity, and radiancy of native cleverness, intelligence, and dignity, towards the great ladies and great gentlemen; it seems to me at this moment, I have never seen a more beautiful expression of a human face. Oh, my dearest! my dearest, that cannot now know how dear! There are glimpses of heaven, too, given us on this earth, though sorely drowned in terrestrial vulgarities, and sorely "flamed-on from the hell beneath," too. This must have been about 1843 or so?

A year or two before, going to see her mother, she had landed in total wreck of seasickness (miserable always at sea, but had taken it as cheapest doubtless), and been brought up almost speechless, and set down at the Queensberry Arms Inn, Annan. Having no maid, no sign but of trouble and (unprofitable) ladyhood, they took her to a remote bedroom, and left her to her solitary shifts there. Very painful to me, yet beautiful and with a noble pathos in it, to look back upon (from her narrative of it) here and now! How Mary, my poor but ever faithful "Sister Mary," came to her (on notice), her resources few, but her heart overflowing; could hardly get admittance to the flunkey house of entertainment at all; got it, however, had a "pint of sherry" with her, had this and that, and perhaps on the third day, got her released from the base place; of which that is my main recollection now, when I chance to pass it, in its now dim enough condition. Perhaps this was about 1840; Mary's husband (now farmer at the Gill, not a clever man, but a diligent and good-natured) was then a carter with two horses in Annan, gradually becoming unable to live in that poor capacity there. They had both been Craigenputtoch figures; and might have been most sordid to my bright darling, but never were at all; gradually far from it, Mary at least. She loved Mary for her kind-heartedness; admired and respected her skill and industry in domestic management of all kinds; and often contrasted to me her perfect talent in that way, compared to sister Jean's, who intellectually was far the superior (and had once been her own pupil and protégée, about the time we left Comley Bank; always very kind and grateful to her since, too, but never such a favorite as the other). Mary's cottage was well known to me too, as I came home by the steamer, on my visits, and was often riding down to bathe, etc. These visits, "once a year to my mother," were pretty faithfully paid; and did my heart always some good; but for the rest were unpleasantly chaotic (especially when my poor old mother, worthiest and dearest of simple hearts, became incapable of management by her own strength, and of almost all enjoyment even from me). I persisted in them to the last, as did my woman; but I think they comprised for both of us (such skinless creatures), in respect of outward physical hardship, an amount larger than all the other items of our then life put together.

How well I remember the dismal evening, when we had got word of her mother's dangerous crisis of illness (a stroke, in fact, which ended it); and her wildly impressive look, laden as if with resolution, affection, and prophetic woe, while she sate in the railway carriage and rolled away from me into the dark. "Poor, poor Jeannie!" thought I; and yet my sympathy how paltry and imperfect was it to what hers would have been for me! Stony-hearted; shame on me! She was stopped at Liverpool by news of the worst; I found her sharply wretched, on my following, and had a strange two or three months, slowly settling everything at Templand; the "last country spring," and my first for many long years. Bright, sad, solitary (letters from Lockhart, etc.), nocturnal mountain heather burning, by day the courses of the hail-storms from the mountains, how they came pouring down their respective valleys, deluge-like, and blotted out the sunshine, etc., spring of 1843 or '42 ?

I find it was in 1842 (February 20) that my poor mother-in-law died. Wild night for me from Liverpool, through Dumfries (sister Jean out with tea, etc.), arrival at waste Templand (only John Welsh, etc., there; funeral quite over); all this and the lonesome, sad, but not unblessed three months almost which I spent there, is still vividly in my mind. I was for trying to keep Templand once, as a summer refuge for us, one of the most picturesque of locations; but her filial heart repelled the notion; and I have never seen more than the chimney-tops of Templand since. Her grief, at my return and for months afterwards, was still poignant, constant; and oh, how inferior my sympathy with her to what hers would have been with me; woe on my dull hard ways in comparison! To her mother she had been the kindest of daughters; liferent of Craigenputtoch settled frankly on her, and such effort to make it practically good to the letter when needful. I recollect one gallop of hers, which Geraldine has not mentioned, gallop from Craigenputtoch to Dumfries Bank, and thence to Templand at a stretch, with the half-year's rent, which our procrastinating brother Alick seldom could or would be punctual with (ah me! gallop which pierces my heart at this moment, and clothes my darling with a sad radiancy to me); but she had many remorses, and indeed had been obliged to have manifold little collisions with her fine, high-minded, but often fanciful and fitful mother, who was always a beauty, too, and had whims and thin-skinned ways, distasteful enough to such a daughter. All which, in cruel aggravation (for all were really small, and had been ridiculous rather than deep or important), now came remorsefully to mind, and many of them, I doubt not, stayed.

Craigenputtoch lapsed to her in 1842, therefore; to me she had left the fee-simple of it by will (in 1824, two years before our marriage), as I remember she once told me thereabouts, and never but once. Will found, the other day, after some difficulty, since her own departure, and the death of any Welsh to whom she could have wished me to bequeath it. To my kindred it has no relation, nor shall it go to them; it is much a problem with me how I shall leave it settled ("Bursaries for Edinburgh College," or what were best?) after my poor interest in it is over. Considerably a problem; and what her wish in it would have actually been? "Bursaries" had come into my own head when we heard that poor final young Welsh was in consumption, but to her I never mentioned it ("wait till the young man's decease do suggest it?"); and now I have only hypothesis and guess. She never liked to speak of the thing, even on question, which hardly once or twice ever rose; and except on question, a stone was not more silent. Beautiful queen-like woman, I did admire her complete perfection on this head of the actual "dowry" she had now brought, £200 yearly or so, which to us was a highly considerable sum, and how she absolutely ig-

nored it, and as it were had not done it at all. Once or so I can
dimly remember telling her as much (thank God I did so), to which
she answered scarcely by a look, and certainly without word, except
perhaps " Tut !"

Thus from this date onward we were a little richer, easier in circumstances; and the pinch of poverty, which had been relaxing
latterly, changed itself into a gentle pressure, or into a limit, and
little more. We did not change our habits in any point, but the
grim collar round my neck was sensibly slackened. Slackened, not
removed at all, for almost twenty years yet. My books were not
nor ever will be "popular," productive of money to any but a contemptible degree. I had lost by the death of Bookseller Fraser,
and change to Chapman and Hall; in short, to judge by the running after me by owls of Minerva in those times, and then to hear
what day's wages my books brought me, would have astonished
the owl mind. I do not think my literary income was above £200
a year in those decades, in spite of my continual diligence day by
day. "Cromwell" I must have written, I think, in 1844, but for
four years prior it had been a continual toil and misery to me. I
forget what was the price of "Cromwell," greater considerably
than in any previous case, but the annual income was still somewhat as above. I had always £200 or £300 in bank, and continually forgot all about money. My darling rolled it all over upon
me, and not one straw about it; only asked for assurance or prom-
issory engagement from me. "How little, then ?" and never failed
to make it liberally and handsomely do. Honor to her (beyond
the ownership of California, I say now), and thanks to poverty that
showed me how noble, worshipful, and dear she was.

In 1849, after an interval of deep gloom and bottomless dubita-
tion, came "Latter-Day Pamphlets," which unpleasantly astonished
everybody, set the world upon the strangest suppositions (" Carlyle got deep into whiskey !" said some), ruined my "reputation"
(according to the friendliest voices, and, in effect, divided me altogether from the mob of "Progress-of-the-species" and other vulgar),
but were a great relief to my own conscience as a faithful citizen,
and have been ever since. My darling gayly approved, and we left
the thing to take its own sweet will, with great indifferency and
loyalty on our part. This did not help our incomings; in fact, I
suppose it effectually hindered, and has done so till quite recently,
any "progress" of ours in that desirable direction, though I did
not find that the small steady sale of my books was sensibly
altered from year to year, but quietly stood where it used to

be. Chapman (hard-fisted cautious bibliographer) would not, for about ten years farther, go into any edition of my "Collected Works." I did once transiently propose it, once only, and remember being sometimes privately a good deal sulky towards the poor man for his judgment on that matter, though decided to leave him strictly to his own light in regard to it, and indeed to avoid him altogether when I had not clear business with him. The "recent return of popularity greater than ever" which I hear of seems due alone to that late Edinburgh affair, especially to the Edinburgh "address," and affords new proof of the singularly dark and feeble condition of "public judgment" at this time. No idea, or shadow of an idea, is in that address but what had been set forth by me tens of times before, and the poor gaping sea of Prurient Blockheadism receives it as a kind of inspired revelation, and runs to buy my books (it is said) now when I have got quite done with their buying or refusing to buy. If they would give me £10,000 a year and bray unanimously their hosannas heaven-high for the rest of my life, who now would there be to get the smallest joy or profit from it? To me I feel as if it would be a silent sorrow rather, and would bring me painful retrospections, nothing else. On the whole, I feel often as if poor England had really done its very kindest to me, after all. Friends not a few I do at last begin to see that I have had all along, and these have all, or all but two or three, been decorously silent; enemies I cannot strictly find that I have had any (only blind blockheads running athwart me on their own errand); and as for the speaking and criticising multitude, who regulate the paying ditto, I perceive that their labors on me have had a twofold result: 1°. that, after so much nonsense said in all dialects, so very little sense or real understanding of the matter, I have arrived at a point of indifferency towards all that, which is really very desirable to a human soul that will do well; and 2°. that, in regard to money, and payment, etc., in the money kind, it is essentially the same, to a degree which, under both heads (if it were safe for me to estimate it), I should say was really a far nearer than common approach to completeness. And which, under both heads, so far as it is complete, means victory, and the very highest kind of "success." Thanks to poor anarchic, crippled, and bewildered England, then; hasn't it done "its very best" for me, under disguised forms, and seeming occasionally to do its worst? Enough of all that; I had to say only that my dear little helpmate, in regard to these things also, has been throughout as one sent from heaven to me. Never for a moment did she take

to blaming England or the world on my behalf; rather to quizzing
my despondencies (if any on that head), and the grotesque stupidities of England and the world. She cared little about criticisms
of me, good or bad, but I have known her read, when such came
to hand, the unfriendliest specimens with real amusement, if their
stupidity was of the readable or amusing kind to by-standers. Her
opinion of me was curiously unalterable from the first. In Edinburgh, for example, in 1826 still, Bookseller Tait (a foolish goosey,
innocent but very vulgar kind of mortal), "Oh, Mrs. Carlyle, fine
criticism in the 'Scotsman;' you will find it at—I think you will
find it at—" "But what good will it do me?" answered Mrs. Carlyle, with great good-humor, to the miraculous collapse of Tait,
who stood (I dare say) with eyes staring.

In 1845, late autumn, I was first at the Grange for a few days (doing D'Ewes's "Election to the Long Parliament," I recollect); she
with me the next year, I think; and there, or at Addiscombe, Al-
verstoke, Bath House, saw on frequent enough occasions, for twelve
years coming, or indeed for nineteen (till the second Lord Ashburton's death), the choicest specimens of English aristocracy; and
had no difficulty in living with them on free and altogether
human terms, and learning from them by degrees whatever they
had to teach us. Something actually, though perhaps not very
much, and surely not the best. To me, I should say, more than to
her, came what lessons there were. Human friendships we also
had, and she too was a favorite with the better kind. Lord Lansdowne, for example, had at last discovered what she was; not
without some amazement in his old retrospective mind, I dare say!
But to her the charm of such circles was at all times insignificant;
human was what she looked at, and what she was, in all circles.
Ay de mi? it is a mingled yarn, all that of our "Aristocratic" history, and I need not enter on it here. One evening, at Bath House,
I saw her in a grand soirée, softly step up, and (unnoticed as she
thought, by anybody) kiss the old Duke of Wellington's shoulder!
That perhaps was one of the prettiest things I ever saw there.
Duke was then very old, and hitched languidly about, speaking
only when spoken to, some "wow-wow," which perhaps had little
meaning in it; he had on his Garter order, his gold-buckle stock,
and was very clean and trim; but except making appearance in
certain evening parties, half an hour in each, perhaps hardly knew
what he was doing. From Bath House we saw his funeral proces-
sion, a while after; and, to our disgust, in one of the mourning
coaches, some official or dignitary reading a newspaper. The

hearse (seventeen tons of bronze), the arrangements generally,
were vulgar and disgusting; but the fact itself impressed everybody; the street rows all silently doffed hat as the body passed;
and London, altogether, seemed to be holding its breath. A dim,
almost wet kind of day; adieu! adieu! With Wellington I don't
think either of us had ever spoken, though we both esteemed him
heartily. I had known his face for nearly thirty years; he also, I
think, had grown to know mine, as that of somebody who wished
him well; not otherwise, I dare say, or the proprietor's name at all;
but I have seen him gaze at me a little as we passed on the streets.
To speak to him, with my notions of his ways of thinking, and of his
articulate endowments, was not among my longings. I went once
to the House of Lords, expressly to hear the sound of his voice, and so
complete my little private physiognomical portrait of him; a fine
aquiline voice, I found it, quite like the face of him; and got a great
instruction and lesson, which has staid with me, out of his little
speech itself (Lord Ellenborough's "Gates of Somnauth" the subject, about which I cared nothing); speech of the most haggly,
hawky, pinched, and meagre kind, so far as utterance and "eloquence" went; but potent for conviction beyond any other; nay, I
may say, quite exclusively of all the others that night, which were
mere "melodious wind" to me (Brougham's, Derby's, etc., etc.), while
this hitching, stunted, haggling discourse of ten or thirteen minutes had made the Duke's opinion completely mine too. I thought
of O. Cromwell withal, and have often since, oftener than ever before, said to myself, "Is not this (to make your opinion mine) the
aim of all 'eloquence,' rhetoric, and Demosthenic artillery practice?" And what is it good for? Fools! get a true insight and
belief of your own as to the matter; that is the way to get your
belief into me, and it is the only way!

One of the days while I was first at the Grange (in 1845) was
John Sterling's death-day. I had well marked it, with a sad, al-
most remorseful contrast; we were at St. Cross and Winchester
Cathedral that day. I think my wife's latest favorites, and in a
sense friends and intimates, among the aristocracy, were the old
Dowager Lady Sandwich (died about four years ago, or three),
young Lady Lothian (recent acquaintance), and the (Dowager)
Lady William Russell, whom I think she had something of real
love to, and in a growing condition for the last two or three years.
This is a clever, high-mannered, massive-minded old lady, now
seventy-two; admirable to me, this good while, as a finished piece
of social art, but hardly otherwise much. My poor little wife!

what a capacity of liking, of sympathy, of giving and getting pleasure, was in her heart, to the very last, compared with my gaunt
mournful darkness in that respect. This Lady William wrote
many notes, etc., in these past seven weeks; I was really sorry for
her withal; and, with an effort, near a month ago, went and saw
her. Alas! she had nothing to speak to me of but of letters received (such "sympathy" from Rome, from Vienna, by persons I
knew not, or knew to be fools; as if this could have been of comfort to me!)—and I could perceive the real "affection" (to whatever extent) had been mostly on my poor darling's side, the alone
opulent in that kind! "Pleasant at our little bits of artistic dinners" (the lady seemed to feel); "a sweet orange, which has
dropped from one's hand into the dust!" I came away, not angry
(oh no), but full of miserable sorrowful feelings of the poverty of
life; and have not since been back.

She liked London constantly, and stood in defense of it against
me and my atrabilious censures of it, never had for herself the
least wish to quit it again, though I was often talking of that, and
her practice would have been loyal compliance for my behoof. I
well remember my first walking her up to Hyde Park Corner in
the summer evening, and her fine interest in everything. At the
corner of the Green Park I found something for her to sit on;
"Hah, there is John Mill coming!" I said, and her joyful, ingenuous
blush is still very beautiful to me. The good child! It did not
prove to be Mill (whom she knew since 1831, and liked for my
sake); but probably I showed her the Duke of Wellington, whom
one often used to see there, striding deliberately along, as if home
from his work, about that hour; him (I almost rather think, that
same evening), and at any rate, other figures of distinction or no-
toriety. And we said to one another, "How strange to be in big
London here; isn't it?" Our purchase of household kettles and
saucepans, etc., in the mean iron-mongery, so noble in its poverty
and loyalty on her part, is sad and infinitely lovely to me at this
moment.

We had plenty of "company" from the very first; John Mill,
down from Kensington once a week or oftener; the "Mrs. Austin"
of those days, so popular and almost famous, on such exiguous
basis (translations from the German, rather poorly some, and of
original nothing that rose far above the rank of twaddle); "_femme
alors célèbre_," as we used to term the phenomenon, parodying some
phrase I had found in Thiers. Mrs. A. affected much sisterhood
with us (affected mainly, though in kind wise), and was a cheery,

sanguine, and generally acceptable member of society—already up to the Marquis of Lansdowne (in a slight sense), much more to all the Radical officials and notables; Charles Buller, Sir W. Molesworth, etc., etc., of "*alors.*" She still lives, this Mrs. A., in quiet though eclipsed condition; spring last she was in town for a couple of weeks; and my dear one went twice to see her, though I couldn't manage quite. Erasmus Darwin, a most diverse kind of mortal, came to seek us out very soon ("had heard of Carlyle in Germany," etc.), and continues ever since to be a quiet house-friend, honestly attached; though his visits latterly have been rarer and rarer, health so poor, I so occupied, etc., etc. He had something of original and sarcastically ingenious in him, one of the sincerest, naturally truest, and most modest of men; elder brother of Charles Darwin (the famed Darwin on Species of these days), to whom I rather prefer him for intellect, had not his health quite doomed him to silence and patient idleness—grandsons, both, of the first famed Erasmus ("Botanic Garden," etc.), who also seems to have gone upon "species" questions, "*omnia ex conchis*" (all from oysters) being a dictum of his (even a stamp he sealed with still extant), as the present Erasmus once told me, many long years before this of Darwin on Species came up among us! Wonderful to me, as indicating the capricious stupidity of mankind; never could read a page of it, or waste the least thought upon it. E. Darwin it was who named the late Whewell, seeing him sit, all ear (not all assent) at some of my lectures, "the Harmonious Blacksmith"—a really descriptive title. My dear one had a great favor for this honest Darwin always; many a road, to shops and the like, he drove her in his cab ("Darwingium Cabbum," comparable to Georgium Sidus), in those early days when even the charge of omnibuses was a consideration, and his sparse utterances, sardonic often, were a great amusement to her. "A perfect gentleman," she at once discerned him to be, and of sound worth and kindliness, in the most unaffected form. "Take me now to Oxygen Street, a dyer's shop there!" Darwin, without a wrinkle or remark, made for Oxenden Street, and drew up at the required door. Amusingly admirable to us both when she came home.

Our commonest evening sitter, for a good while, was Leigh Hunt, who lived close by, and delighted to sit talking with us (free, cheery, idly melodious as bird on bough), or listening, with real feeling, to her old Scotch tunes on the piano, and winding up with a frugal morsel of Scotch porridge (endlessly admirable to Hunt). I think I spoke of this above? Hunt was always accurately dressed these evenings, and had a fine, chivalrous, gentlemanly carriage, polite, affectionate, respectful (especially to her), and yet so free and natural. Her brilliancy and faculty he at once recognized, none better, but there rose gradually in it, to his astonished eye, something of positive, of practically steadfast, which scared him off a good deal; the like in my own case too, still more, which he would call "Scotch," "Presbyterian," who knows what; and which gradually repelled him, in sorrow, not in anger, quite away from us, with rare exceptions, which, in his last years, was almost pathetic to us both. Long before this he had gone to live in Kensington, and we scarcely saw him except by accident. His household, while in "4 Upper Cheyne Row," within few steps of us here, almost at once disclosed itself to be huggermugger, unthrift, and sordid collapsed, once for all, and had to be associated with on cautious terms, while he himself emerged out of it in the chivalrous figure I describe. Dark complexion (a trace of the African, I believe), copious, clean, strong black hair, beautifully shaped head, fine beaming serious hazel eyes; seriousness and intellect the main expression of the face (to our surprise at first); he would lean on his elbow against the mantel-piece (fine, clean, elastic figure, too, he had, five feet ten or more), and look round him nearly in silence, before taking leave for the night, "as if I were a Lar," said he once, "or permanent household god here" (such his polite, aerial-like way). Another time, rising from this Lar attitude, he repeated (voice very fine) as if in sport of parody, yet with something of very sad perceptible, "While I to sulphurous and penal fire" . . . . as the last thing before vanishing. Poor Hunt! no more of him. She, I remember, was almost in tears during some last visit of his, and kind and pitying as a daughter to the now weak and time-worn old man.

Allan Cunningham, living in Pimlico, was well within walking distance, and failed not to come down now and then, always friendly, smooth, and fond of pleasing; "a solid Dumfries stonemason at any rate!" she would define him. He had very smooth manners, much practical shrewdness, some real tone of melody lodged in him, item a twinkle of bright mockery where he judged it safe, culture only superficial (of the surface, truly); reading, information, ways of thinking, all mainly ditto, ditto. Had a good will to us evidently; not an unwelcome face, when he entered, at rare intervals; always rather rarer, as they proved to be; he got at once into Nithsdale, recalled old rustic comicalities (seemed ha-

LEIGH HUNT.

bitually to dwell there), and had not much of instruction either to give or receive. His resort seemed to be much among Scotch City people, who presented him with punch-bowls, etc.; and in his own house there were chiefly unprofitable people to be met. We admired always his sense for managing himself in strange London; his stalwart healthy figure and ways (bright hazel eyes, bald open brow, sonorous hearty tone of voice, a tall, perpendicular, quietly manful-looking figure), and were sorry sincerely to lose him, as we suddenly did. His widow too is now gone; some of the sons (especially Colonel Frank, the youngest, and a daughter, who lives with Frank) have still a friendly though far-off relation to this house.

Harriet Martineau had for some years a much more lively intercourse here, introduced by Darwin possibly, or I forget by whom, on her return from America; her book upon which was now in progress. Harriet had started into lionhood since our first visit to London, and was still run much after, by a rather feeble set of persons chiefly. She was not unpleasant to talk with for a little, though through an ear-trumpet, without which she was totally deaf. To admire her literary genius, or even her solidity of common-sense, was never possible for either of us; but she had a sharp eye, an imperturbable self-possession, and in all things a swiftness of positive decision which, joined to her evident loyalty of intention, and her frank, guileless, easy ways, we both liked. Her adorers, principally, not exclusively, "poor whinnering old moneyed women in their well-hung broughams, otherwise idle," did her a great deal of mischief; and indeed as it proved were gradually turning her fine clear head (so to speak), and leading to sad issues for her. Her talent, which in that sense was very considerable, I used to think, would have made her a quite shining matron of some big female establishment, mistress of some immense dress shop, for instance (if she had a dressing faculty, which perhaps she hadn't); but was totally inadequate to grapple with deep spiritual and social questions, into which she launched at all turns, nothing doubting. However, she was very fond of us, me chiefly, at first, though gradually of both, and I was considerably the first that tired of her. She was much in the world, we little or hardly at all; and her frank friendly countenance, eager for practical help had it been possible, was obliging and agreeable in the circumstances, and gratefully acknowledged by us. For the rest, she was full of Nigger fanaticisms; admirations for (e. g.) her brother James (a Socinian preacher of due quality). The "exchange of ideas"

12*

with her was seldom of behoof in our poor sphere. But she was practically very good. I remember her coming down, on the sudden when it struck her, to demand dinner from us; and dining pleasantly, with praise of the frugal terms. Her soirées were frequent and crowded (small house in Fludyer Street full to the door); and we, for sake of the notabilities or notorieties wandering about there, were willing to attend; gradually learning how insignificant such notabilities nearly all were. Ah me, the thing which it is now touching to reflect on, was the thrift we had to exercise, my little heroine and I! My darling was always dressed to modest perfection (talent conspicuous in that way, I have always understood and heard confirmed), but the expense of 10s. 6d. for a "neat fly" was never to be thought of; omnibus, with clogs and the best of care, that was always our resource. Painful at this moment is the recollection I have of one time, muddy night, between Regent Street and our goal in Fludyer Street, when one of her clogs came loose; I had to clasp it, with what impatience compared to her fine tolerance, stings me with remorse just now. Surely, even I might have taken a cab from Regent Street; 1s., 1s. 6d.; and there could have been no "quarrel about fare" (which was always my horror in such cases); she, beautiful high soul, never whispered or dreamt of such a thing, possibly may have expressly forbidden it, though I cannot recollect that it was proposed in this case. Shame on me! However, I cleaned perfectly my dirty fingers again (probably in some handy little rain-pool in the Park, with diligent wiping); she entered faultless into the illumination (I need not doubt), and all still went well enough.

In a couple of years or so our poor Harriet, nerves all torn by this racket, of "fame" so called, fell seriously ill; threatening of tumor, or I know not what; removed from London (never has resided there since, except for temporary periods); took shelter at Tynemouth, "to be near her brother-in-law, an expert surgeon in Newcastle, and have solitude, and the pure sea air." Solitude she only sometimes had; and, in perfection, never; for it soon became evident she was constantly in spectacle there, to herself and to the sympathetic adorers (who refreshed themselves with frequent personal visits and continual correspondings); and had, in sad effect, so far as could be managed, the whole world, along with self and company, for a theatre to gaze upon her. Life in the sick-room, with "Christus Consolator" (a paltry print then much canted of), etc., etc.; this, and other sad books, and actions full of ostentation, done there, gave painful evidence, followed always by painfuller, till the atheism, etc., etc., which I heard described (by the first Lady Ashburton once) as "a stripping of yourself naked, not to the skin only, but to the bone, and walking about in that guise!" (clever of its kind).

Once in the earliest stage of all this, we made her a visit, my Jane and I; returning out of Scotland by that route. We were very sorry for her; not censorious in any measure, though the aspects were already questionable, to both of us (as I surmise). We had our lodging in the principal street (rather noisy by night), and staid about a week, not with much profit, I think, either to her or ourselves; I at least with none.

There had been, before this, some small note or two of correspondence; with little hope on my part, and now I saw it to be hopeless. My hopefuller and kindlier little darling continued it yet awhile, and I remember scrubbyish (lively enough, but "sawdustish") Socinian didactic little notes from Tynemouth for a year or two hence; but the vapidly didactic, etc., vein continuing more and more, even she, I could perceive, was getting tired of it, and at length, our poor good Harriet, taking the sublime terror "that her letters might be laid hold of by improper parties in future generations," and demanding them all back that she herself might burn them, produced, after perhaps some retiring pass or two, a complete cessation. We never quarrelled in the least, we saw the honest ever self-sufficient Harriet, in the company of common friends, still once or twice, with pleasure rather than otherwise; but never had more to do with her or say to her. A soul clean as river sand; but which would evidently grow no flowers of our planting! I remember our return home from that week at Tynemouth; the yelling flight through some detestable smoky chaos, and midnight witch-dance of base-looking nameless dirty towns (or was this some other time, and Lancashire the scene?) I remember she was with me, and her bright laugh (long after, perhaps towards Rugby now) in the face of some innocent young gentleman opposite, who had ingeniously made a night-cap for himself of his pocket-handkerchief, and looked really strange (an improvised "Camus crowned with sedge"), but was very good-humored too. During the week I also recollect reading one play (never any since or before) of Knight's edition of "Shakspeare," and making my reflections on that fatal brood of people, and the nature of "fame," etc. Sweet friends, for Jesus' sake, forbear!

In those first years, probably from about 1839, we had got acquainted with the Leeds Marshall family; especially with old Mr.

(John) Marshall, the head and founder of it, and the most or really almost only interesting item of it. He had made immense moneys ("wealth now no object to him," Darwin told us in the name of everybody), by skilful, faithful, and altogether human conduct in his flax and linen manufactory at Leeds, and was now settled in opulently shining circumstances in London, endeavoring to enjoy the victory gained. Certain of his sons were carrying on the Leeds "business" in high, quasi-"patriotic" and "morally exemplary," though still prudent and successful style; the eldest was in Parliament, "a landed gentleman," etc., etc.; wife and daughters were the old man's London household, with sons often incidentally present there. None of them was entertaining to speak with, though all were honest, wholesome people. The old man himself, a pale, sorrow-stricken, modest, yet dignified-looking person, full of respect for intellect, wisdom, and worth (as he understood the terms); low-voiced, almost timidly inarticulate (you would have said), yet with a definite and mildly precise imperativeness to his subalterns, as I have noticed once or twice, was an amicable, humane, and thoroughly respectable phenomenon to me. The house (Grosvenor Street, western division), was resplendent, not gaudy, or offensive with wealth and its fruits and furnishings; the dinners large, and splendidly served; guests of distinction (especially on the Whig or Radical side) were to be met with there, and a good sprinkling of promising younger people of the same or a superior type. Soirées extensive, and sumptuously illuminated in all senses, but generally not entertaining. My astonishment at the "Reform" M.P.'s whom I met there, and the notions they seemed "reforming" (and radicalling and quarrelling with their superiors) upon! We went pretty often (I think I myself far the oftener, as in such cases, my loyal little darling taking no manner of offence not to participate in my lionings, but behaving like the royal soul she was, I, dullard egoist, taking no special recognition of such nobleness till the bar was quite passed, or even not fully then!). Alas, I see it now (perhaps better than I ever did!), but we seldom had much real profit, or even real enjoyment for the hour. We never made out together that often-urged " visit to Halsteads" (grand mansion and establishment, near Greystoke, head of Ullswater in Cumberland). I myself, partly by accident, and under convoy of James Spedding, was there once, long after, for one night, and felt very dull and wretched, though the old man and his good old wife, etc., were so good. Old Mr. Marshall was a man worth having known; evidently a great deal of human worth and wisdom lying funded in him. And the world's

resources, even when he had victory over it to the full, were so exiguous, and perhaps to himself almost contemptible! I remember well
always he gave me the first horse I ever had in London, and with
what noble simplicity of unaffected politeness he did it! "Son
William" (the gentleman son, out near Watford) "will be glad to
take it off your hands through winter; and in summer it will help
your health, you know!" And in this way it continued two summers (most part of two), till in the second winter William brought
it down; and it had to be sold for a trifle, £17 if I recollect, which
William would not give to the Anti-Corn-Law Fund (then struggling in the shallows) as I urged, but insisted on handing over to
me. And so it ended. I was at Headingely (by Leeds) with James
Marshall, just wedded to Spring-Rice's daughter, a languishing
patroness of mine; staid till third day; and never happened to
return. And this was about the sum of my share in the Marshall
adventure. It is well known the Marshall daughters were all
married off (each of them had £50,000), and what intricate inter-
marrying with the Spring-Rices there was, "Dowager Lady Monteagle," that now is, being quasi-mother-in-law of James Marshall,
her own brother, wife, etc., etc.! "Family so used up!" as old
Rogers used to snuffle and say. My Jeannie quarrelled with nothing in Marshalldom; quite the contrary; formed a kind of friendship (conquest I believe it was, on her side generously converted
into something of friendship) with Cordelia Marshall, a prim, affectionate, but rather puling, weak, and sentimental elderly young
lady, who became, shortly after, wife, first wife, of the late big
Whewell, and aided his position and advancement toward Mastership of Trinity, etc. I recollect seeing them both here, and Cordelia's adoration of her "Harmonious Blacksmith," with friendly
enough assent, and some amusement, from us two; and I don't
think I ever saw Cordelia again. She soon ceased to write hither;
we transiently heard, after certain years, that she was dead, and
Whewell had married again.

I am weary, writing down all this; so little has my lost one to
do with it, which alone could be its interest for me! I believe I
should stop short. The London years are not definite, or fertile in
disengaged remembrances, like the Scotch ones: dusty, dim, unbeautiful they still seem to me in comparison; and my poor Jeannie's "problem" (which I believe was sorer, perhaps far sorer, than
ever of old, but in which she again proved not to be vanquishable,
and at length to be triumphant!) is so mixed with confusing intricacies to me that I cannot sort it out into clear articulation at all,

or give the features of it, as before. The general type of it is shiningly clear to me. A noble fight at my side; a valiant strangling of serpents day after day done gayly by her (for most part), as I had to do it angrily and gloomily; thus we went on together. *Ay de mi! Ay de mi!*

[June 28. Note from Dods yesterday that the tablet* was not come, nor indeed had been expected; note to-day that it did come yesterday; at this hour probably the mason is hewing out a bed for it; in the silence of the Abbey Kirk yonder, as completion of her father's tomb. The eternities looking down on him, and on us poor Sons of Time! Peace, peace!]

By much the tenderest and beautifullest reminiscence to me out of those years is that of the Lecture times. The vilest welter of odious confusions, horrors, and repugnancies; to which, meanwhile, there was compulsion absolute, and to which she was the one irradiation; noble loving soul, not to be quenched in any chaos that might come. Oh, her love to me; her cheering, unaffected, useful practicality of help: was not I rich, after all? She had a steady hope in me, too, while I myself had habitually none (except of the desperate kind); nay, a steady contentment with me, and with our lot together, let hope be as it might. "Never mind him, my dear," whispered Miss Wilson to her one day, as I stood wriggling in my agony of incipiency; "people like it; the more of that, the better does the Lecture prove." Which was a truth, though the poor sympathizer might, at the moment, feel it harsh. This Miss Wilson and her brother still live (2 Eccleston Street); opulent, fine, Church of England people (scrupulously orthodox to the secularities not less than the spiritualities of that creed), and Miss Wilson very clever, too (i. e., full of strong just insight in her way), who had from the first taken to us, and had us much about them (Spedding, Maurice, etc., attending) then and for some years afterward; very desirous to help us, if that could have much done it (for indeed, to me, it was always mainly an indigestion purchased by a loyal kind of weariness). I have seen Sir James Stephen there, but did not then understand him, or that he could be a "clever man," as reported by Henry Taylor and other good judges. "He shuts his eyes on you," said the elder Spring-Rice (Lord Monteagle), "and talks as if he were dictating a Colonial Despatch" (most true; "teaching you how not to do it," as Dickens defined

---

* For the church at Haddington, where Mrs. Carlyle was buried.

afterwards); one of the pattest things I ever heard from Spring-Rice, who had rather a turn for such. Stephen ultimately, when on half-pay and a Cambridge Professor, used to come down hither pretty often on an evening, and we heard a great deal of talk from him, recognizably serious and able, though always in that Colonial Office style, more or less. Colonial Office being an Impotency (as Stephen inarticulately, though he never said or whispered it, well knew), what could an earnest and honest kind of man do but try and teach you how not to do it? Stephen seemed to me a master in that art.

The lecture time fell in the earlier part of the Sterling period, which latter must have lasted in all, counting till John's death, about ten years (autumn, 1845, when John died). To my Jeannie, I think, this was clearly the sunniest and wholesomest element in her then outer life. All the household loved her, and she had virtually, by her sense, by her felt loyalty, expressed oftenest in a gay mildly quizzing manner, a real influence, a kind of light command one might almost call it, willingly yielded her among them. Details of this are in print (as I said above). In the same years Mrs. Buller (Charles's mother) was a very cheerful item to her. Mrs. B. (a whilom Indian beauty, wit, and finest fine lady), who had at all times a very recognizing eye for talent, and real reverence for it, very soon made out something of my little woman, and took more and more to her, all the time she lived after. Mrs. B.'s circle was gay and populous at this time (Radical chiefly; Radical lions of every complexion), and we had as much of it as we would consent to. I remember being at Leatherhead too, and after that a pleasant rustic week at Troston Parsonage (in Suffolk, where Mrs. B.'s youngest son "served," and serves), which Mrs. B. contrived very well to make the best of, sending me to ride for three days in Oliver Cromwell's country, that she might have the wife more to herself. My Jane must have been there altogether, I dare say, near a month (had gone before me, returned after me), and I regretted never to have seen the place again. This must have been in September or October, 1842; Mrs. Welsh's death in early spring past. I remember well my feelings in Ely Cathedral, in the close of sunset or dusk; the place was open, free to me without witnesses; people seemed to be tuning the organ, which went in solemn gusts far aloft. The thought of Oliver, and his "Leave off your fooling, sir, and come down!" was almost as if audible to me. Sleepless night, owing to cathedral bells, and strange ride next day to St. Ives to Hinchinbrook, etc., and thence to Cambridge, with thun-

der-cloud and lightning dogging me to rear and bursting into tor-
rents few minutes after I got into the Hoop Inn.

My poor darling had, for constant accompaniment to all her bits
of satisfactions, an altogether weak state of health, continually
breaking down, into violent fits of headache in her best times, and
in winter season into cough, etc., in lingering forms of a quite sad
and exhausting sort. Wonderful to me how she, so sensitive a
creature, maintained her hoping cheerful humor to such a degree,
amidst all that; and, except the pain of inevitable sympathy, and
vague fluttering fears, gave me no pain.   Careful always to screen
me from pain, as I by no means always reciprocally was; alas, no,
miserable egoist in comparison.   At this time I must have been in
the thick of " Cromwell;" four years of abstruse toil, obscure speculations, futile wrestling, and misery, I used to count it had cost
me, before I took to editing the "Letters and Speeches" ("to have
them out of my way"), which rapidly drained off the sour swamp
water bodily, and left me, beyond all first expectation, quite free
of the matter.   Often I have thought how miserable my books
must have been to her, and how, though they were none of her
choosing, and had come upon her like ill weather or ill-health, she
at no instant, never once I do believe, made the least complaint of
me or my behavior (often bad, or at least thoughtless and weak)
under them.   Always some quizzing little lesson, the purport and
effect of which was to encourage me; never once anything worse.
Oh, it was noble, and I see it so well now, when it is gone from me,
and no return possible.

"Cromwell" was by much the worst book time, till this of "Friedrich," which, indeed, was infinitely worse; in the dregs of our
strength too; and lasted for about thirteen years. She was generally in quite weak health too, and was often, for long weeks or
months, miserably ill.

It was strange how she contrived to sift out of such a troublous
forlorn day as hers in each case was, all available little items, as
she was sure to do, and used to have them ready for me in the
evening when my work was done, in the prettiest little narrative
anybody could have given of such things. Never again shall I
have such melodious, humanly beautiful half-hours; they were the
rainbow of my poor dripping day, and reminded me that there otherwise was a sun. At this time, and all along, she "did all the
society;" was all brightness to the one or two (oftenest rather
dull and prosaic fellows, for the better sort respected my seclusion,
especially during that last "Friedrich" time) whom I needed to

see on my affairs in hand, or who, with more of brass than others, managed to intrude upon me. For these she did, in their several kinds, her very best. Her own people whom I might be apt to feel wearisome (dislike any of them I never did, or his or her discharge from service would have swiftly followed) she kept beautifully out of my way, saving my "politeness" withal; a very perfect skill she had in all this; and took my dark toiling periods, however long, sullen, and severe they might be, with a loyalty and heart acquiescence that never failed, the heroic little soul!

"Latter-Day Pamphlet" time, and especially the time that preceded it (1848, etc.), must have been very sore and heavy. My heart was long overloaded with the meanings at length uttered there, and no way of getting them set forth would answer. I forget what ways I tried, or thought of. "Times" newspaper was one (alert, airy, rather vacant editorial gentleman I remember going to once, in Printing House Square; but this, of course, proved hypothetical merely, as all others did, till we, as last shift, gave the rough MSS. to Chapman (in Forster's company one winter Sunday). About half of those ultimately printed might be in Chapman's hands, but there was much manipulation as well as addition needed. Forster soon fell away, I could perceive, into terror and surprise, as indeed everybody did. "A lost man!" thought everybody. Not she at any moment; much amused by the outside pother she, and glad to see me getting delivered of my black electricities and consuming fires in that way. Strange letters came to us during those nine months of pamphleteering, strange visitors (of moon-struck unprofitable type for most part), who had, for one reason or another, been each of them wearing himself half mad on some one of the public scandals I was recognizing and denouncing. I still remember some of their faces and the look their paper bundles had. She got a considerable entertainment out of all that, went along with me in everything (probably counselling a little here and there, a censorship well worth my regarding, and generally adoptable, here as everywhere), and minded no whit any results that might follow this evident speaking of the truth. Somebody, writing from India, I think, and clearly meaning kindness, "did hope" (some time afterwards) "the tide would turn, and this lamentable hostility of the press die away into friendship again;" at which I remember our innocent laughter, ignorant till then what "The Press's" feelings were, and leaving "The Press" very welcome to them then. Neuberg helped me zealously, as volunteer amanuensis, etc., through all this business, but I know not

that even he approved it all, or any of it to the bottom. In the
whole world I had one complete approver; in that, as in other
cases, one, and it was worth all.

On the back of "Latter-Day Pamphlets" followed "Life of Sterling;" a very quiet thing, but considerably disapproved of too, as
I learned, and utterly revolting to the religious people in particular (to my surprise rather than otherwise). "Doesn't believe in
us, then, either?" Not he, for certain; can't, if you will know!
Others urged disdainfully, "What has Sterling done that he should
have a Life?" "Induced Carlyle somehow to write him one!" answered she once (to the Ferguses, I think) in an arch airy way
which I can well fancy, and which shut up that question there.
The book was afterward greatly praised, again on rather weak
terms I doubt. What now will please me best in it, and alone will,
was then an accidental quality, the authentic light, under the due
conditions, that is thrown by it on her. Oh, my dear one, sad is
my soul for the loss of thee, and will to the end be, as I compute!
Lonelier creature there is not henceforth in this world; neither
person, work, nor thing going on in it that is of any value, in comparison, or even at all. Death I feel almost daily in express fact,
death is the one haven; and have occasionally a kind of kingship,
sorrowful, but sublime, almost godlike, in the feeling that that is
nigh. Sometimes the image of her, gone in her car of victory (in
that beautiful death), and as if nodding to me with a smile, "I am
gone, loved one; work a little longer, if thou still carest; if not,
follow. There is no baseness, and no misery here. Courage, courage to the last!" that, sometimes, as in this moment, is inexpressibly beautiful to me, and comes nearer to bringing tears than it
once did.

In 1852 had come the new modelling of our house, attended with
infinite dusty confusion (head-carpenter, stupid though honest, fell
ill, etc., etc.); confusion falling upon her more than me, and at
length upon her altogether. She was the architect, guiding and
directing and contriving genius, in all that enterprise, seemingly
so foreign to her. But indeed she was ardent in it, and she had a
talent that way which was altogether unique in my experience.
An "eye" first of all; equal in correctness to a joiner's square, this,
up almost from her childhood, as I understood. Then a sense of
order, sense of beauty, of wise and thrifty convenience; sense of
wisdom altogether in fact, for that was it; a human intellect shining luminous in every direction, the highest and the lowest (as I
remarked above). In childhood she used to be sent to seek when

things fell lost; "the best seeker of us all," her father would say, or look (as she thought); for me also she sought everything, with such success as I never saw elsewhere. It was she who widened our drawing-room (as if by a stroke of genius) and made it zealous-ly (at the partial expense of three feet from her own bedroom) into what it is, one of the prettiest little drawing-rooms I ever saw, and made the whole house into what it now is. How frugal, too, and how modest about it! House was hardly finished, when there arose that of the "demon fowls," as she appropriately named them; macaws, Cochin Chinas, endless concert of crowing, cackling, shriek-ing roosters (from a bad or misled neighbor, next door) which cut us off from sleep or peace, at times altogether, and were like to drive me mad, and her through me, through sympathy with me. From which also she was my deliverer, had delivered and contrived to deliver me from hundreds of such things (oh, my beautiful little Alcides, in the new days of anarchy and the mud-gods, threatening to crush down a poor man, and kill him with his work still on hand!). I remember well her setting off, one winter morning, from the Grange on this enterprise, probably having thought of it most of the night (sleep denied). She said to me next morning the first thing: "Dear, we must extinguish those demon fowls, or they will extinguish us! Rent the house (No. 6, proprietor mad, etc., etc.) ourselves! it is but some £40 a year; pack away those vile people, and let it stand empty. I will go this very day upon it, if you assent;" and she went accordingly, and slew altogether this Lerna hydra, at far less expense than taking the house, nay almost at no expense at all, except by her fine intellect, tact, just discernment, swiftness of decision, and general nobleness of mind (in short). Oh, my bonny little woman, mine only in memory now!

I left the Grange two days after her, on this occasion, hastening through London, gloomy of mind, to see my dear old mother yet once (if I might) before she died. She had, for many months be-fore, been evidently and painfully sinking away, under no disease, but the ever-increasing infirmities of eighty-three years of time. She had expressed no desire to see me, but her love from my birth upwards, under all scenes and circumstances, I knew to be emphat-ically a mother's. I walked from the Kirtlebridge Station that dim winter morning; my one thought "Shall I see her yet alive?" She was still there; weary, very weary, and wishing to be at rest. I think she only at times knew me; so bewildering were her contin-ual distresses; once she entirely forgot me; then, in a minute or two, asked my pardon. Ah me! ah me! It was my mother and not my mother; the last pale rim or sickle of the moon, which had once been full, now sinking in the dark seas. This lasted only three days. Saturday night she had her full faculties, but was in nearly unendurable misery, not breath sufficient, etc., etc. John tried various reliefs, had at last to give a few drops of laudanum, which eased the misery, and in an hour or two brought sleep. All next day she lay asleep, breathing equally but heavily, her face grand and solemn, almost severe, like a marble statue; about four P.M. the breathing suddenly halted, recommenced for half an instant, then fluttered, ceased. "All the days of my appointed time," she had often said, "will I wait till my change come." The most beautifully religious soul I ever knew. Proud enough she was, too, though piously humble, and full of native intellect, humor, etc., though all undeveloped. On the religious side, looking into the very heart of the matter, I always reckon her rather superior to my Jane, who in other shapes, and with far different exemplars and conditions, had a great deal of noble religion too. Her death filled me with a kind of dim amazement and crush of confused sorrows, which were very painful, but not so sharply pathetic as I might have expected. It was the earliest terror of my childhood "that I might lose my mother;" and it had gone with me all my days. But, and that is probably the whole account of it, I was then sunk in the miseries of "Friedrich," etc., etc., in many miseries; and was then fifty-eight years of age. It is strange to me, in these very days, how peaceable, though still sacred and tender, the memory of my mother now lies in me. (This very morning, I got into dreaming confused nightmare stuff about some funeral and her; not hers, nor obviously my Jane's, seemingly my father's rather, and she sending me on it— the saddest bewildered stuff. What a dismal debasing and confusing element is that of a sick body on the human soul or thinking.part!)

It was in 1852 (September–October, for about a month) that I had first seen Germany, gone on my first errand as to "Friedrich:" there was a second, five years afterwards; this time it was to inquire (of Preuss and Co.); to look about me, search for books, portraits, etc., etc. I went from Scotsbrig (my dear old mother painfully weak, though I had no thought it would be the last time I should see her afoot); from Scotsbrig for Leith by Rotterdam, Köln, Bonn (Neuberg's); and on the whole never had nearly so (outwardly) unpleasant a journey in my life; till the second and last I made thither. But the Chelsea establishment was under carpenters, painters; till those disappeared, no work possible, scarcely any living possible (though my brave woman did make it possible without complaint). "Stay so many weeks, all painting at least shall then be off!" I returned, near broken down utterly, at the set time; and alas! was met by a foul dabblement of paint oozing down stairs; the painters had proved treacherous to her; time could not be kept! It was the one instance of such a thing here: and, except the first sick surprise, I now recollect no more of it.

"Mamma, wine makes cosy!" said the bright little one, perhaps between two and three years old, her mother, after some walk with sprinkling of wet or the like, having given her a dram-glass of wine on their getting home: "mamma, wine makes cosy!" said the small silver voice, gayly sipping, getting its new bits of insight into natural philosophy! What "pictures" has my beautiful one left me; what joys can surround every well-ordered human heart! I said, long since, I never saw so beautiful a childhood. Her little bit of a first chair, its wee, wee arms, etc., visible to me in the closet at this moment, is still here, and always was. I have looked at it hundreds of times; from of old, with many thoughts. No daughter or son of hers was to sit there; so it had been appointed us, my darling. I have no book a thousandth part so beautiful as thou; but these were our only "children"—and, in a true sense, these were verily ours; and will perhaps live some time in the world after we are both gone; and be of no damage to the poor brute chaos of a world, let us hope! The Will of the Supreme shall be accomplished. Amen. But to proceed.

Shortly after my return from Germany (next summer, I think, while the Cochin Chinas were at work, and we could not quit the house, having spent so much on it, and got a long lease), there began a new still worse hurlyburly of the building kind, that of the new top story—whole area of the house to be thrown into one sublime garret room, lighted from above, thirty feet by thirty say, and at least eleven feet high, double-doored, double-windowed, impervious to sound, to—in short, to everything but self and work. I had my grave doubts about all this; but John Chorley, in his friendly zeal, warmly urged it on, pushed, superintended—and was a good deal disgusted with my dismal experience of the result. Something really good might have come of it in a scene where good and faithful work was to be had on the part of all, from architect downwards; but here, from all (except one good young man of the carpenter trade, whom I at length noticed thankfully in small matters), the "work," of planning to begin with, and then of executing, in all its details, was mere work of Belial, i. e., of the Father of lies; such "work" as I had not conceived the possibility of among the sons of Adam till then. By degrees I perceived it to be the ordinary English "work" of this epoch; and, with manifold reflections, deep as Tophet, on the outlooks this offered for us all, endeavored to be silent as to my own little failure. My new illustrious "study" was definable as the least inhabitable, and most entirely detestable and despicable, bit of human workmanship in that kind, sad and odious to me very. But, by many and long-continued efforts, with endless botherations which lasted for two or three years after (one winter starved by "Arnott's improved grate," I recollect), I did get it patched together into something of supportability; and continued, though under protest, to inhabit it during all working hours, as I had indeed from the first done. The whole of the now printed "Friedrich" was written there (or in summer in the back court and garden, when driven down by baking heat). Much rawer matter, I think, was tentatively on paper, before this sublime new "study." "Friedrich" once done, I quitted the place forever, and it is now a bedroom for the servants. The "architect" for this beautiful bit of masonry and carpentry was one "Parsons," really a clever creature, I could see, but swimming as for dear life in a mere "mother of dead dogs" (ultimately did become bankrupt). His men of all types, Irish hodmen and upwards, for real mendacity of hand, for drunkenness, greediness, mutinous nomadism, and anarchic malfeasance throughout, excelled all experience or conception. Shut the lid on their "unexampled prosperity" and them forevermore.

The sufferings of my poor little woman, throughout all this, must have been great, though she whispered nothing of them—the rather as this was my enterprise (both the "Friedrich" and it);—indeed, it was by her address and invention that I got my sooterkin of a "study" improved out of its worst blotches; it was she, for example, that went silently to Bramah's smith people, and got me a fireplace, of merely human sort, which actually warmed the room, and sent Arnott's miracle about its business. But undoubtedly that "Friedrich" affair, with its many bad adjuncts, was much the worst we ever had, and sorely tried us both. It lasted thirteen years or more. To me a desperate dead-lift pull all that time; my whole strength devoted to it; alone, withdrawn from all the world (except some bores who would take no hint, almost nobody came to see me, nor did I wish almost anybody then left living for me), all the world withdrawing from me; I, desperate of ever getting through (not to speak of "succeeding"), left solitary "with the nightmares" (as I sometimes expressed it), "hugging unclean creatures" (Prussian Blockheadism) "to my bosom, trying to caress and flatter their secret out of them!" Why do I speak of all this? It is now become κόπρος to me, insignificant as the dung of a thousand centuries ago. I did get through, thank God; let it now wander into the belly of oblivion forever. But what I do still, and shall more and more, remember with loving admiration is her behavior in it. She was habitually in the feeblest health; often, for long whiles, grievously ill. Yet by an alchemy all her own, she had extracted grains as of gold out of every day, and seldom or never failed to have something bright and pleasant to tell me, when I reached home after my evening ride, the most fordone of men. In all, I rode, during that book, some 30,000 miles, much of it (all the winter part of it) under cloud of night, sun just setting when I mounted. All the rest of the day I sat silent aloft, insisting upon work, and such work, *invitissimâ Minervâ* for that matter. Home between five and six, with mud mackintoshes off, and, the nightmares locked up for a while, I tried for an hour's sleep before my (solitary, dietetic, altogether simple) bit of dinner; but first always came up for half an hour to the drawing-room and her; where a bright kindly fire was sure to be burning (candles hardly lit, all in trustful chiar-oscuro), and a spoonful of brandy in water, with a pipe of tobacco (which I had learned to take sitting on the rug, with my back to the jamb, and door never so little open, so that all the smoke, if I was careful, went up the chimney), this was the one bright portion of my black day.

Oh, those evening half-hours, how beautiful and blessed they were, not awaiting me now on my home-coming, for the last ten weeks! She was oftenest reclining on the sofa; wearied enough, she too, with her day's doings and endurings. But her history, even of what was bad, had such grace and truth, and spontaneous tinkling melody of a naturally cheerful and loving heart, that I never anywhere enjoyed the like. Her courage, patience, silent heroism, meanwhile, must often have been immense. Within the last two years or so she has told me about my talk to her of the Battle of Mollwitz on these occasions, while that was on the anvil. She was lying on the sofa, weak, but I knew little how weak, and patient, kind, quiet, and good as ever. After tugging and wriggling through what inextricable labyrinth and slough of despond I still remember, it appears I had at last conquered Mollwitz, saw it all clear ahead and round me, and took to telling her about it, in

my poor bit of joy, night after night. I recollect she answered little, though kindly always. Privately, she at that time felt convinced she was dying—dark winter, and such the weight of misery
and utter decay of strength, and, night after night, my theme to
her, Mollwitz! This she owned to me, within the last year or two,
which how could I listen to without shame and abasement? Never in my pretended superior kind of life, have I done, for love of
any creature, so supreme a kind of thing. It touches me at this
moment with penitence and humiliation, yet with a kind of soft
religious blessedness too. She read the first two volumes of "Friedrich," much of it in printer's sheets (while on visit to the aged Miss-
es Donaldson at Haddington); her blame was unerringly straight
upon the blot, her applause (should not I collect her fine notekins
and reposit them here?) was beautiful and as sunlight to me, for
I knew it was sincere withal, however exaggerated by her great
love of me. The other volumes (hardly even the third, I think)
she never read—I knew too well why; and submitted without
murmur, save once or twice perhaps a little quiz on the subject,
which did not afflict her, either. Too weak, too weak by far for a
dismal enterprise of that kind, as I knew too well! But those
Haddington visits were very beautiful to her (and to me through
her letters and her), and by that time we were over the hill, and
"the worst of our days were passed" (as poor Irving used to give
for toast, long ago), worst of them past, though we did not yet
quite know it.

   [July 3.] Voll. 1 and 2 of "Friedrich" were published, I find, in
1858. Probably about two years before that was the nadir of my
wife's sufferings—internal sufferings and dispiritments; for outward fortune, etc., had now, for about ten years, been on a quite
tolerable footing, and indeed evidently fast on the improving hand:
nor had this, at any worse time, ever disheartened her, or darkened
her feelings. But in 1856, owing to many circumstances, my en-
grossment otherwise (sunk in "Friedrich," in, etc., etc.; far less exclusively, very far less, than she supposed, poor soul!)—and owing
chiefly, one may fancy, to the deeper downbreak of her own poor
health, which from this time, as I now see better, continued its ad-
vance upon the citadel, or nervous system, and intrinsically grew
worse and worse:—in 1856, too evidently, to whatever owing, my
poor little darling was extremely miserable! Of that year there is
a bit of private diary, by chance left unburnt; found by me since
her death, and not to be destroyed, however tragical and sternly
sad are parts of it. She had written, I sometimes knew (though

she would never show to me or to mortal any word of them), at
different times, various bits of diary; and was even, at one time,
upon a kind of autobiography (had not C——, the poor C——
now just gone, stept into it with swine's foot, most intrusively,
though without ill intention—finding it unlocked one day—and
produced thereby an instantaneous burning of it; and of all like it
which existed at that time). Certain enough, she wrote various
bits of diary and private record, unknown to me: but never anything so sore, down-hearted, harshly distressed and sad as certain
pages (right sure am I!) which alone remain as specimen! The
rest are all burnt; no trace of them, seek where I may.

*　　　*　　　*　　　*　　　*　　　*　　　*

A very sad record! We went to Scotland soon after; she to
Auchtertool (cousin Walter's), I to the Gill (sister Mary's).

In July, 1856, soon after, may have been about middle of month,
we went to Edinburgh; a blazing day, full of dust and tumult,
which I still very well remember. Lady Ashburton had got for
herself a grand "Queen's saloon," or *ne plus ultra* of railway carriages (made for the Queen some time before), costing no end of
money. Lady sat, or lay, in the saloon. A common six-seat carriage, immediately contiguous, was accessible from it. In this the
lady had insisted we should ride, with her doctor and her maid; a
mere partition, with a door, dividing us from her. The lady was
very good, cheerful though much unwell; bore all her difficulties,
and disappointments with an admirable equanimity and magnanimity; but it was physically almost the uncomfortablest journey
I ever made. At Peterborough the *ne plus ultra* was found to have
its axle-tree on fire; at every station afterwards buckets were copiously dashed and poured (the magnanimous lady saying never a
syllable to it); and at Newcastle-on-Tyne they flung the humbug
ne plus away altogether, and our whole party into common carriages.
Apart from the burning axle, we had suffered much from dust and
even from foul air, so that at last I got the door opened, and sat
with my head stretched out backward into the wind. This had
alarmed my poor wife, lest I should tumble out altogether; and
she angrily forbade it, dear loving woman, and I complied, not at
first knowing why she was angry. This and Lady A.'s opening
her door to tell us, "Here is Hinchinbrook!" (a long time before, and
with something of pathos traceable in her cheery voice) are nearly
all that I now remember of the base and dirty hurly-burly. Lord
A. had preceded by some days, and was waiting for our train at
Edinburgh, 9.30 P.M.; hurly-burly greater and dirtier than ever.

They went for Barry's Hotel at once, servants and all; no time to inform us (officially) that we too were their guests. But that, too, passed well. We ordered apartments, refreshments of our own there (first of all baths; inside of my shirt collar was as black as ink!), and before the refreshments were ready we had a gay and cordial invitation, etc., etc.; found the "old bear" (Ellis) in their rooms, I remember, and Lord A. and he with a great deal to say about Edinburgh and its people and phenomena. Next morning the Ashburtons went for Kinloch-Luichart (fine hunting seat in Ross-shire); and my dear little woman to her cousins' at Auchtertool, where I remember she was much soothed by their kindness, and improved considerably in health for the time. The day after seeing her settled there, I made for Annandale, and my sister Mary's at the Gill. (Maggie Welsh, now here with me, has helped in adjusting into clearness the recollection of all this.) I remember working on final corrections of books ii. and iii. of "Friedrich," and reading in "Plato" (translation, and not my first trial of him) while there. My darling's letters I remember, too (am on search for them just now), also visits from sister Jean and to Dumfries and her, silent nocturnal rides from that town, etc., and generally much riding on the (Priestside) Solway Sands, and plenty of sombre occupation to my thoughts.

Late on in autumn I met my Jeannie at Kirkcaldy again; uncomfortably lodged, both of us, and did not loiter (though the people very kind); I was bound for Ross-shire and the Ashburtons (miserable journey thither, sombre, miserable stay there, wet weather, sickly, solitary mostly, etc., etc.); my wife had gone to her aunts' in Edinburgh for a night or two; to the Haddington Miss Donaldsons; and in both places, the latter especially, had much to please her, and came away with the resolution to go again.

Next year, 1857, she went accordingly, staid with the Donaldsons (eldest of these old ladies, now well above eighty, and gone stone-blind, was her "godmother," had been at Craigenputtoch to see us, the dearest of old friends my wife now had). She was at Auchtertool too, at Edinburgh with her aunts, once and again; but the chief element was "Sunny Bank, Haddington," which she began with and ended with; a stay of some length each time. Happy to her, and heart-interesting to a high degree, though sorrowfully involved in almost constant bodily pain. It was a tour for health, urged on her by me for that end; and the poor little darling seemed inwardly to grudge all along the expense on herself (generous soul!) as if she were not worth money spent, though money was in no scarcity with us now! I was printing "Fried-rich," voll. i. and ii., here; totally solitary, and recollect her letters of that tour as altogether genial and delightful, sad and miserable as the view is which they now give me of her endless bodily distresses and even torments, now when I read them again after nine years, and what has befallen me eleven weeks ago!

Sunday, July 8. Began writing again at the second line of this page; the intermediate time has been spent in a strenuous search for, and collection of all her letters now discoverable (by Maggie Welsh and me), which is now completed, or nearly so, 1843–2 the earliest found (though surely there ought to be others, of 1837, etc.?), and some of almost every year onward to the last. They are exceedingly difficult to arrange, not having in general any date, so that place often enough, and day and even year throughout, are mainly to be got by the Post-office stamp, supported by inference and inquiry such as is still possible, at least to me.

The whole of yesterday I spent in reading and arranging the letters of 1857; such a day's reading as I perhaps never had in my life before. What a piercing radiancy of meaning to me in those dear records, hastily thrown off, full of misery, yet of bright eternal love; all as if on wings of lightning, tingling through one's very heart of hearts! Oh, I was blind not to see how brittle was that thread of noble celestial (almost more than terrestrial) life; how much it was all in all to me, and how impossible it should long be left with me. Her sufferings seem little short of those in a hospital fever-ward, as she painfully drags herself about; and yet constantly there is such an electric shower of all-illuminating brilliancy, penetration, recognition, wise discernment, just enthusiasm, humor, grace, patience, courage, love, and in fine of spontaneous nobleness of mind and intellect, as I know not where to parallel! I have asked myself, Ought all this to be lost, or kept for myself, and the brief time that now belongs to me? Can nothing of it be saved, then, for the worthy that still remain among these roaring myriads of profane unworthy? I really must consider it farther; and already I feel it to have become uncertain to me whether at least this poor note-book ought to be burnt ere my decease, or left to its chances among my survivors? As to "talent," epistolary and other, these letters, I perceive, equal and surpass whatever of best I know to exist in that kind; for "talent," "genius," or whatever we may call it, what an evidence, if my little woman needed that to me! Not all the Sands and Eliots and babbling *cohue* of "celebrated scribbling women" that have strutted over the world, in my time, could, it seems to me, if all boiled down and distilled to essence, make one such woman. But it is difficult to make these letters fairly legible; except myself there is nobody at all that can completely read them as they now are. They abound in allusions, very full of meaning in this circle, but perfectly dark and void in all others. *Coterie-sprache*, as the Germans call it, "family circle dialect," occurs every line or two; nobody ever so rich in that kind as she; ready to pick up every diamond-spark out of the common floor-dust, and keep it brightly available; so that hardly, I think, in any house, was there more of *coterie-sprache*, shining innocently, with a perpetual expressiveness and twinkle generally of quiz and real humor about it, than in ours. She mainly was the creatress of all this; unmatchable for quickness (and trueness) in regard to it, and in her letters it is continually recurring; shedding such a lambency of "own fireside" over everything, if you are in the secret. Ah me, ah me! At least, I have tied up that bundle (the two letters touching on "Friedrich" have a paper round them; the first written in Edinburgh, it appears now!)

July 9. Day again all spent in searching and sorting a box of hers, full of strange and sad memorials of her mother, with a few of father and infant self (put up in 1842), full of poignant meanings to her then and to me now. Her own christening cap is there, e. g.; the lancet they took her father's blood with (and so killed him, as she always thought); father's door-plate; "commission in Perth Fencibles," etc.; two or three Christmas notes of mine, which I could not read without almost sheer weeping.

It must have been near the end of October, 1863, when I returned home from my ride, weather soft and muddy, humor dreary and oppressed as usual (nightmare "Friedrich" still pressing heavily as ever), but as usual also, a bright little hope in me that now I was across the muddy element, and the lucid twenty minutes of my day were again at hand. To my disappointment my Jeannie was not here; "had gone to see her cousin in the city"—a Mrs. Godby, widow of an important post-official, once in Edinburgh, where he had wedded this cousin, and died leaving children; and in virtue of whom she and they had been brought to London a year or two ago, to a fine situation as "matron of the Post-office establishment" ("forty maids under her, etc., etc., and well managed by her") in St. Martin's-le-Grand. She was a good enough creature, this Mrs. Godby (Binnie had been her Scotch name; she is now Mrs. Something-else, and very prosperous). My Jeannie, in those early times, was anxious to be kind to her in the new scene, and had her often here (as often as, for my convenience, seemed to the loyal heart permissible), and was herself, on calls and little tea-visits, perhaps still oftener there. A perfectly harmless Scotch cousin, polite and prudent; almost prettyish (in spite of her projecting upper teeth); with good wise instincts, but no developed intelligence in the articulate kind. Her mother, I think, was my mother-in-law's cousin or connection; and the young widow and her London friend were always well together. This was, I believe, the last visit my poor wife ever made her; and the last but two she ever received from her, so miserably unexpected were the issues on this side of the matter!

We had been at the Grange for perhaps four or five weeks that autumn; utterly quiet, nobody there besides ourselves; Lord Ashburton being in the weakest state, health and life visibly decaying. I was permitted to be *perdue* till three o'clock daily, and sat writing about Poland, I remember; mournful, but composed and dignifiedly placid the time was to us all. My Jeannie did not complain of health beyond wont, except on one point, that her right arm was strangely lame, getting lamer and lamer, so that at last she could not "do her hair herself," but had to call in a maid to fasten the hind part for her. I remember her sadly dispirited looks, when I came in to her in the morning with my inquiries; "No sleep," too often the response; and this lameness, though little was said of it, a most discouraging thing. Oh, what discouragements, continual distresses, pains and miseries my poor little darling had to bear; remedy for them nowhere, speech about them useless, best to be avoided—as, except on pressure from myself, it nobly was! This part of her life-history was always sad to me; but it is tenfold more now, as I read in her old letters, and gradually realize, as never before, the continual grinding wretchedness of it, and how, like a winged Psyche, she so soared above it, and refused to be chained or degraded by it. "Neuralgic rheumatism," the doctors called this thing: "neuralgia" by itself, as if confessing that they knew not what to do with it. Some kind of hot half-corrosive ointment was the thing prescribed; which did, for a little while each time remove the pain mostly, the lameness not; and I remember to have once seen her beautiful arm (still so beautiful) all stained with spots of burning, so zealous had she been in trying, though with small faith in the prescription. This lasted all the time we were at the Grange; it had begun before, and things rather seemed to be worsening after we returned. Alas, I suppose it was the siege of the citadel that was now going on; disease and pain had for thirty or more years been trampling down the outworks, were now got to the nerves, to the citadel, and were bent on storming that.

I was disappointed, but not sorry at the miss of my "twenty minutes;" that my little woman, in her weak languid state, had got out for exercise, was gladness; and I considered that the "twenty minutes" was only postponed, not lost, but would be repaid me presently with interest. After sleep and dinner (all forgotten now), I remember still to have been patient, cheerfully hopeful; "she is coming, for certain, and will have something nice to tell me of news, etc., as she always has!" In that mood I lay on the sofa, not sleeping, quietly waiting, perhaps for an hour-and-half more. She had gone in an omnibus, and was to return in one. At this time she had no carriage. With great difficulty I had got her induced, persuaded, and commanded to take two drives weekly in a hired brougham ("more difficulty in persuading you to go into expense, than other men have to persuade their wives to keep out of it!"). On these terms she had agreed to the two drives weekly, and found a great benefit in them; but on no terms could I get her to consent to go, herself, into the adventure of purchasing a brougham, etc., though she knew it to be a fixed purpose, and only delayed by absolute want of time on my part. She could have done it, too, employed the right people to do it, right well, and knew how beneficial to her health it would likely be; but no, there was a refined delicacy which would have perpetually prevented her; and my "time," literally, was Zero. I believe, for the last seven years of that nightmare "Friedrich," I did not write the smallest message to friends, or undertake the least business, except upon plain compulsion of necessity. How lucky that, next autumn, I did actually, in spite of "Friedrich," undertake this of the brougham; it is a mercy of Heaven to me for the rest of my life! and oh! why was it not undertaken, in spite of all "Friedrichs" and nightmares, years before! That had been still luckier, perhaps endlessly so? but that was not to be.

The visit to Mrs. Godby had been pleasant, and gone all well; but now, dusk falling, it had to end—again by omnibus as ill luck would have it. Mrs. G. sent one of her maids as escort. At the corner of Cheapside the omnibus was waited for (some excavations going on near by, as for many years past they seldom cease to do); Chelsea omnibus came; my darling was in the act of stepping in (maid stupid and of no assistance), when a cab came rapidly from behind, and, forced by the near excavation, seemed as if it would drive over her, such her frailty and want of speed. She desperately determined to get on the flag pavement again; desperately leaped, and did get upon the curbstone; but found she was falling over upon the flags, and that she would alight on her right or neuralgic arm, which would be ruin; spasmodically struggled against this for an instant or two (maid nor nobody assisting), and had to fall on the neuralgic arm—ruined otherwise far worse, for, as afterwards appeared, the muscles of the thigh-bone, or sinews attaching them, had been torn in that spasmodic instant or two; and for three days coming the torment was excessive, while in the right arm there was no neuralgia perceptible during that time, nor any very manifest new injury afterwards either. The calamity had happened, however, and in that condition my poor darling, "put into a cab" by the humane people, as her one request to them, arrived at this door—"later" than I expected; and after such "a drive from Cheapside" as may be imagined!

I remember well my joy at the sound of her wheels ending in a knock; then my surprise at the delay in her coming up; at the singular silence of the maids when questioned as to that. Thereupon my rushing down, finding her in the hands of Larkin and them, in the greatest agony of pain and helplessness I had ever seen her in. The noble little soul, she had determined I was not to be shocked by it; Larkin then lived next door, assiduous to serve us in all things (did maps, indexes, even joinerings, etc., etc.); him she had resolved to charge with it; alas, alas, as if you could have saved me, noble heroine and martyr? Poor Larkin was standing helpless; he and I carried her up stairs in an arm-chair to the side of her bed, into which she crept by aid of her hands. In few minutes, Barnes (her wise old doctor) was here, assured me there were no bones broken, no joint out, applied his bandagings and remedies, and seemed to think the matter was slighter than it proved to be—the spasmodic tearing of sinews being still a secret to him.

For fifty hours the pain was excruciating; after that it rapidly abated, and soon altogether ceased, except when the wounded limb was meddled with never so little. The poor patient was heroic, and had throughout been. Within a week, she had begun contriving rope machineries, leverages, and could not only pull her bell, but lift and shift herself about, by means of her arms, into any coveted posture, and was, as it were, mistress of the mischance. She had her poor little room arranged, under her eye, to a perfection of beauty and convenience. Nothing that was possible to her had been

omitted (I remember one little thing the apothecary had furnished; an artificial champagne cask; turn a screw and your champagne
spurted up, and when you had a spoonful, could be instantly closed
down; with what a bright face she would show me this in action!)
In fact her sick-room looked pleasanter than many a drawing-room
(all the weakness and suffering of it nobly veiled away); the select
of her lady-friends were admitted for short whiles and liked it well;
to me, whenever I entered, all spoke of cheerfully patient hope, the
bright side of the cloud always assiduously turned out for me, in my
dreary labors! I might have known, too, better than I did, that it
had a dark side withal; sleeplessness, sickliness, utter weakness;
and that "the silver lining" was due to my darling's self mainly,
and to the inextinguishable loyalty and hope that dwelt in her.
But I merely thought, "How lucky beyond all my calculations!"

I still right well remember the night when her bedroom door
(double-door) suddenly opened upon me into the drawing-room,
and she came limping and stooping on her staff, so gracefully and
with such a child-like joy and triumph, to irradiate my solitude.
Never again will any such bright vision of gladdening surprise
illuminate the darkness for me in that room or any other? She
was in her Indian dressing-gown, absolutely beautiful, leaning on
her nibby staff (a fine hazel, cut and polished from the Drumlanrig
woods, by some friend for my service); and with such a kindly
brilliancy and loving innocence of expression, like that of a little
child, unconquerable by weakness and years! A hot-tempered
creature, too, few hotter, on momentary provocation; but what a
fund of soft affection, hope, and melodious innocence and goodness,
to temper all that lightning! I doubt, candidly, if I ever saw a
nobler human soul than this which (alas, alas, never rightly valued
till now!) accompanied all my steps for forty years. Blind and
deaf that we are: oh, think, if thou yet love anybody living, wait
not till death sweep down the paltry little dust-clouds and idle
dissonances of the moment, and all be at last so mournfully clear
and beautiful, when it is too late!

We thought all was now come or fast coming right again, and
that, in spite of that fearful mischance, we should have a good winter, and get our dismal "misery of a book" done, or almost done.
My own hope and prayer was, and had long been, continually that;
hers, too, I could not doubt, though hint never came from her to
that effect—no hint or look, much less the smallest word, at any
time, by any accident. But I felt well enough how it was crushing
down her existence, as it was crushing down my own; and the

thought that she had not been at the choosing of it, and yet must suffer so for it, was occasionally bitter to me. But the practical conclusion always was, "Get done with it, get done with it! For the saving of us both, that is the one outlook." And, sure enough, I did stand by that dismal task with all my time and all my means; day and night wrestling with it, as with the ugliest dragon, which blotted out the daylight and the rest of the world to me, till I should get it slain. There was perhaps some merit in this; but also, I fear, a demerit. Well, well, I could do no better; sitting smoking up-stairs, on nights when sleep was impossible, I had thoughts enough; not permitted to rustle amid my rugs and wrappages lest I awoke her, and startled all chance of sleep away from her. Weak little darling, thy sleep is now unbroken; still and serene in the eternities (as the Most High God has ordered for us), and nobody more in this world will wake for my wakefulness.

My poor woman was what we called "getting well" for several weeks still; she could walk very little, indeed, she nevermore walked much in this world; but it seems she was out driving, and again out, hopefully for some time.

Towards the end of November (perhaps it was in December), she caught some whiff of cold, which, for a day or two, we hoped would pass, as many such had done; but, on the contrary, it began to get worse, soon rapidly worse, and developed itself into that frightful universal "neuralgia," under which it seemed as if no force of human vitality would be able long to stand. "Disease of the nerves" (poisoning of the very channels of sensation); such was the name the doctors gave it, and, for the rest, could do nothing farther with it; well had they only attempted nothing! I used to compute that they, poor souls, had at least reinforced the disease to twice its natural amount; such the pernicious effect of all their "remedies" and appliances, opiates, etc., etc.; which every one of them (and there came many) applied anew, and always with the like result. Oh, what a sea of agony my darling was immersed in, month after month! Sleep had fled. A hideous pain, of which she used to say that "common honest pain, were it cutting off one's flesh or sawing of one's bones, would be a luxury in comparison," seemed to have begirdled her, at all moments and on every side. Her intellect was clear as starlight, and continued so; the clearest intellect among us all; but she dreaded that this too must give way. "Dear," said she to me on two occasions, with such a look and tone as I shall never forget, "promise me that you will not put me into a madhouse, however this go. Do you promise me, now?" I solemnly

13*

did. "Not if I do quite lose my wits?" "Never, my darling; oh, compose thy poor terrified heart!" Another time she punctually directed me about her burial; how her poor bits of possessions were to be distributed—this to one friend, that to another (in help of their necessities, for it was the poor sort she had chosen, old indigent Haddington figures). What employment in the solitary night-watches, on her bed of pain! Ah me! ah me!

The house, by day especially, was full of confusion; Maggie Welsh had come at my solicitation, and took a great deal of patient trouble (herself of an almost obstinate placidity), doing her best among the crowd of doctors, sick-nurses, visitors. I mostly sat aloft, sunk, or endeavoring to be sunk, in work; and, till evening, only visited the sick-room at intervals, first thing in the morning, perhaps about noon again, and always (if permissible) at three P.M., when riding - time came, etc., etc. If permissible, for sometimes she was reported as "asleep" when I passed, though it oftenest proved to have been quiescence of exhaustion, not real sleep. To this hour it is inconceivable to me how I could continue "working," as I nevertheless certainly for much the most part did. About three times or so, on a morning, it struck me, with a cold shudder as of conviction, that here did lie death; that my world must go to shivers, down to the abyss; and that "victory" never so complete, up in my garret, would not save her, nor indeed be possible without her. I remember my morning walks, three of them or so, crushed under that ghastly spell. But again I said to myself, "No man, doctor or other, knows anything about it. There is still what appetite there was; that I can myself understand;" and generally, before the day was done, I had decided to hope again, to keep hoping and working. The aftercast of the doctors' futile opiates were generally the worst phenomena: I remember her once coming out to the drawing-room sofa, perhaps about midnight, decided for trying that. Ah me! in vain, palpably in vain; and what a look in those bonny eyes, vividly present to me yet; unaidable, and like to break one's heart!

One scene with a Catholic sick-nurse I also remember well.

A year or two before this time, she had gone with some acquaintance who was in quest of sick-nurses to an establishment under Catholic auspices, in Brompton somewhere (the acquaintance, a Protestant herself, expressing her "certain knowledge" that this Catholic was the one good kind); where, accordingly, the aspect of matters, and especially the manner of the old French lady who was matron and manager, produced such a favorable impression that I recollect my little woman saying, "If I need a sick-nurse, that is the place I will apply at." Appliance now was made; a nun duly sent in consequence: this was in the early weeks of the illness; household sick-nursing (Maggie's and that of the maids alternately) having sufficed till now. The nurse was a good-natured young Irish nun, with a good deal of brogue, a tolerable share of blarney too, all varnished to the due extent; and, for three nights or so, she answered very well. On the fourth night, to our surprise, though we found afterwards it was the common usage, there appeared a new nun, new and very different—an elderly French "young lady," with broken English enough for her occasions, and a look of rigid earnestness, in fact with the air of a life broken down into settled despondency and abandonment of all hope that was not ultra-secular. An unfavorable change; though the poor lady seemed intelligent, well-intentioned; and her heart-broken aspect inspired pity and good wishes, if no attraction. She commenced by rather ostentatious performance of her nocturnal prayers, "Beata Maria," or I know not what other Latin stuff; which her poor patient regarded with great vigilance, though still with what charity and tolerance were possible. "You won't understand what I am saying or doing," said the nun; "don't mind me." "Perhaps I understand it better than yourself," said the other, who had Latin from of old, and did "mind" more than was expected. The dreary hours, no sleep, as usual, went on; and we heard nothing, till about three A.M. I was awakened (I, what never happened before or after, though my door was always left slightly ajar, and I was right above, usually a deep sleeper)— awakened by a vehement continuous ringing of my poor darling's bell. I flung on my dressing-gown, awoke Maggie by a word, and hurried down. "Put away that woman!" cried my poor Jeannie, vehemently; "away, not to come back." I opened the door into the drawing-room; pointed to the sofa there, which had wraps and pillows plenty; and the poor nun at once withdrew, looking and murmuring her regrets and apologies. "What was she doing to thee, my own poor little woman?" No very distinct answer was to be had then (and afterwards there was always a dislike to speak of that hideous bit of time at all, except on necessity); but I learned, in general, that during the heavy hours, loaded, every moment of them, with its misery, the nun had gradually come forward with ghostly consolations, ill received, no doubt; and at length with something more express, about "Blessed Virgin," "Agnus Dei," or whatever it might be; to which the answer had been, "Hold your tongue, I tell you, or I will ring the bell!" Upon which the nun had rushed forward with her dreadfullest supernal admonitions, "impenitent sinner," etc., and a practical attempt to prevent the ringing. Which only made it more immediate and more decisive. The poor woman expressed to Miss Welsh much regret, disappointment, real vexation, and self-blame; lay silent, after that, amid her rugs; and disappeared, next morning, in a polite and soft manner: never to reappear, she or any consort of hers. I was really sorry for this heavy-laden, pious or quasi-pious, and almost broken-hearted Frenchwoman—though we could perceive she was under the foul tutelage and guidance, probably, of some dirty muddy-minded semi-felonious proselytizing Irish priest. But there was no help for her in this instance; probably, in all England, she could not have found an agonized human soul more nobly and hopelessly superior to her and her poisoned gingerbread "consolations." This incident threw suddenly a glare of strange and far from pleasant light over the sublime Popish "sister of charity" movement; and none of us had the least notion to apply there henceforth.

The doctors were many; Dr. Quain (who would take no fees) the most assiduous; Dr. Blakiston (ditto) from St. Leonard's, express one time; speaking hope, always, both of these, and most industrious to help, with many more, whom I did not even see. When any new miraculous kind of doctor was recommended as such, my poor struggling martyr, conscious, too, of grasping at mere straws, could not but wish to see him; and he came, did his mischief, and went away. We had even (by sanction of Barnes and, indeed, of sound sense never so sceptical) a trial of "animal magnetism;" two magnetizers, first a man, then a quack woman (evidently a conscious quack I perceived her to be), who at least did no ill, except entirely disappoint (if that were much an exception). By everybody it had been agreed that a change of scene (as usual, when all else has failed was the thing to be looked to: "St. Leonard's as soon as the weather will permit!" said Dr. Quain and everybody, especially Dr. Blakiston, who generously offered his house withal; "Definitely more room than we need!" said the sanguine B. always; and we dimly understood, too, from his wife (Bessie Barnet, an old inmate here, and of distinguished qualities and fortunes) that the doctor would accept remuneration, though this proved quite a mistake. The remuneration he had expected was to make a distinguished cure over the heads of so many London rivals. Money for the use of two rooms in his house, we might have anticipated, but did not altogether, he would regard with sovereign superiority.

It was early in March, perhaps March 2, 1864, a cold-blowing damp and occasionally raining day, when the flitting thither took effect. Never shall I see again so sad and dispiriting a scene; hardly was the day of her last departure for Haddington, departure of what had once been she (the instant of which they contrived to hide from me here), so miserable; for she, at least, was now suffering nothing, but safe in victorious rest for evermore, though then beyond expression suffering. There was a railway invalid carriage, so expressly adapted, so, etc., and evidently costing some ten or twelve times the common expense: this drove up to the door; Maggie and she to go in this. Well do I recollect her look as they bore her down-stairs: full of nameless sorrow, yet of clearness, practical management, steady resolution; in a low, small voice she gave her directions, once or twice, as the process went on, and practically it was under her wise management. The invalid carriage was hideous to look upon; black, low, base-looking, and you entered it by window, as if it were a hearse. I knew well what she was thinking; but her eye never quailed, she gave her directions as heretofore; and, in a minute or two, we were all away. Twice or oftener in the journey I visited Maggie and her in their prison. No complaint: but the invalid carriage, in which I doubt if you could actually sit upright (if you were of man's stature or of tall woman's), was evidently a catchpenny humbug, and she freely admitted afterwards that she would never enter it again, and that in a coupé to ourselves she would have been far better. At St. Leonard's, I remember, there was considerable waiting for the horses that should have been ready, a thrice bleak and dreary scene to us all (she silent as a child) : the arrival, the dismounting, the ascent of her quasi-bier up Blakiston's long stairs, etc., etc. Ah me! Dr. Blakiston was really kind. The sea was hoarsely moaning at our hand, the bleared skies sinking into darkness overhead. Within doors, however, all was really nice and well provided (thanks to the skilful Mrs. B.) ; excellent drawing-room, and sitting-room, with bed for her; bedroom up-stairs for Maggie, ditto; for servant, within call, etc., etc.; all clean and quiet. A kind of hope did rise, perhaps even in her, at sight of all this. My mood, when I bethink me, was that of deep misery frozen torpid; singularly dark and stony, strange to me now; due in part to the "Friedrich" incubus then. I had to be home again that night, by the last train; miscalculated the distance, found no vehicle;

and never in my life saved a train by so infinitesimally small a miss. I had taken mournfully tender leave of my poor, much-suffering heroine (speaking hope to her, when I could readily have lifted up my voice and wept). I was to return in so many days, if nothing went wrong; at once, if anything did. I lost nothing by that hurried ride, except, at London Station, or in the final cab, a velvet cap, of her old making, which I much regretted, and still regret. "I will make you another cap, if I get better," said she, lovingly, at our next meeting; but she never did, or perhaps well could. What matter? That would have made me still sorrier, had I had it by me now. Wae's me, wae's me!*

I was twice or perhaps thrice at St. Leonard's (Warrior Square, Blakiston's house right end of it to the sea). Once I recollect being taken by Forster, who was going on a kind of birthday holiday with his wife. Blakiston spoke always in a tone of hope, and there really was some improvement; but, alas! it was small and slow. Deep misery and pain still too visible: and all we could say was, "We must try St. Leonard's farther; I shall be able to shift down to you in May!" My little darling looked sweet gratitude upon me (so thankful always for the day of small things!); but heaviness, sorrow, and want of hope was written on her face; the sight filling me with sadness, though I always strove to be of B.'s opinion. One of my volumes (fourth, I conclude) was coming out at that time; during the Forster visit, I remember there was some review of this volume, seemingly of a shallow, impudent description, concerning which I privately applauded F.'s silent demeanor, and not B.'s vocal, one evening at F.'s inn. The dates, or even the number of these sad preliminary visits, I do not now recollect: they were all of a sad and ambiguous complexion. At home, too, there daily came a letter from Maggie; but this, in general, though it strove to look hopeful, was ambiguity's own self! Much driving in the open air, appetite where it was, sleep at least ditto; all this, I kept saying to myself, must lead to something good.

Dr. Blakiston, it turned out, would accept no payment for his rooms; "a small furnished house of our own" became the only outlook, therefore; and was got, and entered into, some time in April, some weeks before my arrival in May. Brother John, before this, had come to visit me here; ran down to St. Leonard's one day: and, I could perceive, was silently intending to pass the sum-

---

* Wae is the Scotch adjective, too. Wae, wae; there is no word in English that will express what I feel. Wae is my habitual mood in these months.

mer with us at St. Leonard's. He did so, in an innocent, self-soothing, kindly, and harmless way (the good soul, if good wishes would always suffice!); and occasionally was of some benefit to us, though occasionally also not. It was a quiet sunny day of May when we went down together; I read most of "Sterne's Life" (just out, by some Irishman, named Fitz-something); looked out on the old Wilhelmus Conquestor localities; on Lewes, for one thing (de "Le Ouse"—Ouse the dirty river there is still named); on Pevensey, Bexhill, etc., with no unmixed feeling, yet not with absolute misery, as we rolled along. I forget if Maggie Welsh was still there at St. Leonard's. My darling, certain enough, came down to meet us, attempting to sit at dinner (by my request, or wish already signified); but too evidently it would not do. Mary Craik was sent for (from Belfast) instead of Maggie Welsh, who "was wanted" at Liverpool, and did then or a few days afterwards return thither, Mary Craik succeeding, who was very gentle, quiet, prudent, and did well in her post.

I had settled all my book affairs the best I could. I got at once installed into my poor closet on the ground-floor, with window to the north (keep that open, and, the door ajar, there will be fresh air!). Book-box was at once converted into book-press (of rough deal, but covered with newspaper veneering where necessary), and fairly held and kept at hand the main books I wanted; camp-desk, table or two, drawer or two, were put in immediate seasonablest use. In this closet there was hardly room to turn; and I felt as if crushed, all my apparatus and I, into a stocking, and there bidden work. But I really did it withal, to a respectable degree, printer never pausing for me, work daily going on; and this doubtless was my real anchorage in that sea of trouble, sadness, and confusion for the two months it endured. I have spoken elsewhere of my poor darling's hopeless wretchedness, which daily cut my heart, and might have cut a very stranger's: those drives with her ("daily, one of your drives is with me," and I saw her gratitude, poor soul, looking out through her despair; and sometimes she would try to talk to me about street sights, persons, etc.; and it was like a bright lamp flickering out into extinction again); drives mainly on the streets to escape the dust, or still dismaller if we did venture into the haggard, parched lanes, and their vile whirlwinds. Oh, my darling, I would have cut the universe in two for thee, and this was all I had to share with thee, as we were!

St. Leonard's, now that I look back upon it, is very odious to my fancy, yet not without points of interest. I rode a great deal too, two hours and a half my lowest stint; bathed also, and remember the bright morning air, bright Beachy Head and everlasting sea, as things of blessing to me; the old lanes of Sussex too, old cottages, peasants, old vanishing ways of life, were abundantly touching; but the new part, and it was all getting "new," was uniformly detestable and even horrible to me. Nothing but dust, noise, squalor, and the universal tearing and digging as if of gigantic human swine, not finding any worm or roots that would be useful to them! The very "houses" they were building, each "a congeries of rotten bandboxes" (as our own poor "furnished house" had taught me, if I still needed teaching), were "built" as if for nomad apes, not for men. The "moneys" to be realized, the etc., etc., does or can God's blessing rest on all that? My dialogues with the dusty sceneries there (Fairlight, Crowhurst, Battle, Rye even, and Winchelsea), with the novelties and the antiquities, were very sad for most part, and very grim; here and there with a kind of wild interest too. Battle I did arrive at, one evening, through the chaotic roads; Battle, in the rustle or silence of incipient dusk, was really affecting to me; and I saw to be a good post of fence for King Harold, and wondered if the Bastard did "land at Pevensey," or not near Hastings somewhere (Bexhill or so?), and what the marchings and preliminaries had really been. Faithful study, continued for long years or decades, upon the old Norman romances, etc., and upon the ground, would still tell some fit person, I believe; but there shriek the railway "shares" at such and such a premium; let us make for home! My brother, for a few times at first, used to accompany me on those rides, but soon gave in (not being bound to it like me); and Noggs* and I had nothing for it but solitary contemplation and what mute "dialogue" with nature and art we could each get up for himself. I usually got home towards nine P.M. (half-past eight the rigorous rule); and in a gray dusty evening, from some windy hill-tops, or in the intricate old narrow lanes of a thousand years ago, one's reflections were apt to be of a sombre sort. My poor little Jeannie (thanks to her, the loving one!) would not fail to be waiting for me, and sit trying to talk or listen, while I had tea; trying her best, sick and weary as she was; but always very soon withdrew after that; quite worn down and longing for solitary silence, and even a sleepless bed, as was her likeliest prospect for most part. How utterly sad is all that! yes; and there is a kind of devout blessing in it too (so nobly

---

* Carlyle's horse.

was it borne, and conquered in a sort); and I would not have it altered now, after what has come, if I even could.

We lived in the place called "Marina" (what a name!), almost quite at the west end of St. Leonard's; a new house (bearing marks of thrifty, wise, and modestly elegant habits in the old lady owners just gone from it); and, for the rest, decidedly the worst-built house I have ever been within. A scandal to human nature, it and its fellows; which are everywhere, and are not objected to by an enlightened public, as appears! No more of it, except our farewell malison; and pity for the poor old ladies who perhaps are still there!

My poor suffering woman had at first, for some weeks, a vestige of improvement, or at least of new hope and alleviation thereby. She "slept" (or tried for sleep) in the one tolerable bedroom; second floor, fronting the sea, darkened and ventilated, made the tidiest we could; Miss Craik slept close by. I remember our settlings for the night; my last journey up, to sit a few minutes, and see that the adjustments were complete; a "nun's lamp" was left glimmering within reach. My poor little woman strove to look as contented as she could, and to exchange a few friendly words with me as our last for the night. Then in the morning, there sometimes had been an hour or two of sleep; what news for us all! And even brother John, for a while, was admitted to step up and congratulate, after breakfast. But this didn't last; hardly into June, even in that slight degree. And the days were always heavy; so sad to her, so painful, dreary without hope. What a time, even in my reflex of it! Dante's Purgatory I could now liken it to; both of us, especially my loved one by me, "bent like corbels," under our unbearable loads, as we wended on, yet in me always with a kind of steady, glimmering hope! Dante's Purgatory, not his Hell, for there was a sacred blessedness in it withal; not wholly the society of devils, but among their hootings and tormentings something still pointing afar off towards heaven withal. Thank God!

At the beginning of June she still had the feeling we were better here than elsewhere; by her direction, I warned the people we would not quit "at the end of June," as had been bargained, but of "July," as was also within our option, on due notice given. End of June proved to be the time, all the same; the old ladies (justly) refusing to revoke, and taking their full claim of money, poor old souls; very polite otherwise. Middle of June had not come when that bedroom became impossible; "roaring of the sea," once a lullaby, now a little too loud, on some high tide or west wind, kept her entirely awake. I exchanged bedrooms with her; "sea always a lullaby to me;" but, that night, even I did not sleep one wink; upon which John exchanged with me, who lay to rearward, as I till then had done. Rearward we looked over a Mews (from this room); from her now room, into the paltry little "garden;" overhead of both were clay cliffs, multifarious dog and cock establishments (unquenchable by bribes paid), now and then stray troops of asses, etc., etc.; what a lodging for poor sufferers! Sleep became worse and worse; we spoke of shifting to Bexhill; "fine airy house to be let there" (fable when we went to look); then some quiet old country inn? She drove one day (John, etc., escorting) to Battle, to examine; nothing there, or less than nothing. Chelsea home was at least quiet, wholesomely aired and clean; but she had an absolute horror of her old home bedroom and drawing-room, where she had endured such torments latterly. "We will new - paper them, rearrange them," said Miss Bromley; and this was actually done in August following. That "new - papering" was somehow to me the saddest of speculations. "Alas, darling! is that all we can do for thee?" The weak, weakest of resources; and yet what other had we? As June went on, things became worse and worse. The sequel is mentioned elsewhere. I will here put down only the successive steps and approximate dates of it.

June 29. After nine nights totally without sleep she announced to us, with a fixity and with a clearness all her own, that she would leave this place to-morrow for London; try there, not in her own house, but in Mrs. Forster's (Palace Gate house, Kensington), which was not yet horrible to her. June 30 (John escorting), she set off by the noon train. Miss Bromley had come down to see her; could only be allowed to see her in stepping into the train, so desperate was the situation, the mood so adequate to it; a moment never to be forgotten by me! How I "worked" afterwards that day is not on record. I dimly remember walking back with Miss Bromley and her lady friend to their hotel; talking to them (as out of the heart of icebergs); and painfully, somehow, sinking into icy or stony rest, worthy of oblivion.

At Forster's there could hardly be a more dubious problem. My poor wandering martyr did get snatches of sleep there; but found the room so noisy, the scene so foreign, etc., she took a farther resolution in the course of the night and its watchings. Sent for John, the first thing in the morning; bade him get places in the night train for Annandale (my sister Mary's; all kindness poor Mary, whom she always liked); "The Gill; we are not yet at the

end there; and Nithsdale, too, is that way!" John failed not, I
dare say, in representations, counter-considerations, but she was
coldly positive; and go they did, express of about 330 miles. Poor
Mary was loyal kindness itself; poor means made noble and more
than opulent by the wealth of love and ready will and invention.
I was seldom so agreeably surprised as by a letter in my darling's
own hand, narrating the heads of the adventure briefly, with a kind
of defiant satisfaction, and informing me that she had slept that
first Gill night for almost nine hours! Whose joy like ours, durst
we have hoped it would last, or even though we durst not! She
stayed about a week still there; Mary and kindred eager to get her
carriages (rather helplessly in that particular), to do and attempt
for her whatever was possible; but the success, in sleep especially,
grew less and less. In about a week she went on to Nithsdale, to
Dr. and Mrs. Russell, and there, slowly improving, continued. Improvement pretty constant; fresh air, driving, silence, kindness.
By the time Mary Craik had got me flitted home to Chelsea, and
herself went for Belfast, all this had steadily begun; and there were
regular letters from her, etc., and I could work here with such an
alleviation of spirits as had long been a stranger to me. In August
(rooms all "new-papered," poor little Jeannie!) she came back to
me, actually there in the cab (John settling), when I ran down-
stairs, looking out on me with the old kind face, a little graver, I
might have thought, but as quiet, as composed and wise and good
as ever. This was the end, I might say, of by far the most tragic
part of our tragedy: Act 5th, though there lay death in it, was
nothing like so unhappy.

The last epoch of my darling's life is to be defined as almost
happy in comparison. It was still loaded with infirmities, bodily
weakness, sleeplessness, continual or almost continual pain, and
weary misery, so far as body was concerned; but her noble spirit
seemed as if it now had its wings free, and rose above all that to
a really singular degree. The battle was over, and we were sore
wounded; but the battle was over, and well. It was remarked by
everybody that she had never been observed so cheerful and bright
of mind as in this last period. The poor bodily department, I constantly hoped too was slowly recovering; and that there would remain to us a "sweet farewell" of sunshine after such a day of rains
and storms, that would still last a blessed while, all my time at
least, before the end came. And, alas! it lasted only about twenty
months, and ended as I have seen. It is beautiful still, all that period, the death very beautiful to me, and will continue so; let me

not repine, but patiently bear what I have got! While the autumn weather continued good, she kept improving. I remember mornings when I found her quite wonderfully cheerful, as I looked in upon her bedroom in passing down, a bright ray of mirth in what she would say to me, inexpressibly pathetic, shining through the wreck of such storms as there had been. How could I but hope? It was an inestimable mercy to me, as I often remark, that I did at last throw aside everything for a few days, and actually get her that poor brougham. Never was soul more grateful for so small a kindness; which seemed to illuminate, in some sort, all her remaining days for her. It was, indeed, useful and necessary as a means of health; but still more precious, I doubt not, as a mark of my regard for her. Ah me! she never knew fully, nor could I show her, in my heavy-laden miserable life, how much I had at all times regarded, loved, and admired her. No telling of her now. "Five minutes more of your dear company in this world. Oh that I had you yet for but five minutes, to tell you all!" this is often my thought since April 21.

She was surely very feeble in the Devonshire time (March, etc., 1865); but I remember her as wonderfully happy. She had long dialogues with Lady A.; used to talk so prettily with me, when I called, in passing up to bed and down from it; she made no complaint, went driving daily through the lanes—sometimes regretted her own poor brougham and "Bellona" (as "still more one's own "), and contrasted her situation as to carriage convenience with that of far richer ladies. "They have £30,000 a year, cannot command a decent or comfortable vehicle here; their vehicles all locked up, 400 miles off, in these wanderings; while we—!" The Lady Ashburton was kindness itself to her; and we all came up to town together, rather in improved health she, I not visibly so, being now vacant and on the collapse, which is yet hardly over, or fairly on the turn. Will it ever be? I have sometimes thought this dreadful unexpected stroke might perhaps be providential withal upon me; and that there lay some little work to do, under changed conditions, before I died. God enable me, if so; God knows.

In Nithsdale, last year, it is yet only fourteen months ago (ah me!), how beautiful she was; for three or four half or quarter days together, how unique in their sad charm as I now recall them from beyond the grave! That day at Russell's, in the garden, etc., at Holmhill; so poorly she, forlorn of outlook, one would have said (one outlook ahead, that of getting me this room trimmed up, the darling, ever-loving soul!); and yet so lively, sprightly even, for my poor sake. "Sir William Gomm" (old Peninsular and Indian General, who had been reading "Friedrich" when she left), what a sparkle that was! her little slap on the table, and arch look, when telling us of him and it! And her own right hand was lame, she had only her left to slap with. I cut the meat for her, on her plate, that day at dinner, and our drive to the station at seven P.M., so sweet, so pure and sad. "We must retrench, dear! (in my telling her of some foolish bank adventure with the draft I had left her); retrench," oh dear, oh dear! Amongst the last things she told me that evening was, with deep sympathy, "Mr. Thomson (a Virginian who sometimes came) called one night; he says there is little doubt they will hang President Davis!" upon which I almost resolved to write a pamphlet upon it, had not I myself been so ignorant about the matter, so foreign to the whole abominable fratricidal " war" (as they called it; "self-murder of a million brother Englishmen, for the sake of sheer phantasms, and totally false theories upon the Nigger," as I had reckoned it). In a day or two I found I could not enter upon that thrice abject Nigger - delirium (viler to me than old witchcraft or the ravings of John of Münster, considerably viler), and that probably I should do poor Davis nothing but harm.

The second day, at good old Mrs. Ewart's, of Nithbank, is still finer to me. Waiting for me with the carriage. "Better, dear, fairly better since I shifted to Nithbank;" the "dinner" ahead there (to my horror), her cautious charming preparation of me for it; our calls at Thornhill (new servant, "Jessie," admiring old tailor-women—no, they were not of the Shankland kind—wearisome old women, whom she had such an interest in, almost wholly for my sake); then our long drive through the Drumlanrig woods, with such talk from her (careless of the shower that fell battering on our hood and apron); in spite of my habitual dispiritment and helpless gloom all that summer, I, too, was cheered for the time. And then the dinner itself, and the bustling rustic company, all this, too, was saved by her; with a quiet little touch here and there, she actually turned it into something of artistic, and it was pleasant to everybody. I was at two, or perhaps three, dinners after this, along with her in London. I partly remarked what is now clearer to me, with what easy perfection she had taken her position in these things—that of a person recognized for quietly superior, if she cared to be so—and also of a suffering, aged woman, accepting her age and feebleness with such a grace, polite composure, and simplicity, as—as all of you might imitate, impartial bystanders would have said! The minister's assistant, poor young

fellow, was gently ordered out by her to sing me "Hame cam' our
gudeman at e'en," which made him completely happy, and set the
dull drawing-room all into illumination till tea ended. He, the assistant, took me to the station (too late for her that evening).

The third day was at Dumfries; sister Jean's and the railway-
station : more hampered and obstructed, but still good and beautiful as ever on her part. Dumb Turner, at the station, etc.; evening falling, ruddy opulence of sky; how beautiful, how brief and
wae! The fourth time was only a ride from Dumfries to Annan, as
she went home, sad and afflictive to me, seeing such a journey ahead
for her (and nothing but the new "Jessie" as attendant, some carriages off); I little thought it was to be the last bit of railwaying
we did together. These, I believe, were all our meetings in Scotland of last year. One day I stood watching "her train" at the
Gill, as appointed; brother Jamie too had been summoned over by
her desire; but at Dumfries she felt so weak in the hot day, she
could only lie down on the sofa, and sadly send John in her stead.
Brother Jamie, whose rustic equipoise, fidelity, and sharp vernacular sense she specially loved, was not to behold her at this time or
evermore. She was waiting for me the night I returned hither;
she had hurried back from her little visit to Miss Bromley (after
the "room" operation); must and would be here to receive me.
She stood there, bright of face and of soul, her drawing-room all
bright, and everything to the last fibre of it in order; had arrived
only two or three hours before; and here again we were. Such
welcome, after my vile day of railwaying, like Jonah in the whale's
belly! That was always her way; bright home, with its bright
face, full of love and victorious over all disorder, always shone on
me like a star as I journeyed and tumbled along amid the shriek-
eries and miseries. Such welcomes could not await me forever; I
little knew this was the last of them on earth. My next, for a thousand years I should never forget the next (of April 23, 1866) which
now was lying only some six months away. I might have seen she
was very feeble; but I noticed only how refinedly beautiful she
was, and thought of no sorrow ahead—did not even think, as I now
do, how it was that she was beautifuller than ever; as if years and
sorrows had only " worn" the noble texture of her being into greater
fineness, the color and tissue still all complete! That night she
said nothing of the room here (down below), but next morning,
after breakfast, led me down, with a quiet smile, expecting her
little triumph—and contentedly had it; though I knew not at first
the tenth part of her merits in regard to that poor enterprise, or

how consummately it had been done to the bottom in spite of her weakness (the noble heart!); and I think (remorsefully) I never praised her enough for her efforts and successes in regard to it. Too late now!

My return was about the middle of September; she never travelled more, except among her widish circle of friends, of whom she seemed to grow fonder and fonder, though generally their qualities were of the affectionate and faithfully honest kind, and not of the distinguished, as a requisite. She was always very cheerful, and had business enough; though I recollect some mornings, one in particular, when the sight of her dear face (haggard from the miseries of the past night) was a kind of shock to me. Thoughtless mortal—she rallied always so soon, and veiled her miseries away—I was myself the most collapsed of men, and had no sunshine in my life but what came from her. Our old laundress, Mrs. Cook, a very meritorious and very poor and courageous woman, age eighty or more, had fairly fallen useless that autumn, and gone into the workhouse. I remember a great deal of trouble taken about her, and the search for her, and settlement of her; such driving and abstruse inquiry in the slums of Westminster, and to the workhouses indicated; discovery of her at length, in the chaos of some Kensington Union (a truly cosmic body, herself, this poor old cook); with instantaneous stir in all directions (consulting with Rector Blunt, interviews with Poor-law Guardians, etc., etc.), and no rest till the poor old Mrs. Cook was got promoted into some quiet cosmic arrangement; small cell or cottage of your own somewhere, with liberty to read, to be clean, and to accept a packet of tea, if any friend gave you one, etc., etc. A good little triumph to my darling; I think, perhaps, the best she had that spring or winter, and the last till my business and the final one.

"Frederick" ended in January, 1865, and we went to Devonshire together, still prospering, she chiefly, though she was so weak. And her talk with me and with others there! nobody had such a charming tongue for truth, discernment, graceful humor, and ingenuity; ever patient too, and smiling, over her many pains and sorrows. We were peaceable and happy, comparatively, through autumn and winter; especially she was wonderfully bearing her sleepless nights and thousandfold infirmities, and gently picking out of them more bright fragments for herself and me than many a one in perfect health and overflowing prosperity could have done. She had one or two select quality friends among her many others. Lady William Russell is the only one I will name, who loved her like a daughter, and was charmed with her talents and graces. "Mr. Carlyle a great man? Yes! but Mrs. Carlyle, let me inform you, is no less great as a woman!" Lady William's pretty little dinners of three were every week or two an agreeable and beneficial event to me also, who heard the report of them given with such lucidity and charm.

End of October came somebody about the Edinburgh Rectorship, to which she gently advised me. Beginning of November I was elected; and an inane though rather amusing hurlyburly of empty congratulations, imaginary businesses, etc., etc., began, the end of which has been so fatally tragical! Many were our plans and speculations about her going with me; to lodge at Newbattle, at etc., etc. The heaps of frivolous letters lying every morning at breakfast, and which did not entirely cease all winter, were a kind of entertainment to her into March, when the address and journey had to be thought of as practical and close at hand. She decided unwillingly, and with various hesitations, *not* to go with me to Edinburgh, in the inclement weather, not to go even to Fryston (Lord Houghton's; Richard Milnes's). As to Edinburgh, she said one day, " You are to speak extempore" (this was more than once clearly advised, and with sound insight); "now, if anything should happen to you, I find, on any sudden alarm, there is a sharp twinge comes into my back, which is like to cut my breath, and seems to stop the heart almost. I should take some fit in the crowded house; it will never do, really!" Alas! the doctors now tell me this meant an affection in some ganglion near the spine, and was a most serious thing; though I did not attach importance to it, but only assented to her practical conclusion as perfectly just. She loving-ly bantered, and beautifully encouraged me about my speech, and its hateful ceremonials and empty botherations; which, for a couple of weeks, were giving me, and her through me, considerable trouble, interruption of sleep, etc.. . . so beautifully borne by her (for my sake), so much less so by me for hers. In fact, I was very miser-able (angry with myself for getting into such a coil of vanity, sad-ly ill in health), and her noble example did not teach me as it should. Sorrow to me now, when too late!

Thursday, March 29, about nine A.M., all was ready here; she softly regulating and forwarding, as her wont was. Professor Tyndall, full of good spirits, appeared with a cab for King's Cross Station. Fryston Hall to be our lodgings till Saturday. I was in the saddest, sickly mood, full of gloom and misery, but striving to hide it; she, too, looked very pale and ill, but seemed intent only on forgetting nothing that could further me. A little flask, holding perhaps two glasses of fine brandy, she brought me as a thought of her own; I did keep a little drop of that brandy (hers, such was a superstition I had), and mixed it in a tumbler of water in that wild scene of the address, and afterwards told her I had done so; thank Heaven that I remembered that in one of my hurried notes. The last I saw of her was as she stood with her back to the parlor door to bid me her good-bye. She kissed me twice (she me once, I her a second time); and—oh, blind mortals! my one wish and hope was to get back to her again, and be in peace under her bright welcome, for the rest of my days, as it were!

Tyndall was kind, cheery, inventive, helpful; the loyalest son could not have more faithfully striven to support his father under every difficulty that rose; and they were many. At Fryston, no sleep was to be had for railways, etc., and the terror lay in those nights that speaking would be impossible, that I should utterly break down; to which, indeed, I had in my mind said, "Well, then," and was preparing to treat it with the best contempt I could. Tyndall wrote daily to her, and kept up better hopes; by a long gallop with me the second day he did get me one good six hours of sleep, and to her made doubtless the most of it: I knew dismally what her anxieties would be, but trust well he reduced them to their minimum. Lord Houghton's, and Lady's, kindness to me was unbounded; *she* also was to have been there, but I was thankful not. Saturday (to York, etc., with Houghton; thence, after long evil loiterings, to Edinburgh with Tyndall and Huxley) was the acme of the three road days. My own comfort was that there could be no post to her; and I arrived in Edinburgh the forlornest of all physical wretches; and had it not been for the kindness of the good Erskines, and of their people, too, I should have had no sleep there either, and have gone probably from bad to worse. But Tyndall's letter of Sunday would be comforting; and my poor little darling would still be in hope that Monday morning, though, of course, in the painfullest anxiety, and I know she had quite "gone off her sleep" in those five days since I had left.

Monday, at Edinburgh, was to me the gloomiest chaotic day, nearly intolerable for confusion, crowding, noisy inanity and misery, till once I got done. My speech was delivered as in a mood of defiant despair, and under the pressure of nightmares. Some feeling that I was not speaking lies alone sustained me. The applause, etc., I took for empty noise, which it really was not altogether. The instant I found myself loose, I hurried joyfully out of it over to

14

my brother's lodging (73 George Street, near by); to the students all crowding and shouting round me, I waved my hand prohibitively at the door, perhaps lifted my hat: and they gave but one cheer more; something in the tone of *it* which did for the first time go into my heart. "Poor young men! so well-affected to the poor old brother or grandfather; and in such a black whirlpool of a world here all of us!" Brother Jamie and son, etc., were sitting within. Erskine and I went silently walking through the streets; and at night was a kind, but wearing and wearying, congratulatory dinner, followed by other such, unwholesome to me, not joyful to me; and endured as duties, little more. But that same afternoon Tyndall's telegram, emphatic to the uttermost ("A perfect triumph" the three words of it), arrived here; a joy of joys to my own little heroine, so beautiful her description of it to me, which was its one value to me; nearly nought otherwise (in very truth), and the last of such that could henceforth have any such addition made to it. Alas! all "additions" are now ended, and the thing added to has become only a pain. But I do thank Heaven for this last favor to her that so loved me; and it will remain a joy to me, if my last in this world. She had to dine with Forster and Dickens that evening, and their way of receiving her good news charmed her as much almost as the news itself.

From that day forward her little heart appears to have been fuller and fuller of joy; newspapers, etc., etc., making such a jubilation (foolish people, as if the address were anything, or had contained the least thing in it which had not been told you already!). She went out for two days to Mrs. Oliphant, at Windsor; recovered her sleep to the old poor average, or nearly so; and by every testimony and all the evidence I myself have, was not for many years, if ever, seen in such fine spirits and so hopeful and joyfully serene and victorious frame of mind, till the last moment. Noble little heart! her painful, much-enduring, much-endeavoring little history, now at last crowned with plain victory, in sight of her own people and of all the world: everybody now obliged to say my Jeannie was not wrong; she was right, and has made it good! Surely for this I should be grateful to Heaven, for this amidst the immeasurable wreck that was preparing for us. She had from an early period formed her own little opinion about me (what an El Dorado to me, ungrateful being—blind, ungrateful, condemnable, and heavy-laden, and crushed down into blindness by great misery as I oftenest was!), and she never flinched from it an instant, I think, or cared, or counted, what the world said to the contrary (very brave, magnanimous, and noble, truly she was in all this); but to have the world confirm her in it was always a sensible pleasure, which she took no pains to hide, especially from me.

She lived nineteen days after that Edinburgh Monday; on the nineteenth (April 21, 1866, between three and four P.M., as near as I can gather and sift), suddenly, as by a thunderbolt from skies all blue, she was snatched from me; a "death from the gods," the old Romans would have called it; the kind of death she many a time expressed her wish for; and in all my life (and as I feel ever since) there fell on me no misfortune like it, which has smitten my whole world into universal wreck (unless I can repair it in some small measure), and extinguished whatever light of cheerfulness and loving hopefulness life still had in it to me.

[Here follows a letter from Miss Jewsbury, with part of a second, which tell their own tale, and after them Mr. Carlyle's closing words.]

43 Markham Square, Chelsea, May 26, 1866.

DEAR MR. CARLYLE,—I think it better to write than to speak on the miserable subject about which you told me to inquire of Mr. Sylvester.* I saw him to-day. He said that it would be about twenty minutes after three o'clock, or thereabouts, when they left Mr. Forster's house; that he then drove through the Queen's Gate, close by the Kensington Gardens; that there, at the uppermost gate, she got out, and walked along the side of the Gardens very slowly, about two hundred paces, with the little dog running, until she came to the Serpentine Bridge, at the southern end of which she got into the carriage again, and he drove on until they came to a quiet place on the Tyburnia side, near Victoria Gate, and then she put out the dog to run along. When they came opposite to Albion Street, Stanhope Place (lowest thoroughfare of Park towards Marble Arch), a brougham coming along upset the dog, which lay on its back screaming for a while, and then she pulled the check-string; and he turned round and pulled up at the side of the foot-path, and there the dog was (he had got up out of the road and gone there); almost before the carriage stopped she was out of it. The lady whose brougham had caused the accident got out also, and several other ladies who were walking had stopped round the dog. The lady spoke to her; but he could not hear what she said, and the other ladies spoke. She then lifted the dog into the car-

---

* Mrs. Carlyle's coachman.

riage, and got in herself. He asked if the little dog were hurt; but, he thinks, she did not hear him, as carriages were passing. He heard the wretched vermin of a dog squeak as if she had been feeling it (nothing but a toe was hurt); this was the last sound or sigh he ever heard from her place of fate. He went on towards Hyde Park Corner, turned there and drove past the Duke of Wellington's Achilles figure, up the drive to the Serpentine and past it, and came round by the road where the dog was hurt, past the Duke of Wellington's [house] and past the gate opposite St. George's; getting no sign (noticing only the two hands laid on the lap, palm uppermost the right hand, reverse way the left, and all motionless), he turned into the Serpentine drive again; but after a few yards, feeling a little surprised, he looked back, and seeing her in the same posture, became alarmed, made for the streetward entrance into the Park (few yards westward of gate-keeper's lodge), and asked a lady to look in; and she said what we know, and she addressed a gentleman who confirmed her fears. It was then fully a quarter past four; going on to twenty minutes (but nearer the quarter), of this he is quite certain. She was leaning back in one corner of the carriage, rugs spread over her knees; her eyes were closed, and her upper lip slightly, slightly opened. Those who saw her at the hospital, and when in the carriage, speak of the beautiful expression upon her face.

I asked him how it was that so long a time was put over in so short a drive? He said he went very slowly on account of the distractions, etc., and he did not seem to think the time taken up at all remarkable (fifty-five minutes): nor did he tell me if he noticed the time as he passed the Marble Arch clock, either of the two times.

If there be any other question you wish asked of him, if you will tell me, I will ask him. He said he heard the little dog cry out as though she were feeling to find if it were hurt.

Very respectfully and affectionately,

GERALDINE E. JEWSBURY.

On that miserable night, when we were preparing to receive her, Mrs. Warren* came to me and said that one time, when she was very ill, she said to her that when the last had come, she was to go up-stairs into the closet of the spare room, and there she would find two wax candles wrapped in paper, and that those were to be lighted and burned. She said that after she came to live in Lon-

---

* The housekeeper in Cheyne Row.

don, she wanted to give a party. Her mother wished everything to be very nice, and went out and bought candles and confectionery, and set out a table, and lighted up the room quite splendidly, and called her to come and see it when all was prepared. She was angry; she said people would say she was extravagant, and would ruin her husband. She took away two of the candles and some of the cakes. Her mother was hurt and began to weep [I remember the "soirée" well; heard nothing of this! — T. C.]. She was pained at once at what she had done; she tried to comfort her, and was dreadfully sorry. She took the candles and wrapped them up, and put them where they could be easily found. We found them and lighted them, and did as she had desired.

G. E. J.

What a strange, beautiful, sublime, and almost terrible little action; silently resolved on, and kept silent from all the earth, for perhaps twenty-four years! I never heard a whisper of it, and yet see it to be true. The visit must have been about 1837; I remember the "soirée" right well; the resolution, bright as with heavenly tears and lightning, was probably formed on her mother's death, February, 1842. My radiant one! Must question Warren the first time I have heart (May 29, 1866).

I have had from Mrs. Warren a clear narrative (shortly after the above date). Geraldine's report is perfectly true; fact with Mrs. Warren occurred in February or March, 1866, "perhaps a month before you went to Edinburgh, sir." I was in the house, it seems, probably asleep up-stairs, or gone out for my walk, evening about eight o'clock. My poor darling was taken with some bad fit ("nausea," and stomach misery, perhaps), and had rung for Mrs. Warren, by whom, with some sip of warm liquid, and gentle words, she was soon gradually relieved. Being very grateful and still very miserable and low, she addressed Mrs. Warren as above, "When the last has come, Mrs. Warren;" and gave her, with brevity, a statement of the case, and exacted her promise; which the other, with cheering counter-words ("Oh, madam, what is all this! you will see me die first!"), hypothetically gave. All this was wiped clean away before I got in; I seem to myself to half recollect one evening, when she did complain of "nausea so habitual now," and looked extremely miserable, while I sat at tea (pour it out she always would, herself drinking only hot water, O heavens!). The candles burned for two whole nights, says Mrs. W. (July 24, 1866).

The paper of this poor note-book of hers is done; all I have to say, too (though there lie such volumes yet unsaid), seems to be almost done, and I must sorrowfully end it, and seek for something else. Very sorrowfully still, for it has been my sacred shrine and religious city of refuge from the bitterness of these sorrows during all the doleful weeks that are past since I took it up; a kind of devotional thing (as I once already said), which softens all grief into tenderness and infinite pity and repentant love, one's whole, sad life drowned as if in tears for one, and all the wrath and scorn and other grim elements silently melted away. And now, am I to leave it, to take farewell of her a second time? Right silent and serene is she, my lost darling yonder, as I often think in my gloom, no sorrow more for her, nor will there long be for me.

APPENDIX

REMINISCENCES OF SUNDRY.

[Begun at Mentone (Alpes Maritimes), Monday, January 28, 1867.]

MANY literary, and one or two political and otherwise public persons, more or less superior to the common run of men I have met with in my life, but perhaps none of them really great or worth more than a transient remembrance, loud as the talk about them once may have been; and certainly none of them, what is more to the purpose, ever vitally interesting or consummately admirable to myself; so that if I do, for want of something else to occupy me better, mark down something of what I recollect concerning some of them, who seemed the greatest, or stood the nearest to me, it surely ought to be with extreme brevity, with rapid succinctness (if I can); at all events, with austere candor, and avoidance of anything which I can suspect to be untrue. Perhaps nobody but myself will ever read this—but that is not infallibly certain—and even in regard to myself, the one possible profit of such a thing is that it be not false or incorrect in any point, but correspond to the fact in all.

When it was that I first got acquainted with Southey's books I do not now recollect, except that it must have been several years after he had been familiar to me as a name, and many years after the public had been familiar with him as a poet, and poetically and otherwise didactic writer. His laureateship provoked a great deal of vulgar jesting; about the "butt of sack," etc.; for the newspaper public, by far the greater number of them radically given, had him considerably in abhorrence, and called him not only Tory, but "renegade," who had traitorously deserted, and gone over to the bad cause. It was at Kirkcaldy that we all read a "slashing article" (by Brougham, I should now guess, were it of the least moment) on Southey's "Letters to W. Smith, M.P.," of Norwich, a Small Socinian personage, conscious of meaning grandly and well, who had been denouncing him as "renegade" (probably contrasting the once "Wat Tyler" with the now laureateship) in the House of Commons; a second back stroke, which, in the irritating circumstances of the "Wat" itself (republished by some sneaking bookseller) had driven Southey to his fighting gear or polemical pen. The pamphlet itself we did not see, except in review quotations, which were naturally the shrillest and weakest discoverable, with citations from "Wat Tyler" to accompany; but the flash reviewer understood his trade; and I can remember how we all cackled and triumphed over Southey along with him, as over a slashed and well-slain foe to us and mankind; for we were

14*

all Radicals in heart, Irving and I as much as any of the others, and were not very wise, nor had looked into the *per contra* side. I retract now on many points, on that of "Barabbas" in particular, which example Southey cited as characteristic of democracy, greatly to my dissent, till I had much better, and for many years, considered the subject.

That bout of pamphleteering had brought Southey much nearer me, but had sensibly diminished my esteem of him, and would naturally slacken my desire for farther acquaintance. It must have been a year or two later when his "Thalaba," "Curse of Kehama," "Joan of Arc," etc., came into my hands, or some one of them came, which awakened new effort for the others. I recollect the much kindlier and more respectful feeling these awoke in me, which has continued ever since. I much recognize the piety, the gentle, deep affection, the reverence for God and man, which reigned in these pieces: full of soft pity, like the wailings of a mother, and yet with a clang of chivalrous valor finely audible too. One could not help loving such a man; and yet I rather felt, too, as if he were a shrillish, thin kind of man, the feminine element perhaps considerably predominating and limiting. However, I always afterwards looked out for his books, new or old, as for a thing of value, and in particular read his articles in the "Quarterly," which were the most accessible productions. In spite of my Radicalism, I found very much in these Toryisms which was greatly according to my heart; things rare and worthy, at once pious and true, which were always welcome to me, though I strove to base them on a better ground than his—his being no eternal or time-defying one, as I could see, and time, in fact, in my own case, having already done its work then. In this manner our innocently pleasant relation, as writer and written for, had gone on, without serious shock, though, after "Kehama," not with much growth in quality or quantity, for perhaps ten years.

It was probably in 1836 or 7, the second or third year after our removal to London, that Henry Taylor, author of "Artevelde," and various similar things, with whom I had made acquaintance, and whose early regard, constant esteem, and readiness to be helpful and friendly, should be among my memorabilia of those years, invited me to come to him one evening, and have a little speech with Southey, whom he judged me to be curious about, and to like, perhaps, more than I did. Taylor himself, a solid, soundheaded, faithful man, though of morbid vivacity in all senses of that deepreaching word, and with a fine readiness to apprehend new truth, and stand by it, was in personal intimacy with the "Lake" sages and poets, especially with Southey; he considered that in Wordsworth and the rest of them was embodied all of pious wisdom that our age had, and could not doubt but the sight of Southey would be welcome to me. I readily consented to come, none but we three present, Southey to be Taylor's guest at dinner, I to join them after—which was done. Taylor, still little turned of thirty, lived miscellaneously about, in bachelor's lodgings, or sometimes for a month or two during "the season" in furnished houses, where he

ROBERT SOUTHEY.

could receive guests. In the former I never saw him, nor to the latter did I go but when invited. It was in a quiet ground-floor, of the latter character as I conjectured, somewhere near Downing Street, and looking into St. James's Park, that I found Taylor and Southey, with their wine before them, which they hardly seemed to be minding; very quiet this seemed to be, quiet their discourse, too; to all which, not sorry at the omen, I quietly joined myself. Southey was a man towards well up in the fifties; hair gray, not yet hoary, well setting off his fine clear brown complexion; head and face both smallish, as indeed the figure was while seated; features finely cut; eyes, brow, mouth, good in their kind—expressive all, and even vehemently so, but betokening rather keenness than depth either of intellect or character; a serious, human, honest, but sharp, almost fierce-looking, thin man, with very much of the militant in his aspect—in the eyes especially was visible a mixture of sorrow and of anger, or of angry contempt, as if his indignant fight with the world had not yet ended in victory, but also never should in defeat. A man you were willing to hear speak. We got to talk of Parliament, public speaking and the like (perhaps some electioneering then afoot?). On my mentioning the candidate at Bristol, with his "I say ditto to Mr. Burke"—"Hah, I myself heard that" (had been a boy listening when that was said!). His contempt for the existing set of parties was great and fixed, especially for what produced the present electoral temper; though in the future, too, except through Parliaments and elections, he seemed to see no hope. He took to repeating in a low, sorrowfully mocking tone, certain verses (I supposed of his own), emphatically in that vein which seemed to me bitter and exaggerative, not without ingenuity, but exhibiting no trace of genius. Partly in response, or rather as sole articulate response, I asked who had made those verses. Southey answered, carelessly, "Praed, they say; Praed, I suppose." My notion was, he was merely putting me off, and the verses were his own, though he disliked confessing to them. A year or two ago, looking into some review of a reprint of Praed's works, I came upon the verses again, among other excerpts of a similar genus, and found that they verily were Praed's; my wonder now was that Southey had charged his memory with the like of them. This Praed was a young M.P. who had gained distinction at Oxford or Cambridge. As he spoke and wrote without scruple against the late illustrious Reform Bill and sovereign Reform doctrine in general, great things were expected of him by his party, now sitting cowed into silence, and his name was very current in the newspapers for a few months; till suddenly (soon after this of Southey), the poor young man died, and sank at once into oblivion, tragical, though not unmerited, nor extraordinary, as I judged from the contents of that late reprint and Biographical Sketch, by some pious and regretful old friend of his. That Southey had some of Praed's verses by heart (verses about Hon. Mr. this moving, say, to abolish death and the devil; Hon. Mr. B., to change, for improvement's sake, the obliquity of the Ecliptic, etc., etc.) is, perhaps, a kind of honor to poor

Praed, who (inexorable fate cutting short his "career of ambition" in that manner) is, perhaps, as sad and tragical to me as to another. After Southey's bit of recitation I think the party must have soon broken up. I recollect nothing more of it, except my astonishment when Southey at last completely rose from his chair to shake hands. He had only half risen and nodded on my coming in; and all along I had counted him a lean little man; but now he shot suddenly aloft into a lean tall one, all legs, in shape and stature like a pair of tongs, which peculiarity my surprise doubtless exaggerated to me, but only made it the more notable and entertaining. Nothing had happened throughout that was other than moderately pleasant; and I returned home (I conclude) well enough satisfied with my evening. Southey's sensitiveness I had noticed on the first occasion as one of his characteristic qualities, but was nothing like aware of the extent of it till our next meeting.

This was a few evenings afterwards, Taylor giving some dinner, or party, party in honor of his guest; if dinner, I was not at that, but must have undertaken for the evening sequel, as less incommodious to me, less unwholesome more especially. I remember entering, in the same house, but up-stairs this time, a pleasant little drawing-room, in which, in well-lighted, secure enough condition, sat Southey in full dress, silently reclining, and as yet no other company. We saluted suitably; touched ditto on the vague initiatory points; and were still there, when, by way of coming closer, I asked mildly, with no appearance of special interest, but with more than I really felt, "Do you know De Quincey?" (the opium-eater, whom I knew to have lived in Cumberland as his neighbor). "Yes, sir," said Southey, with extraordinary animosity, "and if you have opportunity, I'll thank you to tell him he is one of the greatest scoundrels living!" I laughed lightly, said I had myself little acquaintance with the man, and could not wish to recommend myself by that message. Southey's face, as I looked at it, was become of slate-color, the eyes glancing, the attitude rigid, the figure altogether a picture of Rhadamanthine rage—that is, rage conscious to itself of being just. He doubtless felt I would expect some explanation from him. "I have told Hartley Coleridge," said he, "that he ought to take a strong cudgel, proceed straight to Edinburgh, and give De Quincey, publicly in the streets there, a sound beating, as a calumniator, cowardly spy, traitor, base betrayer of the hospitable social hearth, for one thing!" It appeared De Quincey was then, and for some time past, writing in "Blackwood's Magazine" something of autobiographic nature, a series of papers on the "Lake" period of his life, merely for the sake of the highly needful trifle of money, poor soul, and with no wish to be untrue (I could believe) or hurt anybody, though not without his own bits of splenetic conviction, and to which latter, in regard of Coleridge in particular, he had given more rein than was agreeable to parties concerned. I believe I had myself read the paper on Coleridge, one paper on him I certainly read, and had been the reverse of tempted by it to look after the others; finding in this, e. g., that Coleridge had the greatest intellect perhaps ever given to man, "but that he wanted, or as good as wanted, common honesty in applying it;" which seemed to me a miserable contradiction in terms, and threw light, if not on Coleridge, yet on De Quincey's faculty of judging him or others. In this paper there were probably withal some domestic details or allusions, to which, as familiar to rumor, I had paid but little heed; but certainly, of general reverence for Coleridge and his gifts and deeds, I had traced, not deficiency in this paper, but glaring exaggeration, coupled with De Quincean drawbacks, which latter had alone struck Southey with such poignancy; or perhaps there had been other more criminal papers, which Southey knew of, and not I? In few minutes we let the topic drop, I helping what I could, and he seemed to feel as if he had done a little wrong, and was bound to show himself more than usually amicable and social, especially with me, for the rest of the evening, which he did in effect, though I quite forget the details, only that I had a good deal of talk with him, in the circle of the others, and had again more than once to notice the singular readiness of the blushes; amiable red blush, beautiful like a young girl's, when you touched genially the pleasant theme, and serpent-like flash of blue or black blush (this far, very far the rarer kind, though it did recur too) when you struck upon the opposite. All details of the evening, except that primary one, are clean gone; but the effect was interesting, pleasantly stimulating, and surprising. I said to myself, "How has this man contrived, with such a nervous system, to keep alive for near sixty years? Now blushing under his gray hairs, rosy like a maiden of fifteen; now slaty almost, like a rattlesnake or fiery serpent? How has he not been torn to pieces long since, under such furious pulling this way and that? He must have somewhere a great deal of methodic virtue in him; I suppose, too, his heart is thoroughly honest, which helps considerably." I did not fancy myself to have made personally much impression on Southey; but on those terms I accepted him for a loyal kind of man; and was content and thankful to know of his existing in the world, near me, or still far from me, as the fates should have determined. For perhaps two years I saw no more of him; heard only from Taylor in particular, that he was overwhelmed in misery, and imprudently refusing to yield, or screen himself in any particular. Imprudently, thought Taylor and his other friends; for not only had he been, for several continuous years, toiling and fagging at a collective edition of his works, which cost him a great deal of incessant labor, but, far worse, his poor wife had sunk into insanity, and moreover he would not, such his feeling on this tragic matter, be persuaded to send her to an asylum, or trust her out of his own sight and keeping. Figure such a scene; and what the most sensitive of mankind must have felt under it. This, then, is the garland and crown of "victory" provided for an old man, when he survives, spent with his fifty years of climbing and of running, and has what you call won the race!

It was after I had finished the "French Revolution," and perhaps after my Annandale journey to recover from this adventure, that I heard of Southey's being in town again. His collective edition was complete, his poor wife was dead and at rest; his work was done; in fact (had he known it), all his work in the world was done; and he had determined on a few weeks of wandering, and trying to repose and recreate himself, among old friends and scenes. I saw him twice or thrice on this occasion; it was our second and last piece of intercourse, and much the more interesting, to me at least, and for a reason that will appear. My wild excitation of nerves, after finishing that grim book on "French Revolution," was something strange. The desperate nature of our circumstances and outlooks while writing it, the thorough possession it had taken of me, dwelling in me day and night, keeping me in constant fellowship with such a "flamy cut-throat scene of things," infernal and celestial both in one, with no fixed prospect but that of writing it, though I should die, had held me in a fever blaze for three years long; and now the blaze had ceased, problem *taliter qualiter* was actually done, and my humor and way of thought about all things was of an altogether ghastly, dim-smouldering, and as if preternatural sort. I well remember that ten minutes' survey I had of Annan and its vicinity the forenoon after my landing there. Brother Alick must have met me at the steamboat harbor, I suppose; at any rate, we were walking towards Scotsbrig together, and at Mount Annan Gate, bottom of Landhead hamlet, he had left me for a moment till he called somewhere. I stood leaning against a stone or mile-stone, face towards Annan, of which with the two miles of variegated cheerful green slope that intervened, and then of the Solway Frith, far and wide from Gretna, St. Bees Head and beyond it, of the grand and lovely Cumberland mountains, with Helvellyn and even with Ingleborough in the rearward, there was a magnificent view well known to me. Stone itself was well known to me; this had been my road to Annan School from my tenth year upward; right sharp was my knowledge of every item in this scene, thousandfold my memories connected with it, and mournful and painful rather than joyful, too many of them. And now here it was again; and here was I again. Words cannot utter the wild and ghastly expressiveness of that scene to me; it seemed as if Hades itself, and the gloomy realms of death and eternity, were looking out on me through those poor old familiar objects; as if no miracle could be more miraculous than this same bit of space and bit of time spread out before me. I felt withal how wretchedly unwell I must be; and was glad, no doubt, when Alick returned, and we took the road again. What precedes and what follows this clear bit of memory are alike gone; but for seven or more weeks after, I rode often down and up this same road, silent, solitary, weird of mood, to bathe in the Solway; and not even my dear old mother's love and cheery helpfulness (for she was then still strong for her age) could raise my spirits out of utter grimness and fixed contemptuous disbelief in the future. Hope of having succeeded, of ever succeeding, I had not the faintest, was not even at the pains to wish it; said only, in a dim, mute way, " Very well, then; be it just so, then!" A foolish young neighbor, not an ill-disposed, sent me a number of the "Athenæum" (literary journal of the day), in which I was placidly, with some elaboration, set down as blockhead and strenuous failure: the last words were, "Readers, have we made out our case?" I read it without pain, or pain the least to signify; laid it aside for a day or two; then one morning, in some strait about our breakfast tea-kettle, slipt the peccant number under that, and had my cup of excellent hot tea from it. The foolish neighbor who was filing the "Athenæum" (more power to him!) found a *lacuna* in his set at this point; might know better, another time, it was hoped. Thackeray's laudation in the "Times," I also recollect the arrival of (how pathetic now her mirth over it to me!). But neither did Thackeray inspire me with any emotion, still less with any ray of exultation. "One other poor judge voting," I said to myself; "but what is he, or such as he? The fate of that thing is fixed! I have written it; that is all my result." Nothing now strikes me as affecting in all this but her noble attempt to cheer me on my return home to her, still sick and sad; and how she poured out on me her melodious joy, and all her bits of confirmatory anecdotes and narratives. "Oh, it has had a great success, dear!" and not even she could irradiate my darkness, beautifully as she tried for a long time, as I sat at her feet again by our own parlor fire. "Oh, you are an unbelieving nature!" said she at last, starting up, probably to give me some tea. There was, and is, in all this something heavenly; the rest is all of it smoke; and has gone up the chimney, inferior in benefit and quality to what my pipe yielded me. I was rich once, had I known it— very rich; and now I am become poor to the end.

Such being my posture and humor at that time, fancy my surprise at finding Southey full of sympathy, assent and recognition of the amplest kind, for my poor new book! We talked largely on the huge event itself, which he had dwelt with openly or privately ever since his youth, and tended to interpret, exactly as I, the suicidal explosion of an old wicked world, too wicked, false, and impious for living longer; and seemed satisfied and as if grateful that a strong voice had at last expressed that meaning. My poor "French Revolution" evidently appeared to him a good deed, a salutary bit of "scriptural" exposition for the public and for mankind; and this, I could perceive, was the soul of a great many minor approbations and admirations of detail, which he was too polite to speak of. As Southey was the only man of eminence that had ever taken such a view of me, and especially of this my first considerable book, it seems strange that I should have felt so little real triumph in it as I did. For all other eminent men, in regard to all my books and writings hitherto, and most of all in regard to this latest, had stood pointedly silent, dubitative, disapprobatory, many of them shaking their heads. Then, when poor "Sartor" got passed through "Fraser," and was done up from the Fraser types as a separate thing, perhaps about fifty copies being struck off, I sent six copies to six Edinburgh literary friends, from not one of whom did I get the smallest whisper even of receipt—a thing disappointing more or less to human nature, and which has silently and insensibly led me never since to send any copy of a book to Edinburgh, or, indeed, to Scotland at all, except to my own kindred there, and in one or two specific unliterary cases more. The Plebs of literature might be divided in their verdicts about me, though, by count of heads, I always suspect the "guilties" clean had it; but the conscript fathers declined to vote at all. And yet here was a conscript father voting in a very pregnant manner; and it seems I felt but little joy even in that. Truly I can say for myself, Southey's approbation, though very privately I doubtless had my pride in it, did not the least tend to swell me; though, on the other hand, I must own to very great gloom of mind, sullen some part of it, which is possibly a worse fault than what it saved me from. I remember now how polite and delicate his praises of me were; never given direct or in overmeasure, but always obliquely, in the way of hint or inference left for me; and how kind, sincere, and courteous his manner throughout was. Our mutual considerations about French Revolution, about its incidents, catastrophes, or about its characters, Danton, Camille, etc., and contrasts and comparisons of them with their (probable) English compeers of the day, yielded pleasant and copious material for dialogue when we met. Literature was hardly touched upon: our discourse came almost always upon moral and social topics. Southey's look, I remarked, was strangely careworn, anxious, though he seemed to like talking, and both talked and listened well; his eyes especially were as if filled with gloomy bewilderment and incurable sorrows. He had got to be about sixty-three, had buried all his suffering loved ones, wound up forty years of incessant vehement labor, much of it more or less ungenial to him; and, in fact, though he knew it not, had finished his work in the world, and might well be looking back on it with a kind of ghastly astonishment rather than with triumph or joy.

I forget how often we met; it was not very often; it was always at H. Taylor's, or through Taylor. One day, for the first and last time, he made us a visit at Chelsea. A certain old lady cousin of Taylor's, who sometimes presided in his house for a month or two in the town season—a Miss Fenwick, of provincial accent and type, but very wise, discreet, and well-bred—had come driving down with him. Their arrival, and loud thundering knock at the door, is very memorable to me—the moment being unusually critical in our poor household. My little Jeannie was in hands with the marmalade that day: none ever made such marmalade for me, pure as liquid amber, in taste and in look almost poetically delicate, and it was the only one of her pretty and industrious comfitures that I individually cared for; which made her doubly diligent and punctual about it. (Ah, me! ah, me!) The kitchen fire, I suppose, had not been brisk enough, free enough, so she had had the large brass pan and contents brought up to the brisker parlor fire, and was there victoriously boiling it, when it boiled over, in huge blaze, set the chimney on fire — and I (from my writing up-stairs, I suppose) had been suddenly summoned to the rescue. What a moment! what an outlook! The kindling of the chimney soot was itself a grave matter, involving fine of £10 if the fire-engines had to come. My first and immediate step was to parry this, by at once letting down the grate valve, and cutting quite off the supply of oxygen or atmosphere, which, of course, was effectual, though at the expense of a little smoke in the room meanwhile. The brass pan, and remaining contents (not much wasted or injured), she had herself snatched off and set on the hearth; I was pulling down the back windows, which would have completed the temporary settlement, when, hardly three yards from us, broke out the thundering doorknocker; and before the brass pan could be got away, Miss Fenwick and Southey were let in. Southey, I don't think my darling had yet seen; but her own fine, modest composure and presence of mind never in any greatest other presence forsook her. I remember how daintily she made the salutations, brief, quizzical bit of explanation, got the wreck to vanish, and sate down as member of our little party. Southey and I were on the sofa together; she nearer Miss Fenwick, for a little of feminine " aside " now and then. The colloquy did not last long: I recollect no point of it, except that Southey and I got to speaking about Shelley (whom, perhaps, I remembered to have lived in the Lake country for some time, and had started on Shelley as a practicable topic). Southey did not rise into admiration of Shelley either for talent or conduct; spoke of him and his life without bitterness, but with contemptuous sorrow, and evident aversion mingled with his pity. To me also poor Shelley always was, and is, a kind of ghastly object, colorless, pallid, without health, or warmth, or vigor; the sound of him shrieky, frosty, as if a ghost were trying to " sing to us;" the temperament of him spasmodic, hysterical, instead of strong or robust; with fine affections and aspirations, gone all such a road: a man infinitely too weak for that solitary scaling of the Alps, which he undertook in spite of all the world. At some point of the dialogue I said to Southey, " A haggard existence that of his." I remember Southey's pause, and the tone and air with which he answered, " It is a haggard existence!" His look at this moment was unusually gloomy and heavy-laden, full of confused distress—as if in retrospect of his own existence, and the haggard battle it too had been.

He was now about sixty-three; his work all done, but his heart as if broken. A certain Miss Bowles, given to scribbling, with its affectations, its sentimentalities, and perhaps twenty years younger than he, had (as I afterwards understood) heroically volunteered to marry him, " for the purpose of consoling," etc., etc., to which he heroically had assented, and was now on the road towards Bristol, or the western region where Miss Bowles lived, for completing that poor hope of his and hers. A second wedlock; in what contrast almost dismal, almost horrible, with a former there had been! Far away that former one; but it had been illuminated by the hopes and radiances of very heaven; this second one was to be celebrated

under sepulchral lamps, and as if in the forecoast of the charnel-house!
Southey's deep misery of aspect I should have better understood had this
been known to me; but it was known to Taylor alone, who kept it locked
from everybody.

The last time I saw Southey was on an evening at Taylor's, nobody there
but myself; I think he meant to leave town next morning, and had wished
to say farewell to me first. We sat on the sofa together; our talk was
long and earnest; topic ultimately the usual one, steady approach of democracy, with revolution (probably explosive), and a finis incomputable to
man; steady decay of all morality, political, social, individual; this once
noble England getting more and more ignoble and untrue in every fibre of
it, till the gold (Goethe's composite king) would all be eaten out, and noble
England would have to collapse in shapeless ruin, whether forever or not
none of us could know. Our perfect consent on these matters gave an
animation to the dialogue, which I remember as copious and pleasant.
Southey's last word was in answer to some tirade of mine against universal mammon worship, gradual accelerating decay of mutual humanity, of
piety and fidelity to God or man, in all our relations and performances, the
whole illustrated by examples, I suppose; to which he answered, not with
levity, yet with a cheerful tone in his seriousness, "It will not and it cannot come to good!" This he spoke standing; I had risen, checking my
tirade, intimating that, alas! I must go. He invited me to Cumberland, to
"see the lakes again," and added, "Let us know beforehand that the rites of
hospitality—" I had already shaken hands, and now answered from beyond the door of the apartment, "Ah, yes; thanks, thanks!" little thinking
that it was my last farewell of Southey.

He went to the Western country, got wedded, went back to Keswick, and
I heard once or so some shallow jest about his promptitude in wedding;
but before long the news came, first in whispers, then public and undeniable, that his mind was going and gone, memory quite, and the rest hopelessly following it. The new Mrs. Southey had not succeeded in "consoling and comforting" him, but far the reverse. We understood afterwards that the grown-up daughters and their step-mother had agreed ill;
that perhaps neither they nor she were very wise, nor the arrangement itself very wise or well contrived. Better, perhaps, that poor Southey was
evicted from it, shrouded away in curtains of his own, and deaf to all dis-
cords henceforth! We heard of him from Miss Fenwick now and then (I
think for a year or two more) till the end came. He was usually altogether placid and quiet, without memory, more and more without thought.
One day they had tried him with some fine bit of his own poetry; he woke
into beautiful consciousness, eyes and features shining with their old
brightness (and perhaps a few words of rational speech coming); but it
lasted only some minutes, till all lapsed into the old blank again. By degrees all intellect had melted away from him, and quietly, unconsciously, he
died. There was little noise in the public on this occurrence, nor could his

private friends do other than, in silence, mournfully, yet almost gratefully,
acquiescè. There came out by-and-by, two lives of him—one by his widow,
one by his son (such the family discrepancies, happily inaudible where
they would have cut sharpest); neither of these books did I look into.

Southey I used to construe to myself as a man of slight build, but of
sound and elegant, with considerable genius in him, considerable faculty
of speech and rhythmic insight, and with a morality that shone distinguished among his contemporaries. I reckoned him (with those blue
blushes and those red) to be the perhaps excitablest of all men, and that
a deep mute monition of conscience had spoken to him, "You are capable
of running mad, if you don't take care. Acquire habitudes; stick firm as
adamant to them at all times, and work—continually work!"

This, for thirty or forty years, he had punctually and impetuously done ;
no man so habitual, we were told; gave up his poetry, at a given hour, on
stroke of the clock, and took to prose, etc., etc.; and as to diligence and
velocity, employed his very walking hours, walked with a book in his hand;
and by these methods of his, had got through, perhaps, a greater amount
of work, counting quantity and quality, than any other man whatever in
those years of his; till all suddenly ended. I likened him to one of those
huge sandstone grinding cylinders which I had seen at Manchester, turning
with inconceivable velocity (in the condemned room of the iron factory,
where "the men die of lung disease at forty," but are permitted to smoke
in their damp cellar, and think that a rich recompense!), screaming
harshly, and shooting out each of them its sheet of fire (yellow, starlight,
etc., according as it is brass or other kind of metal that you grind and
polish there)—beautiful sheets of fire, pouring out each as if from the
paper cap of its low-stooping-backed grinder, when you look from rearward. For many years these stones grind so, at such a rate; till at last
(in some cases) comes a moment when the stone's cohesion is quite worn
out, overcome by the stupendous velocity long continued; and while grinding its fastest, it flies off altogether, and settles some yards from you, a
grinding-stone no longer, but a cart-load of quiet sand.

Of Wordsworth I have little to write that could ever be of use to myself
or others. I did not see him much, or till latish in my course see him at
all; nor did we deeply admire one another at any time. Of me in my first
times he had little knowledge; and any feeling he had towards me, I suspect, was largely blended with abhorrence and perhaps a kind of fear.
His works I knew, but never considerably reverenced; could not, on attempting it. A man recognizably of strong intellectual powers, strong
character; given to meditation, and much contemptuous of the unmeditative
world and its noisy nothingnesses; had a fine limpid style of writing and
delineating, in his small way; a fine limpid vein of melody too in him (as
of an honest rustic fiddle, good, and well handled, but wanting two or
more of the strings, and not capable of much!). In fact, a rather dull,
hard-tempered, unproductive, and almost wearisome, kind of man; not

adorable, by any means, as a great poetic genius, much less as the Trismegistus of such; whom only a select few could ever read, instead of misreading, which was the opinion his worshippers confidently entertained of him! Privately I had a real respect for him withal, founded on his early biography (which Wilson of Edinburgh had painted to me as of antique greatness). "Poverty and Peasanthood! Be it so! but we consecrate ourselves to the Muses, all the same, and will proceed on those terms, Heaven aiding!" This, and what of faculty I did recognize in the man, gave me a clear esteem of him, as of one remarkable and fairly beyond common; not to disturb which, I avoided speaking of him to his worshippers; or, if the topic turned up, would listen with an acquiescing air. But to my private self his divine reflections and unfathomabilities seemed stinted, scanty, palish, and uncertain—perhaps in part a feeble reflex (derived at second hand through Coleridge) of the immense German fund of such—and I reckoned his poetic store-house to be far from an opulent or well-furnished apartment. It was perhaps about 1840 that I first had any decisive meeting with Wordsworth, or made any really personal acquaintance with him. In parties at Taylor's I may have seen him before; but we had no speech together, nor did we specially notice one another. One such time I do remember (probably before, as it was in my earlier days of Sterling acquaintanceship, when Sterling used to argue much with me); Wordsworth sat silent, almost next to me, while Sterling took to asserting the claims of Kotzebue as a dramatist ("recommended even by Goethe," as he likewise urged), whom I with pleasure did my endeavor to explode from that mad notion, and thought (as I still recollect), "This will perhaps please Wordsworth too," who, however, gave not the least sign of that or any other feeling. I had various dialogues with him in that same room; but those, I judge, were all or mostly of after-date.

On a summer morning (let us call it 1840 then) I was apprised by Taylor that Wordsworth had come to town, and would meet a small party of us at a certain tavern in St. James's Street, at breakfast, to which I was invited for the given day and hour. We had a pretty little room, quiet, though looking streetward (tavern's name is quite lost to me); the morning sun was pleasantly tinting the opposite houses; a balmy, calm, and sunlight morning. Wordsworth, I think, arrived just along with me; we had still five minutes of sauntering and miscellaneous talking before the whole were assembled. I do not positively remember any of them, except that James Spedding was there, and that the others, not above five or six in whole, were polite, intelligent, quiet persons, and, except Taylor and Wordsworth, not of any special distinction in the world. Breakfast was pleasant, fairly beyond the common of such things. Wordsworth seemed in good tone, and, much to Taylor's satisfaction, talked a great deal; about "poetic," correspondents of his own (i. e., correspondents for the sake of his poetry; especially one such who had sent him, from Canton, an excellent chest of tea; correspondent grinningly applauded by us all); then about ruralities

WILLIAM WORDSWORTH.

and miscellanies; "Countess of Pembroke," antique she-Clifford, glory of those northern parts, who was not new to any of us, but was set forth by Wordsworth with gusto and brief emphasis—"you lily-livered," etc.; and now the only memorable item under that head. These were the first topics. Then, finally, about literature, literary laws, practices, observances, at considerable length, and turning wholly on the mechanical part, including even a good deal of shallow enough etymology, from me and others, which was well received. On all this Wordsworth enlarged with evident satisfaction, and was joyfully reverent of the "wells of English undefiled," though stone-dumb as to the deeper rules and wells of Eternal Truth and Harmony, which you were to try and set forth by said undefiled wells of English, or what other speech you had! To me a little disappointing, but not much; though it would have given me pleasure had the robust veteran man emerged a little out of vocables into things now and then, as he never once chanced to do. For the rest, he talked well in his way; with veracity, easy brevity, and force, as a wise tradesman would of his tools and workshop, and as no unwise one could. His voice was good, frank, and sonorous, though practically clear, distinct, and forcible rather than melodious; the tone of him business-like, sedately confident; no discourtesy, yet no anxiety about being courteous. A fine wholesome rusticity, fresh as his mountain breezes, sat well on the stalwart veteran, and on all he said and did. You would have said he was a usually taciturn man; glad to unlock himself to audience sympathetic and intelligent, when such offered itself. His face bore marks of much, not always peaceful, meditation; the look of it not bland or benevolent so much as close, impregnable, and hard: a man *multa tacere loquive paratus*, in a world where he had experienced no lack of contradictions as he strode along. The eyes were not very brilliant, but they had a quiet clearness; there was enough of brow, and well shaped; rather too much of cheek ("horse face" I have heard satirists say); face of squarish shape, and decidedly longish, as I think the head itself was (its "length" going horizontal); he was large-boned, lean, but still firm-knit, tall, and strong-looking when he stood, a right good old steel-gray figure, with rustic simplicity and dignity about him, and a vivacious strength looking through him which might have suited one of those old steel-gray markgrafs whom Henry the Fowler set up to ward the "marches," and do battle with the intrusive heathen in a stalwart and judicious manner.

On this and other occasional visits of his, I saw Wordsworth a number of times, at dinner, in evening parties; and we grew a little more familiar, but without much increase of real intimacy or affection springing up between us. He was willing to talk with me in a corner, in noisy, extensive circles, having weak eyes, and little loving the general babble current in such places. One evening, probably about this time, I got him upon the subject of great poets, who, I thought, might be admirable equally to us both; but was rather mistaken, as I gradually found. Pope's partial failure I was prepared for; less for the narrowish limits visible in Milton and

others. I tried him with Burns, of whom he had sung tender recognition;
but Burns also turned out to be a limited, inferior creature, any genius he
had a theme for one's pathos rather; even Shakspeare himself had his
blind sides, his limitations. Gradually it became apparent to me that of
transcendent unlimited there was, to this critic, probably but one specimen
known—Wordsworth himself! He by no means said so, or hinted so, in
words; but on the whole it was all I gathered from him in this considerable *tête-à-tête* of ours; and it was not an agreeable conquest. New notion as
to poetry or poet I had not in the smallest degree got; but my insight into
the depths of Wordsworth's pride in himself had considerably augmented,
and it did not increase my love of him; though I did not in the least hate
it either, so quiet was it, so fixed, unappealing, like a dim old lichened crag
on the way-side, the private meaning of which, in contrast with any public
meaning it had, you recognized with a kind of not wholly melancholy grin.

Another and better corner dialogue I afterwards had with him, possibly
also about this time, which raised him intellectually some real degrees higher in my estimation than any of his deliverances, written or oral, had ever
done, and which I may reckon as the best of all his discoursings or dialogues with me. He had withdrawn to a corner, out of the light and of
the general babble, as usual with him. I joined him there, and knowing
how little fruitful was the literary topic between us, set him on giving me
an account of the notable practicalities he had seen in life, especially of the
notable men. He went into all this with a certain alacrity, and was willing to speak whenever able on the terms. He had been in France in the
earlier or secondary stage of the Revolution; had witnessed the struggle of
Girondins and Mountain, in particular the execution of Gorsas, "the first
deputy sent to the scaffold;" and testified strongly to the ominous feeling
which that event produced in everybody, and of which he himself still seemed to retain something: "Where will it end, when you have set an example in this kind?" I knew well about Gorsas, but had found in my read-
ings no trace of the public emotion his death excited, and perceived now
that Wordsworth might be taken as a true supplement to my book, on this
small point. He did not otherwise add to or alter my ideas on the Revolution, nor did we dwell long there; but hastened over to England, and to
the noteworthy, or at least noted, men of that and the subsequent time.
"Noted" and named, I ought, perhaps, to say, rather than "noteworthy;"
for in general I forget what men they were, and now remember only the
excellent sagacity, distinctness, and credibility of Wordsworth's little bio-
graphic portraitures of them. Never, or never but once, had I seen a stronger intellect, a more luminous and veracious power of insight, directed upon
such a survey of fellow-men and their contemporary journey through the
world. A great deal of Wordsworth lay in the mode and tone of drawing,
but you perceived it to be faithful, accurate, and altogether life-like, though
Wordsworthian. One of the best remembered sketches (almost the only
one now remembered at all) was that of Wilberforce, the famous Nigger

philanthropist, drawing-room Christian, and busy man and politician. In all which capacities Wordsworth's esteem of him seemed to be privately as small as my own private one, and was amusing to gather. No hard word of him did he speak or hint; told in brief firm business terms, how he was born at or near the place called Wilberforce in Yorkshire ("force" signifying torrent or angry brook as in Cumberland?); where, probably, his forefathers may have been possessors, though he was poorish; how he did this and that of insignificant (to Wordsworth insignificant) nature; "and then," ended Wordsworth, "he took into the oil trade" (I suppose the Hull whaling); which lively phrase, and the incomparable historical tone it was given in—"the oil trade"—as a thing perfectly natural and proper for such a man, is almost the only point in the delineation which is now vividly present to me. I remember only the rustic picture, sketched as with a burnt stick on the board of a pair of bellows, seemed to me completely good; and that the general effect was, one saw the great Wilberforce and his existence visible in all their main lineaments, but only as through the reversed telescope, and reduced to the size of a mouse and its nest, or little more! This was, in most or in all cases, the result brought out: one's self and telescope of natural (or perhaps preternatural) size; but the object, so great to vulgar eyes, reduced amazingly, with all its lineaments recognizable. I found a very superior talent in these Wordsworth delineations. They might have reminded me, though I know not whether they did at the time, of a larger series like them, which I had from my father during two wet days, which confined us to the house, the last time we met at Scotsbrig. These were of select Annandale figures whom I had seen in my boyhood, and of whom, now that they were all vanished, I was glad to have, for the first time, some real knowledge as facts; the outer *simulacra*, in all their equipments, being still so pathetically vivid to me. My father's, in rugged simple force, picturesque ingenuity, veracity and brevity, were, I do judge, superior to even Wordsworth's as bits of human portraiture, without flavor of contempt, too, but given out with judicial indifference, and intermixed here and there with flashes of the poetical and soberly pathetic (e. g., the death of Ball of Dunnaby, and why the two joiners were seen sawing wood in a pour of rain), which the Wordsworth sketches, mainly of distant and indifferent persons, altogether wanted. Oh, my brave, dear, and ever-honored peasant father, where among the grandees, sages, and recognized poets of the world, did I listen to such sterling speech as yours, golden product of a heart and brain all sterling and royal? That is a literal fact, and it has often filled me with strange reflections, in the whirlpools of this mad world.

During the last seven or ten years of his life Wordsworth felt himself to be a recognized lion in certain considerable London circles, and was in the habit of coming up to town with his wife for a month or two every season, to enjoy his quiet triumph, and collect his bits of tribute *tales quales*. The places where I met him oftenest were Marshall's (the great Leeds linen manufacturer, an excellent and very opulent man), Spring-Rice's (i. e., Lord Monteagle's, who and whose house was strangely intermarried with this Marshall's), and the first Lord Stanley's of Alderly (who then, perhaps, was still Sir Thomas Stanley). Wordsworth took his bit of lion-ism very quietly, with a smile sardonic rather than triumphant, and cer-tainly got no harm by it, if he got or expected little good. His wife, a small, withered, puckered, winking lady, who never spoke, seemed to be more in earnest about the affair, and was visibly and sometimes ridicu-lously assiduous to secure her proper place of precedence at table. One evening at Lord Monteagle's—ah, who was it that then made me laugh as we went home together? ah me! Wordsworth generally spoke a little with me on those occasions; sometimes, perhaps, we sate by one another; but there came from him nothing considerable, and happily at least nothing with an effort. "If you think me dull, be it just so!"—this seemed to a most respectable extent to be his inspiring humor. Hardly above once (perhaps at the Stanleys') do I faintly recollect something of the contrary on his part for a little while, which was not pleasant or successful while it lasted. The light was always afflictive to his eyes; he carried in his pock-et something like a skeleton brass candlestick, in which, setting it on the dinner table, between him and the most afflictive or nearest of the chief lights, he touched a little spring, and there flirted out, at the top of his brass implement, a small vertical green circle which prettily enough threw his eyes into shade, and screened him from that sorrow. In proof of his equanimity as lion, I remember, in connection with this green shade, one ilttle glimpse which shall be given presently as finis. But first let me say that all these Wordsworth phenomena appear to have been indifferent to me, and have melted to steamy oblivion in a singular degree. Of his talk to others in my hearing I remember simply nothing, not even a word or gesture. To myself it seemed once or twice as if he bore suspicions, thinking I was not a real worshipper, which threw him into something of embarrassment, till I hastened to get them laid, by frank discourse on some suitable thing; nor, when we did talk, was there on his side or on mine the least utterance worth noting. The tone of his voice when I got him afloat on some Cumberland or other matter germane to him had a braced rustic vivacity, willingness, and solid precision, which alone rings in my ear when all else is gone. Of some Druid circle, for example, he prolonged his response to me with the addition, "And there is another some miles off, which the country people call Long Meg and her Daugh-ters;" as to the now ownership of which " It " etc.; " and then it came into the hands of a Mr. Crackenthorpe;" the sound of those two phrases is still lively and present with me; meaning or sound of absolutely noth-ing more. Still more memorable is an ocular glimpse I had in one of these Wordsworthian lion-dinners, very symbolic to me of his general de-portment there, and far clearer than the little feature of opposite sort, am-biguously given above (recollection of that viz. of unsuccessful exertion at a Stanley dinner being dubious and all but extinct, while this is still vivid to me as of yesternight). Dinner was large, luminous, sumptuous. I sate a long way from Wordsworth; dessert I think had come in, and certainly there reigned in all quarters a cackle as of Babel (only politer, perhaps), which, far up in Wordsworth's quarter (who was leftward on my side of the table), seemed to have taken a sententious, rather louder, logical, and quasi-scientific turn, heartily unimportant to gods and men, so far as I could judge of it and of the other babble reigning. I look upwards, leftwards, the coast being luckily for a moment clear; then, far off, beautifully screened in the shadow of his vertical green circle, which was on the farther side of him, sat Wordsworth, silent, slowly but steadily gnawing some portion of what I judged to be raisins, with his eye and attention placidly fixed on these and these alone. The sight of whom, and of his rock-like indifference to the babble, quasi-scientific and other, with attention turned on the small practical alone, was comfortable and amusing to me, who felt like him, but could not eat raisins. This little glimpse I could still paint, so clear and bright is it, and this shall be symbolical of all.

In a few years, I forget in how many and when, these Wordsworth appearances in London ceased; we heard, not of ill-health, perhaps, but of increasing love of rest; at length of the long sleep's coming; and never saw Wordsworth more. One felt his death as the extinction of a public light, but not otherwise. The public itself found not much to say of him, and staggered on to meaner but more pressing objects. Why should I continue these melancholy jottings, in which I have no interest; in which the one figure that could interest me is almost wanting! I will cease. [Finished, after many miserable interruptions, catarrhal and other, at Mentone, March 8, 1867.]

THE END.

ENGLISH MEN OF LETTERS.

EDITED BY JOHN MORLEY.

The following volumes are now ready:

JOHNSON .... LESLIE STEPHEN.
GIBBON .... J. C. MORISON.
SCOTT .... R. H. HUTTON.
SHELLEY .... J. A. SYMONDS.
HUME .... Professor HUXLEY.
GOLDSMITH .... WILLIAM BLACK.
DEFOE .... WILLIAM MINTO.
BURNS .... Principal SHAIRP.
SPENSER .... The DEAN OF ST. PAUL'S.
THACKERAY .... ANTHONY TROLLOPE.
BURKE .... JOHN MORLEY.
MILTON .... MARK PATTISON.
SOUTHEY .... Professor DOWDEN.
CHAUCER .... Professor A. W. WARD.
BUNYAN .... J. A. FROUDE.
COWPER .... GOLDWIN SMITH.
POPE .... LESLIE STEPHEN.
BYRON .... JOHN NICHOL.
LOCKE .... THOMAS FOWLER.
WORDSWORTH .... F. MYERS.
DRYDEN .... G. SAINTSBURY.

12mo, Cloth, 75 cents per volume.

HAWTHORNE. By HENRY JAMES, Jr. .... 12mo, Cloth, $1 00.

VOLUMES IN PREPARATION:

SWIFT .... JOHN MORLEY.
GRAY .... JOHN MORLEY.
ADAM SMITH .... LEONARD H. COURTNEY.
LANDOR .... Professor SIDNEY COLVIN.
BENTLEY .... Professor JEBB.
DICKENS .... Professor A. W. WARD.
DE QUINCEY .... Professor D. MASSON.
LAMB .... The Rev. ALFRED AINGER.

Others will be announced.

PUBLISHED BY HARPER & BROTHERS, NEW YORK.

☞ HARPER & BROTHERS *will send any of the above works by mail, postage prepaid, to any part of the United States, on receipt of the price.*

By ROBERT SOUTHEY.

THE COMMON-PLACE BOOK. By ROBERT SOUTHEY, LL.D. Edited by his Son-in-Law, JOHN WOOD WARTER, B.D. 2 vols., 8vo, Cloth, $3 00.

Full of rare and rich quotations. There is hardly a subject on which some striking observations, some memorable facts, are not recorded.

THE DOCTOR. By ROBERT SOUTHEY, LL.D. 12mo, Cloth, $1 25.

What wisdom and poetry lie scattered about the pages! On one we see the amplitude of his learning; on another, the author's peculiar strain of sentiment; his pure Saxon English in a third. The common-place book of a reader of such out-of-the-way lore as Southey loved could not fail to be replete with amusement and substantial information.—*Critic*, London.

THE LIFE OF LORD NELSON. By ROBERT SOUTHEY, LL.D. 18mo, Cloth, 75 cents.

Southey's Life of Nelson will live as long as the English language.—*Fraser's Magazine*, London.

THE LIFE OF JOHN WESLEY; and Rise and Progress of Methodism. By ROBERT SOUTHEY, LL.D. With Notes by the late SAMUEL T. COLERIDGE, and Remarks on the Life and Character of John Wesley by the late ALEXANDER KNOX. Edited by the Rev. CHARLES C. SOUTHEY, M.A. With Notes, &c., by the Rev. DANIEL CURRY, D.D. 2 vols., Cloth, $2 50.

O dear and honored Southey (referring to the Life of Wesley), the favorite of my library among many favorites! the book I can read for the twentieth time with delight when I can read nothing else at all—this darling book! I never met a human being who, in his mien and aspect, as well as in the whole habit of life, manifested such a stamp and signature of virtue as to make one's judgment of them matter of intuition rather than the result of continued examination.—COLERIDGE.

THE LIFE AND CORRESPONDENCE OF ROBERT SOUTHEY, LL.D. Edited by his Son, Rev. C. C. SOUTHEY, M.A. Portrait. 8vo, Cloth, $2 00.

A work presenting a charming picture of the domestic habits, literary enterprises, and characteristic moral features of its eminent subject. Mr. Southey's connection with the progress of English literature during the early part of this century, his strong political predilections, the extent and variety of his productions, and his singular devotion to a purely intellectual life, make his biography a most entertaining and instructive record.

Published by HARPER & BROTHERS, New York.

☞ *Any of the above works sent by mail, postage prepaid, to any part of the United States, on receipt of the price.*

OLIVER GOLDSMITH.

POETICAL WORKS OF OLIVER GOLDSMITH.

With a Biographical Memoir, and Notes on the Poems. Edited by BOLTON CORNEY. Illustrated. 8vo, Cloth, $3 00; Cloth, Gilt Edges, $3 75; Turkey Morocco, Gilt Edges, $7 50.

SELECT POEMS OF OLIVER GOLDSMITH.

Edited, with Notes, by WILLIAM J. ROLFE, A.M. Illustrated. Small 4to, Flexible Cloth, 70 cents; Paper, 50 cents.

GOLDSMITH'S POEMS.

32mo, Paper, 25 cents; Cloth, 40 cents.

GOLDSMITH'S PLAYS.

32mo, Paper, 20 cents; Cloth, 35 cents.

THE VICAR OF WAKEFIELD.

By OLIVER GOLDSMITH. 18mo, Cloth, 50 cents. 32mo, Paper, 25 cents; Cloth, 40 cents.

GOLDSMITH. By WILLIAM BLACK.

Goldsmith. By WILLIAM BLACK. A Critical and Biographical Sketch. (In the series entitled "English Men of Letters.") 12mo, Cloth, 75 cents.

GOLDSMITH.—BUNYAN.—MADAME D'ARBLAY.

By LORD MACAULAY. 32mo, Paper, 25 cents; Cloth, 40 cents.

HISTORY OF GREECE.

By OLIVER GOLDSMITH. Abridged by the Author. 18mo, Cloth, 75 cents.

HISTORY OF ROME.

By OLIVER GOLDSMITH. Abridged by the Author. 18mo, Cloth, 75 cents.

OLIVER GOLDSMITH. By WASHINGTON IRVING.

Life of Oliver Goldsmith. With Selections from his Writings. By WASHINGTON IRVING. 2 vols., 18mo, Cloth, $1 50.

Published by **HARPER & BROTHERS**, New York.

☞ *Any of the above works will be sent by mail, postage prepaid, to any part of the United States, on receipt of the price.*

SAMUEL JOHNSON.

BOSWELL'S JOHNSON.

The Life of Samuel Johnson, LL.D. Including a Journal of a Tour to the Hebrides. By JAMES BOSWELL, Esq. Portrait of Boswell. 2 vols., 8vo, Cloth, $4 00; Sheep, $5 00; Half Calf, $8 50.

JOHNSON'S WORKS.

The Complete Works of Samuel Johnson, LL.D. With an Essay on his Life and Genius, by ARTHUR MURPHY, Esq. 2 vols., 8vo, Cloth, $4 00; Sheep, $5 00; Half Calf, $8 50.

SAMUEL JOHNSON. By LESLIE STEPHEN.

Samuel Johnson. By LESLIE STEPHEN. A Critical and Biographical Sketch. (In the series entitled "English Men of Letters.") 12mo, Cloth, 75 cents.

JOHNSON'S LIFE AND WRITINGS.

Selected and Arranged by the Rev. WILLIAM P. PAGE. 2 vols., 18mo, Cloth, $1 50.

JOHNSON. By Lord MACAULAY.

Samuel Johnson, LL.D. By Lord MACAULAY. 32mo, Paper, 25 cents.

JOHNSON'S RELIGIOUS LIFE.

The Religious Life and Death of Dr. Johnson. 12mo, Cloth, $1 50.

SAMUEL JOHNSON. By E. T. MASON.

Samuel Johnson: His Words and his Ways; What he Said, What he Did, and What Men Thought and Spoke Concerning Him. Edited by E. T. MASON. 12mo, Cloth, $1 50.

Published by HARPER & BROTHERS, New York.

THE LIFE

OF

JOHN LOCKE.

BY

H. R. FOX BOURNE.

2 vols., 8vo, Cloth, $5 00.

The biographer of Locke has interwoven the private and public events of the period skilfully together, so that we see Locke not as an abstract philosopher, but as the child of his age, who was to a large degree the outcome of a period which, nevertheless, he powerfully helped to mould. He has given us a work which supplies an unmistakable want in the literature of English philosophy, and which will make the thoroughly English features of the philosopher familiar to the present generation. He has shown us Locke in connection with his time, and has traced the various ways in which he exercised healthful influence upon it, and became the source of similar influence to succeeding generations. We cordially welcome this excellent piece of biography, and we have little doubt that it will become a standard work.—*British Quarterly Review*, London.

Mr. Fox Bourne has added considerably to our knowledge of the details of Locke's life. We have now a complete picture of the man and his surroundings.—*Examiner*, London.

To revive the memory of such a man is obviously an undertaking of much moment, and Mr. Fox Bourne has felt the responsibility of his task. He spares no pains; his life of Locke evinces much editorial care, and contains novel information.—*Athenæum*, London.

Mr. Fox Bourne is able to state most justly in his Preface that more than half of the contents of this work is derived from hitherto unused manuscripts, and that by them, apart from their independent worth, altogether new light is thrown on most of the information that is not actually new. * * * A conscientious and painstaking performance, and will well repay a careful reading.—*Academy*, London.

It is clear and interesting to read, and will be of permanent value to students of Locke's work and times.—*Saturday Review*, London.

PUBLISHED BY HARPER & BROTHERS, NEW YORK.

☞ HARPER & BROTHERS *will send the above work by mail, postage prepaid, to any part of the United States, on receipt of the price.*

BURNS'S LIFE AND WORKS.

The Life and Works of Robert Burns.   Edited
by ROBERT CHAMBERS.   4 vols., 12mo, Cloth,
$6 00; Half Calf, $13 00.

Mr. Chambers's edition is the completest presentation of the Scottish poet in existence.   The various compositions are here strung in strict chronological order upon the Memoir, that they may render up the whole light which they are qualified to throw upon the history of the life and mental progress of Burns, while a new significance is given to them by their being read in connection with the current of events and emotions which led to their production.   The result of this plan is not merely a great amount of new biographical detail, but a new sense, efficacy, and feeling in the writings of the poet himself.

All that remains of Burns, the writings he has left, seem to us no more than a poor mutilated fraction of what was in him; brief, broken glimpses of a genius that could never show itself complete; that wanted all things for completeness—culture, leisure, true effort, nay, even length of life. * * * There is something in his poems which forbids the most fastidious student of poetry to pass them by. * * * The excellence of Burns is, indeed, among the *rarest*, whether in poetry or prose; but, at the same time, it is plain, and easily recognized—his indisputable air of truth.—THOMAS CARLYLE.

Burns is by far the greatest poet that ever sprung from the bosom of the people, and lived and died in an humble condition.   He was born a poet, if ever man was, and to his native genius alone is owing the perpetuity of his fame. * * * Whatever be the faults or the defects of the poetry of Burns—and no doubt it has many—it has, beyond all that was ever written, this greatest of all merits, intense, life-pervading, and life-breathing truth.—Professor WILSON (*Christopher North*).

PUBLISHED BY HARPER & BROTHERS, NEW YORK.

☞ *Sent by mail, postage prepaid, to any part of the United States,
on receipt of the price.*

cunetation 203
239